THE URBAN VISION

Selected Interpretations of the
Modern American City

THE DORSEY SERIES IN AMERICAN HISTORY

EDITOR   IRVIN G. WYLLIE   *University of Wisconsin, Parkside Campus*

COLE   *An Interpretive History of American Foreign Relations*

CRONON (ed.)   *Twentieth Century America: Selected Readings* Volumes I and II

CROWE (ed.)   *The Age of Civil War and Reconstruction, 1830–1900: A Book of Interpretative Essays*

FILENE (ed.)   *American Views of Soviet Russia, 1917–1965*

FULLINWIDER   *The Mind and Mood of Black America: 20th Century Thought*

GLAAB   *The American City: A Documentary History*

KAPLAN   *Recent American Foreign Policy: Conflicting Interpretations*

NEWBY (ed.)   *The Development of Segregationist Thought*

PESSEN   *Jacksonian America: Society, Personality, and Politics*

QUINT, ALBERTSON, & CANTOR (eds.)   *Main Problems in American History*   rev. ed.   Volumes I and II

SALE & KARN   *American Expansion: A Book of Maps*

SHAFER   *A Guide to Historical Method*

TAGER & GOIST (eds.)   *The Urban Vision: Selected Interpretations of the Modern American City*

VAN TASSEL & HALL (eds.)   *Science and Society in the United States*

WILSON (ed.)   *Darwinism and the American Intellectual: A Book of Readings*

THE URBAN VISION

Selected Interpretations of the Modern American City

EDITED BY

JACK TAGER
University of Massachusetts

AND

PARK DIXON GOIST
Case Western Reserve University

1970

**The
Dorsey
Press** HOMEWOOD, ILLINOIS
IRWIN-DORSEY LIMITED, GEORGETOWN, ONTARIO

First Printing, May, 1970
Second Printing, August, 1971

Library of Congress Catalog Card No. 70-118191
Printed in the United States of America

for
Gina and Doris

INTRODUCTION

The underlying assumption of this book is that what men think about their cities is basic to how they live and act in them. Thus, the following selections are meant to illustrate the variety of human response to the modern city; to present some of the important attitudes toward, and interpretations of, the American industrial metropolis, its problems and opportunities. Because the readings are selective and not intended to reflect all possible reactions to the city, something should be said by way of introduction as to why specific selections have been singled out for consideration.

Over the past century the city has been a matter of increasing concern to Americans. During two periods covered by this book, the 25 years prior to World War I and the years since World War II, there was a particularly pervasive concern with the city: in the first instance with "civic consciousness" and more recently with the "urban crisis." An intervening period between the two wars was marked by efforts to provide an understanding of the modern city, and by the regional approach to city planning.

In the first of our time spans (1890-1915), efforts to deal with the "challenge of the city" reveal basic concerns which have continued to be uppermost in the minds of those trying to cope with urban problems. The city was—and is—a challenge, because its rapid growth called for political and economic reform as well as social readjustment and physical reconstruction. Various efforts to come to grips with these issues have been grouped in this first period under the headings of social reform and physical reconstruction. In the first category, the spokesmen represented reflect a singular, hopeful vision that emerged from a wide diversity of concerns focused on the city. Regardless of the specific reform which each spokesman advocated, these men fully shared in the growing civic consciousness which saw in the city not only a challenge, but "the hope of democracy." The "City Beautiful Movement" was one aspect of this civic reform movement, and its representatives belong in our second category of architectural reformers. A consideration of this first modern planning movement is important because it raises a fundamental question about the feasibility of a "civic art" or city planning which is largely unresponsive to underlying social changes. As we shall see, this is a question which has continued in various forms into our own time.

During the next years to which we turn our attention (1919-45), two important areas of urban concern have been chosen for consideration. These by no means exhaust the attitudes toward, or interpretations of, the city during the 1920's and 1930's, but they do reflect some of the most interesting urban thought in the period. In the first group are those students of society who sought to understand the effect of the industrial metropolis upon society. Their various writings were aimed at understanding the impact of the urban environment on individual and group behavior, at delineating what urbanism means as a distinctive way of life, and at tracing the emergence of a "metropolitan community." One set of approaches to this complex metropolitan entity is found in regional planning efforts, which constitute the second set of readings in this section. Regionalism as a system of planning is in sharp contrast to the City Beautiful Movement. However, the two approaches to regional planning represented in the readings are quite distinct from one another, and offer two different ways of thinking about, and acting toward, the modern metropolis.

In the third and final section of readings we turn to the years since 1945. Because of the plethora of material dealing with the city in the past two decades, and because of its contemporary nature, it is somewhat more difficult to select characteristic readings. We have divided the period along two lines, focusing first on the fragmented character of the "metropolis," and then shifting to various suggestions for what is now called "megalopolis." The readings under the first heading reflect some of the important problems resulting from the existence of two rather distinct urban components, the white suburb and the increasingly black core. With these issues in mind, we turn to a consideration of a few suggestions made recently in response to the current urban crises. Again, the purpose is not to present all possible views, but to indicate some of the most meaningful thought being devoted to urban problems. The discussions of city planning, urban renewal, and housing touch on some of the key issues in current urban redevelopment efforts, as well as echoing the hopes of earlier civic reformers.

The selections in this volume are preceded by a descriptive essay on the development of the industrial city written by one of the co-authors, Professor Jack Tager. This essay provides a concise summary of the significant facts and processes of modern American urbanization. With this overview as a reference, the reader is then asked to consider the various responses to this urban development, efforts aimed at understanding, reforming, and rebuilding our cities.

April, 1970   P. D. G.

CONTENTS

A NARRATIVE OF THE RISE OF THE INDUSTRIAL CITY

The city is an ancient phenomenon; its origins have been traced back to early human settlements of paleolithic times. Generations of scholars have attempted to isolate the main cultural factors which drove men to congregate in cities. Whether the city's origin was as marketplace, religious hearth, fortress, autonomous legal corporation, or communal association is much disputed, but all agree that the city as a societal construct has played a pervasive role in the history of mankind. However, the process of urbanization that took place in the 19th and 20th centuries has resulted in the formation of a markedly different kind of city for a changing modern world. [Urbanization represents the contrast between a preindustrial and an industrial society. Urbanization is a process of radical social change which has attenuated the difference between city and country and produced a new kind of urban environment.]

Simply put, urbanized means that the majority of people lives in urban areas or their surroundings and follows nonagricultural pursuits. Today over 70 percent of Americans live in cities, and nearly half of the urbanites live in metropolitan areas of over one million. While cities are more than 5,000 years old, the proportion of human population concentrated in cities did not begin to increase significantly until 200 years ago. In 1900 only Great Britain could be classified as urbanized; today, all the industrial nations of the West are urbanized, with the expectation that by 1990 more than half the world's population will be living in cities of 100,000 or more. The Industrial Revolution, a major cause of this urbanization process in the West, gave rise to a new social institution—the industrial city.

[The crucial factor which determined the transition of a preindustrial city to an industrial city was technology. The ability of a society to produce a sizeable surplus, based upon the control of inanimate sources of energy, brought about the circumstances of urbanization.] The change from an agricultural to a manufacturing economic system, the shift from land to factory, caused gigantic population swings which quickly distorted older patterns of natality, mortality and

1

social mobility. Growth of new areas of economic power, the relocation of centers of capital accumulation, and the alteration of the makeup of the labor force, all stimulated further transfigurations of the community. The social matrix of society—attitudes, morals, manners, ideology, the family structure, religion, class and political patterns—was significantly affected by industrialization.

There are superficial similarities between the new industrial cities and the cities of the past; Rome had slums and congestion, preindustrial London had water pollution and crime. But the urban problems of the Londoner or Roman had little importance or impact for the basically agricultural societies of which the cities were only a small part. Preindustrial cities were service areas, centers of commerce and culture, the axis for totally rural folk structures. Some of the values of the preindustrial societies were maintained, and even mythicized into the industrial era. But in overall outlook and response, in that which differentiates modern society from the past, the industrial city, as sociologist Leonard Riessman, among others, maintains, signifies a radical break from earlier "urban history." It is the recognition of an "urban revolution" of recent occurrence which justifies the chronological limits of this book of readings. And it is the sudden appearance of the industrial city that marks the breakdown of continuity between a rural past and the urban present.

The Industrial Revolution that began in 19th century America was, and still is, a complicated and far-reaching occurrence. The causes and attributes of such a social revolution are not our concern here. But those particular aspects of industrialization which fostered urbanization need to be specified. At times in the 19th century city growth ran parallel to, or even lagged behind, the development and expansion of the western frontier. People moved to cities in the first half of the century, but they more readily migrated according to the availability of arable land. The three main periods of 19th-century urban growth were the 1840's, when the Transportation Revolution seemed to take hold, the 1860's, when the Civil War served to check western settlement and spurred an industrial burgeoning in the Northeast, and the 1880's, when the United States felt the full brunt of industrialization. While the trend of urban growth was maintained throughout the century, it was industrialization during the latter period that accelerated the process beyond all expectation. The proliferation of factories, the establishment of efficient transportation systems, the migration of farmers to the cities, the immigration from across the seas, the innovations in technology, all tended to force the concentration of human beings into particular geographic areas called cities.

The factory became the nucleus of the new urban growth. Over 90 percent of the industrial production of the United States took place in urban factories. Laborers concentrated around the factories and a host of others—storekeepers, merchants, artisans, entertainers of all sorts—flocked to supply the needs of the workers. By the turn of the century the value of manufactured goods exceeded that of agricultural goods, and the urban population increased 87 times while the population of the countryside increased 12 times. Cities of all sizes, and in all areas of the nation, were growing rapidly. While in 1860 there were 9 cities of 100,000, by 1910 there were 50 such cities. In 1860 there were only 58 areas of over 10,000, by 1910 there were 369 such places, with more developing every year. Whether in transforming older urban settlements, or in creating new towns and cities, it was the factory system that was to dominate many aspects of urban life.

The spread of a viable urban complex of factories was intertwined with the completion of an efficient national transportation system. Manufacturing enterprises usually were located at strategic geographic areas that provided a means of transportation for the goods produced. Factories sprang up in locales situated near rivers, canals, highways and railroad junctions. Transportation systems that brought in raw materials and foodstuffs to satiate the appetites of both factory and worker were imperative to support the rapid expansion of the economy. The success of American industrial growth was assured with the coming of the railroad because there was no longer any need to rely on local markets for the consumption of manufactured and agricultural products. Railroads opened up national markets that created pressures for the production of more goods, which in turn meant a demand for increased productivity in the factories.

The completion of a transcontinental railroad network by 1890, with the United States having one third of the world's total railroad mileage, contributed in many ways to the rapid maturation of the economy. The railroads were also one of the early consumers of industrial products. In the decade of the 1880's for example, the railroads purchased nearly 15 million tons of rails, bought countless other products of the steel mills, and provided employment for armies of workers. The combination of railroads and real estate speculators virtually founded the cities of the West, using transportation as the lure for commercial development and settlement. Many a western town was established, or bankrupted, on the hope of the coming of the railroad. Thus, a national transportation system based upon railroads, so much a part of the industrialization process, provided the fillip for even greater urbanization.

The technological progress which produced a nationwide railroad complex also stimulated city growth by promoting more efficacious intraurban transportation systems. The introduction of electric trolleys, elevated railroads, cable cars, subways, and steel bridges played a significant role in furthering the enlargement of the urban environs. These industrial innovations allowed workers to remove themselves from the proximity of the drab factories to more habitable surroundings. While suburban living had been a part of city life for the rich, the motorized streetcar of the turn of the century was the force that made suburban living economically feasible and attractive for large numbers of city dwellers. Increased urban transportation facilities permitted shoppers to travel conveniently to downtown areas where major stores and businesses were to become centrally located. The greater volume of business brought to the downtown area by the progress in urban transit systems caused a concentration of commercial facilities that became the typical central business district of every American city.

As real estate values soared, businessmen sought out practical and less expensive means to expand their operations. The functional approach was to build upwards, and the skyscraper, made possible by the introduction of the elevator, became the dominant architectural form in the skyline of the modern city. The improvements in urban transportation made the economic and social opportunities of the city even more alluring, and greater numbers of people gave up their old ways of life to move to the city and become urbanites.

Cities mean the congregation of masses of people, and the major force illustrating urban growth in the United States is the staggering population displacement that occurred in the late 19th and early 20th centuries. The higher rate of mortality in the grimy industrial city was more than offset by the continuous influx of population. The lure of the city was based on the economic conditions of industrialization. Adna Weber, one of the first demographers of the industrial city, wrote: "It is now clear that the growth of cities must be studied as a part of the question of the distribution of population, which is always dependent upon the economic organization of society—upon the constant striving to maintain as many people as possible upon a given area." The movement of vast numbers of human beings migrating from rural areas into cities, or into small towns that became cities, was not entirely voluntary. Again, industrialization had created conditions which for many resulted in their being forced to change their way of life in order to survive.

In Europe, beginning in England in the late 18th century, refinements of agricultural techniques—utilization of machines and scientific methods—led to the evolution of large-scale industrial farming by rich landowners. Machines forced the inefficient peasants and landless cottagers off the soil and into the fast-growing industrial cities of Western Europe. But many Europeans chose to emigrate to the New World during the 18th and 19th centuries, ending up in the cities of the United States.

Although the majority of those who flocked to the United States between 1870 and 1920 were either of peasant origin or had been involved in the sale and distribution of agricultural goods, they became locked and bound in the strange and alien environment of the new industrial city. On the one hand, they lacked the funds necessary to travel from seaport cities to the far-flung agricultural heartland of the Middle West and western states. Moreover, few immigrants could acquire the sizeable capital outlay needed to buy land, machinery and seed, for farming on the Great Plains. Thus, the impoverished European immigrants were reluctantly absorbed into the countless unskilled jobs provided by the mushrooming American cities.

European immigration greatly affected population growth in the cities of the United States, but more significant was the large-scale internal rural-urban migration process. Among the first products of the American factories were farm implements—steel plows, tractors, threshers, harvesters—all of which increased farm productivity and cut down on the need for farm labor. The demand for greater capital expenditures to purchase these machines, and the necessity to consolidate farm holdings to maintain a high level of profitability, led to the squeezing out of the small farmer. Jefferson's nation of independent yeoman farmers was drastically transformed. Farming became a big business concerned with credit and market fluctuations. The tremendous capability of an industrialized American agriculture resulted in the overproduction of farm products which glutted markets at home and abroad and caused a spiraling fall of farm prices. The harried farmers were forced to produce more in order to sell enough at low market prices to earn a profit. The growing surpluses further deranged prices and the outcome was severe farm depressions in the 1870's and the 1880's. Many small farmers were adversely affected; poverty-stricken, they left the soil to seek work wherever it was available. In the long run that meant relocation to the nearest industrial city.

The movement of farmers to American cities—whether European immigrants or natives—was not entirely based upon economic motives. Indeed, for many the city was a symbol of hope, holding out the possibility of a better, more enjoyable existence. Clearly, many Europeans left their generally depressed economic condition behind them without consciously pinpointing their reasons. Brutalizing governments, severe taxation, rigid class distinctions, political and religious persecution, and oppressive legal codes were prime factors in their leave-taking. The possibility of somehow improving their lives enabled them to leave a situation which heretofore had immobilized them. For many Americans, life on the isolated farm represented a dreary and drab existence with few social events and meager cultural activities. The excitement and stimulation of urban life, its superior cultural and educational facilities, its "fleshpots," all acted to work on the psyche of the poor farmer who left his patrimony for some vague beckoning emanating from the city.

The concentration of forces, economic or psychological, which stirred the movement of people to the cities resulted in severe congestion. Congestion meant the overcrowding of people into social areas which had not been planned or developed to service large numbers of people. In the process, normal standards (that is to say, the norm for the 19th century) of health, housing, social control, and political behavior were drastically affected. The presence of newly arrived workers' armies jeopardized the vague standards and values of rural America simply because industrialization exaggerated those urban problems that previously had been easily ignored.

There had always been localized areas of poverty or deterioration in the commercial cities of the United States, but in a generally prosperous agricultural nation these spots of blight represented eccentric variations. Primitive standards of health, for instance, were acceptable when people were scattered over the countryside and could not easily infect or pollute their neighbors, the isolation of farm life serving as the best quarantine. Theories or practices or legal codes pertaining to multiple dwelling were nonexistent because the problem of housing factory workers had never before arisen to such an extent. The commercial centers had few operative municipal facilities—police and fire departments were generally voluntary—largely because little expenditure or effort was forthcoming from an indifferent populace of an overwhelmingly agricultural nation. The principles that governed the rise of the industrial city were the result of the rural tradition and its inherent distrust of government. To deal with the conditions of industrialization the rugged individualism of an agricultural society was transformed, without difficulty, into an individualistic ethos based upon laissez-faire capitalism.

The 19th-century belief that the maximum public good is realized through efforts based upon individual self-seeking was to determine the haphazard and makeshift growth of cities. In an age of harsh industrial warfare, with selfish "Robber Barons" waxing rich from a free enterprise system opposed to governmental interference, the industrial city grew amoeba-like around the factory. Improvisation was the practice, utility was the standard, and profit and the demands of competition determined the nature of the urban environment. As Lewis Mumford succinctly put it, the cost of believing in the "mythic struggle for existence" was urban chaos: "Considering this new urban area on its lowest physical terms, without reference to its social facilities or its culture, it is plain that never before in recorded history has such vast masses of people lived in such a savagely deteriorated environment, ugly in form, debased in content . . . [and] never before has human blight so universally been accepted as normal: normal and inevitable."

Never before had so many people jammed together in areas which seemed unable to provide the barest amenities. Urban crowding gave rise to serious public health problems. The existing facilities for the removal of garbage and human waste were totally inadequate. A report of a Philadelphia sanitary commission in 1880 was typical of American cities everywhere when it noted "the custom almost universally practised of turning sink-and-slop water on the ground, allowing it to flow across the sidewalks, and stagnate in the street gutters." Use of privies and outhouses led to unsanitary conditions and foul odors. For instance, a fast-growing Indianapolis, with a population of 75,000 in 1880 had toilet plumbing for only 10 percent of its inhabitants. The proverbial stench of Chicago had already become widely known as the "infinite stink." The pervasiveness of fetid odors and garbage-strewn streets led to demands for sewer systems, sanitation departments, and water purification plants. Indeed, because it was an obvious necessity, it was in the realm of health and sanitation problems that the greatest measure of success has taken place in cities. While most cities quickly found the means to build sewers, purify drinking water and establish waste disposal systems, they seemed reluctant or unable to cope with the problem of slum housing.

The slum tenement was a product of the need to provide housing for great numbers of poorly paid workers in areas where real estate values were extremely high. At first workers were housed around the factories in older one-family structures converted into rent barracks. The growing insistence on more housing construction was met by the real estate developers and the building industry—often with the industrialist taking an active part. The soaring land costs of the city encouraged builders to erect tenements which utilized every square foot possible and were cheap to produce. The six-story walk-up, sometimes of "dumbbell" shape, was efficient in stacking up over 200 human beings into airtight, virtually windowless structures, which provided exorbitant profits for the builders and a dreary existence for the inhabitants. By the turn of the century more than two-thirds of New York City's 3½ million people lived in 90,000 tenements.

Attempts at promoting housing reform were sporadic and largely ineffectual. The major focus was on restrictive legislation, based on the passage of codes that would prevent abuses and maintain helpful conditions. Largely the inspiration of Lawrence Veiller, a housing reformer in New York City, the State of New York passed the Tenement House Law of 1901, which forced builders and landlords to observe minimum standards of safety and health. But restrictive codes served to eliminate only the most severe of housing abuses. While the New York State law greatly influenced the passage of similar restrictive codes all over the nation, the problem of providing sufficient and decent housing for people with low incomes was not solved.

Efforts were made by various individuals and groups to build superior "models" of tenement house design. A few model tenements were built in order to demonstrate that satisfactory housing was possible and would still provide a profitable return on a capital investment. These semiphilanthropic attempts, such as Brooklyn's Riverside Apartments built by Alfred T. White in 1890, were never successfully copied, because the need to maintain a 5 percent annual profit forced rents to be higher than the majority of poorly paid workers could afford.

The satellite town of Pullman, Illinois, near Chicago, begun in the 1880's by sleeping car tycoon George Pullman, was a paternalistic attempt to prevent labor discontent through the creation of a planned model community with substantial low-cost housing. George Pullman's experiment with town planning was based upon his desire to illustrate the virtues and capabilities of the private enterprise system. The town was to be run like any profitable corporation, with the prime focus on the collection of rents. "Strictly a business proposition," said Pullman, "it is simplicity itself—we are landlords and employers. That is all there is of it." Operating under this principle, he cut the wages of his workers during the depression of 1893 but refused to lower the rent of their homes. The outcome was the famous Strike of 1894 which destroyed the model community of Pullman, and seriously retarded further ventures at town planning by private industry.

One manifestation of the inadequacy of housing in the industrial city was the spawning of ethnic and racial ghettos. A ghetto, as defined by the National Advisory Commission on Civil Disorders of 1967, "refers to an area within a city characterized by poverty and acute social disorganization and inhabited by

members of a racial or ethnic group under conditions of involuntary segregation." The urban ghettos arose from two tides of migration—that of Europeans
between 1870 and 1920, and that of southern blacks from 1890 to the present
(gaining real momentum after 1920). Racial and ethnic prejudice, plus economic
subordination, forced these migrants to congregate in the poorest wards of the
city. While it was reasonable for both European immigrants and southern blacks
to seek out their own kind as a means of adjusting to their new environment, the
process was, for the most part, involuntary.

Without resources these migrants could settle only in neighborhoods on the
decline. When one group of workers acquired substantial material wealth and
higher social status they fled the poorer districts to better residential areas,
finally ending up in the suburbs. Depending on the city, generally it was the Irish
who took the place of the native Americans, and they, in turn, were followed by
the Jews and East Europeans and Italians, who then left the deteriorated ghettos
to the arriving blacks. While the European immigrants faced intense and often
xenophobic prejudice, their children became Americanized and were quickly
assimilated into the mainstream of American life. But the racial prejudice of
white Americans against black skins has prevented the Negro from taking part in
this important assimilation process.

Untutored and lacking experience in the forms of democratic government,
the ghetto dwellers—southern blacks as well as European peasants—were easy
prey for the politicians who sought their votes. A sympathetic social worker,
Jane Addams of Chicago's celebrated Hull House, commented that the newly
arrived immigrants were "densely ignorant of civic duties." But lessons in civics
were inappropriate for ghetto residents who were witness daily to the ineffectual
management of the municipality by powerless mayors and weak city councils.
Hamstrung by state legislatures and without the legal means to raise funds,
municipal governments found it virtually impossible to govern the industrial
city. Into this power vacuum strode the political Boss, wielding authority by his
ability to garner votes through the system of the "Big Payoff."

Men like William Tweed and George Washington Plunkitt of New York's
Tammany Hall, "Bath House" John Coughlin of Chicago, Ed Butler of St. Louis,
George Cox of Cincinnati, Abe Ruef of San Francisco, Martin Lomasney of
Boston, Ed Crump of Memphis, Frank Hauge of Jersey City, Tom Pendergast of
Kansas City, headed political machines whose major activity was the dispensation of patronage, favors, and lucrative contracts, largely for the purpose of
self-enrichment. Yet for all its corruption, the machine carried out the two-fold
function of providing social welfare service to the needy and special privileges to
businessmen; both activities gave some measure of stability and coherence to the
teeming industrial city.

The political party was the only agency organized at precinct or ward levels,
close enough to be sensitive to the needs and demands of its lowliest followers.
In return for providing jobs for relatives, charity for needy families, protection
and counsel for the workers, the Bosses were supplied the votes to keep them-

selves in power. The Boss was able to distribute social services to neighborhoods and communities that were not being served by a largely inefficient and disorganized municipality. One Boston ward leader remarked to a journalist: "I think that there's got to be in every ward somebody that any bloke can come to . . . no matter what he's done . . . and get help. Help, you understand; none of your law and justice, but help." As sociologist Robert K. Merton pointed out, "politics was transformed into personal ties," with the machine providing essential functions to the deprived classes of the ghettos whose desires had not been satisfied by the existing social structure.

In order to meet the public service needs of the community, the Boss and machine gave away the resources of the city, in the form of monopolies on public utilities, construction contracts, franchises on public transportation systems, and the like. The Boss regulated competition and promoted monopoly, which meant immediate economic gains for the businessmen and the politician, and, inadvertently, public service for the city dweller. This has been the standard way by which American cities have coped with the disorganization and complexity engendered by industrialization. From time to time, Bosses and machines have been ousted by reformers who have created their own political followings in the cities. But their endeavors have brought forth few improvements in the art of governing a large metropolis. Since the First World War new forms of municipal government, such as the council-manager system, have been tried, but they seem satisfactory for smaller, well-to-do towns rather than the problem-ridden big cities. Up to the present, only the political party, or some variation of it, has been able to centralize and collect the fragments of power scattered throughout the city to satisfy the needs of the diverse groups within the larger urban community.

The inability to govern the municipality effectively is connected to the failure of Americans to visualize the entirety of forces that make up the modern city. To search for the meaning of the city is to plumb the uncertain depths of diverse American views on the subject. But a precise definition of an imprecise and incalculable phenomenon may not be possible to construct. In the last decade many Americans sensitive to the urbanization process have tried to define the term *city* and all that it implies—central core, suburbs, metropolis, megalopolis.

What emerges is a basic disagreement among social scientists and those in the humanities as to what characterizes a city. A common approach is to set an arbitrary figure either stressing a minimum of population in an area, or the density of population per square mile in an area. Others would argue that a city is a recognizable image due to its tall buildings and totality of man-made structures. There is the argument that a city is made up of people who follow nonagricultural pursuits. Furthermore, there are those who maintain that living in a city determines a special mode of life based on the cognizance of time, on the ability to calculate, and on the anonymity of human relations. Less precise, and thus more alluring for some, are the concepts that the city is an area in which there are multiple opportunities to exercise choice or seek out diversity, or more simply, the city is something people can recognize intuitively—it is an idea.

Since all these notions ring true, the possibility of constructing a viable definition of the modern city becomes an academic procedure of little consequence. It may prove more profitable to categorize the particular views of the city generated by thoughtful Americans, and to demonstrate how these variegated interpretations evolved. Then the student of urban affairs can correlate these views with the prominent realities of the urban condition in order to discover their relevancy. Inherent in these viewpoints are value systems that cannot be reduced to social science formulas of truth, but these values can be understood in relation to the origins and evolution of modern city life in the United States and its imprint upon the culture and ethos of Americans.

PART I

The Challenge of the
City, 1890–1915

CHAPTER ONE

AMELIORATION AND THE CITY: THE SOCIAL REFORMERS

One of the few noncontroversial statements that can be made about the modern American city is that it was a product of the Industrial Revolution. The factory and the railroad, as Lewis Mumford has explained, were the generating agents— and the pace of urbanization increased as the rhythm of industrialization quickened. By the beginning of this century most Americans accepted the burgeoning city as the inevitable result of a far-reaching economic change. Reformer Frederic C. Howe characterized this urbanization process as an "industrial accident," an "economic happening."

This new city—with its fascinating mixtures of ugliness and culture, poverty and affluence—was soon recognized as "the essential ground of modern existence."[1] The belief that for the first time men had the power to alter their environment through the use of advanced technology, gave birth to the notion that the new industrial city might be the potential site for the erection of a utopian commonwealth of undreamed dimensions.

That many of those concerned with urban problems in the 1960's share this hope that the city might be the scene of real progress is obvious. Paul Goodman romantically writes about the city as a place of "escape into freedom from social rules."[2] Jane Jacobs possesses the same optimistic estimate about what the city can be: "The surplus wealth, the productivity, the close grained juxtaposition of talents that permit society to support advances . . . are themselves products of our organization into cities, and especially into big and dense cities."[3] Indeed, it is this faith in the city as the locale of future progress or the source of future civilization or the refuge of future freedom, which characterizes all those who might be termed urbanologists. The faith in the city's potential has marked the present day Housing and Urban Development official as clearly as it marked the turn-of-the-century social reformer.

---

[1] Carl E. Schorske, "The Idea of the City in European Thought: Voltaire to Spengler," *The Historian and the City* (ed. O. Handlin and J. Burchard, Cambridge, 1963), p. 109.

[2] Paul Goodman, "Two Issues in Planning," *Commentary,* 44 (Aug., 1967), pp. 75-77.

[3] Jane Jacobs, *The Death and Life of Great American Cities* (New York, 1961), p. 448.

Those pioneers who first came to grips with the emerging industrial city pitted themselves against its most blatant evils—slums, municipal corruption and inefficiency, the breakdown of the democratic process. Striving for social betterment and human rehabilitation, the early urban reformers sought to realize the promise of the city as an agent of democracy and civilization.

The readings in this first chapter emphasize that, while reformers differed in their specific approaches to urban problems, they agreed about two important matters. First, they saw the same enemies; they found themselves confronting the same obstacles to reform. And second, they shared a common assumption: men, by wrestling with these problems, might solve them, might actually transform the squalid urban environment into the shining "city on the hill."

An obvious method to tackle the problems of the industrial city was to reshape its economic roots. Frederic Howe early declared himself an "economic determinist," and suggested that the only hope for real social reform was in a restructuring of the "economic foundations" of the city. A disciple of single-taxer Henry George, Howe advocated the simplistic device of a tax upon the unearned rise in the value of land. This single tax, he was convinced, would be the lever to set in motion the machinery that would create an "industrial democracy." It would be the source of public wealth sufficient to erect an equalitarian society with the state as the guardian of the populace. Once poverty and squalor had been safely eliminated, the city would become a pure democratic society, akin to the city states of Athens and Rome.

But for others, like the minister Josiah Strong, the economic possibilities of the industrial city generated new dangers—the growth of an uncontrollable and corrupting materialism. He feared that the new materialistic ethos, engendered by the Industrial Revolution and nourished in the new cities, would stifle man's spirituality, threaten even his commitment to Christ. Strong believed that the means to avoid a materialistic society lay within the city itself. Christian patriotism, he hoped, would save the city yet; in turn the city might be the vehicle to bring closer the possibility of salvation for the whole society.

To achieve this urban transformation Josiah Strong preached for a "socialized church," and a "social spirit." Like Howe, he believed that the state must take a more active part in curbing individual excesses in the interest of the whole community.

This conflict between community welfare and private license was of particular interest to the advocates of city planning. Enthusiasts like Charles Beard, the famous political scientist and historian, believed that politics offered the most hopeful arena for securing the public interest. Swept along by the wave of reform politics in the Progressive Era, Beard felt that an awakened democracy might overcome the economic and social ills of the city. Concerning himself with what he called "the political implications" or urbanization, Beard observed that the economic forces of the city were transforming its class structure. The middle class, he was sure, would soon be pressured into accepting some kind of municipal socialism in order to prevent an open revolution. Rational, centralized city planning could easily help to alleviate problems of housing, transportation, and education.

But before city planning could work, the municipality needed to deal with the problem of land ownership within the city proper. The fundamental question of land usage was (and is) the crux of any scheme of urban redevelopment based upon city planning. Echoing the argument of Charles Beard, city-planners of the 1960's, like Charles Abrams, plead for "land reform." "To convert chaos into order," Abrams has written, "to make cities workable, to bar bad development and encourage the building of necessary facilities, governments must establish control over the use of land."[4] As early as 1912 Charles Beard envisioned the strengthening of municipal authority, particularly over land ownership and use, as the indispensable means for insuring a habitable city for men.

Some men were looking beyond the establishment of this hospitable urban environment to the creation of an atmosphere of cultural excellence. While Brand Whitlock was the hard-working mayor of Toledo between 1905 and 1913, he was also a novelist, keenly interested in art and literature, numbering among his friends the cultural leaders of the nation. Whitlock, "the artist in politics," extolled the city as the "cradle of civilization." Those who sentimentally rhapsodized the virtues of rural America, he thought, ignored the fact that the city was the center of all that was vibrant and alive in modern society. Not only the birthplace of liberty and industry, the city was also the home of art and of learning. Freeing men from poverty and want, Whitlock argued, would enable individuals to indulge in the highest cultural pursuit of artistic creativity.

The vision of the social reformers of the early 20th century, then, was a hopeful vision. They would ameliorate the excesses of industrialism in the city—whether by a new kind of tax, a moral reawakening, or a political revival. This social amelioration of the industrial city would inevitably lead, for the first time in the history of the world, to an urbanized community where freedom and equality were guaranteed for all men.

---

[4]Charles Abrams, "The Uses of Land in Cities," *Cities: A Scientific American Book* (New York, 1966), p. 126.

The City: The Hope of Democracy

by Frederic C. Howe*

In the discussion of municipal problems it is necessary to bear in mind that the issue of city life has become one of decent human existence. In England, it has become the most vital of imperial problems, for town disease has already affected her army, her industry, her life itself. Even in America the barest conveniences of life are denied to millions, conveniences that make life endurable to the majority of us. Every social adjustment involves some cost. Advancing society exacts some sacrifice. But under our present adjustment the sacrifice is borne by the many for the enjoyment of the few.

That democracy will seek to adjust these burdens so as to improve conditions of life is inevitable. The gain which has been made in the past ten years has been tremendous. Things that were denounced as socialistic but a few years ago are now accepted as commonplace. And greater and greater demands are being made in this direction each year. The time is not far distant when equality of chance, in so far as education is concerned, will be offered to all, while opportunities for recreation, which are now confined to a few and which a few years since were unknown to any, will become the common accessories of city life.

It is along these lines that the advance of society is to be made. It is to come about through the city. For here life is more active, while the government is close to the people. It is already manifest on every hand. Through the divorce of the city from state control this progress will be stimulated. The city will become a centre of pride and patriotism. Here art and culture will flourish. The citizen will be attached to his community just as were the burghers of the mediaeval towns. Through direct legislation the city will be democratized. Public opinion will be free to act. Then the official will be holden to a real responsibility, while national politics will no longer dominate local affairs, for the test of the candidate for office will be his citizenship in the community which he serves.

At the same time the burden of existence will be materially relieved. The great cost of living within the city is largely attributable to ground rent on the one hand, and the cost of such services as transportation, gas, water, and fuel on the other. From one-fourth to one-half of the worker's income is absorbed by

*Frederic C. Howe, *The City: The Hope of Democracy* (New York: Charles Scribners' Sons, 1906), pp. 291-305, 311-313.

these charges. By the municipalization of the latter services and the reduction of charges to cost, a portion of this loss can be regained. Likewise, by a beautiful law of social adjustment, the burdens created by the growth of society, the ground rents of our cities, can be used to compensate the individual for the losses which he has incurred in making the city his home. Such a programme of tax reform is demanded by justice, not by charity. For if it be true that organized society creates this fund, then society should retake it for its own needs and the satisfaction of the wants which are created, and which are everywhere incidental to existence in the city.

Just as by a wonderful provision of nature the moisture is gathered up from the sea, to be later deposited upon the land, which it refreshes and renders productive, whence it is carried back again from mountain-side, hill, and prairie to the sea; so there is open to us a law of social life which performs the same refreshing and productive service. For the gathering together of mankind into close association, with its varied energies and activities, creates a social treasure; a treasure whose magnitude we are now able to measure, and which treasure, if retaken by society, will enable all of the burdens which close association involves, to be borne without cost to the dwellers therein.

This cycle of social production and social distribution, of rent and taxation, is like the circulation of the blood in the body. Surging from the heart, it is carried to the extremities, stimulating activities and enabling life to be carried on. From the extremities again, it is returned to the lungs, where it is purified and again returned to the heart.

Within the city there is a similar cycle. The crowding of mankind together has created a social fund. This fund is in excess of present needs, and the needs of government can never exceed it. In the creation of this fund mankind pays a price, a tribute for the privilege of city life; but a price that is now assumed by private collectors. Were society to retake this fund, it would repay the individual who has made the sacrifice what he has lost, it would offer him many of the common necessities of life and usher in an elevated standard of existence.

All this can be brought about through a reform in our methods of taxation. For the taxation of ground rents does not increase rents nor the cost of living. It merely shifts the burden on to him who enjoys the benefit. It cannot be shifted to any one else. It is like special assessments for paving, sewers, and the like. From this source all of the needs of the city can be satisfied. In many communities this principle has already been recognized. The city of Liverpool receives a half-million dollars annually from the lease of its common land. In certain cities in Germany, it has become the policy to buy up surrounding land in advance of the city's growth, and thus retain the benefits and the unearned increment of the city's expansion.

Through these means poverty would be relieved. For poverty is an eradicable thing. It is not a dispensation of Providence, as we interpret the scriptural expression with which we justify our inaction. Nor is it true that the poverty, which is everywhere increasing in our cities, is traceable to "Nature or the Devil, which has made some men weak and imbecile, and others lazy and worthless." Such men there are, and such there will probably always be. But poverty in city and country is largely the result of human laws. It is the natural, as it is the inevitable, product of legal institutions, which are open to correction. These institutions are most aggressively operative in Great Britain and America, where industrial progress is most advanced and wealth is most abundant. Especially in America is poverty traceable to the monopoly of the land and its withholding from use by those who would work it. In our cities it is the burden of rent, along with the franchise monopolies, that imposes the heaviest burden on the poor. Aside from this, within and about every large city, land is held out of use for speculative purposes, while the city is filled with men eager for an opportunity. It is this dog in the manger policy of acquiring and holding out of use land which other men would work that has changed the character of America within the past twenty years from a nation incredulous of poverty into a nation of rapidly increasing tenancy and landless men. It is this that closes opportunity and must of necessity reduce both nominal as well as real wages. Whatever may be the extent of poverty to-day, (and we have recently had some alarming testimony, if not proof, of its widespread existence from the pen of Mr. Robert Hunter) the poverty of the next generation will be very great. For in no nation of western civilization has monopoly affixed its hold to industry as it has in the United States. With it has gone a marked increase in the cost of living, as well as a closing of opportunity. To this is to be added the injustice of our federal taxes, which are designed like an exaggerated poll-tax and fall almost exclusively on the poor. America is to-day struggling under a burden of monopoly charges in rent, franchise and railway privileges, and taxes on the necessities of life, unparalleled in the civilized world outside of Russia. The poor are held between the burden of unjust taxation on the one hand and monopoly on the other, and the result must inevitably be a decrease in wages, a reduction of the standard of living, and a great increase in poverty.

In the cities it is within our power to lift the burden. The extension of the activities of the city and the reduction of the cost of service on municipal monopolies will do something. But the greatest gain will come through a change in our methods of taxation and the assumption of the unearned increment of the land for public uses.

But the fiscal advantages of the single tax upon land values are not the chief of the advantages which would follow. Through its introduction the bad tenement would disappear, while the vacant lands within and without the city would invite building. A stimulus to industry would result which would increase the demand for labor. This, in turn, would increase wages. But beyond all this a new freedom would arise, while the opportunity of access to the undeveloped resources of America would be like the discovery of a new continent. For while America is the richest country in the world in resources, its population per square mile is still less than one-tenth of that of many European countries.

Through such means as these the city will cease to be a necessary abyss of poverty. It is our institutions and our laws, not a divine ordinance or the inherent viciousness of humankind, that are at fault. Our evils are economic, not personal. Relief is possible through a change in our laws, in an increase in the positive agencies of the government, and the taxing for the common weal of those values which are now responsible for much of the common woe. It is not personal goodness that is demanded so much as public intelligence. For the worst of the evils under which America suffers are traceable to laws creating privileges. The evils can be largely corrected through their abolition. This is most easily obtainable in the city, for it is in the city that democracy is organizing and the power of privilege most rampant.

In the past, the extension of the functions of society has proceeded with an utter indifference to theoretical ideas as to the proper sphere of public activity. While political philosophers have debated the subject, society has ignored the proposals of individualism or socialism. While a priori philosophers have reduced the functions of the state to those of the constable, to the protection of life, liberty, and property from external and internal violence, public sentiment, unaided by the logic of any school, has contentedly accepted the formula of Locke that "the end of government was the welfare of mankind," which Thomas Huxley has said was "the noblest and at the same time briefest statement of the purpose of government known to man."

The Twentieth Century opens with two distinguishing features—the dominant city and militant democracy. These phenomena are not confined to America. They characterize England, Germany, France, Belgium, and Italy. These features are permanent. This is assured by the nature of things. The life, the industry, the culture of the future will be urbanized, even though some revolution in the means of transit should lead to a decentralization of population. The city may change in many ways—undoubtedly it will. In the city of ten or possibly twenty million people there will be a redistribution of centres, possibly a redivision of political functions. But, in a historical sense, the city has resumed the commanding position which it enjoyed in the days of Athens, Rome, and the mediaeval towns.

In external form and appearance, and methods of administration, the modern city does not differ greatly from its early prototype. The features common to both are a close association of mankind with many cooperative activities. Nor does the analogy stop here, for in every age the great cities of the world have enjoyed a certain degree of freedom; of local control over the conduct of their affairs. In Athens, Rome, and the Italian cities there were democratic forms and a popular flavor to the government, while the free cities of the Middle Ages were private corporations of the merchants, hand-workers, and tradesmen, whose guild organizations elected the magistrates, the mayor, and the aldermen, and through this representation of special interests limited the power of the nobles and the feudal system.

The great difference between the twentieth-century city and those of the past lies in our legalized freedom; in universal education; in an organized machinery backed by years of tradition; but especially in the social instincts and industrial background of the present. Democracy, rather than class or business interest, is becoming intelligently organized. In this respect the Twentieth Century marks the dawning of an epoch in Western civilization. Our politics are reflecting this change. Never before has society been able to better its own condition so easily through the agency of government. The ready responsiveness of democracy, under the close association which the city involves, forecasts a movement for the improvement of human society more hopeful than anything the world has known.

In the past, too, the political unit has been the state, and the theories of philosophers, of the socialist, and the individualist have had in mind a centralized organization, working downwards from the top to the individual.

But a shifting of emphasis has taken place. The tendencies of the present day are towards decentralization, in which the city will command an increasing share of attention. This is apparent in England, where the new democracy at work within the city is rapidly socializing industry with the conscious aim of improving the conditions of life. The same is true of all these reform movements in America that have involved the cooperation of the people.

Everywhere matters affecting the individual in his domestic relations are commanding increased attention. Present-day politics are concerning themselves with the elevation of the standard of living, with equality of opportunity, with the uplifting of life, and the betterment of those conditions which most intimately affect mankind. And these are almost all municipal matters. They bear only a distant relationship to the state at large. They are domestic in character and are being solved by an appeal to manhood suffrage and democratic organization. History offers no parallel to this phenomenon. For the cities of the past have been aristocratic centres, capital cities, industrial guilds, or feudal strongholds. Nowhere and at no time has society been organized through manhood suffrage and the ballot, and free to carry out its philosophy or desires by a direct appeal to its members. This is a new force in the world—a force of unmeasured possibilities. And when the scope of the city is borne in mind, the possibilities of this new power of conscious, organized democracy are apparent. Saving as to matters of taxation, of international dealings, of transportation from place to place, of the administration of justice, the city is complete within itself. All other affairs of life, even industry itself, fall within the city's control. And with the unit reduced to the city, and with its functions determined by popular control, as is done in the New England town meeting, the dangers from bureaucratic or distant control are reduced to a minimum. For the city will then expand its activities only in response to the developing demands of the community; it will assume new burdens only as it justifies its abilities to perform them. Every city will be an experiment station, offering new experiences to the world. Just as one by one the services now performed by society have passed from private hands under the control of the city, and have brought increased liberty through the change, so the activities of the future will come in through a demand for a higher standard of life, and a larger equality of opportunity.

This very process is going on in every city. The steps that are being taken are so reasonable that they commend themselves to all. The English official resents the suggestion that his city is socialistic, even though it involves the management of many of those activities which, in America, are now left to private enterprise. The American feels no fear of socialism when his city assumes the disposal of garbage, the supply of water or electricity, the opening up of schools, kindergartens, lodging houses, parks, playgrounds, and bath houses. Yet his father would have rubbed his eyes in amazement at the suggestion of such undertakings being proper fields of public activity. Even the city of Cincinnati, which has built a railroad, is far from a socialistic commonwealth. And yet, no city in the Old or New World, with the possible exception of Manchester, which has aided in the construction of a ship canal, has gone to this extent in its functions. Yet Cincinnati has made a success of this venture. Threatened, as the city believed, by railway discrimination, it secured powers from the state to construct a railroad to the south. The enterprise was carried to a successful completion, and for years has proven not only self-sustaining, but a source of revenue to the city.

All this but indicates the amplitude of powers resident in the city by which it may solve, not only the needs that now confront it, but work out the larger social problems of industry as well. What the final municipal programme of the new city will be, one can only conjecture, but that it will be a programme making for a better civilization, a larger life, and increased comfort and opportunity, the gradual progression of society gives assurance. That these increased activities will come by gradual steps, approved in time by all, is evidenced by the sanction of experience, which accepts with approval the functions which have thus far been assumed.

. . . .

Many there are who question the ability of democracy to solve the problems of city life along the lines indicated. To some this is not so much reasoned conviction as indolent disinclination to assume the burdens involved. It is so much easier to rely on the boss, the party, and the System which has been inaugurated. Yet, the testimony of all experience shows that society has constantly moved onward through forces from below. The great advances in government have been achieved through the common people slowly breaking down privilege after privilege in the onward movement of human liberty. The lesson of our present industrial achievement is the same. The captain of industry has come up from the sod and the mill. He has exemplified the law of nature, which is as active in government as it is in his own career.

The great problem now before the American people is, how can opportunity be kept open; how can industry be saved from privilege; how can our politics be left to the unimpeded action of talent and ability? This is the problem which the city has to solve, even more than the state or the nation. For in the city the life of the future is to be found. Already the burden of mere existence taxes to the uttermost the energy of an increasing mass of the population. This burden arises in large measure through the increased cost of living, which, in turn, is traceable to rent, to transit, to light, heat, and water, the great natural monopolies, whose values the city creates.

With these services, along with the ground rents of our cities, socialized, the standard of living would be elevated, while through cooperative agencies the city would become in effect an enlarged home, offering to its members many of the comforts and conveniences that are now denied to any save a few. With these opportunities enlarged, the love and affection of the citizen for the city would increase, which, in turn, would bring about a purification of our politics that cannot be obtained so long as the influence of the rich and privileged classes is united against the community.

With such a programme achieved, democracy would cease to be a class struggle. There would be created a union of all the people, seeking in conscious ways the betterment of human conditions. Then the merit system, the party, the ballot, the charter, would be reformed by common demand; for then there would be no class, no powerful influence, whose control of the government was dependent upon the persistence of the *status quo*. With home rule secured, with popular control attained, with the city free to determine what activities it will undertake, and what shall be its sources of revenue, then the city will be consciously allied to definite ideals, and the new civilization, which is the hope as well as the problem of democracy, will be open to realization.

The Challenge of the City

by Josiah Strong*

"A tale of two cities" comes down to us from an ancient book. In its opening pages we see the first city built by the first murderer; and it would seem as if vice and crime had festered in the city ever since. In the closing pages of the book we find a glorious city as a fitting type of civilization perfected—a vision of the kingdom of God fully come in the earth. The city of Destruction is waiting to be supplanted by the New Jerusalem.

The nineteenth century gave birth to many marvels, but beyond question its greatest and most characteristic wonder was the unprecedented and disproportionate development of material civilization.

. . . .

It is a vital question whether the materialism of the nineteenth century is to develop into something higher in the twentieth, or whether our marvelous material development will prove to be at the expense of intellectual and spiritual growth.

The order of development is the lowest first; "Time's noblest offspring is the last." The apostle says: "First that which is natural, then that which is spiritual." Child life is, first, animal; later, intelligence dawns; and, last of all, comes the moral and spiritual life. History would seem to show that this is the natural order in the progress of civilization; that great intellectual expansion and spiritual quickening are usually preceded by a material advance and if such material growth is not followed by an intellectual and moral advance, degeneration takes place.

. . . .

We must not forget that during the past century intellectual and moral progress was real and great. There was a wide diffusion of knowledge, and the average man is now far more intelligent than his grandfather was. There has been an

---

*Josiah Strong, *The Challenge of the City* (New York: Young People's Missionary Movement, 1911), pp. 4, 5, 14-16, 48-52, 82-87, 241, 270-273.

The City: Suggestions for the Investigation of Human Behavior in the Urban Environment

by Robert E. Park*

The city, from the point of view of this paper, is something more than a congeries of individual men and of social conveniences—streets, buildings, electric lights, tramways, and telephones, etc.; something more, also, than a mere constellation of institutions and administrative devices—courts, hospitals, schools, police, and civil functionaries of various sorts. The city is, rather, a state of mind, a body of customs and traditions, and of the organized attitudes and sentiments that inhere in these customs and are transmitted with this tradition. The city is not, in other words, merely a physical mechanism and an artificial construction. It is involved in the vital processes of the people who compose it; it is a product of nature, and particularly of human nature.

The city has, as Oswald Spengler has recently pointed out, its own culture: "What his house is to the peasant, the city is to civilized man. As the house has its household gods, so has the city its protecting Deity, its local saint. The city also, like the peasant's hut, has its roots in the soil."

The city has been studied, in recent times, from the point of view of its geography, and still more recently from the point of view of its ecology. There are forces at work within the limits of the urban community—within the limits of any natural area of human habitation, in fact—which tend to bring about an orderly and typical grouping of its population and institutions. The science which seeks to isolate these factors and to describe the typical constellations of persons and institutions which the co-operation of these forces produce, is what we call human, as distinguished from plant and animal, ecology.

Transportation and communication, tramways and telephones, newspapers and advertising, steel construction and elevators—all things, in fact, which tend to bring about at once a greater mobility and a greater concentration of the urban populations—are primary factors in the ecological organization of the city.

*Robert E. Park, "The City: Suggestions for the Investigation of Human Behavior in the Urban Environment," *The City*, eds. Robert E. Park, Ernest W. Burgess, Roderick McKenzie (Chicago: University of Chicago Press, 1925), pp. 1-4, 7-10, 12-14, 23-31, 33-46. Reprinted by permission of the University of Chicago Press.

The city is not, however, merely a geographical and ecological unit; it is at the same time an economic unit. The economic organization of the city is based on the division of labor. The multiplication of occupations and professions within the limits of the urban population is one of the most striking and least understood aspects of modern city life. From this point of view, we may, if we choose, think of the city, that is to say, the place and the people, with all the machinery and administrative devices that go with them, as organically related; a kind of psychophysical mechanism in and through which private and political interests find not merely a collective but a corporate expression.

Much of what we ordinarily regard as the city—its charters, formal organization, buildings, street railways, and so forth—is, or seems to be, mere artifact. But these things in themselves are utilities, adventitious devices which become part of the living city only when, and in so far as, through use and wont they connect themselves, like a tool in the hand of man, with the vital forces resident in individuals and in the community.

The city is, finally, the natural habitat of civilized man. It is for that reason a cultural area characterized by its own peculiar cultural type:

"It is a quite certain, but never fully recognized, fact," says Spengler, "that all great cultures are city-born. The outstanding man of the second generation is a city-building animal. This is the actual criterion of world-history, as distinguished from the history of mankind: world-history is the history of city men. Nations, governments, politics, and religions—all rest on the basic phenomenon of human existence, the city."

Anthropology, the science of man, has been mainly concerned up to the present with the study of primitive peoples. But civilized man is quite as interesting an object of investigation, and at the same time his life is more open to observation and study. Urban life and culture are more varied, subtle, and complicated, but the fundamental motives are in both instances the same. The same patient methods of observation which anthropologists like Boas and Lowie have expended on the study of the life and manners of the North American Indian might be even more fruitfully employed in the investigation of the customs, beliefs, social practices, and general conceptions of life prevalent in Little Italy on the lower North Side in Chicago, or in recording the more sophisticated folkways of the inhabitants of Greenwich Village and the neighborhood of Washington Square, New York.

We are mainly indebted to writers of fiction for our more intimate knowledge of contemporary urban life. But the life of our cities demands a more searching and disinterested study than even Émile Zola has given us in his "experimental" novels and the annals of the Rougon-Macquart family.

We need such studies, if for no other reason than to enable us to read the newspapers intelligently. The reason that the daily chronicle of the newspaper is so shocking, and at the same time so fascinating, to the average reader is because the average reader knows so little about the life of which the newspaper is the record.

"It would be difficult to overrate the influence of agriculture in forming temperate and virtuous habits among the people." It will be much more difficult to maintain a high moral standard in a nation of cities than it would be among an agricultural people.

. . . .

Civic pride is a quick soil in which to grow civic patriotism. When men glory in the history of their city, in its beauty, its art and architecture, its famous men and great institutions, its power and influence, it is easy to inspire sacrifice in order to render the present worthy of so great a past, or to save one's city from eclipse by a rival. The Free Cities of the Middle Ages could command the enthusiastic devotion of their citizens, who were proud of their citizenship. But modern, and especially American, cities exist under radically different conditions. Their past is not old enough to be overgrown and beautified by legend and romance as ancient castles are with ivy. There is no twilight to stimulate the imagination. Their history, even if it outreaches the memory of the oldest inhabitant, does not escape the noonday light of modern inquiry. There is as little in their past to gratify our love of the marvelous as there is in their present to satisfy our sense of the beautiful. It is not because of generations which have gone, but because of those which are to come, that our cities appeal to the imagination. The future is more roomy than the past, and we may have part in its history, for it is even now in the making.

Few Americans live where they were born. The redistribution of population has uprooted families grown in the country and transplanted them in the town. Migration and immigration have gathered heterogeneous multitudes in new homes. The varying demands of the labor market have increased the fluidity of the industrial population. All this is unfriendly to the growth of local interest and pride, which naturally develop in those who are long resident in the same place. The modern ease of travel and short residence are destroying the sense of ownership expressed in "my city" and "my neighborhood"; and as the local point of view characteristic of the old civilization and of its individualistic spirit is lost, we need to gain the new social, altruistic spirit which is concerned with all that concerns the welfare of others.

A man may closely watch the administration of public funds, chiefly because he is a taxpayer. He may be interested in good sanitation, chiefly because he is concerned for the health of his own family. He may desire good schools, chiefly because he has children to educate. And such public spirit is unspeakably better in its results than the indifference to public affairs which is shamefully common; but it is not Christian patriotism, because it is not unselfish. So-called patriotism is sometimes only a euphemism for some form of selfishness, for narrowness and bigotry as applied to one's own city or country.

Christian patriotism is disinterested devotion to the general welfare—a patriotism which knows no limits of geography, nor yet of race, nor even of time, but which is as wide and as onward-reaching as the kingdom of God. Such is the patriotism needed to save the city and the nation.

We have seen that the problem of the city forces upon us a national crisis. It does more; it forces upon this generation a world crisis. The industrial revolution is beginning to produce the same changes in Asia which it has already produced in Europe and America. If the scope of this work permitted, it might be shown that this revolution means the disintegration of social and religious institutions in Asia which have been rigid for thousands of years; that it means a new civilization during the twentieth century to one half of the human family, and, therefore, an unequaled opportunity to the Christian Church; that the numberless new problems of the new industrial civilization are concentered in the general problem of the city, which is, therefore, the supreme problem of the world's future.

It is difficult to imagine the new life of the twentieth century beating under Asia's ancient ribs of death, but the quickening of Japan is prophetic of the mighty changes already beginning throughout continental Asia. And the city is the microcosm of the new industrial world. To solve its problems for America is to solve them for mankind; and we have exceptional facilities for solving them.

The fathers found inspiration to toil and sacrifice in the statesmanlike work of making a nation. We find ours in the Godlike work of shaping a world.

Such is the challenge which the city offers to the young men and young women of this generation. Rarely do those in middle life accept new ideals, new aims, new methods, new standards of obligation and of success. Old age looks backward; it sees the golden age of the world in the past—"There were giants in those days." All who share the conservatism of old age would reform the evils of the present by going back to the simple ways of "the good old times." But that is as impossible as to reverse the stream of time.

Progress has its perils, as it has always had. But now, as always, safety is to be found in more progress. The backward look never sees the way out, for God's golden age is in the future. We find ourselves in the midst of a new civilization, full of new perils and of new possibilities. We have seen that the city is to dominate this new civilization and determine its character. In a single generation the city is to ascend the throne and receive the scepter. That scepter is to sway the long future; and whether it is to be a scepter of righteousness and peace or one of tyranny and greed is to be determined in one generation, and by *you*, young men and young women, who have "come to the kingdom for such a time as this."

The opportunity of the ages has come to *you*. It is an opportunity for supreme sacrifice and service offered to Christ and country, which shall bless unborn generations. You are called to sacrifice, not at the stake or in the deadly charge, when with one supreme act and in one short moment the crown of martyrdom might be won; you are called to the higher heroism of the *living* sacrifice, which alone can "die daily." Your challenge is not to die for Christ and country and humanity, but to *live* for them. Are you equal to it?

. . . .

Physical and sentimental distances reinforce each other, and the influences of local distribution of the population participate with the influences of class and race in the evolution of the social organization. Every great city has its racial colonies, like the Chinatowns of San Francisco and New York, the Little Sicily of Chicago, and various other less pronounced types. In addition to these, most cities have their segregated vice districts, like that which until recently existed in Chicago, their rendezvous for criminals of various sorts. Every large city has its occupational suburbs, like the Stockyards in Chicago, and its residential enclaves, like Brookline in Boston, the so-called "Gold Coast" in Chicago, Greenwich Village in New York, each of which has the size and the character of a complete separate town, village, or city, except that its population is a selected one.

· ·

II. INDUSTRIAL ORGANIZATION AND THE MORAL ORDER

The ancient city was primarily a fortress, a place of refuge in time of war. The modern city, on the contrary, is primarily a convenience of commerce, and owes its existence to the market place around which it sprang up. Industrial competition and the division of labor, which have probably done most to develop the latent powers of mankind, are possible only upon condition of the existence of markets, of money, and other devices for the facilitation of trade and commerce.

An old German adage declares that "city air makes men free." ... This is doubtless a reference to the days when the free cities of Germany enjoyed the patronage of the emperor, and laws made the fugitive serf a free man if he succeeded for a year and a day in breathing city air. Law, of itself, could not, however, have made the craftsman free. An open market in which he might sell the products of his labor was a necessary incident of his freedom, and it was the application of the money economy to the relations of master and man that completed the emancipation of the serf.

Vocational Classes and Vocational Types. The old adage which describes the city as the natural environment of the free man still holds so far as the individual man finds in the chances, the diversity of interests and tasks, and in the vast unconscious co-operation of city life the opportunity to choose his own vocation and develop his peculiar individual talents. The city offers a market for the special talents of individual men. Personal competition tends to select for each special task the individual who is best suited to perform it.

· ·

Success, under conditions of personal competition, depends upon concentration under some single task, and this concentration stimulates the demand for rational methods, technical devices, and exceptional skill. Exceptional skill, while based on natural talent, requires special preparation, and it has called into existence the trade and professional schools, and finally bureaus for vocational guidance. All of these, either directly or indirectly, serve at once to select and emphasize individual differences.

Every device which facilitates trade and industry prepares the way for a further division of labor and so tends further to specialize the tasks in which men find their vocations.

The outcome of this process is to break down or modify the older social and economic organization of society, which was based on family ties, local associations, on culture, caste, and status, and to substitute for it an organization based on occupation and vocational interests.

In the city every vocation, even that of a beggar, tends to assume the character of a profession and the discipline which success in any vocation imposes, together with the associations that it enforces, emphasizes this tendency—the tendency, namely, not merely to specialize, but to rationalize one's occupation and to develop a specific and conscious technique for carrying it on.

The effect of the vocations and the division of labor is to produce, in the first instance, not social groups, but vocational types: the actor, the plumber, and the lumber-jack. The organizations, like the trade and labor unions which men of the same trade or profession form, are based on common interests. In this respect they differ from forms of association like the neighborhood, which are based on contiguity, personal association, and the common ties of humanity. The different trades and professions seem disposed to group themselves in classes, that is to say, the artisan, business, and professional classes. But in the modern democratic state the classes have as yet attained no effective organization. Socialism, founded on an effort to create an organization based on "class consciousness," has never succeeded, except, perhaps, in Russia, in creating more than a political party.

The effects of the division of labor as a discipline, i.e., as means of molding character, may therefore be best studied in the vocational types it has produced. Among the types which it would be interesting to study are: the shopgirl, the policeman, the peddler, the cabman, the nightwatchman, the clairvoyant, the vaudeville performer, the quack doctor, the bartender, the ward boss, the strike-breaker, the labor agitator, the school teacher, the reporter, the stockbroker, the pawnbroker; all of these are characteristic products of the conditions of city life; each, with its special experience, insight, and point of view determines for each vocational group and for the city as a whole its individuality.

. . . .

III. SECONDARY RELATIONS AND SOCIAL CONTROL

Modern methods of urban transportation and communication—the electric railway, the automobile, the telephone, and the radio—have silently and rapidly changed in recent years the social and industrial organization of the modern city. They have been the means of concentrating traffic in the business districts, have changed the whole character of retail trade, multiplying the residence suburbs and making the department store possible. These changes in the industrial organization and in the distribution of population have been accompanied by corre-

American City Government

by Charles Beard*

The political implications of the industrial revolution and the growth of our cities in size and complexity are manifold. The working class is developing a solidarity and consciousness of identity of interest which is manifesting itself in the trade union and socialist movements whose demands are all collectivist in character. The clerical and shopkeeping sections of the bourgeoisie are willing to approve such communal enterprises as waterworks, gas and electric plants, and street railways, if it can be shown that they promise a reduction in taxes and rates. Moreover, enlightened leaders among the middle classes, either because they fear the development of a purely proletarian movement, or regard the economic and human waste of the present state of affairs as intolerable, are advocating the assumption of new and vital functions by the municipalities. To all appearances, the age of tinkering with political machinery and spectacular "wars on bosses" is passing into an era of constructive municipal undertakings on a large scale.

From city to city and type to type, the problems of government must vary. Education in New York, with its thousands of foreigners is one thing, and in Des Moines recruited largely from native stock it is another. Housing in the anthracite coal regions does not involve the problem of congestion in a small area, but of providing decent, sanitary homes in the place of the miserable shanties—hideous to look at and demoralizing to live in. Housing in Manhattan, pinched as it is in a narrow island, is another matter altogether. The question of transportation where the inhabitants are scattered over an open plain is quite different from transportation in closely crowded cities where the people live in six- and ten-story tenements. And so on through the whole range of the administrative problems which the city must attack.

Nevertheless, each municipality must deal with some aspects of great problems common to them all: election of officers, efficient management, police, education, housing, transportation, recreation, city planning, and the like. And the experience of each city throws light on the questions of all other cities. The positive gains of one are an encouragement to the workers in all; and out of the combined gains in our common municipal experience have come some of the

*Charles A. Beard, *American City Government, A Survey of Newer Tendencies* (New York: The Century Company, 1912), pp. 28-30, 356, 370-386.
30

finest achievements in our political life. It may be, after all, that the American city, which Mr. Bryce thought to be our greatest failure, will prove to be "the hope of democracy."

. . . .

City planning is a new municipal interest in the United States. On the call of the New York City committee on congestion, the first National Conference on City Planning and the Problems of Congestion was held at Washington, D.C., in May, 1909. The attendance at the sessions and the consideration given to the subject by the public generally were such as to warrant the repetition of the experiment. A second conference was held at Rochester, in 1910, a third at Philadelphia, in 1911, and a fourth at Boston, in 1912. Thus every year students, experts in city planning, and officials of cities are brought together to compare ideas and take stock of the latest developments in the improvement of cities.

. . . .

It is difficult to make many observations on the general subject of city planning which are helpful in concrete cases, but it is interesting to note, from a study of the recent works and plans prepared by experts in the United States and Europe, the main lines of attack which are being proposed. New York City, the heart of whose population is congested on a long narrow island, presents one set of circumstances in the matter of housing and transportation, Pittsburgh scattered along river banks and up and down high hills another, and Indianapolis spread out over a wide plain another, and so on throughout all the cities of the country. Nevertheless, certain problems must be treated in each case: transportation, the location of public buildings and factories, and housing.

Naturally, all the recent plans deal extensively with streets, water fronts, terminals, and other means of traffic and intercourse. The business reasons for this are obvious, for as the Pittsburgh civic commission points out in its report on the main thoroughfares of that city prepared by Mr. [Frederick Law] Olmstead: "All delays and congestion of traffic . . . add to the expense of manufacturers, the costs borne by wholesale dealers; in short, inadequate traffic facilities in Pittsburgh as in other cities, add to the cost of doing business and of living." Then there is another element—congested traffic and difficulties in transit make for congestion of population near the factory districts.

Broadly speaking, three general methods of laying out streets are suggested. There is in the first place the "gridiron" "checker-board" plan which is so common in the United States and has little to recommend it. It is true that it affords a maximum area for building, but, except in a few rare instances, lack of room for growth is not a characteristic of American urban sites. Another quality, which has done so much to commend it to the American imagination in esthetic matters, is that it is so simple that any childish engineer can follow it.

In the second place, there is the diagonal avenue scheme which is the basis of L'Enfant's Washington plan, and is followed in a more or less thoroughgoing fashion by some other cities, as in the case of Indianapolis. This scheme has many features to recommend it. As Mr. Charles M. Robinson points out, it offers

cally by a modification of structure. In man it means mental stimulation and greater intelligence, or mental depression, in case of failure.

Under the conditions imposed by city life in which individuals and groups of individuals, widely removed in sympathy and understanding, live together under conditions of interdependence, if not of intimacy, the conditions of social control are greatly altered and the difficulties increased.

The problem thus created is usually characterized as one of "assimilation." It is assumed that the reason for rapid increase of crime in our large cities is due to the fact that the foreign element in our population has not succeeded in assimilating American culture and does not conform to the American mores. This would be interesting, if true, but the facts seem to suggest that perhaps the truth must be sought in the opposite direction.

. . . .

What we do observe, as a result of the crisis, is that control that was formerly based on mores was replaced by control based on positive law. This change runs parallel to the movement by which secondary relationships have taken the place of primary relationships in the association of individuals in the city environment.

It is characteristic of the United States that great political changes should be effected experimentally under the pressure of agitation or upon the initiative of small but militant minorities. There is probably no other country in the world in which so many "reforms" are in progress as at the present time in the United States. Reform has, in fact, become a kind of popular "indoor sport." The reforms thus effected, almost without exception, involve some sort of restriction or governmental control over activities that were formerly "free" or controlled only by the mores and public opinion.

The effect of this extension of what is called the police power has been to produce a change, not merely in the fundamental policy of the law, but in the character and standing of the courts.

The juvenile and morals courts illustrate a change which is perhaps taking place elsewhere. In these courts the judges have assumed something of the functions of administrative officers, their duties consisting less in the interpretation of law than in prescribing remedies and administering advice intended to restore delinquents brought before them to their normal place in society.

A similar tendency to give judges a wide discretion and to impose upon them a further responsibility is manifest in those courts which have to deal with the technical affairs of the business world, and in the growth in popularity of commissions in which judicial and administrative functions are combined, for example, the Interstate Commerce Commission.

In order to interpret in a fundamental way the facts in regard to social control it is important to start with a clear conception of the nature of corporate action.

Corporate action begins when there is some sort of communication between individuals who constitute a group. Communication may take place at different levels; that is, suggestions may be given and responded to on the instinctive, senso-motor, or ideo-motor levels. The mechanism of communication is very subtle, so subtle, in fact, that it is often difficult to conceive how suggestions are conveyed from one mind to another. This does not imply that there is any special form of consciousness, any special sense of kinship or consciousness of kind, necessary to explain corporate action.

. . . .

The important fact is that by means of this comparatively simple device corporate action is made possible.

Individuals not only react upon one another in this reflex way, but they inevitably communicate their sentiments, attitudes, and organic excitements, and in doing so they necessarily react, not merely to what each individual actually does, but to what he intends, desires, or hopes to do. The fact that individuals often betray sentiments and attitudes to others of which they are themselves only dimly conscious makes it possible for individual A, for example, to act upon motives and tensions in B as soon, or even before, B is able to do so. Furthermore, A may act upon the suggestions that emanate from B without himself being clearly conscious of the source from which his motives spring. So subtle and intimate may the reactions be which control individuals who are bound together in a social-psychological process.

It is upon the basis of this sort of instinctive and spontaneous control that every more formal sort of control must be based in order to be effective.

Changes in the form of social control may for the purposes of investigation be grouped under the general heads:

1. The substitution of positive law for custom, and the extension of municipal control to activities that were formerly left to individual initiative and discretion.

2. The disposition of judges in municipal and criminal courts to assume administrative function so that the administration of the criminal law ceases to be a mere application of the social ritual and becomes an application of rational and technical methods, requiring expert knowledge or advice, in order to restore the individual to society and repair the injury that his delinquency has caused.

3. Changes and divergencies in the mores among the different isolated and segregated groups in the city. What are the mores, for example, of the shopgirl? the immigrant? the politician? and the labor agitator?

It should be the aim of these investigations to distinguish not merely the causes of these changes, the direction in which they are moving, but also the forces that are likely to minimize and neutralize them. For example, it is important to know whether the motives which are at present multiplying the positive restrictions on the individual will necessarily go as far in this country as they have already done in Germany. Will they eventually bring about a condition approaching socialism?

. . . .

Party Politics and Publicity.   There is everywhere at present a disposition to increase the power of the executive branch of the government at the expense of assigned for overcrowding in modern cities. It is sometimes remarked that congestion is due to the fact that people prefer to live huddled up in tenement quarters, where the amusements and diversions of life are more abundant, than to endure the humdrum existence of the small towns or country. Of course, it is true that there would be no problem of congestion if people did not come to the cities; but this view overlooks two important facts. In the first place, it ignores the economic forces at work divorcing the people from the soil and carrying them into the cities. And in the second place, it offers no hint as to the problem of congestion; for whatever may be the forces bringing the people to the cities, it is a condition, not a theory, with which we have to deal. The city cannot refuse to attack the problem simply because it does not approve the motives which have led people to come within its borders.

A large and active school of reformers contend that the problem of congestion may be solved by proper systems of transportation and low fares for long rides, supplemented, perhaps, by workmen's trains early in the morning and late at night. That facilities for rapid transit admit of the wider distribution of population cannot be doubted, and often noteworthy improvements in congested centers are observable after the establishment of a new suburb connected with the factory districts by rapid transit lines. Nevertheless, modern students of the municipal transportation problem are coming to the opinion that even a perfect system of transportation will not solve the problem of overcrowding, unless it is accompanied by other measures.

Two of the most recent scientific investigations of the subject, the report of the New York committee on congestion and Dr. Pratt's study of the industrial causes of congestion, give three fundamental causes for overcrowding: congestion of factories, low wages and long hours, and land speculation. The tendency of working people to live within walking distance of their employment is natural and inevitable. Their long hours make them adverse to spending any considerable time in crowded trains or street cars going to and from their work—and large numbers of them cannot afford to spend ten, or even six, cents a day in car fare.

Dr. Pratt shows that the great volume of manufacturing in New York City is carried on in Manhattan below Fourteenth Street within a space which constitutes about one one-hundredth of the city's total area. The forces making for congestion within this area are cumulative. Working people, who are constantly haunted by the specter of unemployment, must live within an area that offers the most chances for jobs. The factory at hand closes down for a week, or indefinitely, and the employee feels more secure in having other opportunities open nearby. This same advantage also invites manufacturers to come into the already overcrowded area, because they want to take advantage of the fluid labor market, from which they may draw their labor supplies freely, and into which they may pour their discharged laborers with little or no compunctions of conscience. It is perfectly clear that as long as manufacturers are permitted to establish their plants wherever they please within the city's area, they will gravitate towards the congested centers, terminal transportation facilities and other similar advantages being equal.

The fact that low wages and long hours contribute heavily to congestion hardly needs any statistical demonstration. No person who works eight or ten hours a day wants to spend another hour or two going to and from his work. The longer the hours the less time the workman is physically able to spend in reaching his work—to say nothing of the wear and tear upon his nerves and efficiency. Then, too, the lower the wages, the smaller will be the amount which can be spared for transportation. The truth of these statements is supported by the results of Dr. Pratt's survey. On the basis of statistical study, he concludes that there is "an intimate and seemingly causal connection between increasing wages and constantly widening distribution."

. . . .

The third cause of congestion is land speculation. The private acquisition of unearned increment in land values is of course strongly emphasized by the advocates of the single tax. Leaving aside the question of the justice of private ownership of land in great cities, there is no doubt that the holding of land for purely speculative purposes, particularly on the outskirts of cities, tends to check the flow of the population from the overcrowded high-rent areas. By the shifting of a large portion of the burden of taxation from improvements to land, the holding of vacant lots would be discouraged and a decided stimulus would be given to the building of tenements and residences. Nevertheless, it is difficult to see how the taxation of increasing land values unaccompanied by control over the location of factories and a general improvement in the condition of the working class so far as the hours and wages of labor are concerned, would of itself approach the solution of the problem of congestion.

Indeed, this is recognized by recent students of the question of congestion. The report of the New York City committee on congestion, published in 1911, marks a distinct advance over the views entertained a decade ago by reformers who looked to tenement-house legislation and the improvement of transit facilities as the really important methods of relieving congestion. This report recognizes the complexity of the situation and comes to the conclusion that any real solution of the problem of relieving and preventing congestion must embrace a long program of measures. Among the projects cited in it are restriction of the height and volume of buildings, including the area of the lot that may be occupied; the forcible distribution of factories; the taxation of land at a higher rate than buildings; stringent legislation against overcrowding and unsanitary conditions; the education of citizens in such a manner as to interest them in removing from congested centers wherever possible; municipal housing and the active coöperation of the city in housing enterprises; the construction of garden cities and garden suburbs; the encouragement of labor unions in maintaining the standard of wages and hours; and national assistance in the distribution of immigrants.

In approaching those graver questions of city planning which involve a more or less drastic interference with private rights in land, city planners grow cautious, although they admit that the land question is, in fact, one of the basic elements in city development. Nevertheless, we are beginning to see in the agency of publicity to bring about radical reforms. The work of the Bureau of Municipal Research in New York has had a similar practical purpose. To these must be added the work accomplished by the child-welfare exhibits, by the social surveys undertaken in different parts of the country, and by similar propaganda in favor of public health.

As a source of social control public opinion becomes important in societies founded on secondary relationships, of which great cities are a type. In the city every social group tends to create its own milieu, and as these conditions become fixed, the mores tend to accommodate themselves to the conditions thus created. In secondary groups and in the city fashion tends to take the place of custom, and public opinion, rather than the mores, becomes the dominant force in social control.

In any attempt to understand the nature of public opinion and its relation to social control it is important to investigate first of all the agencies and devices which have come into practical use in the effort to control, enlighten, and exploit it.

The first and the most important of these is the press, that is, the daily newspaper and other forms of current literature, including books classed as current.

After the newspaper, the bureaus of research which are now springing up in all the large cities are the most interesting and the most promising devices for using publicity as a means of control.

The fruits of these investigations do not reach the public directly, but are disseminated through the medium of the press, the pulpit, and other sources of popular enlightenment.

In addition to these there are the educational campaigns in the interest of better health conditions, the child-welfare exhibits, and the numerous "social advertising" devices which are now employed, sometimes upon the initiative of private societies, sometimes upon that of popular magazines or newspapers, in order to educate the public and enlist the masses of the people in the movement for the improvement of conditions of community life.

The newspaper is the great medium of communication within the city, and it is on the basis of the information which it supplies that public opinion rests. The first function which a newspaper supplies is that which formerly was performed by the village gossip.

In spite, however, of the industry with which newspapers pursue facts of personal intelligence and human interest, they cannot compete with the village gossips as a means of social control. For one thing, the newspaper maintains some reservations not recognized by gossip, in the matters of personal intelligence. For example, until they run for office or commit some other overt act that brings them before the public conspicuously, the private life of individual men or women is a subject that is, for the newspaper, taboo. It is not so with gossip, partly because in a small community no individual is so obscure that his private affairs escape observation and discussion; partly because the field is smaller. In small communities there is a perfectly amazing amount of personal information afloat among the individuals who compose them.

The absence of this in the city is what, in large part, makes the city what it is.

. . . .

IV. TEMPERAMENT AND THE URBAN ENVIRONMENT

Great cities have always been the melting-pots of races and of cultures. Out of the vivid and subtle interactions of which they have been the centers, there have come the newer breeds and the newer social types. The great cities of the United States, for example, have drawn from the isolation of their native villages great masses of the rural populations of Europe and America. Under the shock of the new contacts the latent energies of these primitive peoples have been released, and the subtler processes of interaction have brought into existence not merely vocational, but temperamental, types.

Mobilization of the Individual Man. Transportation and communication have effected, among many other silent but far-reaching changes, what I have called the "mobilization of the individual man." They have multiplied the opportunities of the individual man for contact and for association with his fellows, but they have made these contacts and associations more transitory and less stable. A very large part of the populations of great cities, including those who make their homes in tenements and apartment houses, live much as people do in some great hotel, meeting but not knowing one another. The effect of this is to substitute fortuitous and casual relationship for the more intimate and permanent associations of the smaller community.

Under these circumstances the individual's status is determined to a considerable degree by conventional signs—by fashion and "front"—and the art of life is largely reduced to skating on thin surfaces and a scrupulous study of style and manners.

Not only transportation and communication, but the segregation of the urban population tends to facilitate the mobility of the individual man. The processes of segregation establish moral distances which make the city a mosaic of little worlds which touch but do not interpenetrate. This makes it possible for individuals to pass quickly and easily from one moral milieu to another, and encourages the fascinating but dangerous experiment of living at the same time in several different contiguous, but otherwise widely separated, worlds. All this tends to give to city life a superficial and adventitious character; it tends to complicate social relationships and to produce new and divergent individual types. It introduces, at the same time, an element of chance and adventure which adds to the stimulus of city life and gives it, for young and fresh nerves, a peculiar attractiveness. The lure of great cities is perhaps a consequence of stimulations which act directly upon the reflexes. As a type of human behavior it may be explained, like the attraction of the flame for the moth, as a sort of tropism.

dence of the city upon the larger social and economic tissue of which it is a part. If the prime cause of congestion, as defined above, is low wages, and the best authorities agree that this is true, how can the city expect to do more than touch the fringe of the question? If long hours, low wages, and extensive periods of unemployment are responsible for a large part of the crime and misery of the city, how can a municipal government hope to make any radical changes when the underlying economic forces are beyond its reach.

All this is not said in disparagement of city planning or any of the newer enlightened activities of American municipalities. A great deal can be done by the city to make the living and working conditions within its borders better, but when the city has done its utmost, many fundamental evils will remain untouched at the real source. That is why non-partizanship, aiming at mere business efficiency in administration, and good city government movements are to be considered as temporary, not permanent, advances in American politics. The social policy of the city cannot be forcibly torn from the larger social policy of the nation which conditions the very problems with which the municipality must deal.

The City and Civilization

by Brand Whitlock*

In concluding his fascinating history of Rome, and as though to close with a brilliant picture of the greatness of the empire under Augustus, Signor Ferrero describes the fair towns and the spendid cities that had sprung up under the *pax Romana;* ... and he goes on to show how "the spirit of country life, the simplicity, the thrift, and the old-fashioned austerity which Virgil had sung in his Georgics was doomed to vanish," and, in turn, the vitality of the country was to be sapped by the towns, which absorbed wealth, intellect, and energy for conversion to vice and luxury. ...

The picture, like many another in which the great modern historian has realized so vividly for us the Rome of that day, is as familiar as the laments which the poets then uttered, for the poets have been deploring the urban and extolling the rural condition ever since, and the tradition of the moral superiority of clodhoppers has been handed down, in a sort of apostolical succession, from Theocritus and Virgil and Horace, to Bacon, who regarded the country as God's garden; to Cowley, who went so far as to make Cain the father of all municipalities; to Cowper, who fixed the tradition in his line, "God made the country, and man made the town," and helped to raise a superstition in America to the dignity of a political principle. For the preachers, the publicists, and the politicians have imitated the poets in these their pious preferences, and whenever the complex social problems of the time become too difficult, they extricate themselves from their perplexities by gliding down to those familiar generalities in which the youth of the land are advised to stay on the farms.

. . . .

The prepossession in favor of this myth on the part of the preachers can better be ascribed to their love of the pagan classics than to their love of the country, since all of them, or all of them who can so do, quickly leave the country and hie to the city like their brother humans, despite a professional distrust of urban life as suggesting the abominations of Nineveh and of Babylon. It may be in part the natural result of that idealism with which the spiritual

*Brand Whitlock, "The City and Civilization," *Scribner's Magazine,* 52 (November, 1912), pp. 623-633.

long genealogies of the Jukes and the tribes of Ishmael would not show such a persistent and distressing uniformity of vice, crime, and poverty unless they were peculiarly fit for the environment in which they are condemned to exist.

We must then accept these "moral regions" and the more or less eccentric and exceptional people who inhabit them, in a sense, at least, as part of the natural, if not the normal, life of a city.

It is not necessary to understand by the expression "moral region" a place or a society that is either necessarily criminal or abnormal. It is intended rather to apply to regions in which a divergent moral code prevails, because it is a region in which the people who inhabit it are dominated, as people are ordinarily not dominated, by a taste or by a passion or by some interest which has its roots directly in the original nature of the individual. It may be an art, like music, or a sport, like horse-racing. Such a region would differ from other social groups by the fact that its interests are more immediate and more fundamental. For this reason its differences are likely to be due to moral, rather than intellectual, isolation.

Because of the opportunity it offers, particularly to the exceptional and abnormal types of man, a great city tends to spread out and lay bare to the public view in a massive manner all the human characters and traits which are ordinarily obscured and suppressed in smaller communities. The city, in short, shows the good and evil in human nature in excess. It is this fact, perhaps, more than any other, which justifies the view that would make of the city a laboratory or clinic in which human nature and social processes may be conveniently and profitably studied.

The Growth of the City: An Introduction to a Research Project

by Ernest W. Burgess*

The outstanding fact of modern society is the growth of great cities. Nowhere else have the enormous changes which the machine industry has made in our social life registered themselves with such obviousness as in the cities. In the United States the transition from a rural to an urban civilization, though beginning later than in Europe, has taken place, if not more rapidly and completely, at any rate more logically in its most characteristic forms.

All the manifestations of modern life which are peculiarly urban—the sky-scraper, the subway, the department store, the daily newspaper, and social work—are characteristically American. The more subtle changes in our social life, which in their cruder manifestations are termed "social problems," problems that alarm and bewilder us, as divorce, delinquency, and social unrest, are to be found in their most acute forms in our largest American cities. The profound and "subversive" forces which have wrought these changes are measured in the physical growth and expansion of cities. That is the significance of the comparative statistics of Weber, Bücher, and other students.

These statistical studies, although dealing mainly with the effects of urban growth, brought out into clear relief certain distinctive characteristics of urban as compared with rural populations. The larger proportion of women to men in the cities than in the open country, the greater percentage of youth and middle-aged, the higher ratio of the foreign-born, the increased heterogeneity of occupation, increase with the growth of the city, and profoundly alter its social structure. These variations in the composition of population are indicative of all the changes going on in the social organization of the community. In fact, these changes are a part of the growth of the city, and suggest the nature of the processes of growth.

The only aspect of growth adequately described by Bücher and Weber was the rather obvious process of the *aggregation* of urban population. Almost as overt a process, that of *expansion,* has been investigated from a different and

*Ernest W. Burgess, "The Growth of the City: An Introduction to a Research Project," *Publications of the American Sociological Society,* 18 (1923), pp. 85-97. Reprinted with the permission of the American Sociological Association.

hopeful the signs may be—he seems to have been justified in this restraint. He has been confirmed by M. Ostrogorski, that able Russian who came over here not long ago and wrote about us, and saw many things in us we had not seen ourselves, because, perhaps, to borrow an expression from the painters, he beheld with a fresher eye.

The young DeTocqueville has said long since that "local assemblies constitute the strength of free nations," that "town meetings are to liberty what primary schools are to science"; and that "a nation may establish a system of free government, but without the spirit of municipal institutions it cannot have the spirit of liberty." In a word, as Mr. Frederic C. Howe has said in his excellent book, "the city is the hope of democracy." The last census shows that about forty-six per cent of our population is urban, the urban increase in the preceding ten years having been thirty-four per cent as against an increase of eleven per cent in the rural population. If democracy is to be justified it must assuredly be justified first in that jurisdiction which is most compact, in that one where the interests vitally affecting the detail of daily life are ever before the citizen, in that one whose government is nearest at hand. The citizen may feel an interest in the amount of indirect tax the tariff compels him to pay in his capacity of ultimate consumer, but what a cold, dispassionate academic interest it will be compared with that warm, personal concern he shows when his street-car fare is under consideration! He may be impressed by a debate in Congress, but interfere by ordinance with the sign he puts out on the sidewalk to advertise the business of his little shop, and see which claims his more vivid attention.

This denial of democracy through constant legislative interference has helped to pile up the tragedy which everywhere and in all times has marked the decadence seemingly inseparable from excessive urbanism. Little need is there to speak of the evil types produced by city life, whether in its higher circles or in the purlieus of the slum and tenderloin. These have been abundantly represented on the stage and in the fiction of every land. The daily newspapers reveal the squalid and saddening phase of city life; it is all too well known, and too constantly noted by the thoughtful and observing; the poets and the preachers have been quite accurate in their descriptions of it, and wholly and nobly right minded in their abhorence of it.

. . . .

If there has been no such study of the rural population in our own land, it may be because of the fact that our writers, when they have not sentimentalized the farmer and his life quite as extravagantly as have the politicians, have chosen to treat them humorously, unless, indeed, it be that they have felt that the official records have spared them the pains. To any one who knows the rural politics of our States the revelations of the last year were not so surprising as they seem to have been to those romanticists who write the startling headlines in the daily press. In Adams County, Ohio, it was shown that two-thirds of the bone and sinew of the land had been regularly selling their votes to the highest bidder, and that the bidders did not have to bid very high either, the price of votes ranging from two dollars to ten dollars, and so many of the guilty ones were disenfranchised that in some precincts there were not enough duly qualified electors remaining to man the polls officially for election day. And Adams County knew few of the corrupting influences of urban civilization; it could not have been the corporations, for Adams County was traversed by but one railway, and that scrupulously ran sixteen miles from the county-seat; it was not to be ascribed to the ignorant foreign vote for there were few if any foreigners in Adams County, the people being of the high, pure American strain; nor could it have been the saloon, for Adams County had been dry for ten years. Here, indeed, was a county ideally rural, where the agricultural and pastoral life were lived in all their sylvan simplicity; one would have said that here, of all places, untouched and uncontaminated by city people and their evil customs, the golden age should have been restored, and that the population of American sovereigns should have developed such Arcadian loveliness of character that the whole State might have been regenerated and redeemed.

And, lest Adams County be thought an exception, revelations about the same time were made of similar political morals in Putnam County, New York, and these were succeeded immediately by exposures quite as distressing in Vermilion County, Illinois. Tammany at its worst could not approach the degradation that was revealed in these rural communities, for while it has been estimated that the purchasable vote in New York is but five per cent of the total electorate, it was shown to be sixty-six and two-thirds per cent in the Ohio instance, while according to the *New York Evening Post* the venality in Putnam County was practically unanimous.

The mere barter and sale of the suffrage does not constitute, of course, all of the corruption in cities, even in New York, and it may be said for the malefactors of small wealth in Adams and Putnam and Vermilion Counties, as for those thousands of other counties in these States exactly like them, that they did not dispose of their suffrages for passes, or for social invitations, or for the smiles and favors of the wicked rich, or for protection, either at the hands of policemen or of the collectors of the customs, or for legal privileges; they seem to have contented themselves with crude and naïve and elemental expressions of the spirit of graft, but, so far as the opportunity was afforded, they seem to have embraced it eagerly and entirely.

But neither the testimony of the criminal records of rural counties nor the evidence adduced by the conscientious novelists of the school of modern realism is needed to prove that the morals of rural communities are no better than those of the urban condition. Any one who has had experience of the atmosphere of the average American State Legislature will readily enough depose that the moral sense of the country member is no better than that of his colleague from the city. The typical exposures in investigations, like those which recently have been made with reference to the election of a distinguished senator from Illinois, have

CHART I. THE GROWTH OF THE CITY

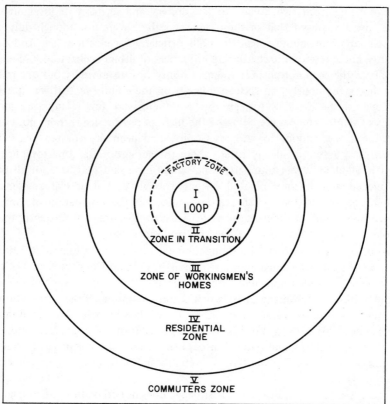

contained the residences of the "best families." It hardly needs to be added that neither Chicago nor any other city fits perfectly into this ideal scheme. Complications are introduced by the lake front, the Chicago River, railroad lines, historical factors in the location of industry, the relative degree of the resistance of communities to invasion, etc.

Besides extension and succession, the general process of expansion in urban growth involves the antagonistic and yet complementary processes of concentration and decentralization. In all cities there is the natural tendency for local and outside transportation to converge in the central business district. In the downtown section of every large city we expect to find the department stores, the skyscraper office buildings, the railroad stations, the great hotels, the theaters, the art museum, and the city hall. Quite naturally, almost inevitably, the economic, cultural, and political life centers here. The relation of centralization to the other processes of city life may be roughly gauged by the fact that over half a million people daily enter and leave Chicago's "loop." More recently sub-business centers have grown up in outlying zones. These "satellite loops" do not, it seems, represent the "hoped for" revival of the neighborhood, but rather a telescoping of several local communities into a larger economic unity. The Chicago of yesterday, an agglomeration of country towns and immigrant colonies, is undergoing a process of reorganization into a centralized decentralized system of local communities coalescing into sub-business areas visibly or invisibly dominated by the central business district. The actual processes of what may be called centralized decentralization are now being studied in the development of the chain store, which is only one illustration of the change in the basis of the urban organization.

Expansion, as we have seen, deals with the physical growth of the city, and with the extension of the technical services that have made city life not only livable, but comfortable, even luxurious. Certain of these basic necessities of urban life are possible only through a tremendous development of communal existence. Three millions of people in Chicago are dependent upon one unified water system, one giant gas company, and one huge electric light plant. Yet, like most of the other aspects of our communal urban life, this economic co-operation is an example of co-operation without a shred of what the "spirit of co-operation" is commonly thought to signify. The great public utilities are a part of the mechanization of life in great cities, and have little or no other meaning for social organization.

Yet the processes of expansion, and especially the rate of expansion, may be studied not only in the physical growth and business development, but also in the consequent changes in the social organization and in personality types. How far is the growth of the city, in its physical and technical aspects, matched by a natural but adequate readjustment in the social organization? What, for a city, is a normal rate of expansion, a rate of expansion with which controlled changes in the social organization might successfully keep pace?

SOCIAL ORGANIZATION AND DISORGANIZATION AS PROCESSES OF METABOLISM

These questions may best be answered, perhaps, by thinking of urban growth as a resultant of organization and disorganization analogous to the anabolic and catabolic processes of metabolism in the body. In what way are individuals incorporated into the life of a city? By what process does a person become an organic part of his society? The natural process of acquiring culture is by birth. A person is born into a family already adjusted to a social environment—in this case the modern city. The natural rate of increase of population most favorable for assimilation may then be taken as the excess of the birth-rate over the death-rate, but is this the normal rate of city growth? Certainly, modern cities have increased and are increasing in population at a far higher rate. However, the grows less and less obscure, as, amid the perplexities of life, reason and the good-will of man discern a better purpose, a better order, and a better way.

. . . .

This sense is already beginning to find a rudimentary expression in the tendency to replan cities, or to plan cities, since they were never planned in the first place, but merely grew, haggard, unkempt, and ugly, as industrial accidents. We are hearing much of the city beautiful in these days; hardly a city or a town that has not its commission and its plan for a unified treatment of its parks, for a civic centre of some sort—in a word, its dream. These are the expressions of that divine craving in mankind for harmony, for beauty, for order, which is the democratic spirit. This, of course, is no new impulse; after the great London fire in 1666, Sir Christopher Wren drew plans for building the city anew, and had the model city he imagined been erected, civilization might have been a lovelier thing than it has been. L'Enfant planned an ideal Washington—amid the jeers of all philistinism, echoing in the halls of Congress even in our own day—but there is now the hope that his dream will be realized; indeed, it is being realized as the result of the intelligence and appreciation which in these matters marked the administrations of Colonel Roosevelt and President Taft.

. . . .

Civilization may well provide better housing for the people, and by means of purified-water supplies, light, and transportation serve the public utility, health, and convenience; it may extend and harmonize parks and breathing-spots, widen boulevards, plant trees and flowers, and make playgrounds, swimming-pools, and skating-ponds for the children, and thus introduce into urban life something of the wholesomeness and charm of rural life. It may plan and arrange its cities so that they will please the aesthetic eye and, with music-halls and art-galleries, refine and ennoble taste; it may build its roads far out on the countryside, and by its myriad conveniences and inventions, the marvels of its genius, alleviate the rigors of rural existence and bring country and city more closely together; all these it may do and is doing. But this is not all. For this city sense, this urge of democracy is but the spirit of good-will in humanity, working now, however blindly however unconsciously, with whatever bungling and mistake to improve the lot of man, and this spirit must contrive cities that shall be not only clean, beautiful, and symmetrical in their physical proportions, but cities, in a word, which by a stupendous and supreme summing up of all the sciences and all the arts shall express the ideals of the people and work wonderful ameliorations in the human soul. This will not be accomplished by the triumph of one class over another, or by any *bouleversement* in which the processes of despotism will be reversed. It will not come out of the clash of parties, or by new formulae, new dogma, or new orthodoxies; these would but replace the old that are no different from them in spirit, or from the brute force on which they rely; they would fail as the others have failed. It will not descend upon the cities from any feudal lord or industrial baron of our time, whether in the hall of legislature or in the counting-house, however gracious and benevolent he may be. It must come up from the people themselves through patient study and careful experiment in the spirit of humility and tolerance and be the expression of their own best longings and aspirations.

For such a freedom the cities themselves must be made free, for the great advancements, the great progressions in the world and in the life of the race have been made where the cities were free. The cities indeed are microcosms. In them the cleavages that divide society are easily beheld, the problems that weary mankind are somehow reduced to simpler factors. Privilege can be seen, almost with the eye; its various despots may be identified, as though they rolled in chariots through the streets, and its victims as they run, begging, after. The cities are the centres of the nation's thought, the citadels of its liberties, and as they were once and originally the trading-posts and the stockades whence the hardy pioneers began their conquest of the physical domain of the continent, so are they now the outposts whence mankind is to set forth on a new conquest of the spiritual world, in which the law of social relations is to be discovered and applied. Already we apprehend a new truth, that in the inspiring tendency of the neo-democratic spirit there is to be realized not only an aesthetic, but an ethic beauty, and the time is foreshadowed when our cities will be beautiful in their morals, in their spirit, and in the common lot and in the individuality, the personality of their citizens. But that time will come only when they are made free of feudal rulers. And, thence, from the city into the State, from the State into the nation, is it, in this old and moody and nervous age, too much to hope?—from the nation into the world? It is the dream of America, at any rate, the goal of democracy and the purpose of civilization.

Greek ice-cream parlors, Chinese laundries, Negro porters, Belgian janitors, etc.

The facts that in Chicago 1,000,000 (996,589) individuals gainfully employed reported 509 occupations, and that over 1,000 men and women in *Who's Who* gave 116 different vocations, give some notion of how in the city the minute differentiation of occupation "analyzes and sifts the population, separating and classifying the diverse elements." These figures also afford some intimation of the complexity and complication of the modern industrial mechanism and the intricate segregation and isolation of divergent economic groups. Interrelated with this economic division of labor is a corresponding division into social classes, and into cultural and recreational groups. From this multiplicity of groups, with their different patterns of life, the person finds his congenial social world, and, what is not feasible in the narrow confines of a village, may move and live in widely separated and, perchance, conflicting worlds. Personal disorganization may be but the failure to harmonize the canons of conduct of two divergent groups.

If the phenomena of expansion and metabolism indicate that a moderate degree of disorganization may and does facilitate social organization, they indicate as well that rapid urban expansion is accompanied by excessive increases in disease, crime, disorder, vice, insanity, and suicide, rough indexes of social disorganization. But what are the indexes of the causes rather than of the effects of the disordered social metabolism of the city? The excess of the actual over the natural increase of population has already been suggested as a criterion. The significance of this increase consists in the immigration into a metropolitan city like New York and Chicago of tens of thousands of persons annually. Their invasion of the city has the effect of a tidal wave inundating first the immigrant colonies, the ports of first entry, dislodging thousands of inhabitants who overflow into the next zone, and so on and on until the momentum of the wave has spent its force on the last urban zone. The whole effect is to speed up expansion, to speed up industry, to speed up the "junking" process in the area of deterioration (II). These internal movements of the population become the more significant for study. What movement is going on in the city, and how may this movement be measured? It is easier, of course, to classify movement within the city than to measure it. There is the movement from residence to residence, change of occupation, labor turnover, movement to and from work, movement for recreation and adventure. This leads to the question: What is the significant aspect of movement for the study of the changes in city life? The answer to this question leads directly to the important distinction between movement and mobility.

MOBILITY AS THE PULSE OF THE COMMUNITY

Movement, per se, is not an evidence of change or of growth. In fact, movement may be a fixed and unchanging order of motion, designed to control a constant situation, as in routine movement. Movement that is significant for growth implies a change of movement in response to a new stimulus or situation. Change of movement of this type is called *mobility*. Movement of the nature of routine finds its typical expression in work. Change of movement, or mobility, is characteristically expressed in adventure. The great city, with its "bright lights," its emporiums of novelties and bargains, its palaces of amusement, its under-world of vice and crime, its risks of life and property from accident, robbery, and homicide, has become the region of the most intense degree of adventure and danger, excitement and thrill.

Mobility, it is evident, involves change, new experience, stimulation. Stimulation induces a response of the person to those objects in his environment which afford expression for his wishes. For the person, as for the physical organism, stimulation is essential to growth. Response to stimulation is wholesome so long as it is a correlated *integral* reaction of the entire personality. When the reaction is *segmental,* that is, detached from, and uncontrolled by, the organization of personality, it tends to become disorganizing or pathological. That is why stimulation for the sake of stimulation, as in the restless pursuit of pleasure, partakes of the nature of vice.

The mobility of city life, with its increase in the number and intensity of stimulations, tends inevitably to confuse and to demoralize the person. For an essential element in the mores and in personal morality is consistency, consistency of the type that is natural in the social control of the primary group. Where mobility is the greatest, and where in consequence primary controls break down completely, as in the zone of deterioration in the modern city, there develop areas of demoralization, of promiscuity, and of vice.

In our studies of the city it is found that areas of mobility are also the regions in which are found juvenile delinquency, boys' gangs, crime, poverty, wife desertion, divorce, abandoned infants, vice.

These concrete situations show why mobility is perhaps the best index of the state of metabolism of the city. Mobility may be thought of in more than a fanciful sense, as the "pulse of the community." Like the pulse of the human body, it is a process which reflects and is indicative of all the changes that are taking place in the community, and which is susceptible of analysis into elements which may be stated numerically.

The elements entering into mobility may be classified under two main heads: (1) the state of mutability of the person, and (2) the number and kind of contacts or stimulations in his environment. The mutability of city populations varies with sex and age composition, the degree of detachment of the person from the family and from other groups. All these factors may be expressed numerically. The new stimulations to which a population responds can be measured in terms of change of movement or of increasing contacts. Statistics on the movement of urban population may only measure routine, but an increase at a higher ratio than the increase of population measures mobility. In 1860 the horse-car lines of New York City carried about 50,000,000 passengers; in 1890 the trolley-cars (and a few surviving horse-cars) transported about 500,000,000;

ington, Manila, and Chicago were derived from the experience of the Fair. His plan of the City of Chicago, commissioned by the Commercial Club (a group of prominent Chicago businessmen), was to stand as his major contribution to American city planning. In this blueprint for city growth, Burnham sought to create a "well ordered, convenient and unified city" which would enhance business activity while introducing a level of architectural coherence and artistic quality. Burnham's work influenced the building of many civic centers throughout the country. The City Beautiful Movement blended together the concepts of civic art and municipal planning and was to dominate American urban planning circles.

But aesthetic factors continued to be subordinate to technical progress. Architecture and urban design were wedded to capitalism, with primary inspiration and initiative coming from the patron and not the artist. Civic art was simply the means to develop and demonstrate civic consciousness; the city planner Charles Mulford Robinson cast art in the role of servant to the municipality when he wrote: "Today, the spirit of the time is commercial and industrial, and our modern civic art reveals itself in forms that commerce and industry comprehend." Robinson, who held the first Chair of Civic Design in the University of Illinois (1913-1917) believed this was to be achieved when utility joined beauty in the pursuit of the city beautiful. The naive belief that civic progress must wait upon the favors of the conscience-stricken businessmen represented the major folly of American city-planners.

There were others who were as attracted and fascinated by the might and success of American technological development as were the city-planners, but who doubted that urban design or civic art had any role to play in the creation of an urbanized society. So long as American art was immature and did not represent a national consciousness or spirit, exclaimed Herbert Croly, erstwhile architectural critic and ideologist of the Progressive Movement, city planning was impossible. Utility, Croly felt, could be the only legitimate force governing city growth.

Unfortunately, by their adherence to the city beautiful concept the early planners and architects ignored the most pressing social problems of their day. The physical inadequacies and economic evils of the city made little impression upon the course of their work. The architects served the rich, thus, like their patrons, engendering an architecture notable primarily for its sheer bulk—what critic Henry-Russell Hitchcock has termed "quantitative architecture." City planning inspired illusions of civic grandeur while municipalities became infested and polluted by slums and brutalizing urban conditions. While stimulating the acceptance of the notion of city planning, and creating islands of architectural achievement amid seas of urban ugliness, the City Beautiful Movement and modern civic art failed in their central purpose: to make the city beautiful.

Report on Choice of Site of the World's Columbian Exposition

by Frederick Law Olmsted*

We have been asked to examine and comment upon several properties that have been suggested to your Board as sites for the Exposition.

Our report of the 12th inst. on Jackson Park having been given by your Board to the public, and having been generally thought, as we are informed, to be wholly unfavorable to that site, we would like to point out that such an understanding of it must be due to the fact that it was written for a body of gentlemen presumed to be specially well informed in the premises, and to be fully aware of many circumstances and of many considerations with which the public could not be expected to be familiar.

. . . .

Assuming these and other considerations to be familiar to those to whom the report was addressed, we did not in our report, think it necessary to specifically refer to them. It had been within our knowledge, gained twenty years before, in wading through the site of Jackson Park, that topographically, it was a morass, divided by a few low, narrow sand dunes; one-third of it below the surface of the Lake at ordinary stages of the water, and the greater part of it subject to be occasionally flooded. We had regarded with admiration, the characteristic Chicago audacity of the proposition to divide a World's Fair between such a situation, and another more than six miles distant from it, on which land was to be created for the purpose, by displacing a part of Lake Michigan. We fell heartily into the bold spirit of the project, and considered that, if carried out creditably, the result would be, in itself, for many, a most interesting circumstance of the Fair. In this spirit we took up the problem which your request presented to us; considered with care certain elements of the case to which no reference was made in our report, and of which we have seen no account publicly taken, and gave you our conclusions without a doubt that they would be considered highly favorable to the proposition. We had at the time no thought of any other site as in competition with that of Jackson Park, and said nothing with an intention to lessen the favor with which we believed it to be regarded by your Board.

. . . .

---
*Frederick Law Olmstead, "Report on Choice of Site of World's Columbian Exposition—Chicago," 1893.

51

Urbanism as a Way of Life

by Louis Wirth*

A SOCIOLOGICAL DEFINITION OF THE CITY

Despite the preponderant significance of the city in our civilization . . . our knowledge of the nature of urbanism and the process of urbanization is meager. Many attempts have indeed been made to isolate the distinguishing character- istics of urban life. Geographers, historians, economists, and political scientists have incorporated the points of view of their respective disciplines into diverse definitions of the city. While in no sense intended to supersede these, the formu- lation of a sociological approach to the city may incidentally serve to call atten- tion to the interrelations between them by emphasizing the peculiar characteris- tics of the city as a particular form of human association. A sociologically significant definition of the city seeks to select those elements of urbanism which mark it as a distinctive mode of human group life.

The characterization of a community as urban on the basis of size alone is obviously arbitrary. It is difficult to defend the present census definition which designates a community of 2,500 and above as urban and all others as rural. The situation would be the same if the criterion were 4,000, 8,000, 10,000, 25,000, or 100,000 population, for although in the latter case we might feel that we were more nearly dealing with an urban aggregate than would be the case in communities of lesser size, no definition of urbanism can hope to be completely satisfying as long as numbers are regarded as the sole criterion. Moreover, it is not difficult to demonstrate that communities of less than the arbitrarily set number of inhabitants lying within the range of influence of metropolitan centers have greater claim to recognition as urban communities than do larger ones leading a more isolated existence in a predominantly rural area. Finally, it should be recognized that census definitions are unduly influenced by the fact that the city, statistically speaking, is always an administrative concept in that the corporate limits play a decisive role in delineating the urban area. Nowhere is this more clearly apparent than in the concentrations of population on the peripheries of great metropolitan centers which cross arbitrary administrative boundaries of city, county, state, and nation.

As long as we identify urbanism with the physical entity of the city, viewing

*Louis Wirth, "Urbanism as a Way of Life," *The American Journal of Sociology,* 44 (July, 1938), pp. 1-24. Reprinted by permission of the University of Chicago Press.

it merely as rigidly delimited in space, and proceed as if urban attributes abruptly ceased to be manifested beyond an arbitrary boundary line, we are not likely to arrive at any adequate conception of urbanism as a mode of life. The technological developments in transportation and communication which virtually mark a new epoch in human history have accentuated the role of cities as dominant elements in our civilization and have enormously extended the urban mode of living beyond the confines of the city itself. The dominance of the city, especially of the great city, may be regarded as a consequence of the concentration in cities of industrial and commercial, financial and administrative facilities and activities, transportation and communication lines, and cultural and recreational equipment such as the press, radio stations, theaters, libraries, museums, concert halls, operas, hospitals, higher educational institutions, research and publishing centers, professional organizations, and religious and welfare institutions. Were it not for the attraction and suggestions that the city exerts through these instrumentalities upon the rural population, the differences between the rural and the urban modes of life would be even greater than they are. Urbanization no longer denotes merely the process by which persons are attracted to a place called the city and incorporated into its system of life. It refers also to that cumulative accentuation of the characteristics distinctive of the mode of life which is associated with the growth of cities, and finally to the changes in the direction of modes of life recognized as urban which are apparent among people, wherever they may be, who have come under the spell of the influences which the city exerts by virtue of the power of its institutions and personalities operating through the means of communication and transportation.

The shortcomings which attach to number of inhabitants as a criterion of urbanism apply for the most part to density of population as well. Whether we accept the density of 10,000 persons per square mile as Mark Jefferson proposed, or 1,000, which Willcox preferred to regard as the criterion of urban settlements, it is clear that unless density is correlated with significant social characteristics it can furnish only an arbitrary basis for differentiating urban from rural communities. Since our census enumerates the night rather than the day population of an area, the locale of the most intensive urban life—the city center—generally has low population density, and the industrial and commercial areas of the city, which contain the most characteristic economic activities underlying urban society, would scarcely anywhere be truly urban if density were literally interpreted as a mark of urbanism. Nevertheless, the fact that the urban community is distinguished by a large aggregation and relatively dense concentration of population can scarcely be left out of account in a definition of the city. But these criteria must be seen as relative to the general cultural context in which cities arise and exist and are sociologically relevant only in so far as they operate as conditioning factors in social life.

The same criticisms apply to such criteria as the occupation of the inhabitants, the existence of certain physical facilities, institutions, and forms of political organization. The question is not whether cities in our civilization or in behind the buildings, however dressed with turf, or bedecked with flowers, shrubs or trees, fountains, statutes, bric-a-brac, and objects of art, should be one *in unity of design* with the buildings; should set off the buildings and should be set off, in matters of light and shadow and tone, by the buildings.

It will be seen that all this class of considerations leads towards the conclusion that the choice of a site should be largely influenced by the facility with which the natural conditions of the locality will be favorable to a great, consistent effect on the imagination, in the buildings, and in all that is to come under the observation of visitors, both in looking toward and in looking from the buildings.

We will simply add to this attempt to indicate the leading artistic principle that should be kept in view in the selection of a site, this other: that if it is possible to associate with the grandeur of architecture in a Great Exhibition, and object of natural grandeur, more is thus to be gained than by the most elaborate and costly artificial decorations in the form of gardening features, terraces, fountains and statues, than it is possible for the mind of man to devise, or the hand of man to carry out. Nor, however desirable, is it necessary to the realization of great value in this respect that these natural features should be in such pictorial composition with the architectural group, as would be the case, for example, if the group were to be seen against a mountain side and with some correspondence between its outlines and the outlines of the mountain. Simple proximity, bringing into association natural grandeur with artificial grandeur, would be of great value. To come at once to the local application of this precept, there is at Chicago, but one natural object at all distinctively local, which can be regarded as an object of much grandeur, beauty or interest. This is the Lake. With regard to the value of this possession of the city in respect to the Exposition of 1892, it is to be considered that the inhabitants of the larger part of the United States, of Canada and of Mexico, from which visitors will come to the Fair, will, until they arrive here, never have seen a broad body of water extending to the horizon; will never have seen a vessel under sail, nor a steamboat of half the tonnage of those to be seen hourly passing in and out of Chicago harbor; and will never have seen such effects of reflected light or of clouds piling up from the horizon, as are to be enjoyed almost every summer's day on the lake margin of the city. Your visitors from Europe will never have seen a body of fresh water comparable in majesty to your Lake. It is to be considered also, that Chicago itself, is, in its history and in its commerce, to be a most interesting, perhaps the *most* interesting, of all the exhibits of the Exposition. What would have been its history, what its commerce, what its interest to the world, if Chicago were without this Lake?

We do not lay it down that such considerations as these, recommending you to make the Lake *a part of the Fair,* should prevent the consideration of any site not commanding an unbroken view of the Lake; but we point out that any such other site must have marked superiority in some other highly important respect, to place it at all in competition with sites upon the Lake.

Yet another word in regard to preliminary considerations. The success of the contemplated Exposition, may turn greatly upon what may be sufficiently suggested by the term—"spectacular effect." This spectacular effect depends upon elements of mass and outline and broad effects of color. Applied decorations when used to combine, strengthen, sustain and emphasize the general scheme in this respect, are greatly to be valued; but used except in perfect subordination to it, they are greatly to be depreciated.

It is rare under ordinary circumstances, that this consideration comes into play in any important way in respect to the base and flanks of great buildings, and the consequent tendency to slight it when studying questions of architecture and landscape, is so strongly fixed in most men's minds, that we feel that we cannot too strongly urge the importance of its application to questions which are even now under consideration by your Board. If the combination of circumstances which you are able to establish, produces unity of spectacular effect in a great way, the Exposition will have won a prestige that will carry it successfully through not a few minor insufficiencies.

. . . .

We have now to consider the several sites you have asked us to examine. Not, we say again, with a view to an expression of opinion as to which of them offers the largest advantages, on the whole, for your purpose; but as to their comparative value in respect to special desiderate of the Fair.

The Jackson Park Site.   Since our report upon this site of the 12th inst., we have learned from the public journals that a good deal of apprehension is felt, that the larger part of the Exposition cannot be quite safely and well provided for on the central Lake-Front as presumed in our original instructions; and though these have not been amended, we think it best to take this doubt into consideration. We believe there is no question that a part of the Lake-Front will be available. If the policy of your Board should be modified as thus suggested, a much larger area for building might be wanted at Jackson Park than we had been led to have in view in framing our former report.

As we pointed out verbally to your Committee on Buildings and Grounds before that report was made, a large amount of additional land for the purpose of the Fair could, in several ways, be obtained without a wasteful destruction of the standing wood or interference with the plans of the South Park Commissioners. We have been told, for example, although not perhaps, with authority, that 100 acres or more of low-lying private land could be had in connection with the park site on the South. The locality is a swamp, and would require filling to a depth of at least three feet to make it at all available. The cost of so filling it would not be forbidding, and the increased value of the land, after the Exposition because of the filling, would probably be a full return for its cost. As we also advised you verbally on the 12th inst., the strip of land called the Midway Plaisance, between Jackson and Washington Parks, might be so cleared of its present standing wood, as to allow a building or buildings to be set upon it three-quarters of a mile in aggregate length, and 400 feet wide. These buildings having been removed at the end of the Fair, the land would be as well adapted as it is at present for carrying out the plans of the South Park Commissioners. As we have also advised you before, 70 acres, probably 80, of the open Green of Washington Park could be well used for buildings of the Exposition without permanent detriment to that Park. Certain other land in Washington Park to the extent of 5 to 10 acres, might also be used. Further, we have been informed, but again, not in an authoritative way, that the stables and race course of the Washington Park Club, lying a short distance to the South of Washington Park, with some adjoining land, might be rented for the live-stock department of the Exposition. This would be a detached ground and over a mile and a half from the principal buildings near the Lake shore.

The obvious objection to this and to all suggestions that so far as we know, have been made for connecting much additional land with that of Jackson Park is the *extremely straggling, disjointed and incoherent* character of the arrangement to which it would lead, and the entire disregard it would involve for the advantages which we have shown to lie in a compact and well-organized primary, and central trunk scheme, with looser, but still compact, radial ramifications. Doubtless expedients could be adopted for lessening this objection in some respects. As, for example, by bringing all the different parts into connection by some form of cheap and rapid transit. But a very serious set-back to the success of the Exposition would thus be only in a measure *mitigated:* by no means *removed.*

We have been asked, by a member of your Board, to explain why we did not propose that any of the land in the Southwestern part of the Jackson Park site should be occupied by the Fair. In the first place, we have shown how 60% more floor room could be provided than your scheme as it then stood, required; in the second place, it appeared to us that a great advantage for an effective grouping of the large buildings of the Jackson Park division of the Fair would be lost if a part were planted near the shore, and another part three-quarters of a mile distant, and on a line diagonally to the frontage of the first; in the third place: the body of wood in that quarter of the Park is, after the view the site commands of the Lake, the most valuable property of the Park, and the most valuable landscape property of the locality; and in studying the landscape and spectacular capabilities of the site, we had reckoned largely upon it; in the fourth place, as no suggestion has been made to us that room for the Live Stock Department would be wanted on Jackson Park, we presumed that some other place was had in view for it, in which the devastation of a body of well grown trees would not be necessary. Finally it occurred to us that if this was not the case, and the question was an open one, flat ground contiguous to the Lake and not more than three feet above its ordinary surface was not that which a good shepherd would choose for the sojourn, even for a month, of a valuable block. We understand that the Lake may possibly be at a higher level in the summer of 1893 than it is at present. This consideration dictated the line or two given to the subject at the close of our former report.

We do not understand that the proposition to plant the whole Fair at and near Jackson Park has ever been entertained by your Board; nor that reasons are now required of us why such a proposition should not be entertained. To what we have here said, and what was said in our former report, we have therefore only to add, that should your Board adopt Jackson Park with any necessary annexations as a site for a considerable part of the Fair, our study of the conditions to be dealt with, has led us to think it would not be impossible to treat the land unoccupied by buildings in a manner that, without marked violence to nature, or much apparent effort, would produce results of a pleasingly becoming character, such as have not hitherto been aimed at in World's Fairs, and that would be refined, interesting and attractive.

Garfield Park Site. On the west side of the City near Garfield Park, a body of land has been considered which would be large enough for all purposes of the Exposition. It would allow a compact symmetrical arrangement of the buildings. The soil is a very retentive, heavy clay, but susceptible of drainage and of a degree of amelioration in other aspects. Compared with the Jackson Park site, its advantages from our point of view, are principally, that it would require no filling or dredging operations; that it would be undivided by any water course, and that the arrangement of buildings would not be complicated by such regard for trees or other local circumstances as should be had in dealing with the Jackson Park site, because of its dedication to Park purposes.

In comparison with Jackson Park, the disadvantages of the Garfield Park site are that the country about it is generally unwooded, flat and monotonous, and that the eye ranges from it to a great distance over an unattractive landscape. Touching this point of the question, it may be observed that as to beauty of prairie scenery, depending upon breadth and simplicity of landscape elements, and an horizon broken by distant bodies of wood following sluggish water courses, and a general expression of nature in pleasing repose; as to landscape qualities of this order, they no longer exist in the outskirts of Chicago, having been everywhere disturbed or wholly broken up by introduced, entirely *discordant* elements of landscape.

We are obliged to say, also, that there is now nothing and there can be nothing on what was once the prairie side of the city that will, in the faintest degree compare, in landscape value, with that which, in the summer of 1893, will everywhere be presented on the Lake side. Saying this, we again point out that we do not mean that the comparative disadvantage of a West side site, in this particular, may not be compensated by its greater accessibility from a majority of homes of the city, the greater and better facilities for the transportation, both of visitors and of the materials which the Exposition will require to be brought to and taken from the site. We recognize that, taking the year through, such part of the West side as is fairly well built up. may be the best residence quarter of the city. But considering what has been so strenuously urged upon the attention of the country in regard to the number and excellence of the sites which Chicago has to offer; considering what advantages the Centennial Fair in

Philadelphia possessed in the neighboring scenery; considering what advantages of the same order would have been possessed by the Fair if it had been given a site in the beautiful Rock Creek Valley at Washington, of which the Nation is just taking possession for a Park; considering what superb views were presented of the Palisades and up the valley of the Hudson on the one hand, and the waters and varied shores of Long Island Sound on the other, from the site offered for the Fair by New York; considering all this, we cannot but fear that the choice of a site in the rear of the city, utterly without natural landscape attraction, would be found a disappointment to the country, and that it would give occasion for not a little ironical reference to the claims of an endless extent of *perfect* sites made last winter before Congress.

The North-West Site.   This site is flat, has much good soil and is partly covered with an extended body of wood, many of the trees of which are of a fine character, superior to any others which we have seen equally near the center of the city. Probably better advantages for horticulture are offered here than on any other of the sites considered. Through the timber winds the river which, as we have formerly seen it, would, in connection with the timber, be a landscape attraction of value. But when the stream of this river dwindles nearly to dead pools, as we believe that it is liable to do any summer, it would, with its raw banks and miry bed, be both an inconvenient and inoffensive feature of a great Fair. It has at present, hardly a perceptible current, and the little matter that remains in it appears foul and stagnant. Considering this circumstance and the fact that the site commands no view of the Lake, it must be considered less desirable than the site which lies a little more than a mile eastward from it—and which is next to be taken up.

The North Lake Site.   This is the only site that we have examined with which we had previously no familiarity. Nor did we hear that it had been proposed until we asked if there was no ground north of the city to be considered. That it had not been more prominently brought forward we presume to be due in part, to the absence of any local interest to have it adopted, and in part to reasons not in our province to weigh, such as those of access by railways. Probably the suggestion of it would not be pleasing to the great body of the citizens of Chicago. But these considerations make it the more our duty to advise you that, before deciding the question of a site for the Fair, certain advantages that it offers would be fully realized.

It has been thought to be possible, as we understand, that the Directors of the Exposition might obtain possession during the period of the Fair, of a body of land to be in part described as follows: A nearly square block of 300 acres, with additions of irregular outline on the North of as much more; less than half of this whole area being, in our judgment, more than ample for all requirements of the Fair, provided it could be had in a suitable form. A frontage of a mile and a half on the Lake, much nearer the center of population of the city than Jackson Park. A surface nearly flat, undivided by gullys or sloughs. A sandy sub-soil, as far as we observed, throughout; covered in the western half by a dark surface soil, largely composed of leaf mould, and which has been considerably used with success for nursery and market gardens. This soil gradually becomes thinner in the eastern part, and near the beach a more or less drifting sand takes its place. Large bodies of wood, not as fine as that on the north west site, but much finer than that of the South Parks. The whole, as far as we could judge by cursory examination at this season, better drained than any other land in the suburbs of the city, and a notable part of it already sewered. Water works are now being constructed near the south east corner of the tract, and it is believed practicable to complete them within a year. As planned, they are of large capacity, being intended to meet the future wants of a great district yet thinly inhabited in the northern part of the city. This is a highly important consideration; for, with an abundant use of water, with other applications, it will be practicable even on the sandy surface near the shore, to establish all desired verdure. Of this, evidence appears in the present conditions of a few of the lawns and gardens closely adjoining the tract. Evidence, also, in the present condition of Lincoln Park to those who remember the condition of its site twenty years ago.

The long line of the Lake Shore at this point is mainly a clean, hard, sandy beach: there is a Lake horizon of nearly 180 degrees. The view over the Lake is even finer than that to be had from the intended esplanade of Jackson Park, in that nearly all the floating commerce of the port of Chicago, the largest in number of craft, and the second in tonnage, of any part of this continent, passes in procession on a line parallel with the beach, and generally at a distance most favorable for an imposing panoramic display.

No other site near Chicago offers equal advantages in respect to an effective grouping of large and small structures and of features of natural landscape, in association with them; and generally, for arrangements of the character which, in the preface to this report, we have described to be most desirable. To suggest the grounds of this opinion, let it be supposed, for example, that the principal group of buildings for the Fair should be placed near the shore; suppose the agricultural and horticultural exhibits should be placed in the Western part; suppose these two divisions should be connected by a broad *allee,* with a viaduct over the railroad which passes through the property on a North and South line at a distance of half a mile from the shore; suppose that a series of smaller buildings and various horticultural and other exhibits not requiring buildings, should be placed in an orderly way, fronting upon this *allee;* suppose that passages should be occasionally left between these buildings, leading to the right and to the left. There would then be, for nearly all these structures and for other exhibits, a back-ground of well-grown natural woods *infinitely* finer than could be provided on any site, by planting, before the time of the Fair. These woods would give a form to all that part of the Exhibition requiring the finest setting of approximately that of a prolonged amphitheatre, the principal group on the lake side forming one end of it, the principal structure of the agricultural or horticultural department, the other. Pursuing the *allees* leading out right and left from the axial line of this amphitheatre, districts would be approached through the woods on each side, in which would be satisfactorily placed all those features of the Fair that, because coming in too late, had not been considered nor given places in the earlier arrangements: or which, for any reason, it would be desirable to set somewhat distinguishingly apart.

It is more than probable that with study, and after proper consultation with the architects and other artists whom you will employ, a general design much better than that thus imperfectly suggested, may be devised. But, with respect, to the advantages offered for a design of the general motives suggested, it will be obvious that the North Lake Site stands by itself.

We do not wish to touch upon the question of approaches, except with respect to natural landscape considerations. Having regard to these, we may say that nothing can surpass what will be offered by the North Shore, or Sheridan Drive Passing as it will for a considerable distance between the foliage of Lincoln Park on the one hand, and the bright, broad waters of the Lake on the other. It is our calling to prepare pleasure drives with borders adapted by the modelling of their surface, their stretches of verdure, their groups and masses of foliage and the perspectives of scenery to be obtained from them, that will be as enjoyable as the conditions imposed upon us admit. For the better pursuit of this calling, we have repeatedly visited and studied all the most notable works of this description in Europe and the United States. Is it necessary that we should testify that nothing of the kind that art can produce as an approach to a World's Fair, is to be held for a moment in comparison with that which, without any draft upon your funds, the city will, before 1893, have provided in the Sheridan Drive?

If we have said enough to secure a prudent consideration of the availability of the territory we have thus described, it is unnecessary that we should, at this time, say more: and we have only to repeat once again, in concluding this contribution to the study of the question of the most suitable site for the World's Fair, that we have aimed to give you no opinion as to which of the places that have been considered, taking everything into account, and looking from all sides, is the best for the purpose; that being a question calling for much study of another kind than that which it has been our professional concern to apply to it.

Plan of Chicago

by Daniel H. Burnham*

The tendency of mankind to congregate in cities is a marked characteristic of modern times. This movement is confined to no one country, but is world-wide. Each year Rome, and the cities of the Orient, as well as Berlin, New York, and Chicago, are adding to their population at an unprecedented rate. Coincident with this urban development there has been a widespread increase in wealth, and also an enlarged participation on the part of the people in the work of government. As a natural result of these causes has come the desire to better the conditions of living. Men are becoming convinced that the formless growth of the city is neither economical nor satisfactory; and that overcrowding and congestion of traffic paralyze the vital functions of the city. The complicated problems which the great city develops are now seen not to be beyond the control of aroused public sentiment; and practical men of affairs are turning their attention to working out the means whereby the city may be made an efficient instrument for providing all its people with the best possible conditions of living.

Chicago, in common with other great cities, realizes that the time has come to bring order out of the chaos incident to rapid growth, and especially to the influx of people of many nationalities without common traditions or habits of life. Among the various instrumentalities designed to accomplish this result, a plan for a well-ordered and convenient city is seen to be indispensable; and to the task of producing such a plan the Commercial Club has devoted its energies for the past three years.

It is not to be expected that any plan devised while as yet few civic problems have received final solution will be perfect in all its details. It is claimed for the plan herein presented, that it is the result of extended and careful study of the needs of Chicago, made by disinterested men of wide experience, amid the very conditions which it is sought to remedy; and that during the years devoted to its preparation the plan has had the benefit of varied and competent criticism. The real test of this plan will be found in its application; for, such is the determina-

---

*Daniel Burnham and Edward H. Bennett, *Plan of Chicago: Prepared under the Direction of the Commercial Club, During the Years 1906, 1907, 1908,* ed. Charles Moore (Chicago: 1909), pp. 1-8, 119-124.

tion of the people to secure more perfect conditions, it is certain that if the plan is really good it will commend itself to the progressive spirit of the times, and sooner or later it will be carried out.

It should be understood, however, that such radical changes as are proposed herein cannot possibly be realized immediately. Indeed, the aim has been to anticipate the needs of the future as well as to provide for the necessities of the present: in short, to direct the development of the city towards an end that must seem ideal, but is practical. Therefore it is quite possible that when particular portions of the plan shall be taken up for execution, wider knowledge, longer experience, or a change in local conditions may suggest a better solution; but, on the other hand, before any departure shall be determined upon, it should be made clear that such a change is justified.

If many elements of the proposed plan shall seem familiar, it should be remembered that the purpose has not been to invent novel problems for solution, but to take up the pressing needs of to-day, and to find the best methods of meeting those requirements, carrying each particular problem to its ultimate conclusion as a component part of a great entity,—a well-ordered, convenient, and unified city.

This conception of the task is the justification of a comprehensive plan of Chicago. To many who have given little consideration to the subject, a plan seems to call for large expenditures and a consequent increase in taxation. The reverse is the case. It is certain that civic improvement will go on at an accelerated rate; and if those improvements shall be marshaled according to a well-ordered plan great saving must result. Good order and convenience are not expensive; but haphazard and ill-considered projects invariably result in extravagance and wastefulness. A plan insures that whenever any public or semi-public work shall be undertaken, it will fall into its proper and predetermined place in the general scheme, and thus contribute to the unity and dignity of the city.

The plan frankly takes into consideration the fact that the American city, and Chicago preeminently, is a center of industry and traffic. Therefore attention is given to the betterment of commercial facilities; to methods of transportation for persons and for goods; to removing the obstacles which prevent or obstruct circulation; and to the increase of convenience. It is realized, also, that good workmanship requires a large degree of comfort on the part of the workers in their homes and their surroundings, and ample opportunity for that rest and recreation without which all work becomes drudgery. Then, too, the city has a dignity to be maintained; and good order is essential to material advancement. Consequently, the plan provides for impressive groupings of public buildings, and reciprocal relations among such groups. Moreover, consideration is given to the fact that in all probability Chicago, within the lifetime of persons now living, will become a greater city than any existing at the present time; and that therefore the most comprehensive plans of to-day will need to be supplemented in a not remote future. Opportunity for such expansion is provided for.

The origin of the plan of Chicago can be traced directly to the World's Columbian Exposition. The World's Fair of 1893 was the beginning, in our day and in this country, of the orderly arrangement of extensive public grounds and buildings. The result came about quite naturally. Chicago had become a commercial community wherein men were accustomed to get together to plan for the general good. Moreover, those at the head of affairs were, many of them, the same individuals who had taken part in every movement since the city had emerged from the condition of a mere village. They were so accustomed to results even beyond their most sanguine predictions, that it was easy for them to believe that their Fair might surpass all fairs that had preceded it.

Then, too, the men of Chicago, trained in intense commercial activity, had learned the lesson that great success cannot be attained unless the special work in hand shall be entrusted to those best fitted to undertake it. It had become the habit of our business men to select some one to take the responsibility in every important enterprise; and to give to that person earnest, loyal, and steadfast support. Thus the design and arrangement of the buildings of the World's Columbian Exposition, which have never been surpassed, were due primarily to the feeling of loyalty to the city and to its undertakings; and secondly, to the habit of entrusting great works to men trained in the practice of such undertakings.

The results of the World's Fair of 1893 were many and far-reaching. To the people of Chicago the dignity, beauty, and convenience of the transitory city in Jackson Park seemed to call for the improvement of the water front of the city. With this idea in mind, the South Park Commissioners, during the year following the Fair, proposed the improvement of the Lake front from Jackson Park to Grant Park. Following out this suggestion, a plan for a connection between the two parks was drawn to a large scale, and the project was presented at a meeting of the West and South Park Commissioners. Later this design was exhibited at a dinner given by the Commercial Club; and many business men were emphatic in expressing their conviction that the proposed scheme would be of enormous value to Chicago, and that it should be adopted and carried into execution. This was the inception of the project for a park out in the Lake, having a lagoon between it and the shore.

During the next three or four years more careful studies of the Lake front scheme were made, and very large drawings were prepared for a meeting at the Women's Club and the Art Institute, and for a Merchants Club dinner at the Auditorium. The newspapers and magazines, both at home and throughout the country, united in commenting on and commending the undertaking; and during the decade that has elapsed since the plans were first presented, the proposed improvement has never been forgotten, but has ever been looked upon as something sure to be accomplished. This was the beginning of a general plan for the city.

While these projects were in course of preparation, an extensive expansion of the South Parks system was in progress, and a plan was formulated for a metropolitan park system, including an outer belt of parks and parkways. These movements were started with energy in 1903, under the general direction of the South Park Commissioners and the Special Park Commission; and the results of their work have been useful to those who have undertaken the present task.

Early in 1906 the Merchants Club arranged for the preparation of a complete project for the future development of Chicago. In order to facilitate the progress of the work, rooms were built on the roof of Railway Exchange Building, where the drawings have been prepared and the studies have been made. The Merchants Club and the Commercial Club having been merged in 1907 under the name of the latter organization, the work has continued under the auspices of that association. The committee on the plan has held several hundred meetings; during many weeks meetings have taken place daily; and throughout the entire time no week has passed without one or more such gatherings. By invitation of the Club, the Governor of Illinois, the Mayor of Chicago, and many other public officials have visited the rooms where the work was in progress, and have become familiar with the entire scheme as it was being worked out. The Department of State, through the United States consuls in various European cities, has furnished valuable information relative to civic developments now in progress. Thus the plans have had the benefit of many criticisms and suggestions, made by persons especially conversant with existing conditions. Moreover, visitors interested in the improvement of cities and in park work of all kinds have come from both our own and foreign towns; and from them also much of value and encouragement has been gained.

In presenting this report, the Commercial Club realizes that from time to time supplementary reports will be necessary to emphasize one feature or another which may come prominently before the public for adoption. At the same time, it is confidently believed that this presentation of the entire subject accomplishes the task which has been recognized from the outset, namely:

First, to make the careful study of the physical conditions of Chicago as they now exist;

Second, to discover how those conditions may be improved;

Third, to record such conclusions in the shape of drawings and texts which shall become a guide for the future development of Chicago.

In creating the ideal arrangement, every one who lives here is better accommodated in his business and his social activities. In bringing about better freight and passenger facilities, every merchant and manufacturer is helped. In establishing a complete park and parkway system, the life of the wage-earner and of his family is made healthier and pleasanter; while the greater attractiveness thus produced keeps at home the people of means and taste, and acts as a magnet to draw those who seek to live amid pleasant surroundings. The very beauty that attracts him who has money makes pleasant the life of those among whom he lives, while anchoring him and his wealth to the city. The prosperity aimed at is for all Chicago.

This same spirit which carried out the Exposition in such a manner as to make it a lasting credit to the city is still the soul of Chicago, vital and dominant; and even now, although many new men are at the front, it still controls and is doing a greater work than it was in 1893. It finds the men; it makes the occasion; it attracts the sincere and unselfish; it vitalizes the organization, and impels it to reach heights not believed possible of attainment. This spirit still exists. It is present to-day among us. Indeed, it seems to gather force with the years and the opportunities. It is even now impelling us to larger and better achievements for the public good. It conceals no private purpose, no hidden ends. This spirit—the spirit of Chicago—is our greatest asset. It is not merely civic pride: it is rather the constant, steady determination to bring about the very best conditions of city life for all the people, with full knowledge that what we as a people decide to do in the public interest we can and surely will bring to pass.

. . . .

The plan of Chicago as presented in illustration and text is the result of a systematic and comprehensive study, carried on during a period of thirty months, with the sole purpose of mapping out an ideal project for the physical development of this city. Perfection of detail is not claimed, but the design as a whole is placed before the public in the confident belief that it points the way to realize civic conditions of unusual economy, convenience, and beauty.

It is fully realized that a plan calling for improvements on a scale larger and more inclusive than any heretofore proposed seems, on first consideration, beyond the financial ability of the community. If, however, the plan meets public approval, it can be executed without seriously increasing present burdens. The very growth of the city, creating as it does wealth greater than mines can produce, gives a basis of bond issues in excess of the utmost cost involved in carrying out this plan. The increase in the assessed value of real estate in the city of Chicago for the past ten years exceeds the expense required to put the plan into execution; and at the same time the very character of the proposed changes is such as to stimulate the increase in wealth. The public, therefore, has the power to put the plan into effect if it shall determine to do so.

It is quite possible that some revision of existing laws may be necessary in order to enable the people to carry out this project; but this is clearly within the power of the people themselves. The realization of the plan, therefore, depends entirely on the strength of the public sentiment in its favor. And what hope is there that the people will desire to make Chicago an ideal city? A brief survey of the past will help to form an opinion on this subject.

Sixty years ago, when Chicago was scarcely more than a village, it became apparent that in order to secure proper drainage the street levels must be fixed to a considerable extent throughout what we know as the old city, from the main river to Twelfth Street, and also for a distance on the West and North Sides. This project, albeit a very formidable one for that time, was promptly entered upon and duly carried out, although it involved raising all the streets and most of the buildings throughout that large territory. For that day and generation the undertaking was much more serious than the reconstruction of the city thoroughfares now proposed.

Again, some fifty years ago, when the idea of creating great metropolitan park areas was new, Chicago undertook to acquire and improve a chain of parks surrounding the city on three sides. This scheme, which has well supplied the needs of Chicago until recent times, was carried out in such a manner that it never was burdensome. The creation of a park system for Chicago was not undertaken from motives of utility, but purely because of a desire to make the city attractive; and the success was magnificent.

Later, in the Eighties, the purification of the water of Lake Michigan by the diversion of the sewage became a public issue. Once again the people of Chicago rose to the occasion; and after years of hard work the Drainage Canal, built at a cost of $60,000,000 has been completed.

Next came the World's Fair, in the early Nineties, and here also a result was accomplished which has never been surpassed either in scope or in architectural beauty. The cost of the Fair (over $20,000,000 for grounds and buildings alone) was very large for that day. The fact that the Fair came into being here indicated that this people, generally regarded as a commercial community, were deeply appreciative of the higher forms of good order and municipal beauty.

The Chicago World's Fair, like the raising of the grades of the city, the creation of a complete system of parks and boulevards, and the building of the · Drainage Canal, went far beyond anything of the same kind ever before undertaken by a city. These four works are the greatest ones which have been achieved by Chicago. They have proved the readiness of the people to take up large schemes of public improvement which at the time of their inception required great foresight and great faith in the future. Two of them were demanded by considerations exclusively practical, while the other two were not so regarded, but on the other hand were the expression of the deeper sense in man of the value of delightful surroundings. If an accurate statement of the costs of the four improvements could be made, it would probably show that about equal sums have been spent on the practical and on the aesthetic side.

Besides the public enterprises mentioned, the people of Chicago, either collectively or as individuals, have established many agencies for the improvement of the intellectual, social, moral, and aesthetic conditions. The Chicago Orchestra occupies land and buildings on Michigan Avenue which have a present value of over a million and a quarter of dollars; and during the past twenty years private subscriptions have amounted to at least another million, all expended for an organization purely artistic. The Art Institute building in Grant Park cost $700,000, and since its completion, in 1893, it has never been closed for a day. Besides its large and excellent art school, there is a good collection of the works of old and modern masters, which is constantly receiving additions. The Crerar Library has an endowment fund of three and a half millions, besides a substantial building fund; and the Newberry Library and the Armour Institute of Technology are other worthy public benefactions.

Especially notable are the educational foundations which contribute so largely to the intellectual life of the city, and exert an influence throughout the Middle West,—Lake Forest University, Northwestern University, and the University of Chicago. The last-named institution, established in 1892, has already taken its place among the foremost universities in this country, not only by reason of its endowment and property (representing more than $23,000,000), but also because of wise administration along a well-considered plan.

Quite in accord with the plan of Chicago is the Benjamin Franklin Ferguson Monument Fund of a million dollars, the income of which is available for defraying the cost of statuary commemorating worthy men and women of America, or important events in American history, to be erected in the parks and boulevards of the city, under the direction of the trustees of the Art Institute. The Field Museum, representing gifts aggregating $9,000,000, is a further instance of loyalty to the city and a desire for its improvement.

Such enterprises and such gifts as those enumerated show what may be expected from individual benefactions as wealth increases and the idea of public service is encouraged. When opportunities for enriching the city are provided, individual citizens rise to the occasion, and find true satisfaction in leaving memorials useful or agreeable to the people.

Mere increase in numbers does not warrant the belief that public sentiment in favor of extensive public works will grow in proportion to the population; but the history of the past does prove that the people of Chicago are always ready and anxious to follow when the way to great benefits is plainly open. We believe that the tendency which the community has shown by its acts points hopefully to the adoption of a great scheme of public improvement. In other words, Chicago having already carried out large projects strictly on the lines of this report, may we not, therefore, confidently expect this people to go on doing as they have done?

There is a still stronger reason for the belief that the public will favor such a plan as is herein presented. It lies in the growing love of good order, due to the advance in education. Every one knows that the civic conditions which prevailed fifty years ago would not now be tolerated anywhere; and every one believes that conditions of to-day will not be tolerated by the men who shall follow us. This must be so, unless progress has ceased. The education of a community inevitably brings about a higher appreciation of the value of systematic improvement, and results in a strong desire on the part of the people to be surrounded by conditions in harmony with the growth of good taste; and as fast as the people can be brought to see the advantage to them of more orderly arrangement of the streets, transportation lines, and parks, it is well-nigh certain that they will bring about such desirable ends. Thus do the dreams of to-day become the commonplaces of tomorrow; and what we now deem fanciful will become mere matter-of-fact to the man of the future.

If the plan as a whole be approved by the majority of our citizens because it is found to be both practical and beautiful, the next question is as to what it commits us. In answering this query a general review of the principal elements composing the plan will be of value. The following list comprises the main items:

First. The improvement of the Lake front.

Second. The creation of a system of highways outside the city.

Third. The improvement of railway terminals, and the development of a complete traction system for both freight and passengers.

Fourth. The acquisition of an outer park system, and of parkway circuits.

Fifth. The systematic arrangement of the streets and avenues within the city, in order to facilitate the movement to and from the business district.

Sixth. The development of centers of intellectual life and of civic administration, so related as to give coherence and unity to the city.

The improvement of the Lake front from Winnetka to the Indiana line is an economic necessity. As has been stated, the aggregate of the waste material seeking dumping ground on the Lake shore because that is the cheapest place to deposit it, is not less than one million cubic yards per annum. This material is sufficient to produce annually from twenty-seven to thirty acres of land if used to build the Lake parkways and park-strips herein recommended. The park authorities would only have to furnish breakwaters and bridges and to finish the grounds. The utilization of this material in thirty years would produce all the Lake front land recommended in the report for the region between Grant and Jackson parks. But long before the expiration of the thirty years the amount of filling urgently seeking the Lake front dump will be enormously increased. This dirt should be utilized for the public benefit, instead of being wasted as at present in the open Lake, where it becomes detrimental to health and an interference to navigation. The dirt to be disposed of in building new traction tunnels under the principal streets of the city will go far toward the completion of the new Lake shore parks. It is evident, therefore, that this improvement, involving the redemption of the entire Lake front from Winnetka to the Indiana state line, and the creation of an extremely beautiful and useful public recreation ground, will involve very little public expense. There can be no doubt that this part of the plan of Chicago will be carried through; and in fact much is already being accomplished along these lines.

The interurban highway system can be realized very cheaply. Ninety-five per cent of the necessary roads now exist as public highways, and the cost of acquiring the other five per cent will be merely nominal. . . . The cost of widening that comparatively small portion of the roadways which require to be widened; the straightening of the few which need such treatment; the planting of trees along the highways; and the macadamizing of the roads are improvements that may be hastened by concerted intelligent action. The expense involved is comparatively small, but the economy and convenience to the public are very large. Is it not evident that this portion of the plan can be realized at no distant day provided a strong organization of active men shall be formed for the purpose of carrying it into effect?

The suggestions in regard to trunk lines, their rights-of-way, stations, and general conditions, are many and serious. The suggestions have been made for the purpose of bringing about the greatest economy of money and time, both in freight and passenger handling. If the recommendations herein contained will produce conditions really beneficial to the individual shipper and passenger, undoubtedly they will be found best for the railroads themselves. The direct object in view is to free a large portion of the South Side from tracks and stations and restore it to business use; to double the capacity of the streets of the whole city by opening circulation to the north, west, and south, and by connecting the outlying parts in the best possible manner with the heart of the city. Over and above all these considerations, highly important as they all are, is economy in the freight handling of Chicago as a shipping center. The object here has been to find that general principle which, if applied, will give to the merchants, manufacturers, and jobbers of this city all the advantages that should naturally be theirs throughout the great territory dominated by Chicago. If the general scheme herein proposed shall not be adopted by the public and the railroads, some other inevitably must be, because the very life of the community is involved in the solution of this problem. The commercial prosperity of the community is represented by the cost per ton of handling freight into and out of this territory as a shipping center. General changes in railroad conditions take years to accomplish. That will be the case if such a scheme as we recommend is carried out; but the public should remember that they will not be taxed to pay for it. When these improvements come they will be railroad enterprises, undertaken by the railroads and carried out by the railroads.

The traction recommendations contained in this report are already in progress, and no question need be raised as to whether or not this portion of work will be carried out. It has practically been decided upon, and no doubt will be accomplished. The cost will be borne in part by the traction lines themselves, and partly by the public.

The additional parks and parkways recommended are extensive, as should be the case. Although it is true that the men of forty years ago did devise a scheme which has been sufficient almost up to the present moment, it is also true that the number, location, and arrangement of the parks and parkways of Chicago to-day are entirely inadequate for its future development; and nothing is suggested in this report except what has seemed to be absolutely required. Fifty years ago, before population had become dense in certain portions of the city, people could live without parks; but we of to-day cannot. We now regard the promotion of robust health of body and mind as necessary public duties, in order that the individual may be benefited, and that the community at large may possess a higher average degree of good citizenship. And after all has been said, good citizenship is the prime object of good city planning. In some locations parks and park-ways are sufficient to accommodate the people in the immediate neighborhoods; other sections of this city, and suburbs which will soon become parts of this city, should be equally well provided. "Nature," says President Charles W. Eliot, "is the greatest factor in the continuous education of man and woman." The extensive woodlands proposed are an addition not usually designed for American cities, although almost invariably used in Europe. The cost of these added parks and woodlands will be considerable, and it must be borne by the public; but it is a sane proposition that the people of Chicago and its suburbs should have the sixty thousand acres of wooded territory as well as the great Bow, . . . which will occupy from six to eight hundred additional acres. The acquisition and completion of an outer park system may easily be carried through in ten years; and if the cost shall be distributed over that period of time, it will not prove burdensome. The returns will come in the shape of increase of health and joy of living for all the people; and incidentally the value of every real estate holding in the city will be enhanced.

The land necessary for the civic center should be secured at once, while values at the point proposed are reasonable. For the time being this land may be treated as park space; but the sites and the general scheme of grouping for the buildings should be approved, so that as the city, the county, and the general government outgrow their present structures, the new ones may take their appointed places, each one contributing its part to an orderly and convenient scheme. The adoption of such a scheme would save a very large amount of money in the purchase of public building sites; and would create stability in real estate values. To the West Side especially the development of a civic center along the lines indicated is a matter of prime importance; for it will give to that portion of the city the needed impetus towards higher standards than now prevail there. At the same time it will benefit all other parts of the city, since it is for the advantage of Chicago as a whole that each portion shall be developed equally with every other portion. The cost of the civic center should be paid by the whole community.

The street plan as laid out involves a very considerable amount of money; but it will be found that in Chicago as in other cities, the opening of new thoroughfares, although involving large initial expense, creates an increase in values, due to increase in convenience and the provision for adequate sites for the increasing retail traffic of the city. The cost will amount to many millions of dollars, but the result will be continuous prosperity for all who dwell here; and such prosperity the city cannot have unless it becomes a convenient and pleasant place in which to live.

Finally, it seems probable that the schemes of outer highways and of all the Lake front improvements may come about quite naturally and with very little expense to the city; that the railways will pay most of the expense of their changes and improvements, thus leaving a portion of the cost of the traction system and all of the cost of the civic center, of the parks and parkways, and of the street development for the general public to meet. The community has ample financial ability to do its part without placing undue burdens upon the people. Paris had not much more than half a million people, and her commercial prospects were far less than ours to-day, when that municipality adopted a street improvement scheme involving over two hundred and sixty million dollars, and carried it to completion in thirty-five years. The motive of the French people in undertaking this enterprise was to create a great attraction for all men: a city so delightful as to insure continuous prosperity to the inhabitants. The success of the undertaking has amply justified the pains and the expense. People from all over the world visit and linger in Paris. No matter where they make their money, they go there to spend it; and every proprietor and workman in Paris benefits by reason of that fact. Conditions in Chicago are such as to repel outsiders and drive away those who are free to go. The cream of our own earnings should be spent here, while the city should become a magnet, drawing to us those who wish to enjoy life. The change would mean prosperity, effective, certain, and forever continuous.

If, therefore, the plan is a good one, its adoption and realization will produce for us conditions in which business enterprises can be carried on with the utmost economy, and with the certainty of successful issue, while we and our children can enjoy and improve life as we cannot now do. Then our own people will become home-keepers, and the stranger will seek our gates.

Modern Civic Art

by Charles Mulford Robinson*

The question properly arises as to what municipal art is. Granted that the progressive modern city develops gradually in beauty and splendour, is this normal improvement, which is yet more or less haphazard, civic art? Is the term, after all, a relative one; stands this art alone among all the arts in having nothing absolute, nothing sure? Is there civic art, or merely progress toward civic art, when macadam is laid where no pavement was, or when a bit of waste ground along a river bank is secured by the municipality in order that it may be never used for private ends to the exclusion of the public? If that be civic art, what shall we say if the town, having secured the plot, never develops it; or if, in an effort to "improve," it follows wrong counsels and degrades with tastelessness what might have been a charming feature? Shall we let the spirit of the thing count and still cry "Hail" to civic art?

In other realms of art there must be a joint worthiness of impulse and execution, else the act is not recognised as art. The child, or untaught man, who would paint a Sistine Madonna and succeeds in making only a daub, is not greeted as a master, nor hears the work called "art," though his impulse be of the highest and most artistic. So in the plastic art and the tonal art, there is something absolute—a standard below which no handiwork is art, whatever be the impulse; above which beauty is surely recognised and where the highest art of all is possible—the coupling of worthy execution to high resolve and noble impulse.

So it is not enough that we should see the progressive city tending normally toward physical improvement, and should lay down therefore a dictum that civic art is a late step in civic evolution. We may well pause to ask ourselves just what is municipal art, and whether we mean only a continuance of improvement, an extension of sequence with never a conclusion, when we talk of civic art as a goal.

Perhaps the common trouble is that our minds are not fixed upon perfection in this art, so that we forget that there may be perfection in it. For most art, it may be noted, serves a useful purpose incidentally, finding in its own perfection, in its own beauty, such justification that often men seek art for art's sake alone; while with municipal art the utilitarian advantages and social benefits become so

*Charles Mulford Robinson, *Modern Civic Art, or the City Made Beautiful* (New York: G. P. Putnam's Sons, 1903), pp. 24-36.

paramount that they are not forgotten, are not overlooked, in straining for the sensual pleasure and for that full rounding of positive attainment which in itself may be the artist's goal. Here, then, in this distinction, comes a suggestion for the first qualifying clause in the definition of municipal art. And how natural this first step of definition is! This art, which serves so many social ends, is *municipal,* in the sense of communal.

It is municipal first of all. If men seek it they seek it not for art's sake, but for the city's; they are first citizens and then, in their own way, artists, and artists in this way only because they are citizens. We do not find men and women banding themselves together to create a public sentiment and fund in order that some sculptor may do a noble bit of work to the glorifying of his field of art. But they so band themselves and so commission sculptors, painters, artists, and landscape designers, for the glorifying of civic art—not just because it is art, but because it is civic. They are not asking the town to help art, but art to help the town; the artists, not to glorify their art, but by their art to glorify the city.

This, then, is the first consideration, and it is worthy of more emphasis than might appear. It does something else than conveniently differentiate civic art from any other art. It explains why its disciples may care little for artists though giving commissions, why its clientage should be all the urban world—the art ignorant as well as the cultured; why it must be delayed in coming until civilisation is at its flower, since not dependent on individual and selfish ambition; and why, when coming, it will magnificently make all other purely art endeavours but handmaids to its one great effort—because this is social and the public is behind it.

Thus is civic art first municipal, and has ever attained its largest victories when cities were mightiest. For in so far as it is art, its principles are eternal as the truth, and its conquests must be at least as old as cities. Down through the Middle Ages, poets and painters dreamed of the "city beautiful"; the Irish Gaelic poets sang of it; barbaric Nero strove to realise it; the inspired apostle transcribed his vision in its terms; Greek philosophers drew inspiration from the measure of Athen's attainment of it, and the great prophet named Babylon as "the glory of kingdoms." As anciently as the dawn with its golden radiance has transformed cities, there has been a dream, a sigh, a reaching forth, with civic art the goal.

And what precisely shall be the definition of this art, ancient as all the arts, but distinguished from them by its contentment to be servant, not mistress, in the glorifying of cities? What is any art but the right, best way of doing a certain thing? This art, which is so utilitarian in its purposes as to be civic first and art afterwards, may be defined, then, as the taking in just the right way of those steps necessary or proper for the comfort of the citizens—as the doing of the necessary or proper civic thing in the right way. Thus is its satisfaction quite as much intellectual as sensual, and for popular appreciation it must wait—because of its very practicalness—upon popular education.

So civic art is not a fad. It is not merely a bit of aestheticism. There is nothing effeminate and sentimental about it,—like tying tidies on telegraph poles and putting doilies on the cross-walks,—it is vigorous, virile, sane. Altruism is its impulse, but it is older than any altruism of the hour—as old as the dreams and aspirations of men. We talk much about it now, because we are living in a period that has witnessed more building and remodeling of cities than any period of history, and therefore in a period that compels us to turn our thoughts to the best ways of making improvements and to the principles that ought to guide in building the modern city. And those are the laws of civic art, of the great art that is of the people and for the people, that is closest to their lives, and that draws more than half its charm from the recognition of perfect fitness in its achievements. There is much said now of civic art because it has become at last a popular goal—this art of doing civic things in the right way, which is ever the beautiful way. Because this is true there is a civic art.

As an art that exists not for its own sake, but mainly for the good of the community, first for the doing of the thing and then for the way of doing it, there can be only one successful civic art. This will be one which joins utility to beauty. Cities are not made to be looked at, but to be lived in; and if in the decoration of them there be any forgetfulness of that, no successful civic art will follow and the effort will defeat itself. Realising this, we should try to discover some general rules for guidance, and if we succeed, by noting the requirements and the various means that have been tried to satisfy them, we should be able to that extent to translate our art into a civic science that will be more or less exact—into the science of city-building, which is the text-book of civic art. Where the art fails, the cause has been neglect of the rules, through forgetfulness or ignorance.

Precedent, of course, to transcribing the science, there are to be considered the functions of civic art. If the end be to clothe utility with beauty, and in providing the beautiful to provide also that which will add to the convenience and comfort of the citizens, we shall best find its opportunities for usefulness by studying what has been happily called the anatomy of cities. In this there appear three groups of requirements: Those that have to do with circulation, those that have to do with hygiene, and those that have to do distinctly with beauty. No hard lines separate these classes. If in the street plan, for instance, we find the convenience of circulation—i.e., readiest adaptability to the traffic—the most pressing point, we come in the broad open space, shaded with trees and planted with grass, to a problem that is to be approached still from the side of circulation—since convenient short cuts may be offered—and yet from the side of hygiene, and from that of aesthetics. But the classification remains convenient, for in seeking urban welfare and comfort we must act in one or more of these groups. It may be briefly asserted, therefore, that the function of civic art is the making of artistic—which is to say, of aesthetically pleasant—provision for the circulation, for hygiene, and for city beauty.

It is important to note that beauty itself is the object in only one of these three departments of effort, and even then, as in the case of a bit of sculpture,

which certainly belongs under neither hygiene nor circulation, other considerations, educational or commemorative, may easily modify the artistic aspiration.
Thus the greater part, if not the best, of civic art is that which first does
something else than please the senses. And that is why public-spirited men of all
interests, striving to ameliorate civic conditions along many lines, find in municipal art one desideratum upon which they all agree, and for the furtherance of
which they all—by many paths—are working.

Having observed the purposes of civic art, we come to the means to be
employed in gaining them. Here we must seek rules for guidance and may take
up art principles. These are not new nor are they novel. They are as old as
beauty and as broad as art. They are the three dominant chords on which is built
up the melody of all art. They are unity, variety, and harmony.

If our civic art will not stand its double test—first, the civic test, as to the
urban good it does; and then the aesthetic test, it fails. And this latter test is a
more rigorous requirement with civic art than it is with any other, for municipal
art cannot stand alone, to be judged without its environment—and the field in
which it stands is so broad to have unity, so varied to have harmony, so much
the same in parts to have variety. Consider how easily civic art may fail with this
test applied: a thrilling statue on an unkempt street is not successful civic art,
because its surroundings are not harmonious; a park, lovely in itself, may fail,
from this broad standpoint, for want of that unity in the city plan which would
lend to its location seeming inevitableness. Building restrictions designed to
insure harmony, but made too severe, may lose their artistic effectiveness by the
repression of variety to the verge of monotony. But if it is easy to fail, as surely
it is, success is better worth the winning; and where a city, or part of a city, is
built up from the ground plan to the street furnishings and construction with
regard for these three principles of art, how beautiful, consistent, and intellec-
tually satisfying is the result!

The desirability of obtaining such a thorough, general, and artistic plan of
improvement for every community is evident. The chance to plan a city on
paper before it is built comes but rarely nowadays, and the best we can do is to
see to it that the cities grow artistically, that their extensions at least are beautiful, and that every change in the city itself shall bring it one step nearer to the
ideal. The trouble with most improvement effort is that it is planned all by itself,
that the benefit to the neighborhood is studied rather than that to the community, and that the first half-dozen years after the improvement is made stand out
with more prominence and importance—receive more consideration from taxpayers and tax-spenders—than all the years that are to come thereafter. But in
wise city-building we would consider not five years, not ten years, but posterity.
And to do this would be cheaper in the end.

In an effort for civic improvement, therefore, the first step that is best is one
very seldom taken. It is almost the only step that can insure the highest type of
modern civic art, for the requirements are greater now than when artists and
master builders, dressing with beauty the narrow streets of Italian and Flemish
cities, created the civic art of five centuries ago. In those cities urban hygiene

and circulation made no demands on civic art. Nowadays these things are fundamental, and unless there be a well thought out, artistically conceived, general plan to work on, our civic art will go astray, with lack of completeness or continuity. So it will fail, because isolated and spasmodic; because it will mean a fine park, some patriotic statuary, three or four good streets, and a few noble buildings rather than a city dignified and lovely as a whole—where the open space does not stop with balancing the slum, but redeems it. We have set for ourselves a more complex problem than was dreamed of by the Renaissance, and unless our modern urban art can gain it the result will not satisfy.

It is no reproach to the present that so much has been done without the guidance of general plans. It merely shows that our art impulse outran our art intelligence—a very common procedure. The architect, the artist, the landscape gardener,—all enthusiastic,—have gone too fast for the civil authorities, who represent the people; and so the underlying principles, the great laws that should determine the laying-out and the up-building of cities, have not been set down and studied, as they should be, from all sides. Many a good thing costs more than it ought to, or has to be done over, and often the people have the common-sense argument—though the ideals of the artists are true and high and their dreams need only a little pruning and a little injection of worldly wisdom to be made thoroughly practical. The great thing, the significant thing in its promise for the future, is that there are such dreams, for it is easy to prune, and worldly wisdom is ever cheaper than inspiration. If, out of the abundant experience now available, out of the many costly experiments of the recent years that have witnessed in so marvellous a degree the rise and growth of cities, we can now find enough lessons that are pertinent and suggestive to formulate a sort of science of city-building, we shall have something to guide the artist and something to awaken the interest and enthusiasm of him who cannot dream. It will be not the gospel—which is in the heart—but the law and the prophets of modern civic art.

That, in fact, is one of the great theoretical wants of the day. The dreamers of the city beautiful, the countless artists and laymen who are working for the improvement of cities, towns, and villages, want a theory of civic art to which they can turn. Practically, the need of the day is the local application of this general theory to every interested community. It is the attainment of this end which is sought in urging that the first step in bringing civic art to a town should be the provision of a general plan of development and improvement; of a complete and consistent plan, to the end that henceforth every step taken should be a sure step of progress.

To the greater part of the population, also, the plan that is thus set forth will represent a new ideal, and one which they will find readily comprehensible because concerned so plainly with the conditions before their very eyes, to the avoidance of abstractions. The value to the community of a civic ideal scarcely needs exposition. Since realisation of this ideal is dependent ultimately upon the public's appreciation, it will be brought a great deal nearer by the public's perception of it. Of course an immense responsibility will be thrown upon its makers. The best expert advice should, unfailingly, be obtained; but if the laws of city-building have been put on paper, it will not be hard to measure the suggestions by these laws; and the very prominence of the work will give to it a publicity broadly inviting criticism, while the fact that the progress toward the ideal must continue through a long series of years will demand that the plan proposed be able to bear the changes in special interest and point of view which lapse of years will bring. The plan once secured, the public spirit and artistic sense of the community can hardly fail to insist that it be adhered to. Educationally, it may be parenthetically remarked, knowledge of this plan, which is the perception of a concrete ideal, will offer a short cut, doing in a few months what can be accomplished only very slowly by the efforts to inculcate in school children civic pride and aesthetic appreciation. These efforts will be continued, but they will be given direction and practicalness.

The provision of this ideal, the setting before all the people of a tangible vision of their own possible city beautiful, will have other value than merely that of popular education. It will offer them inspiration. Nor will this inspiration be material only, but as clearly moral and political and intellectual. The pride that enables a man to proclaim himself "a citizen of no mean city" awakens in his heart high desires that had before been dormant. "To make us love our city we must make our city lovely" was taken as its motto by the Municipal Art Society of New York when it was organised, and he who loves his city is a better citizen and a better man.

There will be other than merely general inspiration, for the dream of what one's city should be, and may be, and even some day must be, will be a special inspiration to all those professions of the fine arts upon which the beauty of the city ultimately depends. There is not an architect of spirit who will not feel a new incentive when he thinks that he is planning buildings that are to be part of the city of the future; not a landscape gardener who will not plant with greater care because of this vision; not a sculptor who will not throw himself more devotedly into the modelling of the civic monument that is to be one of the new city's ornaments. And down from the professions to the workers, and from those who execute the commissions to those who give them, will be felt the spur of the dream, the hope, the goal.

"I do not want art for a few," said William Morris, "any more than education for a few, or freedom for a few"—and civic art is essentially public art. It has been likened to "a fire built upon the market place, where every one may light his torch; while private art is a fire built upon a hearthstone, which will blaze and die out with the rise and fall of fortunes."

What Is Civic Art?

by Herbert Croly*

The question as to what is civic art might seem to be as unnecessary as the question: What is municipal reform? Civic art is obviously the name given to the very general aspiration and movement which aims at the improvement of our cities in convenience and appearance; and an answer to any question about its nature would apparently consist of a description of the movement, its purposes, methods, achievements and principles. This is the way in which the question has been answered for the most part by Mr. Charles Mulford Robinson, in his book on "Modern Civic Art." After a couple of introductory chapters, of which more presently, Mr. Robinson enters into an elaborate explanation and illustration of the general rules which should determine the improvement of cities. He begins by establishing their focal points, such as the land and water approaches, and the administrative centre, goes on to discuss the plan and architecture of the business district, and the proper manner of furnishing its streets, and concludes this division of the book by a similar discussion of the proper disposition and embellishment of a residential neighborhood. Then he winds up with a section dealing with the city at large, with parks, parkways and open spaces generally. On none of these subjects does Mr. Robinson leave very much to say. His book will be the manual of municipal improvement for many years to come, and will render any other book of the kind unnecessary. He has sketched for us the ideal city of the civic art reformers—the city in which the utilitarian lion lies down with the artistic lamb, and in which all things are as they should be.

Mr. Robinson waxes very enthusiastic over his vision. "There is," he says, "the promise in the sky of a new day. The darkness rolls away, and the buildings that had been shadows stand forth distinctly in the gray air. The tall façades glow as the sun rises; their windows shine as topaz; their pennants of steam, tugging flutteringly from high chimneys, are changed to silvery plumes. Whatever was dingy, coarse and ugly is either transformed or hidden in shadow. The streets, bathed in the fresh morning light, fairly sparkle, their pavements from the upper windows appearing smooth and clean. . . . As when the heavens rolled away and St. John beheld the new Jerusalem, so a vision of a new London, a new Washington, Chicago, or New York, breaks with the morning sunshine upon

*Herbert Croly, "What Is Civic Art"? *Architectural Record,* 16, (July, 1904), pp. 41-51.

the degradation, discomfort and baseness of modern city life. There are born a new dream and a new hope." For my own part, I cannot share Mr. Robinson's enthusiasm over his vision. While I believe that the movement towards better-planned and better-looking modern cities is as almost necessary and as praise-worthy as the movement towards political reform, I doubt very much the practical value or the theoretic defensibility of looking forward to a civic art millennium or definitely outlining such a consummation. Mr. Robinson's new Jerusalem, like the heaven of mythological Christianity is merely a bit of poetry, but unlike the heaven of mythological Christianity, it is a bit of poetry out of place. It is seductive and impressive only as it is vague and remote. In proportion as it is made definite, it becomes tame, characterless and uninteresting. The ideal city, which is envisaged by putting together the elements of Mr. Robinson's complete vision, in which the streets were all correctly laid out and furnished, the architecture sufficiently subdued and regulated, and the monuments most immaculately grouped and situated, and in which every suggestion of baseness and discomfort is removed—such a city would be less amusing, less suggestive, and in a real sense less habitable than the degraded but living cities of to-day. It is true that the well-planned, well-regulated and well-furnished ideal city is "cracked up" to be very beautiful; but its beauty is entirely a matter of words. Just as the irregularities and discomforts and degradation of London make a more interesting city than the monotonous machine-made regularity of the newer Paris, so no amount of elaborate and correct planning of streets, monu-ments, furniture and parks will of themselves make a beautiful, habitable and interesting city. The ugly actual cities of to-day make a livelier appeal to the imagination than does an ideal city, which in sacrificing its ugliness on the altar of civic art, sacrifices also its proper character and inherent vitality.

It will be answered immediately that this criticism is founded on a false conception of civic art and of the ideal city. The new Jerusalem, of which Mr. Robinson writes, is, it will be said, a flexible ideal, which can be adapted freely to the local peculiarities of any particular city, and which is described in general terms merely as a matter of literary convenience. Well! No doubt the ideal city is at bottom merely a matter of literary convenience; but the writer holds, never-theless, that the criticism is based on a more wholesome and truer conception of civic art than is the one contained in Mr. Robinson's book and adopted by the majority of civic art reformers. It is the assumption of these gentlemen that the making of habitable, interesting and beautiful cities is fundamentally a matter of highly conscious and well-informed design; that provided sufficient means and authority were placed at their disposal, contemporary American architects and sculptors are quite capable of planning and designing consummate New Yorks and Chicagos—cities, which would not only be devoid of offense and highly convenient, but almost as much a source of permanent aesthetic satisfaction as the great architectural achievements of the past. The writer strongly dissents from this assumption. American art is not sufficiently national and mature to undertake colossal and grandiose schemes. Public opinion is unprepared for such millennial flights of civic art. It is all very well to lay out a comprehensive scheme of development for a city like Washington, which owes its existence to the national government and its individuality to a pre-natal plan. It is all very well to carry out particular improvements in particular cases, for which the necessity is immediate and the times are ripe—such, for instance, as the group of public buildings to be erected in Cleveland, or the proposed rearrangement of the buildings in the City Hall Park of New York. But, at the present stage of American municipal growth and aesthetic capability, we should not try to plan too much and too far. However much we may borrow from Paris (and I do not question the desirability of such borrowing) we do not want a Frenchified New York. We want an American New York at any cost—even at the cost of good looks.

Whether an American New York can be obtained only at the price of good looks remains to be seen; but at least we should not fall into the naïve error of seeking to make either a consummately beautiful or a consummately American city merely by the magic of intelligent effort. A great city cannot be forced to bloom beautiful. Its comeliness must wait on the concurrence of a number of rare and happy conditions. The art, which is capable of making a consummately beautiful city must possess more than intelligence, good taste, and complete information. It must be a mature art, guided by authentic conventions, fertile in great designers, possessed for a passion for propriety and beauty of form, and confirmed by genuine popular appreciation, in every respect the master of its resources. We have plenty of clever and well-informed architects, painters and sculptors in this country, and some few great ones, but it must be recognized that American art is mature only in spots, and that it should be in no hurry about attempting to rear a series of great municipal and national monuments. American art is not as yet guided by authentic conventions. Its methods are experimental. The subjects it uses are abstract and arbitrary. The popular interest it arouses is both lukewarm and restricted. Above all it has not yet succeeded in giving any large propriety to the forms it uses. That which is artistic is very artistic and is loudly declared to be artistic by every aspect of its appearance. That which is useful is very useful, and its grim utility is equally a matter of loud proclamation. Only very few attempts have been made to make the architectural forms really expressive of the honest engineering and utilitarian fact; and until this gulf between the artistic and the useful has been bridged American architecture and the allied arts cannot become national and authentic. The vision of a local pseudo-classic Beaux-Artist New Jerusalem, which is the only kind of an ideal city the civic art reformer ever imagines, seems to the writer a very insipid ideal. For me the skyscraper and the furnace-stack.

The ridiculous extreme to which the idea of the consummate city may be carried was recently illustrated by Mr. Brook Adams. A few years ago he seriously argued in a public address that New York should spend a couple of hundred million dollars on beauty immediately, because history proved that beauty was a profitable investment—as if a great city could make itself permanently comely and effective by much the same methods and arts that an actress uses when she goes upon the stage, and for much the same purpose. Good looks, obtained in this way, if obtained at all, would be no more than a make-up. Should some millionaire be enthusiastic enough to give a few hundred million dollars to a committee of New Yorkers with instructions to spend it in buying a pretty mask for the city, the money would be more wisely spent in case the interest rather than the principle were applied to the task. It is far better, at present, to keep our city improvement plans confined by a comparatively modest ambition. If a city needs new streets and buildings let them be built, of course; but contemporary work should be restricted to contemporary needs, and no attempt should be made to build very much for a future that may be much better capable of building for itself.

In making these criticisms on Mr. Robinson's book, I have no wish to disparage the movement in favor of what is called civic art as such. Confined to its proper limits that movement is wholesome, necessary and promising; but I cannot help thinking that the civic art reformers in the appearance they make to the public over-emphasize the artistic and under-emphasize the utilitarian value of their laborers. Civic art is, properly understood, more of a science than an art, and its purposes and methods are better adapted to scientific and social rather than to artistic results. By all means let American cities be better planned wherever possible; let their streets be wider and more conveniently laid out, let the furniture in those streets be made from good routine designs; let the buildings that line them be regulated in their appearance, so that all of them are subordinated to a general effect; and let the harsh, straight lines of these streets and houses be relieved by trees and parks. These things are well enough; but do not let us confuse them with such a high thing as beauty. They belong to a middle realm of scientific aesthetics, which is assuredly of the utmost importance for the health, convenience and looks of a great city, but which are the better managed and the better understood, the closer they are kept to the utilitarian and engineering level.

Mr. Robinson recognizes the importance of what may be called civic engineering; but he is not content to keep the business at that level. "Engineering," he says, "upon which the aesthetic aspect of cities is so largely dependent, differs from pure art in that it need not be the child of inspiration. It is an exact science, and as such wealth can buy it, bringing to the city the engineer who can make the municipality splendidly correct, if among its own citizens there be no other who has that power. The science of city-building does not wholly depend upon high impulse or inspiration. For its plainer yet essential victories the intellect is sufficient. And yet over and above this requirement which we can hope to meet so easily, there are the high motives, that must surely give birth to inspiration." Surely it would be very much better for the present to cleave to the modest ideal of making our cities wherever possible "splendidly correct." In New York, for instance, the reformers who want to make a city beautiful at the expense of a few hundred million dollars, would accomplish something more and better, in case they merely tried to revise the street plan along practical lines, and so rallied to their support all those interests in the city who will be benefited by a freer movement of traffic, both on the sidewalks and in the streets. The improvement of the mechanism of city life by means of careful and comprehensive planning, while it should not be pushed too far, is much the most fruitful soil for the application of scientific methods and civic enthusiasm, and while it would be absurd to deny that such methods can be applied within limits to great works of public art; still they should be applied in moderation. The beauty of a city life, if it is capable of acquiring any, must issue from more inevitable and less conscious sources.

This brings us back to the question with which I started: "What is civic art?" Mr. Robinson's idea of the essential nature of civic art is contained in his second chapter, which, however, is entitled not "What is Civic Art?" but "What Civic Art Is." The doctrine reads as follows: "It is municipal art, first of all. If men seek it, they seek it not for Art's sake but for the city's; they are first citizens and then in their own artists, and artists in this way only because they are citizens. We do not find men and women banding together to create a public sentiment and fund in order that some sculptor may do a notable bit of work to the glorifying of his field of art. But they so bind themselves together . . . for the glorifying of civic art—not just because it is art, but because it is civic. They are not asking the town to help art, but art to help the town; the artists, not to glorify their art but by their art to glorify the city." It is just this conception of civic art, which we believe to be erroneous and sterile. Good art is not the product of good intentions; high motives do not, as Mr. Robinson says, lead to inspiration. The motives that do issue in a great work of public sculpture are partly the "motives" peculiar to all artistic creation, and partly the peculiar vision proper to the particular art of sculpture. It is an intellectual and not a moral passion—a passion for consummate form and not for a consummate city. Does Mr. Robinson suppose that St. Gaudens had any particular wish to glorify "New York when he spent years of anxious and exhausting work in making his Sherman." He probably never thought about New York, except to regret bitterly the fact that its city officials refused to let him place his statue as he believed it should be placed. If he was "glorifying" anything, he was "glorifying" his subject and his own power of daring and effective sculptural composition. Yet if the Sherman is not a piece of civic art, what would you call it? In truth civic art differs from other kinds of art only in the fact that its opportunities are bigger, and require on the part of the artist a larger vision, a completer training, a higher power of cooperation and a more authentic tradition. There is no reason why an artist who is an artist, should not love his city and want to "glorify" it, but if so, that is only a happy accident. If he cannot "glorify" his art, he cannot "glorify" his city, no matter how much he may love it.

PART II

Urbanism as a Way of
Life, 1915–1945

CHAPTER THREE

THE CITY LABORATORY: ECOLOGISTS AND SOCIOLOGISTS

During the 1920's a number of American sociologists contributed to a unique way of studying the city and its problems. This approach was first developed by Robert E. Park and Ernest W. Burgess, who both taught sociology at the University of Chicago. Two of Park's students, Roderick D. McKenzie and Louis Wirth, were also among the leading representatives of this "Chicago school" of urban sociology. The following essays by Park, Burgess, and Wirth are "classic" statements of the way in which a whole generation of scholars tried to make sense of the city. The reading from McKenzie's study of the metropolitan community is an effort to extend this approach in order to understand the city in its wider social and economic context. Though certain assumptions of the Chicago school have been seriously challenged—the emphasis upon the "disorganized" character of urban life for example—selections from these pioneering urbanists reflect a significant effort to formulate a theory of the city.

These students played an important role in continuing the effort of sociologists to establish social investigation on a more precise foundation than had generally been the case among muckraking journalists. In attempting to be more scientific and less crusading or sensational in dealing with the facts and forces of urban society they shared much in common with such reformers as Frederic Howe and Brand Whitlock. Evolving from the social work, community survey, and social gospel concerns of the Progressive Era, and influenced by a number of 19th- and 20th-century social-psychological, geographic, and biologically oriented disciplines, the Chicago urbanists sought to find a new method for studying the city. As one recent observer has commented, "the Chicago school of urban sociology was strongly motivated by a drive to view the city as an object of detached sociological analysis. These men were fascinated with the complexities of the urban community and the prospect of discovering patterns of regularity in its apparent confusion.[1]

---

[1]Morris Janowitz, "Introduction" to 1967 edition of *The City,* ed., Park, Burgess, McKenzie (Chicago, 1967), viii.

But how does one make sense of the turbulent ebb and flow that is the American city? In their search for an answer to this question the Chicago urban sociologists first shifted their attention somewhat from the progressives' emphasis upon reform and social work. Beyond trying to ameliorate immediate social and political problems they sought a broader perspective—an understanding of those larger forces that seemed to be at work ordering and reorganizing city life. That such forces existed was first suggested to the sociologists by studies of the interaction between living organisms and their environment conducted by plant and animal ecologists. Investigations of various phenomena and "natural areas" in Chicago seemed to confirm the hypothesis that processes were at work sifting and sorting populations and institutions in the city which were not dissimilar from the ways in which plant and animal communities became stabilized. The relationship between the resulting "ecological order" and the "moral order" of the city, based on self-conscious willing and consensus, was a key problem for Robert Park and his colleagues and students. This approach to the city and its problems became known as human ecology.

The effort of the urban sociologists and ecologists in the 1920's to come to grips with urban chaos, to find patterns of regularity, was largely governed by an essential question their generation asked of the expanding industrial city. The way in which they formed that question helped determine the emphasis of their work. "How is it possible," they asked, "with all the social disorganization caused by and rampant in the city, that there can exist any stability whatever?" Their theory of the city, which emerged from fusing an ecological framework and sociological research, was aimed at answering this fundamental question.

The ecological theory envisaged the city as an organism which, in the course of its natural growth, was regulated and ordered by processes that brought about a coherent physical pattern and social organization. The apparent chaos of the city made sense when seen in terms of a growing organism whose parts became differentiated even while being integrated into a larger urban community. The growth of modern industrial cities disrupted traditional forms of human behavior and association indigenous to a rural society, and shattered traditional values; but as an organism with a life of its own, it also provided for the integration of society and its citizens. Such urban institutions as occupational groups, newspapers, political machines, as well as neighborhoods and other natural areas, provided the means of participation in modern city life. For all the social upheaval within the metropolis the leaders of the Chicago school strongly believed that the local community was the core of individual and group life in the city, and therein lay the most significant basis for the reorientation of life in urban America.

Since its formulation, the human ecological approach has been challenged along a number of lines. First of all, the emphasis upon biological analogy, whereby processes which describe plant and animal life are carried over to human society to explain the functioning of the city, has been largely rejected. If such naturalistic processes "explain" the city, it has been asked, what role does human volition play in determining the character of urban environment and social organization? Secondly, critics have charged that by beginning with an emphasis on disorganization in the city, the Chicago sociologists failed to give adequate attention to those "organizing" aspects of urban life which bring people together. In this regard, it has even been charged that their emphasis upon the local community is an expression of the desire to return to a simpler, more uncomplicated, preurban time.

A final body of criticism of the Chicago school is aimed directly at Wirth's essay, "Urbanism as a Way of Life." In that article Wirth establishes a basic definition of the city "as a relatively large, dense and permanent settlement of socially heterogeneous individuals," and from these variables tries to deduce characteristics which make up an urban way of life. Both his definition of the city and the different traits which he attributes to city life have been questioned. One of the most recent critics, in summarizing previous criticism, maintains that Wirth's analysis fails to distinguish between different kinds of urban life such as the inner city and the suburbs.[2] The reader should keep this in mind while reading Wirth's important essay.

Though probably less positive about the city than reformers of the Progressive Era, the sociologists of the 1920's readily accepted the city. Their efforts to understand the city within a larger theoretical framework distinguish them from the majority of current sociologists whose studies of urban phenomena are more particular and specialized. The question which Park, Burgess, McKenzie, and Wirth asked of the city made sense to many who lived through the drastic changes taking place in the first half of the 20th century. In attempting to answer that question they formulated the nearest thing to a comprehensive urban theory that this country has yet produced.

---

[2] Herbert J. Gans, "Urbanism and Suburbanism as Ways of Life: A Re-evaluation of Definitions" in Arnold Rose (ed.), *Human Behavior and Social Processes* (Boston, 1962).

The City: Suggestions for the Investigation of Human Behavior in the Urban Environment

by Robert E. Park*

The city, from the point of view of this paper, is something·more than a conge-ries of individual men and of social conveniences—streets, buildings, electric lights, tramways, and telephones, etc.; something more, also, than a mere con-stellation of institutions and administrative devices—courts, hospitals, schools, police, and civil functionaries of various sorts. The city is, rather, a state of mind, a body of customs and traditions, and of the organized attitudes and sentiments that inhere in these customs and are transmitted with this tradition. The city is not, in other words, merely a physical mechanism and an artificial construction. It is involved in the vital processes of the people who compose it; it is a product of nature, and particularly of human nature.

The city has, as Oswald Spengler has recently pointed out, its own culture: "What his house is to the peasant, the city is to civilized man. As the house has its household gods, so has the city its protecting Deity, its local saint. The city also, like the peasant's hut, has its roots in the soil."

The city has been studied, in recent times, from the point of view of its geography, and still more recently from the point of view of its ecology. There are forces at work within the limits of the urban community—within the limits of any natural area of human habitation, in fact—which tend to bring about an orderly and typical grouping of its population and institutions. The science which seeks to isolate these factors and to describe the typical constellations of persons and institutions which the co-operation of these forces produce, is what we call human, as distinguished from plant and animal, ecology.

Transportation and communication, tramways and telephones, newspapers and advertising, steel construction and elevators—all things, in fact, which tend to bring about at once a greater mobility and a greater concentration of the urban populations—are primary factors in the ecological organization of the city.

*Robert E. Park, "The City: Suggestions for the Investigation of Human Behavior in the Urban Environment," *The City*, eds. Robert E. Park, Ernest W. Burgess, Roderick McKenzie (Chicago: University of Chicago Press, 1925), pp. 1-4, 7-10, 12-14, 23-31, 33-46. Reprinted by permission of the University of Chicago Press.

The city is not, however, merely a geographical and ecological unit; it is at the same time an economic unit. The economic organization of the city is based on the division of labor. The multiplication of occupations and professions within the limits of the urban population is one of the most striking and least understood aspects of modern city life. From this point of view, we may, if we choose, think of the city, that is to say, the place and the people, with all the machinery and administrative devices that go with them, as organically related; a kind of psychophysical mechanism in and through which private and political interests find not merely a collective but a corporate expression.

Much of what we ordinarily regard as the city—its charters, formal organization, buildings, street railways, and so forth—is, or seems to be, mere artifact. But these things in themselves are utilities, adventitious devices which become part of the living city only when, and in so far as, through use and wont they connect themselves, like a tool in the hand of man, with the vital forces resident in individuals and in the community.

The city is, finally, the natural habitat of civilized man. It is for that reason a cultural area characterized by its own peculiar cultural type:

"It is a quite certain, but never fully recognized, fact," says Spengler, "that all great cultures are city-born. The outstanding man of the second generation is a city-building animal. This is the actual criterion of world-history, as distinguished from the history of mankind: world-history is the history of city men. Nations, governments, politics, and religions—all rest on the basic phenomenon of human existence, the city."

Anthropology, the science of man, has been mainly concerned up to the present with the study of primitive peoples. But civilized man is quite as interesting an object of investigation, and at the same time his life is more open to observation and study. Urban life and culture are more varied, subtle, and complicated, but the fundamental motives are in both instances the same. The same patient methods of observation which anthropologists like Boas and Lowie have expended on the study of the life and manners of the North American Indian might be even more fruitfully employed in the investigation of the customs, beliefs, social practices, and general conceptions of life prevalent in Little Italy on the lower North Side in Chicago, or in recording the more sophisticated folkways of the inhabitants of Greenwich Village and the neighborhood of Washington Square, New York.

We are mainly indebted to writers of fiction for our more intimate knowledge of contemporary urban life. But the life of our cities demands a more searching and disinterested study than even Émile Zola has given us in his "experimental" novels and the annals of the Rougon-Macquart family.

We need such studies, if for no other reason than to enable us to read the newspapers intelligently. The reason that the daily chronicle of the newspaper is so shocking, and at the same time so fascinating, to the average reader is because the average reader knows so little about the life of which the newspaper is the record.

The observations which follow are intended to define a point of view and to indicate a program for the study of urban life: its physical organization, its occupations, and its culture.

I. THE CITY PLAN AND LOCAL ORGANIZATION

The city, particularly the modern American city, strikes one at first blush as so little a product of the artless processes of nature and growth, that it is difficult to recognize it as a living entity. The ground plan of most American cities, for example, is a checkerboard. The unit of distance is the block. This geometrical form suggests that the city is a purely artificial construction which might conceivably be taken apart and put together again, like a house of blocks.

The fact is, however, that the city is rooted in the habits and customs of the people who inhabit it. The consequence is that the city possesses a moral as well as a physical organization, and these two mutually interact in characteristic ways to mold and modify one another. It is the structure of the city which first impresses us by its visible vastness and complexity. But this structure has its basis, nevertheless, in human nature, of which it is an expression. On the other hand, this vast organization which has arisen in response to the needs of its inhabitants, once formed, imposes itself upon them as a crude external fact, and forms them, in turn, in accordance with the design and interests which it incorporates. Structure and tradition are but different aspects of a single cultural complex which determines what is characteristic and peculiar to city, as distinguished from village, life and the life of the open fields.

. . . .

The Neighborhood.   Proximity and neighborly contact are the basis for the simplest and most elementary form of association with which we have to do in the organization of city life. Local interests and associations breed local sentiment, and, under a system which makes residence the basis for participation in the government, the neighborhood becomes the basis of political control. In the social and political organization of the city it is the smallest local unit.

. . . .

The neighborhood exists without formal organization. The local improvement society is a structure erected on the basis of the spontaneous neighborhood organization and exists for the purpose of giving expression to the local sentiment in regard to matters of local interest.

Under the complex influences of the city life, what may be called the normal neighborhood sentiment has undergone many curious and interesting changes, and produced many unusual types of local communities. More than that, there are nascent neighborhoods and neighborhoods in process of dissolution. Consider, for example, Fifth Avenue, New York, which probably never had an improvement association, and compare with it 135th Street in the Bronx (where the Negro population is probably more concentrated than in any other single

spot in the world), which is rapidly becoming a very intimate and highly organized community.

. . . .

It is important to know what are the forces which tend to break up the
tensions, interests, and sentiments which give neighborhoods their individual
character. In general these may be said to be anything and everything that tends
to render the population unstable, to divide and concentrate attentions upon
widely separated objects of interest.

. . . .

On the other hand, certain urban neighborhoods suffer from isolation. Efforts
have been made at different times to reconstruct and quicken the life of city
neighborhoods and to bring them in touch with the larger interests of the community. Such is, in part, the purpose of the social settlements. These organizations and others which are attempting to reconstruct city life have developed
certain methods and a technique for stimulating and controlling local communities. We should study, in connection with the investigation of these agencies,
these methods and this technique, since it is just the method by which objects
are practically controlled that reveals their essential nature, that is to say, their
predictable character. . . .

In many of the European cities, and to some extent in this country, reconstruction of city life has gone to the length of building garden suburbs, or
replacing unhealthful and run-down tenements with model buildings owned and
controlled by the municipality.

In American cities the attempt has been made to renovate evil neighborhoods by the construction of playgrounds and the introduction of supervised
sports of various kinds, including municipal dances in municipal dance halls.
These and other devices which are intended primarily to elevate the moral tone
of the segregated populations of great cities should be studied in connection
with the investigation of the neighborhood in general. They should be studied, in
short, not merely for their own sake, but for what they can reveal to us of
human behavior and human nature generally.

Colonies and Segregated Areas. In the city environment the neighborhood
tends to lose much of the significance which it possessed in simpler and more
primitive forms of society. The easy means of communication and of transportation, which enable individuals to distribute their attention and to live at the
same time in several different worlds, tend to destroy the permanency and
intimacy of the neighborhood. On the other hand, the isolation of the immigrant
and racial colonies of the so-called ghettos and areas of population segregation
tend to preserve and, where there is racial prejudice, to intensify the intimacies
and solidarity of the local and neighborhood groups. Where individuals of the
same race or of the same vocation live together in segregated groups, neighborhood sentiment tends to fuse together with racial antagonisms and class interests.

Physical and sentimental distances reinforce each other, and the influences of local distribution of the population participate with the influences of class and race in the evolution of the social organization. Every great city has its racial colonies, like the Chinatowns of San Francisco and New York, the Little Sicily of Chicago, and various other less pronounced types. In addition to these, most cities have their segregated vice districts, like that which until recently existed in Chicago, their rendezvous for criminals of various sorts. Every large city has its occupational suburbs, like the Stockyards in Chicago, and its residential enclaves, like Brookline in Boston, the so-called "Gold Coast" in Chicago, Greenwich Village in New York, each of which has the size and the character of a complete separate town, village, or city, except that its population is a selected one.

. . . .

II. INDUSTRIAL ORGANIZATION AND THE MORAL ORDER

The ancient city was primarily a fortress, a place of refuge in time of war. The modern city, on the contrary, is primarily a convenience of commerce, and owes its existence to the market place around which it sprang up. Industrial competition and the division of labor, which have probably done most to develop the latent powers of mankind, are possible only upon condition of the existence of markets, of money, and other devices for the facilitation of trade and commerce.

An old German adage declares that "city air makes men free." ... This is doubtless a reference to the days when the free cities of Germany enjoyed the patronage of the emperor, and laws made the fugitive serf a free man if he succeeded for a year and a day in breathing city air. Law, of itself, could not, however, have made the craftsman free. An open market in which he might sell the products of his labor was a necessary incident of his freedom, and it was the application of the money economy to the relations of master and man that completed the emancipation of the serf.

Vocational Classes and Vocational Types. The old adage which describes the city as the natural environment of the free man still holds so far as the individual man finds in the chances, the diversity of interests and tasks, and in the vast unconscious co-operation of city life the opportunity to choose his own vocation and develop his peculiar individual talents. The city offers a market for the special talents of individual men. Personal competition tends to select for each special task the individual who is best suited to perform it.

. . . .

Success, under conditions of personal competition, depends upon concentration under some single task, and this concentration stimulates the demand for rational methods, technical devices, and exceptional skill. Exceptional skill, while based on natural talent, requires special preparation, and it has called into existence the trade and professional schools, and finally bureaus for vocational guidance. All of these, either directly or indirectly, serve at once to select and emphasize individual differences.

Every device which facilitates trade and industry prepares the way for a further division of labor and so tends further to specialize the tasks in which men find their vocations.

The outcome of this process is to break down or modify the older social and economic organization of society, which was based on family ties, local associations, on culture, caste, and status, and to substitute for it an organization based on occupation and vocational interests.

In the city every vocation, even that of a beggar, tends to assume the character of a profession and the discipline which success in any vocation imposes, together with the associations that it enforces, emphasizes this tendency—the tendency, namely, not merely to specialize, but to rationalize one's occupation and to develop a specific and conscious technique for carrying it on.

The effect of the vocations and the division of labor is to produce, in the first instance, not social groups, but vocational types: the actor, the plumber, and the lumber-jack. The organizations, like the trade and labor unions which men of the same trade or profession form, are based on common interests. In this respect they differ from forms of association like the neighborhood, which are based on contiguity, personal association, and the common ties of humanity. The different trades and professions seem disposed to group themselves in classes, that is to say, the artisan, business, and professional classes. But in the modern democratic state the classes have as yet attained no effective organization. Socialism, founded on an effort to create an organization based on "class consciousness," has never succeeded, except, perhaps, in Russia, in creating more than a political party.

The effects of the division of labor as a discipline, i.e., as means of molding character, may therefore be best studied in the vocational types it has produced. Among the types which it would be interesting to study are: the shopgirl, the policeman, the peddler, the cabman, the nightwatchman, the clairvoyant, the vaudeville performer, the quack doctor, the bartender, the ward boss, the strike-breaker, the labor agitator, the school teacher, the reporter, the stockbroker, the pawnbroker; all of these are characteristic products of the conditions of city life; each, with its special experience, insight, and point of view determines for each vocational group and for the city as a whole its individuality.

. . . .

III. SECONDARY RELATIONS AND SOCIAL CONTROL

Modern methods of urban transportation and communication—the electric railway, the automobile, the telephone, and the radio—have silently and rapidly changed in recent years the social and industrial organization of the modern city. They have been the means of concentrating traffic in the business districts, have changed the whole character of retail trade, multiplying the residence suburbs and making the department store possible. These changes in the industrial organization and in the distribution of population have been accompanied by corresponding changes in the habits, sentiments, and character of the urban population.

The general nature of these changes is indicated by the fact that the growth of cities has been accompanied by the substitution of indirect, "secondary," for direct, face-to-face, "primary" relations in the associations of individuals in the community.

> By primary groups I [Charles Horton Cooley] mean those characterized by intimate face-to-face association and co-operation. They are primary in several senses, but chiefly in that they are fundamental in forming the social nature and ideals of the individual. The result of intimate association, psychologically, is a certain fusion of individualities in a common whole, so that one's very self, for many purposes at least, is the common life and purpose of the group. Perhaps the simplest way of describing this wholeness is by saying that it is a "we"; it involves the sort of sympathy and mutual identification for which "we" is the natural expression. One lives in the feeling of the whole and finds the chief aims of his will in that feeling.

Touch and sight, physical contact, are the basis for the first and most elementary human relationships. Mother and child, husband and wife, father and son, master and servant, kinsman and neighbor, minister, physician, and teacher—these are the most intimate and real relationships of life, and in the small community they are practically inclusive.

The interactions which take place among the members of a community so constituted are immediate and unreflecting. Intercourse is carried on largely within the region of instinct and feeling. Social control arises, for the most part spontaneously, in direct response to personal influences and public sentiment. It is the result of a personal accommodation, rather than the formulation of a rational and abstract principle.

The Church, the School, and the Family.   In a great city, where the population is unstable, where parents and children are employed out of the house and often in distant parts of the city, where thousands of people live side by side for years without so much as a bowing acquaintance, these intimate relationships of the primary group are weakened and the moral order which rested upon them is gradually dissolved.

Under the disintegrating influences of city life most of our traditional institutions, the church, the school, and the family, have been greatly modified. The school, for example, has taken over some of the functions of the family. It is around the public school and its solicitude for the moral and physical welfare of the children that something like a new neighborhood and community spirit tends to get itself organized.

The church, on the other hand, which has lost much of its influence since the printed page has so largely taken the place of the pulpit in the interpretation of life, seems at present to be in process of readjustment to the new conditions.

. . . .

It is probably the breaking down of local attachments and the weakening of the restraints and inhibitions of the primary group, under the influence of the urban environment, which are largely responsible for the increase of vice and crime in great cities. It would be interesting in this connection to determine by investigation how far the increase in crime keeps pace with the increasing mobility of the population and to what extent this mobility is a function of the growth of population. It is from this point of view that we should seek to interpret all those statistics which register the disintegration of the moral order, for example, the statistics of divorce, of truancy, and of crime.

. . . .

Crisis and the Courts. It is characteristic of city life that all sorts of people meet and mingle together who never fully comprehend one another. The anarchist and the club man, the priest and the Levite, the actor and the missionary who touch elbows on the street still live in totally different worlds. So complete is the segregation of vocational classes that it is possible within the limits of the city to live in an isolation almost as complete as that of some remote rural community.

. . . .

The difference is that each one of these little colonies has a more or less independent political and social organization of its own, and is the center of a more or less vigorous nationalist propaganda. For example, each one of these groups has one or more papers printed in its own language. In New York City there were, a few years ago, 270 publications, most of them supported by the local population, printed in 23 different languages. In Chicago there were 19 daily papers published in 7 foreign languages with a combined daily circulation of 368,000 papers.

Under these conditions the social ritual and the moral order which these immigrants brought with them from their native countries have succeeded in maintaining themselves for a considerable time under the influences of the American environment. Social control, based on the home mores, breaks down, however, in the second generation.

We may express the relation of the city to this fact in general terms by saying that the effect of the urban environment is to intensify all effects of crisis.

The term "crisis" is not to be understood in a violent sense. It is involved in any disturbance of habit. There is a crisis in the boy's life when he leaves home. The emancipation of the Negro and the immigration of the European peasant are group crises. Any strain of crisis involves three possible changes: greater fitness, reduced efficiency, or death. In biological terms, "survival" means successful adjustment to crisis, accompanied typically by a modification of structure. In man it means mental stimulation and greater intelligence, or mental depression, in case of failure.

Under the conditions imposed by city life in which individuals and groups of individuals, widely removed in sympathy and understanding, live together under conditions of interdependence, if not of intimacy, the conditions of social control are greatly altered and the difficulties increased.

The problem thus created is usually characterized as one of "assimilation." It is assumed that the reason for rapid increase of crime in our large cities is due to the fact that the foreign element in our population has not succeeded in assimilating American culture and does not conform to the American mores. This would be interesting, if true, but the facts seem to suggest that perhaps the truth must be sought in the opposite direction.

. . . .

What we do observe, as a result of the crisis, is that control that was formerly based on mores was replaced by control based on positive law. This change runs parallel to the movement by which secondary relationships have taken the place of primary relationships in the association of individuals in the city environment.

It is characteristic of the United States that great political changes should be effected experimentally under the pressure of agitation or upon the initiative of small but militant minorities. There is probably no other country in the world in which so many "reforms" are in progress as at the present time in the United States. Reform has, in fact, become a kind of popular "indoor sport." The reforms thus effected, almost without exception, involve some sort of restriction or governmental control over activities that were formerly "free" or controlled only by the mores and public opinion.

The effect of this extension of what is called the police power has been to produce a change, not merely in the fundamental policy of the law, but in the character and standing of the courts.

The juvenile and morals courts illustrate a change which is perhaps taking place elsewhere. In these courts the judges have assumed something of the functions of administrative officers, their duties consisting less in the interpretation of law than in prescribing remedies and administering advice intended to restore delinquents brought before them to their normal place in society.

A similar tendency to give judges a wide discretion and to impose upon them a further responsibility is manifest in those courts which have to deal with the technical affairs of the business world, and in the growth in popularity of commissions in which judicial and administrative functions are combined, for example, the Interstate Commerce Commission.

In order to interpret in a fundamental way the facts in regard to social control it is important to start with a clear conception of the nature of corporate action.

Corporate action begins when there is some sort of communication between individuals who constitute a group. Communication may take place at different levels; that is, suggestions may be given and responded to on the instinctive, senso-motor, or ideo-motor levels. The mechanism of communication is very subtle, so subtle, in fact, that it is often difficult to conceive how suggestions are conveyed from one mind to another. This does not imply that there is any special form of consciousness, any special sense of kinship or consciousness of kind, necessary to explain corporate action.

. . . .

The important fact is that by means of this comparatively simple device corporate action is made possible.

Individuals not only react upon one another in this reflex way, but they inevitably communicate their sentiments, attitudes, and organic excitements, and in doing so they necessarily react, not merely to what each individual actually does, but to what he intends, desires, or hopes to do. The fact that individuals often betray sentiments and attitudes to others of which they are themselves only dimly conscious makes it possible for individual A, for example, to act upon motives and tensions in B as soon, or even before, B is able to do so. Furthermore, A may act upon the suggestions that emanate from B without himself being clearly conscious of the source from which his motives spring. So subtle and intimate may the reactions be which control individuals who are bound together in a social-psychological process.

It is upon the basis of this sort of instinctive and spontaneous control that every more formal sort of control must be based in order to be effective.

Changes in the form of social control may for the purposes of investigation be grouped under the general heads:

1. The substitution of positive law for custom, and the extension of munici-pal control to activities that were formerly left to individual initiative and discre-tion.

2. The disposition of judges in municipal and criminal courts to assume administrative function so that the administration of the criminal law ceases to be a mere application of the social ritual and becomes an application of rational and technical methods, requiring expert knowledge or advice, in order to restore the individual to society and repair the injury that his delinquency has caused.

3. Changes and divergencies in the mores among the different isolated and segregated groups in the city. What are the mores, for example, of the shopgirl? the immigrant? the politician? and the labor agitator?

It should be the aim of these investigations to distinguish not merely the causes of these changes, the direction in which they are moving, but also the forces that are likely to minimize and neutralize them. For example, it is im-portant to know whether the motives which are at present multiplying the positive restrictions on the individual will necessarily go as far in this country as they have already done in Germany. Will they eventually bring about a condition approaching socialism?

. . . .

Party Politics and Publicity. There is everywhere at present a disposition to increase the power of the executive branch of the government at the expense of the legislative. The influence of state legislatures and of city councils has been diminished in some instances by the introduction of the referendum and the recall. In others they have been largely superseded by the commission form of government. The ostensible reason for these changes is that they offer a means for overthrowing the power of the professional politicians. The real ground seems to me the recognition of the fact that the form of government which had its origin in the town meeting and was well suited to the needs of a small community based on primary relations is not suitable to the government of the changing and heterogeneous populations of cities of three or four millions.

. . . .

For one thing, the problems of city government have become, with the growth and organization of city life, so complicated that it is no longer desirable to leave them to the control of men whose only qualification for handling them consists in the fact that they have succeeded in gaining office through the ordinary machinery of ward politics.

Another circumstance which has made the selection of city officials by popular vote impractical under the conditions of city life is the fact that, except in special cases, the voter knows little or nothing about the officials he is voting for; knows little or nothing about the functions of the office to which that official is to be elected; and, besides all the rest, is too busy elsewhere to inform himself about conditions and needs of the city as a whole.

At a recent election in Chicago, for example, voters were called upon to select candidates from a ballot containing 250 names, most of them unknown to the voters. Under these circumstances the citizen who wishes to vote intelligently relies on some more or less interested organization or some more or less interested advisor to tell him how to vote.

To meet this emergency, created primarily by conditions imposed by city life, two types of organization have come into existence for controlling those artificial crises that we call elections. One of these is the organization represented by the political boss and the political machine. The other is that represented by the independent voters' leagues, taxpayers' associations, and organizations like the bureaus of municipal research.

It is an indication of the rather primitive conditions in which our political parties were formed that they sought to govern the country on the principle that the remedy for all sorts of administrative evils was to "turn the rascals out," as the popular phrase expressed it, a change of government. The political machine and the political boss have come into existence in the interest of party politics. The parties were necessarily organized to capture elections. The political machine is merely a technical device invented for the purpose of achieving this end. The boss is the expert who runs the machine. He is as necessary to the winning of an election as a professional coach is necessary to success at football.

It is characteristic of the two types of organization which have grown up for the purpose of controlling the popular vote that the first, the political machine, is based, on the whole, on local, personal, that is to say, primary, relationships. The second, the good-government organizations, make their appeal to the public, and the public, as we ordinarily understand that expression, is a group based on secondary relationships. Members of a public are not as a rule personally acquainted.

The political machine is, in fact, an attempt to maintain, inside the formal administrative organization of the city, the control of a primary group. The organizations thus built up, of which Tammany Hall is the classic illustration, appear to be thoroughly feudal in their character. The relations between the boss and his ward captain seem to be precisely that, of personal loyalty on one side and personal protection on the other, which the feudal relation implies. The virtues which such an organization calls out are the old tribal ones of fidelity, loyalty, and devotion to the interests of the chief and the clan. The people within the organization, their friends and supporters, constitute a "we" group, while the rest of the city is merely the outer world, which is not quite alive and not quite human in the sense in which the members of the "we" group are. We have here something approaching the conditions of primitive society.

. . . .

Advertising and Social Control. In contrast with the political machine, which has founded its organized action on the local, personal, and immediate interests represented by the different neighborhoods and localities, the good-government organizations, the bureaus of municipal research, and the like have sought to represent the interests of the city as a whole and have appealed to a sentiment and opinion neither local nor personal. These agencies have sought to secure efficiency and good government by the education of the voter, that is to say, by investigating and publishing the facts regarding the government.

In this way publicity has come to be a recognized form of social control, and advertising—"social advertising"—has become a profession with an elaborate technique supported by a body of special knowledge.

It is one of the characteristic phenomena of city life and of society founded on secondary relationships that advertising should have come to occupy so important a place in its economy.

In recent years every individual and organization which has had to deal with the public, that is to say the public outside the smaller and more intimate communities of the village and small town, has come to have its press agent, who is often less an advertising man than a diplomatic man accredited to the newspapers, and through them to the world at large. Institutions like the Russell Sage Foundation, and to a less extent, the General Education Board have sought to influence public opinion directly through the medium of publicity. The Carnegie Report upon Medical Education, the Pittsburgh Survey, the Russell Sage Foundation Report on Comparative Costs of Public-School Education in the several states, are something more than scientific reports. They are rather a high form of journalism, dealing with existing conditions critically, and seeking through the agency of publicity to bring about radical reforms. The work of the Bureau of Municipal Research in New York has had a similar practical purpose. To these must be added the work accomplished by the child-welfare exhibits, by the social surveys undertaken in different parts of the country, and by similar propaganda in favor of public health.

As a source of social control public opinion becomes important in societies founded on secondary relationships, of which great cities are a type. In the city every social group tends to create its own milieu, and as these conditions become fixed, the mores tend to accommodate themselves to the conditions thus created. In secondary groups and in the city fashion tends to take the place of custom, and public opinion, rather than the mores, becomes the dominant force in social control.

In any attempt to understand the nature of public opinion and its relation to social control it is important to investigate first of all the agencies and devices which have come into practical use in the effort to control, enlighten, and exploit it.

The first and the most important of these is the press, that is, the daily newspaper and other forms of current literature, including books classed as current.

After the newspaper, the bureaus of research which are now springing up in all the large cities are the most interesting and the most promising devices for using publicity as a means of control.

The fruits of these investigations do not reach the public directly, but are disseminated through the medium of the press, the pulpit, and other sources of popular enlightenment.

In addition to these there are the educational campaigns in the interest of better health conditions, the child-welfare exhibits, and the numerous "social advertising" devices which are now employed, sometimes upon the initiative of private societies, sometimes upon that of popular magazines or newspapers, in order to educate the public and enlist the masses of the people in the movement for the improvement of conditions of community life.

The newspaper is the great medium of communication within the city, and it is on the basis of the information which it supplies that public opinion rests. The first function which a newspaper supplies is that which formerly was performed by the village gossip.

In spite, however, of the industry with which newspapers pursue facts of personal intelligence and human interest, they cannot compete with the village gossips as a means of social control. For one thing, the newspaper maintains some reservations not recognized by gossip, in the matters of personal intelligence. For example, until they run for office or commit some other overt act that brings them before the public conspicuously, the private life of individual men or women is a subject that is, for the newspaper, taboo. It is not so with gossip, partly because in a small community no individual is so obscure that his private affairs escape observation and discussion; partly because the field is smaller. In small communities there is a perfectly amazing amount of personal information afloat among the individuals who compose them.

The absence of this in the city is what, in large part, makes the city what it is.

. . . .

IV. TEMPERAMENT AND THE URBAN ENVIRONMENT

Great cities have always been the melting-pots of races and of cultures. Out of the vivid and subtle interactions of which they have been the centers, there have come the newer breeds and the newer social types. The great cities of the United States, for example, have drawn from the isolation of their native villages great masses of the rural populations of Europe and America. Under the shock of the new contacts the latent energies of these primitive peoples have been released, and the subtler processes of interaction have brought into existence not merely vocational, but temperamental, types.

Mobilization of the Individual Man. Transportation and communication have effected, among many other silent but far-reaching changes, what I have called the "mobilization of the individual man." They have multiplied the opportunities of the individual man for contact and for association with his fellows, but they have made these contacts and associations more transitory and less stable. A very large part of the populations of great cities, including those who make their homes in tenements and apartment houses, live much as people do in some great hotel, meeting but not knowing one another. The effect of this is to substitute fortuitous and casual relationship for the more intimate and permanent associations of the smaller community.

Under these circumstances the individual's status is determined to a considerable degree by conventional signs—by fashion and "front"—and the art of life is largely reduced to skating on thin surfaces and a scrupulous study of style and manners.

Not only transportation and communication, but the segregation of the urban population tends to facilitate the mobility of the individual man. The processes of segregation establish moral distances which make the city a mosaic of little worlds which touch but do not interpenetrate. This makes it possible for individuals to pass quickly and easily from one moral milieu to another, and encourages the fascinating but dangerous experiment of living at the same time in several different contiguous, but otherwise widely separated, worlds. All this tends to give to city life a superficial and adventitious character; it tends to complicate social relationships and to produce new and divergent individual types. It introduces, at the same time, an element of chance and adventure which adds to the stimulus of city life and gives it, for young and fresh nerves, a peculiar attractiveness. The lure of great cities is perhaps a consequence of stimulations which act directly upon the reflexes. As a type of human behavior it may be explained, like the attraction of the flame for the moth, as a sort of tropism.

The attraction of the metropolis is due in part, however, to the fact that in the long run every individual finds somewhere among the varied manifestations of city life the sort of environment in which he expands and feels at ease; finds, in short, the moral climate in which his peculiar nature obtains the stimulations that bring his innate dispositions to full and free expression. It is, I suspect, motives of this kind which have their basis, not in interest nor even in sentiment, but in something more fundamental and primitive which draw many, if not most, of the young men and young women from the security of their homes in the country into the big, booming confusion and excitement of city life. In a small community it is the normal man, the man without eccentricity or genius, who seems most likely to succeed. The small community often tolerates eccentricity. The city, on the contrary, rewards it. Neither the criminal, the defective, nor the genius has the same opportunity to develop his innate disposition in a small town that he invariably finds in a great city.

Fifty years ago every village had one or two eccentric characters who were treated ordinarily with a benevolent toleration, but who were regarded meanwhile as impracticable and queer. These exceptional individuals lived an isolated existence, cut off by their very eccentricities, whether of genius or of defect, from genuinely intimate intercourse with their fellows. If they had the making of criminals, the restraints and inhibitions of the small community rendered them harmless. If they had the stuff of genius in them, they remained sterile for lack of appreciation or opportunity. Mark Twain's story of *Pudd'n Head Wilson* is a description of one such obscure and unappreciated genius. It is not so true as it was that

Full many a flower is born to blush unseen
And waste its fragrance on the desert air.

Gray wrote the "Elegy in a Country Churchyard" before the rise of the modern metropolis.

In the city many of these divergent types now find a milieu in which, for good or for ill, their dispositions and talents parturiate and bear fruit.

. . . .

The Moral Region. It is inevitable that individuals who seek the same forms of excitement, whether that excitement be furnished by a horse race or by grand opera, should find themselves from time to time in the same places. The result of this is that in the organization which city life spontaneously assumes the population tends to segregate itself, not merely in accordance with its interests, but in accordance with its tastes or its temperaments. The resulting distribution of the population is likely to be quite different from that brought about by occupational interests or economic conditions.

Every neighborhood, under the influences which tend to distribute and segregate city populations, may assume the character of a "moral region." Such, for example, are the vice districts, which are found in most cities. A moral region is not necessarily a place of abode. It may be a mere rendezvous, a place of resort.

In order to understand the forces which in every large city tend to develop these detached milieus in which vagrant and suppressed impulses, passions, and ideals emancipate themselves from the dominant moral order, it is necessary to refer to the fact or theory of latent impulses of men.

The fact seems to be that men are brought into the world with all the passions, instincts, and appetites, uncontrolled and undisciplined. Civilization, in the interests of the common welfare, demands the suppression sometimes, and the control always, of these wild, natural dispositions. In the process of imposing its discipline upon the individual, in making over the individual in accordance with the accepted community model, much is suppressed altogether, and much more finds a vicarious expression in forms that are socially valuable, or at least innocuous. It is at this point that sport, play, and art function. They permit the individual to purge himself by means of symbolic expression of these wild and suppressed impulses. This is the catharsis of which Aristotle wrote in his *Poetic,* and which has been given new and more positive significance by the investigations of Sigmund Freud and the psychoanalysts.

No doubt many other social phenomena such as strikes, wars, popular elections, and religious revivals perform a similar function in releasing the subconscious tensions. But within smaller communities, where social relations are more intimate and inhibitions more imperative, there are many exceptional individuals who find within the limits of the communal activity no normal and healthful expression of their individual aptitudes and temperaments.

The causes which give rise to what are here described as "moral regions" are due in part to the restrictions which urban life imposes; in part to the license which these same conditions offer. We have, until very recently, given much consideration to the temptations of city life, but we have not given the same consideration to the effects of inhibitions and suppressions of natural impulses and instincts under the changed conditions of metropolitan life. For one thing, children, which in the country are counted as an asset, become in the city a liability. Aside from this fact it is very much more difficult to rear a family in the city than on the farm. Marriage takes place later in the city, and sometimes it doesn't take place at all. These facts have consequences the significance of which we are as yet wholly unable to estimate.

. . . .

Temperament and Social Contagion. What lends special importance to the segregation of the poor, the vicious, the criminal, and exceptional persons generally, which is so characteristic a feature of city life, is the fact that social contagion tends to stimulate in divergent types the common temperamental differences, and to suppress characters which unite them with the normal types about them. Association with others of their own ilk provides also not merely a stimulus, but a moral support for the traits they have in common which they would not find in a less select society. In the great city the poor, the vicious, and the delinquent, crushed together in an unhealthful and contagious intimacy, breed in and in, soul and body, so that it has often occurred to me that those long genealogies of the Jukes and the tribes of Ishmael would not show such a persistent and distressing uniformity of vice, crime, and poverty unless they were peculiarly fit for the environment in which they are condemned to exist.

We must then accept these "moral regions" and the more or less eccentric and exceptional people who inhabit them, in a sense, at least, as part of the natural, if not the normal, life of a city.

It is not necessary to understand by the expression "moral region" a place or a society that is either necessarily criminal or abnormal. It is intended rather to apply to regions in which a divergent moral code prevails, because it is a region in which the people who inhabit it are dominated, as people are ordinarily not dominated, by a taste or by a passion or by some interest which has its roots directly in the original nature of the individual. It may be an art, like music, or a sport, like horse-racing. Such a region would differ from other social groups by the fact that its interests are more immediate and more fundamental. For this reason its differences are likely to be due to moral, rather than intellectual, isolation.

Because of the opportunity it offers, particularly to the exceptional and abnormal types of man, a great city tends to spread out and lay bare to the public view in a massive manner all the human characters and traits which are ordinarily obscured and suppressed in smaller communities. The city, in short, shows the good and evil in human nature in excess. It is this fact, perhaps, more than any other, which justifies the view that would make of the city a laboratory or clinic in which human nature and social processes may be conveniently and profitably studied.

The Growth of the City: An Introduction to a Research Project

by Ernest W. Burgess*

The outstanding fact of modern society is the growth of great cities. Nowhere else have the enormous changes which the machine industry has made in our social life registered themselves with such obviousness as in the cities. In the United States the transition from a rural to an urban civilization, though beginning later than in Europe, has taken place, if not more rapidly and completely, at any rate more logically in its most characteristic forms.

All the manifestations of modern life which are peculiarly urban—the skyscraper, the subway, the department store, the daily newspaper, and social work—are characteristically American. The more subtle changes in our social life, which in their cruder manifestations are termed "social problems," problems that alarm and bewilder us, as divorce, delinquency, and social unrest, are to be found in their most acute forms in our largest American cities. The profound and "subversive" forces which have wrought these changes are measured in the physical growth and expansion of cities. That is the significance of the comparative statistics of Weber, Bücher, and other students.

These statistical studies, although dealing mainly with the effects of urban growth, brought out into clear relief certain distinctive characteristics of urban as compared with rural populations. The larger proportion of women to men in the cities than in the open country, the greater percentage of youth and middle-aged, the higher ratio of the foreign-born, the increased heterogeneity of occupation, increase with the growth of the city, and profoundly alter its social structure. These variations in the composition of population are indicative of all the changes going on in the social organization of the community. In fact, these changes are a part of the growth of the city, and suggest the nature of the processes of growth.

The only aspect of growth adequately described by Bücher and Weber was the rather obvious process of the *aggregation* of urban population. Almost as overt a process, that of *expansion*, has been investigated from a different and

*Ernest W. Burgess, "The Growth of the City: An Introduction to a Research Project," *Publications of the American Sociological Society,* 18 (1923), pp. 85-97. Reprinted with the permission of the American Sociological Association.

very practical point of view by groups interested in city planning, zoning, and regional surveys. Even more significant than the increasing density of urban population is its correlative tendency to overflow, and so to extend over wider areas, and to incorporate these areas into a larger communal life. This paper therefore will treat first of the expansion of the city, and then of the less known processes of urban metabolism and mobility, which are closely related to expansion.

EXPANSION AS PHYSICAL GROWTH

The expansion of the city from the standpoint of the city plan, zoning, and regional surveys is thought of almost wholly in terms of its physical growth. Traction studies have dealt with the development of transportation in its relation to the distribution of population throughout the city. The surveys made by the Bell Telephone Company and other public utilities have attempted to forecast the direction and the rate of growth of the city in order to anticipate the future demands for the extension of their services. In the city plan the location of parks and boulevards, the widening of traffic streets, the provision for a civic center, are all in the interest of the future control of the physical development of the city.

This expansion in area of our largest cities is now being brought forcibly to our attention by the Plan for the Study of New York and Its Environs, and by the formation of the Chicago Regional Planning Association, which extends the metropolitan district of the city to a radius of 50 miles, embracing 4,000 square miles of territory. Both are attempting to measure expansion in order to deal with the changes that accompany city growth. In England, where more than one-half of the inhabitants live in cities having a population of 100,000 and over, the lively appreciation of the bearing of urban expansion on social organization is thus expressed by C. B. Fawcett:

> One of the most important and striking developments in the growth of the urban populations of the more advanced peoples of the world during the last few decades has been the appearance of a number of vast urban aggregates, or conurbations, far larger and more numerous than the great cities of any preceding age. These have usually been formed by the simultaneous expansion of a number of neighboring towns, which have grown out towards each other until they have reached a practical coalescence in one continuous urban area. Each such conurbation still has within it many nuclei of denser town growth, most of which represent the central areas of the various towns from which it has grown, and these nuclear patches are connected by the less densely urbanized areas which began as suburbs of these towns. The latter are still usually rather less continuously occupied by buildings, and often have many open spaces.
>
> These great aggregates of town dwellers are a new feature in the distribution of man over the earth. At the present day there are from thirty to

forty of them, each containing more than a million people, whereas only a hundred years ago there were, outside the great centers of population on the waterways of China, not more than two or three. Such aggregations of people are phenomena of great geographical and social importance; they give rise to new problems in the organization of the life and well-being of their inhabitants and in their varied activities. Few of them have yet developed a social consciousness at all proportionate to their magnitude, or fully realized themselves as definite groupings of people with many common interests, emotions and thoughts.

In Europe and America the tendency of the great city to expand has been recognized in the term "the metropolitan area of the city," which far overruns its political limits, and in the case of New York and Chicago, even state lines. The metropolitan area may be taken to include urban territory that is physically contiguous, but it is coming to be defined by that facility of transportation that enables a business man to live in a suburb of Chicago and to work in the loop, and his wife to shop at Marshall Field's and attend grand opera in the Auditorium.

EXPANSION AS A PROCESS

No study of expansion as a process has yet been made, although the materials for such a study and intimations of different aspects of the process are contained in city planning, zoning, and regional surveys. The typical processes of the expansion of the city can best be illustrated, perhaps, by a series of concentric circles, which may be numbered to designate both the successive zones of urban extension and the types of areas differentiated in the process of expansion.

This chart represents an ideal construction of the tendencies of any town or city to expand radially from its central business district—on the map "The Loop" (I). Encircling the downtown area there is normally an area in transition, which is being invaded by business and light manufacture (II). A third area (III) is inhabited by the workers in industries who have escaped from the area of deterioration (II) but who desire to live within easy access of their work. Beyond this zone is the "residential area" (IV) of high-class apartment buildings or of exclusive "restricted" districts of single family dwellings. Still farther, out beyond the city limits, is the commuters' zone—suburban areas, or satellite cities—within a thirty- to sixty-minute ride of the central business district.

This chart brings out clearly the main fact of expansion, namely, the tendency of each inner zone to extend its area by the invasion of the next outer zone. This aspect of expansion may be called *succession*, a process which has been studied in detail in plant ecology. If this chart is applied to Chicago, all four of these zones were in its early history included in the circumference of the inner zone, the present business district. The present boundaries of the area of deterioration were not many years ago those of the zone now inhabited by independent wage-earners, and within the memories of thousands of Chicagoans

CHART I. THE GROWTH OF THE CITY

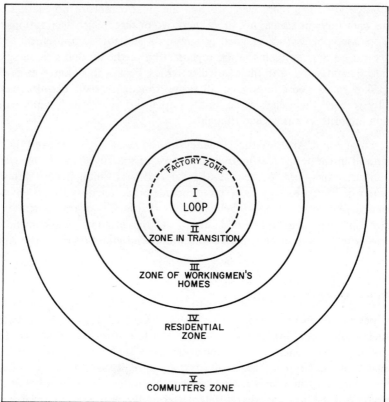

contained the residences of the "best families." It hardly needs to be added that neither Chicago nor any other city fits perfectly into this ideal scheme. Complications are introduced by the lake front, the Chicago River, railroad lines, historical factors in the location of industry, the relative degree of the resistance of communities to invasion, etc.

Besides extension and succession, the general process of expansion in urban growth involves the antagonistic and yet complementary processes of concentration and decentralization. In all cities there is the natural tendency for local and outside transportation to converge in the central business district. In the downtown section of every large city we expect to find the department stores, the skyscraper office buildings, the railroad stations, the great hotels, the theaters, the art museum, and the city hall. Quite naturally, almost inevitably, the economic, cultural, and political life centers here. The relation of centralization to the other processes of city life may be roughly gauged by the fact that over half a million people daily enter and leave Chicago's "loop." More recently sub-business centers have grown up in outlying zones. These "satellite loops" do not, it seems, represent the "hoped for" revival of the neighborhood, but rather a telescoping of several local communities into a larger economic unity. The Chicago of yesterday, an agglomeration of country towns and immigrant colonies, is undergoing a process of reorganization into a centralized decentralized system of local communities coalescing into sub-business areas visibly or invisibly dominated by the central business district. The actual processes of what may be called centralized decentralization are now being studied in the development of the chain store, which is only one illustration of the change in the basis of the urban organization.

Expansion, as we have seen, deals with the physical growth of the city, and with the extension of the technical services that have made city life not only livable, but comfortable, even luxurious. Certain of these basic necessities of urban life are possible only through a tremendous development of communal existence. Three millions of people in Chicago are dependent upon one unified water system, one giant gas company, and one huge electric light plant. Yet, like most of the other aspects of our communal urban life, this economic co-operation is an example of co-operation without a shred of what the "spirit of co-operation" is commonly thought to signify. The great public utilities are a part of the mechanization of life in great cities, and have little or no other meaning for social organization.

Yet the processes of expansion, and especially the rate of expansion, may be studied not only in the physical growth and business development, but also in the consequent changes in the social organization and in personality types. How far is the growth of the city, in its physical and technical aspects, matched by a natural but adequate readjustment in the social organization? What, for a city, is a normal rate of expansion, a rate of expansion with which controlled changes in the social organization might successfully keep pace?

SOCIAL ORGANIZATION AND DISORGANIZATION AS PROCESSES OF METABOLISM

These questions may best be answered, perhaps, by thinking of urban growth as a resultant of organization and disorganization analogous to the anabolic and catabolic processes of metabolism in the body. In what way are individuals incorporated into the life of a city? By what process does a person become an organic part of his society? The natural process of acquiring culture is by birth. A person is born into a family already adjusted to a social environment—in this case the modern city. The natural rate of increase of population most favorable for assimilation may then be taken as the excess of the birth-rate over the death-rate, but is this the normal rate of city growth? Certainly, modern cities have increased and are increasing in population at a far higher rate. However, the

CHART II. URBAN AREAS

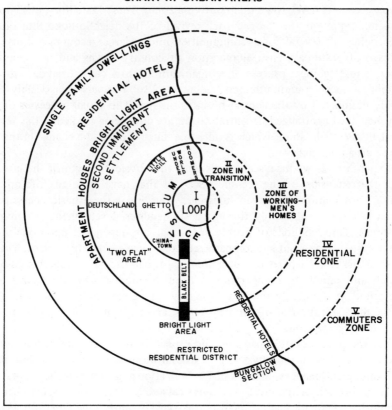

natural rate of growth may be used to measure the disturbances of metabolism caused by any excessive increase, as those which followed the great influx of southern Negroes into northern cities since the war. In a similar way all cities show deviations in composition by age and sex from a standard population such as that of Sweden, unaffected in recent years by any great emigration or immigration. Here again, marked variations, as any great excess of males over females, or of females over males, or in the proportion of children, or of grown men or women, are symptomatic of abnormalities in social metabolism.

Normally the processes of disorganization and organization may be thought of as in reciprocal relationship to each other, and as co-operating in a moving equilibrium of social order toward an end vaguely or definitely regarded as progressive. So far as disorganization points to reorganization and makes for more efficient adjustment, disorganization must be conceived not as pathological, but as normal. Disorganization as preliminary to reorganization of attitudes and conduct is almost invariably the lot of the newcomer to the city, and the discarding of the habitual, and often of what has been to him the moral, is not infrequently accompanied by sharp mental conflict and sense of personal loss. Oftener, perhaps, the change gives sooner or later a feeling of emancipation and an urge toward new goals.

In the expansion of the city a process of distribution takes place which sifts and sorts and relocates individuals and groups by residence and occupation. The resulting differentiation of the cosmopolitan American city into areas is typically all from one pattern, with only interesting minor modifications. Within the central business district or on an adjoining street is the "Main Stem" of "Hobohemia," the teeming Rialto of the homeless migratory man of the Middle West. In the zone of deterioration encircling the central business section are always to be found the so-called "slums" and "bad lands," with their submerged regions of poverty, degradation, and disease, and their underworlds of crime and vice. Within a deteriorating area are rooming-house districts, the purgatory of "lost souls." Near by is the Latin Quarter, where creative and rebellious spirits resort. The slums are also crowded to overflowing with immigrant colonies—the Ghetto, Little Sicily, Greektown, Chinatown—fascinatingly combining Old World heritages and American adaptations. Wedging out from here is the Black Belt, with its free and disorderly life. The area of deterioration, while essentially one of decay, of stationary or declining population, is also one of regeneration, as witness the mission, the settlement, the artists' colony, radical centers—all obsessed with the vision of a new and better world.

The next zone is also inhabited predominatingly by factory and shopworkers, but skilled and thrifty. This is an area of second immigrant settlement, generally of the second generation. It is the region of escape from the slum, the "Deutschland" of the aspiring Ghetto family. For "Deutschland" (literally Germany) is the name given, half in envy, half in derision, to that region beyond the Ghetto where his successful neighbors appear to be imitating German Jewish standards of living. But the inhabitant of this area in turn looks to the "Promised Land" beyond, to its residential hotels, its apartment-house region, its "satellite loops," and its "bright light" areas.

This differentiation into natural economic and cultural groupings gives form and character to the city. For segregation offers the group, and thereby the individuals who compose the group, a place and a rôle in the total organization of city life. Segregation limits development in certain directions, but releases it in others. These areas tend to accentuate certain traits, to attract and develop their kind of individuals, and so to become further differentiated.

The division of labor in the city likewise illustrates disorganization, reorganization, and increasing differentiation. The immigrant from rural communities in Europe and America seldom brings with him economic skill of any great value in our industrial, commercial, or professional life. Yet interesting occupational selection has taken place by nationality, explainable more by racial temperament or circumstance than by Old World economic background, as Irish policemen,

Greek ice-cream parlors, Chinese laundries, Negro porters, Belgian janitors, etc.

The facts that in Chicago 1,000,000 (996,589) individuals gainfully employed reported 509 occupations, and that over 1,000 men and women in *Who's Who* gave 116 different vocations, give some notion of how in the city the minute differentiation of occupation "analyzes and sifts the population, separating and classifying the diverse elements." These figures also afford some intimation of the complexity and complication of the modern industrial mechanism and the intricate segregation and isolation of divergent economic groups. Interrelated with this economic division of labor is a corresponding division into social classes, and into cultural and recreational groups. From this multiplicity of groups, with their different patterns of life, the person finds his congenial social world, and, what is not feasible in the narrow confines of a village, may move and live in widely separated and, perchance, conflicting worlds. Personal disorganization may be but the failure to harmonize the canons of conduct of two divergent groups.

If the phenomena of expansion and metabolism indicate that a moderate degree of disorganization may and does facilitate social organization, they indicate as well that rapid urban expansion is accompanied by excessive increases in disease, crime, disorder, vice, insanity, and suicide, rough indexes of social disorganization. But what are the indexes of the causes rather than of the effects of the disordered social metabolism of the city? The excess of the actual over the natural increase of population has already been suggested as a criterion. The significance of this increase consists in the immigration into a metropolitan city like New York and Chicago of tens of thousands of persons annually. Their invasion of the city has the effect of a tidal wave inundating first the immigrant colonies, the ports of first entry, dislodging thousands of inhabitants who overflow into the next zone, and so on and on until the momentum of the wave has spent its force on the last urban zone. The whole effect is to speed up expansion, to speed up industry, to speed up the "junking" process in the area of deterioration (II). These internal movements of the population become the more significant for study. What movement is going on in the city, and how may this movement be measured? It is easier, of course, to classify movement within the city than to measure it. There is the movement from residence to residence, change of occupation, labor turnover, movement to and from work, movement for recreation and adventure. This leads to the question: What is the significant aspect of movement for the study of the changes in city life? The answer to this question leads directly to the important distinction between movement and mobility.

MOBILITY AS THE PULSE OF THE COMMUNITY

Movement, per se, is not an evidence of change or of growth. In fact, movement may be a fixed and unchanging order of motion, designed to control a constant situation, as in routine movement. Movement that is significant for growth implies a change of movement in response to a new stimulus or situation. Change of movement of this type is called *mobility*. Movement of the nature of routine finds its typical expression in work. Change of movement, or mobility, is characteristically expressed in adventure. The great city, with its "bright lights," its emporiums of novelties and bargains, its palaces of amusement, its under-world of vice and crime, its risks of life and property from accident, robbery, and homicide, has become the region of the most intense degree of adventure and danger, excitement and thrill.

Mobility, it is evident, involves change, new experience, stimulation. Stimulation induces a response of the person to those objects in his environment which afford expression for his wishes. For the person, as for the physical organism, stimulation is essential to growth. Response to stimulation is wholesome so long as it is a correlated *integral* reaction of the entire personality. When the reaction is *segmental,* that is, detached from, and uncontrolled by, the organization of personality, it tends to become disorganizing or pathological. That is why stimulation for the sake of stimulation, as in the restless pursuit of pleasure, partakes of the nature of vice.

The mobility of city life, with its increase in the number and intensity of stimulations, tends inevitably to confuse and to demoralize the person. For an essential element in the mores and in personal morality is consistency, consistency of the type that is natural in the social control of the primary group. Where mobility is the greatest, and where in consequence primary controls break down completely, as in the zone of deterioration in the modern city, there develop areas of demoralization, of promiscuity, and of vice.

In our studies of the city it is found that areas of mobility are also the regions in which are found juvenile delinquency, boys' gangs, crime, poverty, wife desertion, divorce, abandoned infants, vice.

These concrete situations show why mobility is perhaps the best index of the state of metabolism of the city. Mobility may be thought of in more than a fanciful sense, as the "pulse of the community." Like the pulse of the human body, it is a process which reflects and is indicative of all the changes that are taking place in the community, and which is susceptible of analysis into elements which may be stated numerically.

The elements entering into mobility may be classified under two main heads: (1) the state of mutability of the person, and (2) the number and kind of contacts or stimulations in his environment. The mutability of city populations varies with sex and age composition, the degree of detachment of the person from the family and from other groups. All these factors may be expressed numerically. The new stimulations to which a population responds can be measured in terms of change of movement or of increasing contacts. Statistics on the movement of urban population may only measure routine, but an increase at a higher ratio than the increase of population measures mobility. In 1860 the horse-car lines of New York City carried about 50,000,000 passengers; in 1890 the trolley-cars (and a few surviving horse-cars) transported about 500,000,000;

in 1921, the elevated, subway, surface, and electric and steam suburban lines carried a total of more than 2,500,000,000 passengers. In Chicago the total annual rides per capita on the surface and elevated lines were 164 in 1890, 215 in 1900, 320 in 1910, and 338 in 1921. In addition, the rides per capita on steam and electric suburban lines almost doubled between 1916 (23) and 1921 (41), and the increasing use of the automobile must not be overlooked. For example, the number of automobiles in Illinois increased from 131,140 in 1915 to 833,920 in 1923.

Mobility may be measured not only by these changes of movement, but also by increase of contacts. While the increase of population of Chicago in 1912-22 was less than 25 per cent (23.6 per cent), the increase of letters delivered to Chicagoans was double that (49.6 per cent) (from 693,084,196 to 1,038,007,854). In 1912 New York had 8.8 telephones, in 1922, 16.9 per 100 inhabitants. Boston had, in 1912, 10.1 telephones, ten years later, 19.5 telephones per 100 inhabitants. In the same decade, the figures for Chicago increased from 12.3 to 21.6 per 100 population. But increase of the use of the telephone is probably more significant than increase in the number of telephones. The number of telephone calls in Chicago increased from 606,131,928 in 1914, to 944,010,586 in 1922, an increase of 55.7 per cent, while the population increased only 13.4 per cent.

Land values, since they reflect movement, afford one of the most sensitive indexes of mobility. The highest land values in Chicago are at the point of greatest mobility in the city, at the corner of State and Madison streets, in the loop. A traffic count showed that at the rush period 31,000 people an hour, or 210,000 men and women in sixteen and one-half hours passed the southwest corner. For over ten years land values in the loop have been stationary, but in the same time they have doubled, quadrupled, and even sextupled in the strategic corners of the "satellite loops," an accurate index of the changes which have occurred. Our investigations so far seem to indicate that variations in land values, especially where correlated with differences in rents, offer perhaps the best single measure of mobility, and so of all the changes taking place in the expansion and growth of the city.

In general outline, I have attempted to present the point of view and methods of investigation which the department of sociology is employing in its studies in the growth of the city, namely; to describe urban expansion in terms of extension, succession, and concentration; to determine how expansion disturbs metabolism when disorganization is in excess of organization; and, finally, to define mobility and to propose it as a measure both of expansion and metabolism, susceptible to precise quantitative formulation, so that it may be regarded almost literally as the pulse of the community. In a way, this statement might serve as an introduction to any one of five or six research projects under way in the department. The project, however, in which I am directly engaged, is an attempt to apply these methods of investigation to a cross-section of the city—to put this area, as it were, under the microscope, and so to study in more detail and with greater control and precision the processes which have been described here in the large. For this purpose the West Side Jewish community has been selected. This community includes the so-called "Ghetto," or area of first settlement, and Lawndale, the so-called "Deutschland," or area of second settlement. This area has certain obvious advantages for this study, from the standpoint of expansion, metabolism, and mobility. It exemplifies the tendency to expansion radially from the business center of the city. It is now relatively a homogeneous cultural group. Lawndale is itself an area in flux, with the tide of migrants still flowing in from the Ghetto and a constant egress to more desirable regions of the residential zone. In this area, too, it is also possible to study how the expected outcome of this high rate of mobility in social and personal disorganization is counteracted in large measure by the efficient communal organization of the Jewish community.

Urbanism as a Way of Life

by Louis Wirth*

A SOCIOLOGICAL DEFINITION OF THE CITY

Despite the preponderant significance of the city in our civilization . . . our knowledge of the nature of urbanism and the process of urbanization is meager. Many attempts have indeed been made to isolate the distinguishing characteristics of urban life. Geographers, historians, economists, and political scientists have incorporated the points of view of their respective disciplines into diverse definitions of the city. While in no sense intended to supersede these, the formulation of a sociological approach to the city may incidentally serve to call attention to the interrelations between them by emphasizing the peculiar characteristics of the city as a particular form of human association. A sociologically significant definition of the city seeks to select those elements of urbanism which mark it as a distinctive mode of human group life.

The characterization of a community as urban on the basis of size alone is obviously arbitrary. It is difficult to defend the present census definition which designates a community of 2,500 and above as urban and all others as rural. The situation would be the same if the criterion were 4,000, 8,000, 10,000, 25,000, or 100,000 population, for although in the latter case we might feel that we were more nearly dealing with an urban aggregate than would be the case in communities of lesser size, no definition of urbanism can hope to be completely satisfying as long as numbers are regarded as the sole criterion. Moreover, it is not difficult to demonstrate that communities of less than the arbitrarily set number of inhabitants lying within the range of influence of metropolitan centers have greater claim to recognition as urban communities than do larger ones leading a more isolated existence in a predominantly rural area. Finally, it should be recognized that census definitions are unduly influenced by the fact that the city, statistically speaking, is always an administrative concept in that the corporate limits play a decisive role in delineating the urban area. Nowhere is this more clearly apparent than in the concentrations of population on the peripheries of great metropolitan centers which cross arbitrary administrative boundaries of city, county, state, and nation.

As long as we identify urbanism with the physical entity of the city, viewing

---

*Louis Wirth, "Urbanism as a Way of Life," *The American Journal of Sociology,* 44 (July, 1938), pp. 1-24. Reprinted by permission of the University of Chicago Press.

it merely as rigidly delimited in space, and proceed as if urban attributes abruptly ceased to be manifested beyond an arbitrary boundary line, we are not likely to arrive at any adequate conception of urbanism as a mode of life. The technological developments in transportation and communication which virtually mark a new epoch in human history have accentuated the role of cities as dominant elements in our civilization and have enormously extended the urban mode of living beyond the confines of the city itself. The dominance of the city, especially of the great city, may be regarded as a consequence of the concentration in cities of industrial and commercial, financial and administrative facilities and activities, transportation and communication lines, and cultural and recreational equipment such as the press, radio stations, theaters, libraries, museums, concert halls, operas, hospitals, higher educational institutions, research and publishing centers, professional organizations, and religious and welfare institutions. Were it not for the attraction and suggestions that the city exerts through these instrumentalities upon the rural population, the differences between the rural and the urban modes of life would be even greater than they are. Urbanization no longer denotes merely the process by which persons are attracted to a place called the city and incorporated into its system of life. It refers also to that cumulative accentuation of the characteristics distinctive of the mode of life which is associated with the growth of cities, and finally to the changes in the direction of modes of life recognized as urban which are apparent among people, wherever they may be, who have come under the spell of the influences which the city exerts by virtue of the power of its institutions and personalities operating through the means of communication and transportation.

The shortcomings which attach to number of inhabitants as a criterion of urbanism apply for the most part to density of population as well. Whether we accept the density of 10,000 persons per square mile as Mark Jefferson proposed, or 1,000, which Willcox preferred to regard as the criterion of urban settlements, it is clear that unless density is correlated with significant social characteristics it can furnish only an arbitrary basis for differentiating urban from rural communities. Since our census enumerates the night rather than the day population of an area, the locale of the most intensive urban life—the city center—generally has low population density, and the industrial and commercial areas of the city, which contain the most characteristic economic activities underlying urban society, would scarcely anywhere be truly urban if density were literally interpreted as a mark of urbanism. Nevertheless, the fact that the urban community is distinguished by a large aggregation and relatively dense concentration of population can scarcely be left out of account in a definition of the city. But these criteria must be seen as relative to the general cultural context in which cities arise and exist and are sociologically relevant only in so far as they operate as conditioning factors in social life.

The same criticisms apply to such criteria as the occupation of the inhabitants, the existence of certain physical facilities, institutions, and forms of political organization. The question is not whether cities in our civilization or in others do exhibit these distinctive traits, but how potent they are in molding the character of social life into its specifically urban form. Nor in formulating a fertile definition can we afford to overlook the great variations between cities. By means of a typology of cities based upon size, location, age, and function, such as we have undertaken to establish in our recent report to the National Resources Committee, we have found it feasible to array and classify urban communities ranging from struggling small towns to thriving world-metropolitan centers; from isolated trading-centers in the midst of agricultural regions to thriving world-ports and commercial and industrial conurbations. Such differences as these appear crucial because the social characteristics and influences of these different "cities" vary widely.

A serviceable definition of urbanism should not only denote the essential characteristics which all cities—at least those in our culture—have in common, but should lend itself to the discovery of their variations. An industrial city will differ significantly in social respects from a commercial, mining, fishing, resort, university, and capital city. A one-industry city will present different sets of social characteristics from a multi-industry city, as will an industrially balanced from an imbalanced city, a suburb from a satellite, a residential suburb from an industrial suburb, a city within a metropolitan region from one lying outside, an old city from a new one, a southern city from a New England, a middle-western from a Pacific Coast city, a growing from a stable and from a dying city.

A sociological definition must obviously be inclusive enough to comprise whatever essential characteristics these different types of cities have in common as social entities, but it obviously cannot be so detailed as to take account of all the variations implicit in the manifold classes sketched above. Presumably some of the characteristics of cities are more significant in conditioning the nature of urban life than others, and we may expect the outstanding features of the urban-social scene to vary in accordance with size, density, and differences in the functional type of cities. Moreover, we may infer that rural life will bear the imprint of urbanism in the measure that through contact and communication it comes under the influence of cities. It may contribute to the clarity of the statements that follow to repeat that while the locus of urbanism as a mode of life is, of course, to be found characteristically in places which fulfil the requirements we shall set up as a definition of the city, urbanism is not confined to such localities but is manifest in varying degrees wherever the influences of the city reach.

While urbanism, or that complex of traits which makes up the characteristic mode of life in cities, and urbanization, which denotes the development and extensions of these factors, are thus not exclusively found in settlements which are cities in the physical and demographic sense, they do, nevertheless, find their most pronounced expression in such areas, especially in metropolitan cities. In formulating a definition of the city it is necessary to exercise caution in order to avoid identifying urbanism as a way of life with any specific locally or histori-cally conditioned cultural influences which, while they may significantly affect the specific character of the community, are not the essential determinants of its character as a city.

It is particularly important to call attention to the danger of confusing urbanism with industrialism and modern capitalism. The rise of cities in the modern world is undoubtedly not independent of the emergence of modern power-driven machine technology, mass production, and capitalistic enterprise. But different as the cities of earlier epochs may have been by virtue of their development in a preindustrial and precapitalistic order from the great cities of today, they were, nevertheless, cities.

For sociological purposes a city may be defined as a relatively large, dense, and permanent settlement of socially heterogeneous individuals. On the basis of the postulates which this minimal definition suggests, a theory of urbanism may be formulated in the light of existing knowledge concerning social groups.

A THEORY OF URBANISM

In the rich literature on the city we look in vain for a theory of urbanism presenting in a systematic fashion the available knowledge concerning the city as a social entity. We do indeed have excellent formulations of theories on such special problems as the growth of the city viewed as a historical trend and as a recurrent process, and we have a wealth of literature presenting insights of sociological relevance and empirical studies offering detailed information on a variety of particular aspects of urban life. But despite the multiplication of research and textbooks on the city, we do not as yet have a comprehensive body of compendent hypotheses which may be derived from a set of postulates implicitly contained in a sociological definition of the city, and from our general sociological knowledge which may be substantiated through empirical research. The closest approximations to a systematic theory of urbanism that we have are to be found in a penetrating essay, "Die Stadt," by Max Weber, and a memorable paper by Robert E. Park on "The City: Suggestions for the Investigation of Human Behavior in the Urban Environment." But even these excellent contributions are far from constituting an ordered and coherent framework of theory upon which research might profitably proceed.

In the pages that follow we shall seek to set forth a limited number of identifying characteristics of the city. Given these characteristics we shall then indicate what consequences or further characteristics follow from them in the light of general sociological theory and empirical research. We hope in this manner to arrive at the essential propositions comprising a theory of urbanism. Some of these propositions can be supported by a considerable body of already available research materials; others may be accepted as hypotheses for which a certain amount of presumptive evidence exists, but for which more ample and exact verification would be required. At least such a procedure will, it is hoped, show what in the way of systematic knowledge of the city we now have and what are the crucial and fruitful hypotheses for future research.

The central problem of the sociologist of the city is to discover the forms of social action and organization that typically emerge in relatively permanent, compact settlements of large numbers of heterogeneous individuals. We must also infer that urbanism will assume its most characteristic and extreme form in the measure in which the conditions with which it is congruent are present. Thus the larger, the more densely populated, and the more heterogeneous a community, the more accentuated the characteristics associated with urbanism will be. It should be recognized, however, that in the social world institutions and practices may be accepted and continued for reasons other than those that originally brought them into existence, and that accordingly the urban mode of life may be perpetuated under conditions quite foreign to those necessary for its origin.

Some justification may be in order for the choice of the principal terms comprising our definition of the city. The attempt has been made to make it as inclusive and at the same time as denotative as possible without loading it with unnecessary assumptions. To say that large numbers are necessary to constitute a city means, of course, large numbers in relation to a restricted area or high density of settlement. There are, nevertheless, good reasons for treating large numbers and density as separate factors, since each may be connected with significantly different social consequences. Similarly the need for adding heterogeneity to numbers of population as a necessary and distinct criterion of urbanism might be questioned, since we should expect the range of differences to increase with numbers. In defense, it may be said that the city shows a kind and degree of heterogeneity of population which cannot be wholly accounted for by the law of large numbers or adequately represented by means of a normal distribution curve. Since the population of the city does not reproduce itself, it must recruit its migrants from other cities, the countryside, and—in this country until recently—from other countries. The city has thus historically been the melting-pot of races, peoples, and cultures, and a most favorable breeding-ground of new biological and cultural hybrids. It has not only tolerated but rewarded individual differences. It has brought together people from the ends of the earth *because* they are different and thus useful to one another, rather than because they are homogeneous and like-minded.

There are a number of sociological propositions concerning the relationship between (*a*) numbers of population, (*b*) density of settlement, (*c*) heterogeneity of inhabitants and group life, which can be formulated on the basis of observation and research.

Size of the Population Aggregate

Ever since Aristotle's *Politics,* it has been recognized that increasing the number of inhabitants in a settlement beyond a certain limit will affect the relationships between them and the character of the city. Large numbers involve, as has been pointed out, a greater range of individual variation. Furthermore, the greater the number of individuals participating in a process of interaction, the greater is the *potential* differentiation between them. The personal traits, the occupations, the cultural life, and the ideas of the members of an urban community may, therefore, be expected to range between more widely separated poles than those of rural inhabitants.

That such variations should give rise to the spatial segregation of individuals according to color, ethnic heritage, economic and social status, tastes and preferences, may readily be inferred. The bonds of kinship, of neighborliness, and the sentiments arising out of living together for generations under a common folk tradition are likely to be absent or, at best, relatively weak in an aggregate the members of which have such diverse origins and backgrounds. Under such circumstances competition and formal control mechanisms furnish the substitutes for the bonds of solidarity that are relied upon to hold a folk society together.

Increase in the number of inhabitants of a community beyond a few hundred is bound to limit the possibility of each member of the community knowing all the others personally. Max Weber, in recognizing the social significance of this fact, pointed out that from a sociological point of view large numbers of inhabitants and density of settlement mean that the personal mutual acquaintanceship between the inhabitants which ordinarily inheres in a neighborhood is lacking. The increase in numbers thus involves a changed character of the social relationships. As Simmel points out:

> [If] the unceasing external contact of numbers of persons in the city should be met by the same number of inner reactions as in the small town, in which one knows almost every person he meets and to each of whom he has a positive relationship, one would be completely atomized internally and would fall into an unthinkable mental condition.

The multiplication of persons in a state of interaction under conditions which make their contact as full personalities impossible produces that segmentalization of human relationships which has sometimes been seized upon by students of the mental life of the cities as an explanation for the "schizoid" character of urban personality. This is not to say that the urban inhabitants have fewer acquaintances than rural inhabitants, for the reverse may actually be true; it means rather that in relation to the number of people whom they see and with whom they rub elbows in the course of daily life, they know a smaller proportion, and of these they have less intensive knowledge.

Characteristically, urbanites meet one another in highly segmental roles. They are, to be sure, dependent upon more people for the satisfactions of their life-needs than are rural people and thus are associated with a greater number of organized groups, but they are less dependent upon particular persons, and their dependence upon others is confined to a highly fractionalized aspect of the other's round of activity. This is essentially what is meant by saying that the city is characterized by secondary rather than primary contacts. The contacts of the city may indeed be face to face, but they are nevertheless impersonal, superficial, transitory, and segmental. The reserve, the indifference, and the blasé outlook which urbanites manifest in their relationships may thus be regarded as devices for immunizing themselves against the personal claims and expectations of others.

The superficiality, the anonymity, and the transitory character of urban-social relations make intelligible, also, the sophistication and the rationality generally ascribed to city-dwellers. Our acquaintances tend to stand in a relationship of utility to us in the sense that the role which each one plays in our life is overwhelmingly regarded as a means for the achievement of our own ends. Whereas, therefore, the individual gains, on the one hand, a certain degree of emancipation or freedom from the personal and emotional controls of intimate groups, he loses, on the other hand, the spontaneous self-expression, the morale, and the sense of participation that comes with living in an integrated society. This constitutes essentially the state of *anomie* or the social void to which Durkheim alludes in attempting to account for the various forms of social disorganization in technological society.

The segmental character and utilitarian accent of interpersonal relations in the city find their institutional expression in the proliferation of specialized tasks which we see in their most developed form in the professions. The operations of the pecuniary nexus leads to predatory relationships, which tend to obstruct the efficient functioning of the social order unless checked by professional codes and occupational etiquette. The premium put upon utility and efficiency suggests the adaptability of the corporate device for the organization of enterprises in which individuals can engage only in groups. The advantage that the corporation has over the individual entrepreneur and the partnership in the urban-industrial world derives not only from the possibility it affords of centralizing the resources of thousands of individuals or from the legal privilege of limited liability and perpetual succession, but from the fact that the corporation has no soul.

The specialization of individuals, particularly in their occupations, can proceed only, as Adam Smith pointed out, upon the basis of an enlarged market, which in turn accentuates the division of labor. This enlarged market is only in part supplied by the city's hinterland; in large measure it is found among the large numbers that the city itself contains. The dominance of the city over the surrounding hinterland becomes explicable in terms of the division of labor which urban life occasions and promotes. The extreme degree of interdependence and the unstable equilibrium of urban life are closely associated with the division of labor and the specialization of occupations. This interdependence and instability is increased by the tendency of each city to specialize in those functions in which it has the greatest advantage.

In a community composed of a larger number of individuals than can know one another intimately and can be assembled in one spot, it becomes necessary to communicate through indirect mediums and to articulate individual interests by a process of delegation. Typically in the city, interests are made effective through representation. The individual counts for little, but the voice of the representative is heard with a deference roughly proportional to the numbers for whom he speaks.

While this characterization of urbanism, in so far as it derives from large numbers, does not by any means exhaust the sociological inferences that might be drawn from our knowledge of the relationship of the size of a group to the characteristic behavior of the members, for the sake of brevity the assertions made may serve to exemplify the sort of propositions that might be developed.

Density

As in the case of numbers, so in the case of concentration in limited space, certain consequences of relevance in sociological analysis of the city emerge. Of these only a few can be indicated.

As Darwin pointed out for flora and fauna and as Durkheim noted in the case of human societies, an increase in numbers when area is held constant (i.e., an increase in density) tends to produce differentiation and specialization, since only in this way can the area support increased numbers. Density thus reinforces the effect of numbers in diversifying men and their activities and in increasing the complexity of the social structure.

On the subjective side, as Simmel has suggested, the close physical contact of numerous individuals necessarily produces a shift in the mediums through which we orient ourselves to the urban milieu, especially to our fellow-men. Typically, our physical contacts are close but our social contacts are distant. The urban world puts a premium on visual recognition. We see the uniform which denotes the role of the functionaries and are oblivious to the personal eccentricities that are hidden behind the uniform. We tend to acquire and develop a sensitivity to a world of artefacts and become progressively farther removed from the world of nature.

We are exposed to glaring contrasts between splendor and squalor, between riches and poverty, intelligence and ignorance, order and chaos. The competition for space is great, so that each area generally tends to be put to the use which yields the greatest economic return. Place of work tends to become dissociated from place of residence, for the proximity of industrial and commercial establishments makes an area both economically and socially undesirable for residential purposes.

Density, land values, rentals, accessibility, healthfulness, prestige, aesthetic consideration, absence of nuisances such as noise, smoke, and dirt determine the desirability of various areas of the city as places of settlement for different sections of the population. Place and nature of work, income, racial and ethnic characteristics, social status, custom, habit, taste, preference, and prejudice are among the significant factors in accordance with which the urban population is selected and distributed into more or less distinct settlements. Diverse population elements inhabiting a compact settlement thus tend to become segregated from one another in the degree in which their requirements and modes of life are incompatible with one another and in the measure in which they are antagonistic to one another. Similarly, persons of homogeneous status and needs unwittingly drift into, consciously select, or are forced by circumstances into, the same area. The different parts of the city thus acquire specialized functions. The city consequently tends to resemble a mosaic of social worlds in which the transition from one to the other is abrupt. The juxtaposition of divergent personalities and modes of life tends to produce a relativistic perspective and a sense of toleration of differences which may be regarded as prerequisites for rationality and which lead toward the secularization of life.

The close living together and working together of individuals who have no sentimental and emotional ties foster a spirit of competition, aggrandizement, and mutual exploitation. To counteract irresponsibility and potential disorder, formal controls tend to be resorted to. Without rigid adherence to predictable routines a large compact society would scarcely be able to maintain itself. The clock and the traffic signal are symbolic of the basis of our social order in the urban world. Frequent close physical contact, coupled with great social distance, accentuates the reserve of unattached individuals toward one another and, unless compensated for by other opportunities for response, gives rise to loneliness. The necessary frequent movement of great numbers of individuals in a congested habitat gives occasion to friction and irritation. Nervous tensions which derive from such personal frustrations are accentuated by the rapid tempo and the complicated technology under which life in dense areas must be lived.

Heterogeneity

The social interaction among such a variety of personality types in the urban milieu tends to break down the rigidity of caste lines and to complicate the class structure, and thus induces a more ramified and differentiated framework of social stratification than is found in more integrated societies. The heightened mobility of the individual, which brings him within the range of stimulation by a great number of diverse individuals and subjects him to fluctuating status in the differentiated social groups that compose the social structure of the city, tends toward the acceptance of instability and insecurity in the world at large as a norm. This fact helps to account, too, for the sophistication and cosmopolitanism of the urbanite. No single group has the undivided allegiance of the individual. The groups with which he is affiliated do not lend themselves readily to a simple hierarchical arrangement. By virtue of his different interests arising out of different aspects of social life, the individual acquires membership in widely divergent groups, each of which functions only with reference to a single segment of his personality. Nor do these groups easily permit of a concentric arrangement so that the narrower ones fall within the circumference of the more inclusive ones, as is more likely to be the case in the rural community or in primitive societies. Rather the groups with which the person typically is affiliated are tangential to each other or intersect in highly variable fashion.

Partly as a result of the physical footlooseness of the population and partly as a result of their social mobility, the turnover in group membership generally is rapid. Place of residence, place and character of employment, income and interests fluctuate, and the task of holding organizations together and maintaining and promoting intimate and lasting acquaintanceship between the members is difficult. This applies strikingly to the local areas within the city into which persons become segregated more by virtue of differences in race, language, income, and social status, than through choice or positive attraction to people like themselves. Overwhelmingly the city-dweller is not a home-owner, and since a transitory habitat does not generate binding traditions and sentiments, only rarely is he truly a neighbor. There is little opportunity for the individual to obtain a conception of the city as a whole or to survey his place in the total scheme. Consequently he finds it difficult to determine what is to his own "best interests" and to decide between the issues and leaders presented to him by the agencies of mass suggestion. Individuals who are thus detached from the organized bodies which integrate society comprise the fluid masses that make collective behavior in the urban community so unpredictable and hence so problematical.

Although the city, through the recruitment of variant types to perform its diverse tasks and the accentuation of their uniqueness through competition and the premium upon eccentricity, novelty, efficient performance, and inventiveness, produces a highly differentiated population, it also exercises a leveling influence. Wherever large numbers of differently constituted individuals congregate, the process of depersonalization also enters. This leveling tendency inheres in part in the economic basis of the city. The development of large cities, at least in the modern age, was largely dependent upon the concentrative force of steam. The rise of the factory made possible mass production for an impersonal market. The fullest exploitation of the possibilities of the division of labor and mass production, however, is possible only with standardization of processes and products. A money economy goes hand in hand with such a system of production. Progressively as cities have developed upon a background of this system of production, the pecuniary nexus which implies the purchasability of services and things has displaced personal relations as the basis of association. Individuality under these circumstances must be replaced by categories. When large numbers have to make common use of facilities and institutions, an arrangement must be made to adjust the facilities and institutions to the needs of the average person rather than to those of particular individuals. The services of the public utilities, of the recreational, educational, and cultural institutions must be adjusted to mass requirements. Similarly, the cultural institutions, such as the schools, the movies, the radio, and the newspapers, by virtue of their mass clientele, must necessarily operate as leveling influences. The political process as it appears in urban life could not be understood without taking account of the mass appeals made through modern propaganda techniques. If the individual would participate at all in the social, political, and economic life of the city, he must subordinate some of his individuality to the demands of the larger community and in that measure immerse himself in mass movements.

THE RELATION BETWEEN A THEORY OF URBANISM
AND SOCIOLOGICAL RESEARCH

By means of a body of theory such as that illustratively sketched above, the complicated and many-sided phenomena of urbanism may be analyzed in terms of a limited number of basic categories. The sociological approach to the city thus acquires an essential unity and coherence enabling the empirical investigator not merely to focus more distinctly upon the problems and processes that properly fall in his province but also to treat his subject matter in a more integrated and systematic fashion. A few typical findings of empirical research in the field of urbanism, with special reference to the United States, may be indicated to substantiate the theoretical propositions set forth in the preceding pages, and some of the crucial problems for further study may be outlined.

On the basis of the three variables, number, density of settlement, and degree of heterogeneity, of the urban population, it appears possible to explain the characteristics of urban life and to account for the differences between cities of various sizes and types.

Urbanism as a characteristic mode of life may be approached empirically from three interrelated perspectives: (1) as a physical structure comprising a population base, a technology, and an ecological order; (2) as a system of social organization involving a characteristic social structure, a series of social institutions, and a typical pattern of social relationships; and (3) as a set of attitudes and ideas, and a constellation of personalities engaging in typical forms of collective behavior and subject to characteristic mechanisms of social control.

Urbanism in Ecological Perspective

Since in the case of physical structure and ecological processes we are able to operate with fairly objective indices, it becomes possible to arrive at quite precise and generally quantitative results. The dominance of the city over its hinterland becomes explicable through the functional characteristics of the city which derive in large measure from the effect of numbers and density. Many of the technical facilities and the skills and organizations to which urban life gives rise can grow and prosper only in cities where the demand is sufficiently great. The nature and scope of the services rendered by these organizations and institutions and the advantage which they enjoy over the less developed facilities of smaller towns enhances the dominance of the city and the dependence of ever wider regions upon the central metropolis.

The urban-population composition shows the operation of selective and differentiating factors. Cities contain a larger proportion of persons in the prime of life than rural areas which contain more old and very young people. In this, as in so many other respects, the larger the city the more this specific characteristic of urbanism is apparent. With the exception of the largest cities, which have attracted the bulk of the foreign-born males, and a few other special types of cities, women predominate numerically over men. The heterogeneity of the urban population is further indicated along racial and ethnic lines. The foreign born and their children constitute nearly two-thirds of all the inhabitants of cities of one million and over. Their proportion in the urban population declines as the size of the city decreases, until in the rural areas they comprise only about one-sixth of the total population. The larger cities similarly have attracted more Negroes and other racial groups than have the smaller communities. Considering that age, sex, race, and ethnic origin are associated with other factors such as occupation and interest, it becomes clear that one major characteristic of the urban-dweller is his dissimilarity from his fellows. Never before have such large masses of people of diverse traits as we find in our cities been thrown together into such close physical contact as in the great cities of America. Cities generally, and American cities in particular, comprise a motley of peoples and cultures, of highly differentiated modes of life between which there often is only the faintest communication, the greatest indifference and the broadest tolerance, occasionally bitter strife, but always the sharpest contrast.

The failure of the urban population to reproduce itself appears to be a biological consequence of a combination of factors in the complex of urban life, and the decline in the birth-rate generally may be regarded as one of the most significant signs of the urbanization of the Western world. While the proportion of deaths in cities is slightly greater than in the country, the outstanding difference between the failure of present-day cities to maintain their population and that of cities of the past is that in former times it was due to the exceedingly high death-rates in cities, whereas today, since cities have become more livable from a health standpoint, it is due to low birth-rates. These biological characteristics of the urban population are significant sociologically, not merely because they reflect the urban mode of existence but also because they condition the growth and future dominance of cities and their basic social organization. Since cities are the consumers rather than the producers of men, the value of human life and the social estimation of the personality will not be unaffected by the balance between births and deaths. The pattern of land use, of land values, rentals, and ownership, the nature and functioning of the physical structures, of housing, of transportation and communication facilities, of public utilities—these and many other phases of the physical mechanism of the city are not isolated phenomena unrelated to the city as a social entity, but are affected by and affect the urban mode of life.

Urbanism as a Form of Social Organization

The distinctive features of the urban mode of life have often been described sociologically as consisting of the substitution of secondary for primary contacts, the weakening of bonds of kinship, and the declining social significance of the family, the disappearance of the neighborhood, and the undermining of the traditional basis of social solidarity. All these phenomena can be substantially verified through objective indices. Thus, for instance, the low and declining urban-reproduction rates suggest that the city is not conducive to the traditional type of family life, including the rearing of children and the maintenance of the home as the locus of a whole round of vital activities. The transfer of industrial, educational, and recreational activities to specialized institutions outside the home has deprived the family of some of its most characteristic historical functions. In cities mothers are more likely to be employed, lodgers are more frequently part of the household, marriage tends to be postponed, and the proportion of single and unattached people is greater. Families are smaller and more frequently without children than in the country. The family as a unit of social life is emancipated from the larger kinship group characteristic of the country, and the individual members pursue their own diverging interests in their vocational, educational, religious, recreational, and political life.

Such functions as the maintenance of health, the methods of alleviating the hardships associated with personal and social insecurity, the provisions for education, recreation, and cultural advancement have given rise to highly specialized institutions on a community-wide, statewide, or even national basis. The same factors which have brought about greater personal insecurity also underlie the wider contrasts between individuals to be found in the urban world. While the city has broken down the rigid caste lines of preindustrial society, it has sharpened and differentiated income and status groups. Generally, a larger proportion of the adult-urban population is gainfully employed than is the case with the adult-rural population. The white-collar class, comprising those employed in trade, in clerical, and in professional work, are proportionately more numerous in large cities and in metropolitan centers and in smaller towns than in the country.

On the whole, the city discourages an economic life in which the individual in time of crisis has a basis of subsistence to fall back upon, and it discourages self-employment. While incomes of city people are on the average higher than those of country people, the cost of living seems to be higher in the larger cities. Home ownership involves greater burdens and is rarer. Rents are higher and absorb a larger proportion of the income. Although the urban-dweller has the benefit of many communal services, he spends a large proportion of his income for such items as recreation and advancement and a smaller proportion for food. What the communal services do not furnish the urbanite must purchase, and there is virtually no human need which has remained unexploited by commercialism. Catering to thrills and furnishing means of escape from drudgery, monotony, and routine thus become one of the major functions of urban recreation, which at its best furnishes means for creative self-expression and spontaneous group association, but which more typically in the urban world results in passive spectatorism on the one hand, or sensational record-smashing feats on the other.

Being reduced to a stage of virtual impotence as an individual, the urbanite is bound to exert himself by joining with others of similar interest into organized groups to obtain his ends. This results in the enormous multiplication of voluntary organizations directed toward as great a variety of objectives as there are human needs and interests. While on the one hand the traditional ties of human association are weakened, urban existence involves a much greater degree of interdependence between man and man and a more complicated, fragile, and volatile form of mutual interrelations over many phases of which the individual as such can exert scarcely any control. Frequently there is only the most tenuous relationship between the economic position or other basic factors that determine the individual's existence in the urban world and the voluntary groups with which he is affiliated. While in a primitive and in a rural society it is generally possible to predict on the basis of a few known factors who will belong to what and who will associate with whom in almost every relationship of life, in the city we can only project the general pattern of group formation and affiliation, and this pattern will display many incongruities and contradictions.

Urban Personality and Collective Behavior

It is largely through the activities of the voluntary groups, be their objectives economic, political, educational, religious, recreational, or cultural, that the urbanite expresses and develops his personality, acquires status, and is able to carry on the round of activities that constitute his life-career. It may easily be inferred, however, that the organizational framework which these highly differentiated functions call into being does not of itself insure the consistency and integrity of the personalities whose interests it enlists. Personal disorganization, mental breakdown, suicide, delinquency, crime, corruption, and disorder might be expected under these circumstances to be more prevalent in the urban than in the rural community. This has been confirmed in so far as comparable indices are available; but the mechanisms underlying these phenomena require further analysis.

Since for most group purposes it is impossible in the city to appeal individually to the large number of discrete and differentiated individuals, and since it is only through the organizations to which men belong that their interests and resources can be enlisted for a collective cause, it may be inferred that social control in the city should typically proceed through formally organized groups. It follows, too, that the masses of men in the city are subject to manipulation by symbols and stereotypes managed by individuals working from afar or operating invisibly behind the scenes through their control of the instruments of communication. Self-government either in the economic, the political, or the cultural realm is under these circumstances reduced to a mere figure of speech or, at best, is subject to the unstable equilibrium of pressure groups. In view of the ineffectiveness of actual kinship ties we create fictional kinship groups. In the face of the disappearance of the territorial unit as a basis of social solidarity we create interest units. Meanwhile the city as a community resolves itself into a series of tenuous segmental relationships superimposed upon a territorial base with a definite center but without a definite periphery and upon a division of labor which far transcends the immediate locality and is world-wide in scope. The larger the number of persons in a state of interaction with one another the lower is the level of communication and the greater is the tendency for communication to proceed on an elementary level, i.e., on the basis of those things which are assumed to be common or to be of interest to all.

It is obviously, therefore, to the emerging trends in the communication system and to the production and distribution technology that has come into existence with modern civilization that we must look for the symptoms which will indicate the probable future development of urbanism as a mode of social life. The direction of the ongoing changes in urbanism will for good or ill transform not only the city but the world. Some of the more basic of these factors and processes and the possibilities of their direction and control invite further detailed study.

It is only in so far as the sociologist has a clear conception of the city as a social entity and a workable theory of urbanism that he can hope to develop a unified body of reliable knowledge, which what passes as "urban sociology" is certainly not at the present time. By taking his point of departure from a theory of urbanism such as that sketched in the foregoing pages to be elaborated, tested, and revised in the light of further analysis and empirical research, it is to be hoped that the criteria of relevance and validity of factual data can be determined. The miscellaneous assortment of disconnected information which has hitherto found its way into sociological treatises on the city may thus be sifted and incorporated into a coherent body of knowledge. Incidentally, only by means of some such theory will the sociologist escape the futile practice of voicing in the name of sociological science a variety of often unsupportable judgments concerning such problems as poverty, housing, city-planning, sanitation, municipal administration, policing, marketing, transportation, and other technical issues. While the sociologist cannot solve any of these practical problems—at least not by himself—he may, if he discovers his proper function, have an important contribution to make to their comprehension and solution. The prospects for doing this are brightest through a general theoretical, rather than through an *ad hoc* approach.

The Metropolitan Community

by Roderick D. McKenzie*

The history of American settlement may be divided roughly into three periods. The first was the pre-railway era extending from colonial times to about the middle of the nineteenth century. During this period settlement was confined, for the most part, to areas accessible to navigable water; that is, to the Atlantic seaboard and the main river systems east of the Mississippi. As late as 1850 over 90 per cent of the population of the United States resided east of the Mississippi River, and the greater part of this east of the Alleghenies. During this river régime, settlement was of a segmentary character; the various units as determined by geographic conditions had but slight economic or social relations with one another. Settlement was also primarily rural in character; almost four-fifths of the 23,000,000 inhabitants of the United States in 1850 resided in rural territory or in communities of less than 8,000.

The second period of settlement development commenced about 1850 with the expansion of the railroad. Beginning in the eastern part of the country, railroad construction extended westward, first to the river centers of settlement as previously established and, later, into new frontiers beyond the Mississippi. By 1870 there was rail transportation to the Pacific Coast, and by 1900 all the main outlines of the present railway net had been established.

The story of settlement development during this railway era need not be repeated here. Certain features, however, may be called to attention. Freed from the dominance of the river highways, settlement spread under the influence of railroad transportation westward across the continent. The flow was directed and controlled by the opportunities offered in the way of soil and other natural resources. During the 30-year period from 1870 to 1900 more than 495,000,000 acres were added to the cultivated area of the United States, an extent of territory, as E. L. Bogart estimates, equal to the land area of Great Britain and Europe except Spain.

This rush to new areas of agricultural opportunity lost its momentum shortly after the turn of the twentieth century. As early as 1890 the Superintendent of the Census made the significant announcement that the frontier had disap-

*Roderick D. McKenzie, *The Metropolitan Community* (New York: McGraw-Hill, 1933), pp. 3-7, 311-318.

peared, meaning thereby that population had become distributed over the land
to a minimum density of two persons per square mile. In a review of population
growth in the United States for the decade 1910 to 1920, W. S. Rossiter calls
attention to the slackening of this westward drift.

> Until 1900 the flow of population was mainly westward. From that
> census it appeared that the current had slackened, and changes of popula-
> tion became more dependent upon isolated developments in different sec-
> tions of the country, such as irrigation, the settlement of Oklahoma,
> orcharding in the far Northwest, and the mining and oil discoveries of the
> Southwest. . . . The eddies and currents of population tended increasingly
> to follow changing industrial development. This naturally led to an acceler-
> ated increase in urban population.

From the beginning of the westward movement, even before, but more particularly during, the period of railway expansion, city growth was largely a product
of the flow of population into areas from which raw materials could most
readily be obtained to sell in distant markets. As late as 1900 agricultural
products constituted 66 per cent of all foreign exports from the United States.
Since that time, however, their ratio has diminished rapidly; in the period from
1926 to 1930 agricultural exports were only 36 per cent of the total value of all
exports.

During this period of population dispersion the city was for the most part the
child and servant of expanding rural settlement; it followed rather than directed
population spread. Gateway cities arose at entrance points to producing regions
and functioned as collecting centers for the basic products from surrounding
settlement and as distributing points for manufactured goods brought in from
outside territory. These gateway centers maintained contact with tributary territory through a community hierarchy of villages, towns, and cities established on
the basis of railway transportation. Thus the basic pattern of modern American
settlement was formed. No less than 42 of the 93 cities of over 100,000 population in 1930 were incorporated since 1850; that is, since the beginning of railway development, and 5 of these began their official careers since 1890.

Toward the close of the nineteenth century the city began to play a new rôle
in the evolution of settlement in the United States. With the rise of manufacturing, population and wealth became increasingly concentrated in the larger cities.
The demand of the city for raw materials for its growing industries, and for
specialized types of agricultural products for its increasing population, more and
more determined the course of rural settlement. New frontiers continued to
arise, but chiefly in areas from which products might be obtained to supply the
domestic city market. On the other hand, many of the older areas of rural
settlement began to recede in response to the economic forces originating in
metropolitan centers. With the growth of population and wealth throughout the
nation, the city acquired an increasing range of economic and social functions

which it performed not only for its own inhabitants but for rural settlements as well. Accordingly it increased in economic and cultural dominance.

The third period of settlement, and the one with which we are chiefly concerned in this study, began about 1900 or shortly thereafter. It may be referred to as an era of city regionalism which is developing under the influence of motor transportation. As previously indicated, the railroad laid the foundation for modern regionalism by creating a network of large gateway cities which served as focal points in the integration of surrounding territory and which drew the entire nation together into a single economic unity. The motor vehicle has not changed the main outlines of this railway pattern of settlement. The great economic forces in operation when the automobile was introduced compelled accommodation of this new agency of transportation to the existing settlement structure. Despite this fact, it may be fairly stated that the gross effect of motor transportation upon American civilization has been quite as fundamental as that produced by the advent of the railroad. In the first place, motor transportation has grown with a rapidity even greater than that of the railroads in their period of fastest expansion. Within a quarter of a century, 26,000,000 motor vehicles and more than 500,000 miles of surfaced motor highways have been added to the transportation system of the United States. Beginning with city streets and wagon roads as the only routes of traffic, the motor vehicle has developed a system of surface highways adapted to its needs. This new motor-highway net which has been superimposed upon the existing pattern of settlement is developed most intensively around the margins of cities and has brought the city and surrounding territory within a common transportation system. In so doing, it has erased the boundaries and bridged the distances which formerly separated urban from rural territory and has introduced a type of local community entirely without precedent in history.

Generalizing, it may be said that the railways set the main structural outlines of American settlement. By making possible the transfer of products between distant regions, they brought the entire settlement of the United States into a single economic unity integrated through a system of gateway cities of varying importance which function through chains of lesser centers strung like beads along the railway lines. The railroads, however, did not materially change the traditional pattern of life within the local community. Except in the larger cities where mechanical forms of transportation were introduced, first steam and then electric, the horse-drawn vehicle remained as the chief agency of local travel and traffic. Local institutions and social relations persisted in the railway régime on much the same basis as in the previous era. But the coming of motor transportation revolutionized this traditional pattern of local relations and effected institutional and cultural changes more disturbing to the social fabric than the more conspicuous developments induced by the advent of rail transportation.

By reducing the scale of local distance, the motor vehicle extended the horizon of the community and introduced a territorial division of labor among local institutions and neighboring centers which is unique in the history of settlement.

The large center has been able to extend the radius of its influence; its population and many of its institutions, freed from the dominance of rail transportation, have become widely dispersed throughout surrounding territory. Moreover, formerly independent towns and villages and also rural territory have become part of this enlarged city complex. This new type of supercommunity organized around a dominant focal point and comprising a multiple of differentiated centers of activity differs from the metropolitanism established by rail transportation in the complexity of its institutional division of labor and the mobility of its population. Its territorial scope is defined in terms of motor transportation and competition with other regions. Nor is this new type of metropolitan community confined to the great cities. It has become the communal unit of local relations throughout the entire nation. Its development has induced a vast amount of rearrangement of populations and institutions, a process which is still far from having attained an equilibrium.

The object of this study is to trace the rise of this new type of regional community, to note the forces which are bringing it about and determining its form and *modus operandi*. In this connection it is important to note the tendencies in the spatial arrangement of population both within the country as a whole and within the local area; to examine the trend of settlement from the isolated independent communal nucleus to this complex type of supercommunity; and to note problems which arise in the process of reorganization. In undertaking such a task, one is confronted with the limitations of the statistics available by which to measure tendencies and interrelations of phenomena. Many of our generalizations are inadequately supported by factual evidence. Likewise, various lines of approach had to be neglected for lack of quantitative data. This lack of data pertains particularly to the changes that are occurring in the social and cultural life of the metropolitan community. Although it is obvious that the changes in these aspects of community life must be as significant as those in commercial relations, it is not possible to obtain information by which to measure them. If this study, therefore, seems to overstress the economic and to slight the social side of the metropolitan community, it is primarily because of the comparative inadequacies of the social data.

. . . .

It is now possible to take a bird's-eye view of the growth and expansion of the metropolitan community in the United States. Fully one-half of the people of this country now live within 50 miles of a city of 100,000 or more, and over 80 per cent reside within an hour's motor journey of a city of 25,000 or more. Growth has been much more rapid in the territory adjoining the larger cities than in the nation as a whole or even within the large cities themselves. Small cities and rural territory within motor access of a metropolitan center have increased several times as fast as similar territory lying outside the local sphere of influence of a large city. This grouping of population around the larger cities of the country and the reaching out of such communities over larger territories are

the outstanding phases of the recent "drift to the cities." The census classification of all incorporated places of 2,500 or more as urban is increasingly less
significant than a classification based upon whether population is or is not
contained within the sphere of influence of a metropolitan center.

The negative aspect of this concentration process is reflected in an expanding
area of decreasing population. Between 1920 and 1930, 41 per cent of all
counties in the United States suffered an actual loss of population. Not only was
there the migration from rural territory, with which previous censuses have made
us familiar; there was also a shifting within the urban population itself, from the
smaller centers to the greater and from certain areas to certain other areas. The
1930 census recorded 512 cities of over 2,500 inhabitants that lost population
after 1920. Fifteen of these cities had attained the 50,000 mark before decline
set in. These data suggest how inadequate a vision of what is actually taking
place the gross statistics of urban growth convey.

Up to 1920, the leading factor making for population concentration was the
centralization of industry. In other words, the population followed the factories.
The census of 1930 with supplementary evidence now available indicates that
the factors involved in metropolitan growth during the last decade were primarily commercial and institutional, with industry playing a relatively smaller rôle.
The metropolitan community, at least until the advent of the depression in
1929, offered an increasing variety of jobs as well as more steady employment.
It also offered a wider variety of economic and cultural services. It took on more
and more the aspect of a coherent economic and cultural state, more realistic in
many ways than the existing political states.

These supercommunities have not only been increasing in population, but
have been taking on definite attributes. Wherever population concentrates in
aggregations of several hundred thousands, it tends to break up into a multiplicity of communal units. Every large city is the center of a constellation of smaller
centers, some of which are the direct products of the outward movement from
the main city; others were formerly independent centers have have now become
economically and socially integrated with the dominant city. Among these various units of local settlement, there is arising an ever-increasing refinement of
division of labor and interdependence of relationship. This has the effect of
creating within the city region bonds of common interest that are much stronger
than any ties that bind one region to another.

The city region as here defined is largely a product of modern means of
communication, developed more intensively in local areas than throughout the
nation as a whole. Assume that the boundaries of an ancient or medieval city
were largely determined by the distance a man could walk in two hours. This
would give a practical radius of 8 miles and a diameter of 16 miles. The introduction of the motor car would at once multiply these limits at least six times,
extending the practicable radius to at least 50 miles. The case of the modern
supercity is not quite so simple as this, since transportation by horse-drawn

stages, by steam boats where water was adjacent, and by steam railways extended the urban radius long before the coming of the automobile. But the illustration is pertinent. Measured in time, rather than linear expansion, the old boundaries of cities have been outgrown and vast new areas have been brought within the city's influence.

The supercommunity therefore absorbs varying numbers of separate local communities into its economic and cultural organizations. In this pattern, a dominant city—that is, dominant relative to surrounding settlement—functions as the integrating unit. These central cities are becoming increasingly conscious of themselves as centers of commercial provinces and are attempting to define and delineate the territory over which they exercise a dominant economic influence. The evidence at hand clearly indicates that the influence of the central city over surrounding territory tends to diminish with distance outward. There is usually a line, or rather zone, where the territory of one metropolitan center meets and overlaps that of another. We can in fact draw a map tentatively allotting the entire territory of continental United States to a comparatively small number of the larger cities. In other words, there is developing within the United States, and in fact throughout the modern world, a pattern of settlement which may be designated as city regionalism. This new city regionalism differs from the regionalism of former times in that it is a product of contact and division of labor rather than of mere geographic isolation.

These supercommunities throughout the nation appear to be becoming more nearly uniform in their economic and institutional structure. The frontier type of city is gradually developing into a metropolis. This is shown in physical structure—in the growth of tall office buildings and financial institutions. It is also shown in the increasing complexity of the industrial and occupational pattern of the larger cities throughout the nation and by the tendency toward more uniform distribution of cultural traits and cultured persons. The increasing diversity within the city region and the uniformity among the regions result in a higher degree of local autonomy. The regional city tends to grow more self-sufficient and therefore to become a competing unit within the larger interregional economy. But this self-sufficiency is limited by the concentration of certain industries and certain raw materials. There is a countertendency toward a closer functional relation among the metropolitan centers of the nation. Just as communities within the metropolitan region preserve a certain degree of independence and local identity, yet are closely bound within the economic and cultural network of the central city; so the regional communities themselves are independent in many things, yet are parts of a national and international economy.

This situation is brought about, or intensified, by the growth of national organizations, economic and social, of the chain type. The general practice of such organizations is to divide the country into service areas and to select the largest regional city as district headquarters for activities in surrounding territory. This pattern of organization, initiated by the Federal Reserve Banking System in 1913, is becoming common to large-scale organizations of almost every type. Although the number of key centers employed by any organization to reach its clientele varies with the nature of the service, there is a tendency on the part of different organizations to select the same regional headquarters for financial and administrative purposes. The process is cumulative. Once a city becomes established as a regional distributing center, its banking, transportation, and other facilities compel new concerns entering the region to select it as their point of operation. The result is that a rather well-defined pattern of regional office centers is taking shape throughout the nation.

But while the rôle of the great city in the nation at large has been growing in importance and changing in nature, even more radical and important changes have taken place within the city itself. Every large city has experienced rapid shifts in its local population since the end of the World War. The suburban drift has not only increased in volume but has altered in character. The outward movement in recent years has been largely among the white-collar classes, who have created a definite new problem by removing themselves from the political city while remaining within the sphere of influence of the economic and cultural city. They have drawn after them a number of local institutions, business outlets and municipal services, creating a real *rus in urbe* in the suburban territories. Industry likewise has tended to migrate outward, not for the same reasons but because increasing congestion in the more central districts has hampered its activities and added to its production costs.

The general effect of this outward drift, coupled with the more intensive use of land brought about by large structural units, has been to hasten the obsolescence of much of the older pattern of the city. Every large city is confronted, on the one hand, with the problem of increasing congestion in certain areas and, on the other, with that of revitalizing its blighted areas. The deteriorated districts are rarely rehabilitated by private enterprise, though in some cities, notably New York, blighted areas have been restored, at least partially, by the erection of high-class apartment houses. But these blighted areas are always in competition with newer subdivisions which offer a more inviting field for private enterprise. Usually lying close to the main business center of the city, they become the habitats of the vicious and criminal elements of the population. Without the economic incentive toward repair or replacement, buildings are allowed to deteriorate. Land values decline, assessments are lost to the city, transportation problems are aggravated by the fact that residence is further removed from the center of business. This actual misuse and underuse of land create a difficult situation for the city planner, the city assessor, the health department, the police department, the transportation managers, and the housing and welfare agencies.

While many of the older areas have been allowed to deteriorate, there has been an extensive exploitation of new urban territory. The last decade witnessed an unprecedented speculative development of subdivision platting. Most of our cities are now surrounded by unused platted areas—many of which possess some or all of the essential city utilities—sufficient to meet any probable growth requirements for several decades to come. This excessive development of new urban land and the extensive spread of the city's population and services during the last decade are generally recognized as important factors in intensifying the present municipal tax burdens and transportation difficulties. The facilities of mass transportation, except in certain of the very large cities, are not adequate for the needs of the suburban population; nor is it economically feasible to provide transportation except to certain of the more densely occupied areas. The widely scattered suburban residents must rely upon the private automobile as the principal agency of local transportation. In order to meet the requirements of automotive traffic, every large city has been confronted with the problem of constructing arterial motor thoroughfares. This involves condemnation, street widening, terminal facilities, and a host of related problems of taxation and special assessments.

Nearly every one of the new problems of great cities comes home sooner or later to the governmental agencies. The last decade has witnessed a rapid expansion of all types of municipal utilities and services. At the same time, many of the governmental functions have failed to keep pace with the economic and cultural expansion of urban life. The multiplicity of separate governmental and taxation bodies in every large metropolitan aggregation constitutes one of the serious difficulties confronting the metropolitan community today. Because city planning is by definition limited to the obsolescent political city, it is now being rapidly superseded by regional planning. But regional planning on a scale commensurate with actual needs is thwarted by the large number of politically independent communities with which planning bodies have to deal.

The development of the new supercity points, therefore, to the need of some sort of supermetropolitan government. Professor Reed has presented this problem and the steps already taken to cope with it. It is quite apparent that the old procedure of annexation of surrounding territory by a central city is no longer a satisfactory solution. The spread of population under the influence of motor transport is far too rapid and too extensive to be dealt with adequately by annexation, even if annexation were not vigorously resisted by most of the suburban communities. Some plan of coordination of governmental functions must be developed before the political unity of the real functional metropolitan community can be achieved.

From the point of view of individual welfare, most of the graver problems of metropolitan living may be grouped under the general category of insecurity or instability. Our metropolitan communities are organized with the individual rather than the family as the economic unit. This makes possible a high degree of specialization and occupational division of labor within the local population group and thereby increases the efficiency of the corporate whole; but this very specialization makes the individual increasingly dependent upon the smooth operation of the economic system. As population concentrates in larger aggregation units, there is a continual increase in the differentiation of occupations and in the interdependence of tasks. The economic mechanism becomes more intricate and the balance between the interdependent units more delicate. As long as the general economic trend is upward, the individual can shift from task to task and from place to place in response to the conditions of the dynamic process, but once the sensitive system becomes dislocated, as at present, he is left helpless and stranded. His only recourse is to rely upon his scattered kinsfolk for temporary relief or to cast himself upon the mercy of organized charity.

Accommodation to present conditions of dislocation has largely taken the form of attempts to revert to a simpler social order. National governments have attempted to protect their citizens against outside competition by raising tariff barriers and immigration restrictions. Many states and cities have appealed to their inhabitants to confine their purchases as far as possible to goods and products produced within the local area. Individuals have sought refuge in the kinship group, and families have returned to the village and deserted farmstead. Even the ancient system of barter has been revived. These and many similar practices that might be mentioned reveal the natural human impulse to return in times of stress to ways that are more familiar and presumably more secure. But our metropolitan society is too complex a mechanism to be adjusted by such expedients. The outstanding fact to be kept in mind is that our great metropolitan communities are products of the operation of economic and cultural forces that are world-wide in scope. While each metropolitan aggregate is tending to become a more complete economic and social unit, the interdependence among these supercommunities is becoming more sensitive and more extended in space. To attempt to adjust this complex mechanism by reversion to old techniques is analogous to trying to repair a motor car with a crowbar and hammer.

In closing this study, perhaps one might be excused for venturing to speculate about probable future developments. It would seem that the general outlines of American settlement pattern are established for years to come. Our great centers of population are not only deeply rooted in the general economic fabric, but an increasing proportion of our people have become socially and culturally conditioned to urban ways of living. It is highly improbable, within the near future at any rate, that any revolutionary changes will occur in population patterning. In all probability our great cities will continue to decentralize in the sense that population and economic functions will become more widely dispersed throughout the metropolitan areas. But it is not likely that there will be any general exodus to the farm. Modern agriculture is closely integrated with our metropolitan system of living. It has developed in response to the growth of city markets and has been subject to the same technological influences that have invaded other forms of industry, as evidenced by the steady decline in the number of workers required to cultivate the land. There will undoubtedly continue to be much interregional shifting of the urban population as the general rate of population growth diminishes and as new industries arise in different parts of the nation.

As our regional communities become more conscious of their common interests, an increasing amount of purposeful planning is likely to ensue. Nor is this planning likely to be restricted to the mere physical aspects of community structure and municipal functions. It will, in all probability, include an increasing range of economic and social activities. The age of extreme and almost unregulated individual competition appears to be nearing a close. If we are going to consider stability and security as essential aspects of wholesome social living, conscious effort must be directed toward regulating competition in the interest of general welfare.

CHAPTER FOUR

THE LEVIATHAN CITY:
THE REGIONAL PLANNERS

A significant problem for those who faced the emergence of the metropolitan community was how to make sense of, organize, and plan so large and unwieldy an entity. The early urban reformers sought means of bringing order to the city, whether by a single tax, a revitalized church, or municipal control of urban land. The City Beautiful Movement, for all its limitations, nonetheless suggested the possibility, through the harmonious arrangement of public buildings and open spaces, that some order could be brought to the urban chaos. The ecologists and urban sociologists also formulated a way of looking at the city and metropolis which emphasized the patterns of regularity underlying the more apparent disorganization of the urban environment. In city planning, however, as the profession developed and became more specialized, attention often shifted from the larger context to such specific problems as zoning codes and transportation. But there also emerged in the 1920's and 1930's a number of efforts to conceive of and plan for the city in a broader environmental framework.

Members of the Regional Planning Association of America (RPAA), formed in 1923, were sharply critical of prevailing trends in housing and city planning. Architect-planners like Clarence Stein and Henry Wright, and regionalists like Lewis Mumford and Benton MacKaye argued that inadequate housing, water supplies, streets and public transportation were only the most blatant of urban ills in our "dinosaur cities." Stein and his colleagues maintained that unrestricted real estate speculation, accompanied by an increasing dependence on the automobile as the chief form of urban transportation, resulted in the further haphazard agglomeration of people, buildings, and physical apparatus in the cities and their suburbs. Furthermore, the RPAA blamed the manner in which cities were being built—monotonous suburban housing subdivisions, elaborate subway and highway schemes, street widenings and zoning restrictions—for actually facilitating rather than checking this congestion. The question these planners posed was fundamental: what urban form might be established to ease the pressures of meaningless urban massing? Their answer was a form of regionalism which, along with a number of specific community and housing proposals, offered an alternative to largely unregulated metropolitan expansion.

The 1926 *Report* of the New York State Commission of Housing and Regional Planning (CHRP), submitted to Governor Alfred E. Smith, is an example of the regional approach adopted by the RPAA. Prepared largely by Henry Wright, the CHRP *Report* is a regional survey in the genre of the Scottish planner Patrick Geddes (1854-1932), whose maxim, "Diagnosis before treatment," greatly influenced many planners in the years before 1945. Geddes emphasized that any comprehensive plan for city improvement must include a preliminary survey of the geology, climate, economy, and social institutions of the city and its region. Wright's 70-page report is a survey, in this broad sense, of the state of New York, and is divided into two main sections: first, a discussion of the various factors which have given shape to the present, and secondly, a review of those forces likely to influence the future. The report traces the settlement pattern of the state in which a fairly balanced spread of population is transformed by manufacturing and industrialization. The result is the centralization of industry and the concentration of population. Wright saw hope for the future of the state's crowded cities in the decentralizing and community building potentials of modern technology—particularly electricity. The regionalism advocated in Wright's 1926 survey of New York envisioned a more efficient industrial and agricultural utilization of land, and a more rational pattern of human settlement than that offered in the continued heaping of population into overcrowded cities.

An important influence on Stein, Wright, and their regional planning colleagues was the garden city idea of Ebenezer Howard. A London court stenographer and amateur inventor, Howard put forth his scheme in a little book eventually titled *Garden Cities of To-Morrow* (1898, 1902), as a means of alleviating the congestion of huge cities and of checking urban sprawl. Rather than planning existing cities more carefully, Howard advocated building new cities on large plots of land outside the high-density metropolis, each to be surrounded by an agricultural and recreational greenbelt area. A typical middle-class Victorian reformer, Howard hoped to combine in his scheme a "collective" system of land tenure—whereby the usual "unearned increment" of the real estate speculators would accrue to the community—with a regional pattern of controlled urban growth. According to this later proposal, when a garden city attained a population of about 30,000 instead of expanding into its greenbelt it would—"under Parliamentary powers probably"—leap over that zone and establish another city some distance away. Howard did not then project the building of isolated communities, but rather the planning of "town clusters," whereby a number of various-sized towns or "social cities" would each be surrounded by a greenbelt area and linked by interurban railways to a larger metropolitan core or central city. If society adhered to this principle of controlled growth, Howard was confident that a new city pattern would emerge.

In the United States the garden city idea was incorporated by Stein and the regionalists into a number of planned communities built in the 1920's and 1930's. At such places as Radburn, New Jersey, Chatham Village in Pittsburgh, and the New Deal communities of Greenbelt (Maryland), Greenhills (Ohio), and Greendale (Wisconsin), planners substituted a superblock for the normal gridiron street pattern as the basic planning unit. A number of other unique planning features were also employed: the use of specialized roadways for different purposes, the separation of foot and motor traffic, a continuous park-belt system serving as the core of neighborhoods, houses turned away from the street facing gardens and parks, and a neighborhood unit based on an elementary school radius of one-half mile. One of the many features of the Radburn plan was the creation of a "highwayless town," and as an adjunct, Mumford and MacKaye proposed "townless highways." Predicated on the assumption that "Motor traffic and pedestrian 'living' do not go together," the townless highway was conceived as a way of preventing the typical "roadtown slum" of ugly gas stations and hot dog stands, and of linking the highwayless towns like Radburn. In this sense, MacKaye and Mumford were attempting to adapt the regional "social cities" concept of Howard to the realities of the automobile age.

The regional approach of Stein, Wright, Mumford and MacKaye was overshadowed in the 1920's and 1930's by the more conventional methods of the city planning profession and by the work of metropolitan planners. In contrast to Wright's slender report, the monumental *Regional Plan of New York and Its Environs* (1929-1931), directed by Thomas Adams, was far more influential. Adams, a Scottish town planner, was associated with the garden city movement in England, and had been an administrator at Letchworth, Ebenezer Howard's first successful garden city. He was selected by the Russell Sage Foundation to direct the development of a regional plan for New York City, and the result was the publication of ten volumes surveying all aspects of the urban area, and two volumes of plans for the future of the city. Compiled by a staff of experts from various fields, the *Regional Plan of New York* is more typical of how urban planners go about their work and conceive of the city than are the projects and plans of the RPAA. The main distinction between the approach represented by Adams' work on the one hand, and Wright's report on the other, is not the greater comprehensiveness of the former, but an essential difference in attitude toward the problems of metropolitan expansion. While Adams and his colleagues were planning for continued population concentration in a given urban area, Henry Wright and his friends were offering an alternative to the existing metropolitan pattern of centralization.

The approach and proposals of the garden city regionalists have seemed impractical to some observers, and have come under increasing criticism since World War II. One of the first challenges to this concept of urban rebuilding as a viable solution to modern city problems was made by Lloyd Rodwin in 1945. Rodwin, who later became a professor of city and regional planning, argued that

Howard and his American regionalist followers, like Mumford, were motivated by a "primitive agrarian philosophy," and by a negative reaction to large cities. Rodwin also asserted that an interest in building new cities diverts attention from such vital urban concerns as industrial location, municipal administration, metropolitan government, commuting problems, and the need to plan for the future of existing cities. Like other critics of garden city regionalism, Rodwin suggests that it is time to turn from the dreams of "anti-urban" decentralists and take up the hard chore of dealing with the realities of the existing urban world.

One of the questions, which this continuing controversy over the varieties of urban regionalism raises, is, what kind of approach should be adopted in rebuilding our urban environment? Should we continue to plan our metropolitan areas for an ever increasing number of inhabitants, or would it be better to work toward alternatives to our present urban pattern? The next chapter will focus on some of the social problems accompanying the development of the 20th-century American city which make it imperative that citizens confront the issues raised by various approaches to urban planning.

Dinosaur Cities

by Clarence S. Stein*

Most of us see the Great City as in a dream. It is the sum of all our possible aspirations. A picturesque skyline, massive towers, romantic beauty! Crowds swaying through the lighted streets in pursuit of pleasure; flashing lights, dancing feet, and delightful foods with the flavor of Rome, Paris, Vienna, Pekin or London. A far cry from the Ladies' Social of Gopher Prairie! Libraries of rare books, vast museums and universities, the grand opera and the concert hall—the city of culture!

Our dream does not stop here; it has also a practical side. We see successful lawyers, engineers, advertising men, seated behind wide mahogany desks, protected and padded by secretaries, or speeding out to the golf-links and the country estate—the city of great opportunities! Chicago and New York, or at least Philadelphia, Boston, St. Louis and Los Angeles, lie at the end of that long, long trail which winds into the land of our dreams. Even if we remain in the home town, our aim is to make it grow fast enough to put us in the same class as these cities.

It is cruel to put the hard realities of daylight alongside these dream cities. But sooner or later most of us in the great cities awake to find that we have been grasping after a bubble, and that many of the real opportunities of living have slipped through our hands. For the city of our dreams is lost in another city which could occur to a sane mind only in a nightmare. It is in this second city that the great mass of people who swell the census statistics live and work and marry and die.

Look at the great city in its entirety: the turbid mass of traffic blocking the streets and avenues, the slow-moving crowd of people clambering into streetcars, elevateds, subways, their arms pinioned to their sides, pushed and packed like cattle in ill-smelling cars, with a mingling of bodies which would be indecent were it not for the suffocation and discomfort that acts, as it were, as a counter irritant. Look at the dingy slums of the East Side, Long Island City, the stockyard neighborhoods, the Hump, or where you will: there is little enough to choose between the dark unsanitary tenements of lower Manhattan (some of

*Clarence S. Stein, "Dinosaur Cities," *The Survey Graphic,* 54 (May 1, 1925), pp. 134-138.

them among the worst in the world) and the grey minimum of decency that West Philadelphia provides. What part does art, literature, culture, or financial opportunity play in the lives of the millions of men and women who go through the daily routine of life in our great urban districts? The city of dreams is as far away from them as it is from the denizen of Winesburg, Ohio.

To the few the great city gives all: to the millions it gives annually less and less. In spite of sanitary codes, tenement house laws, and various other urban reforms, the prospects for decent human living have become distinctly worse in New York during the last generation. And New York, unfortunately, represents the goal towards which all our bigger centers are striving with might and main. For this reason I propose to examine New York's plight in greater detail, and to ask: Why the Great City? What are we putting into the Great City, and what are we getting out of it? How long can we stand the strains and difficulties that are peculiar to our large congested centers? What particular promise is there in planning for an increasing population in other large centers, if all these efforts are doomed eventually to result in the same difficulties? Is the Great City still the goal of our legitimate desires, or is it a monstrosity, a bloated spider that lures us into its web only to devour us?

One can get a better notion of the present plight of the Great City in general if we follow the greatest city, New York, through a series of breakdowns that have attended its growth.

Historically, the first great breakdown of the metropolis came in housing. The crowding of the population into the growing port of New York had, as early as 1835, created a housing shortage and a slum area. Here conditions were so wretched that they drew down the attention of the Health Commissioner; and the Report of Housing Conditions in 1842 was the first of a long list that dealt with the housing problem. It is safe to say that New York has never caught up with its original shortage. Today half the population of Manhattan are living in quarters which are below the standard fixed as safe and sanitary by the tenement house law of 1901: these tenements are within reach of the unskilled worker because they do not possess running water, the heating apparatus and the sanitary facilities which represent the minimum standard for safe living quarters today. But what of the new law houses? The new tenements meet a minimum standard of sanitation and ventilation; but they do this at a price beyond the reach of two-thirds of the population; while their bleak courts, their white-washed walls, their dull streets, their occasional glimpse of the sun are still a long way from being the kind of environment in which mothers and children can flourish. Jane Addams showed us a long time ago what happened to "the spirit of youth in the city streets" when it was denied normal outlets for its energy and zest of life: but what have these bleak and overcrowded homes to offer the adolescent boy and girl?

Congestion is such a normal process in the great city, and decent living quarters require such a restriction on the profits of the speculative builder, that even on the edge of the city, where the price of land remains comparatively low, four- and five-story tenements are erected. Superficial observers talk of this housing breakdown as if it were a product of the war. On the contrary, there is a chronic deficiency that has been piling up in every great city—in London, Paris, and Berlin, as well as in American cities—for the last hundred years. In the great city there are not enough decent quarters to go round; and even the decent quarters are not good enough. That is the sum and substance of the housing breakdown. In the acutest stages of the housing crisis the smaller centers in New York state did not feel the shortage as keenly as the great city. One can almost put the case in a mathematical form: the bigger the city the remoter are its chances of solving the housing problem. This does not, of course, ignore the fact that other causes than congestion have created housing difficulties quite frequently in small cities, and even villages.

The second breakdown of the big city occurred in its water-system and its sewers. In 1842 New York was compelled to push back into the Croton watershed for a sufficient supply of clear water, and by the beginning of the present century the shortage threatened so acutely that a new system was planned, with reservoirs in the Catskills and the Adirondacks. If the thirst of the big city is not unquenchable, its tendency to grow has not at any rate been diminished: as a result, the necessity for still further aqueducts has already been recognized. This process must come to an end either when the existing areas have been drained dry, or when the cost per capita for watermains reaches a point at which water will become a luxury—supplied at an *uneconomic rate* for the same reason that bread and shows and baths were provided in ancient Rome, namely, to keep the population contented. Through this continual reaching back for new water supplies New York city is draining away, quite literally, an essential resource from other communities, dependent upon their immediate supply.

A different sort of loss and disaster results from sewage-congestion. The difficulties that Chicago has experienced in getting rid of its sewage are notorious. The spread of sewage in the Hudson, the East River, and the Harbor has not merely destroyed the opportunities for bathing and caused the practical disappearance of North River shad; it has also, according to the latest report of the Joint Legislative Committee at Albany, cut the city off from 80 per cent of its shellfish, increased the dangers of typhoid (as nearly a thousand cases in the past winter testify) and now threatens the bathing beaches of Coney Island and Brighton.

In this case, the great city can avoid a complete breakdown only by building an elaborate plant and equipment which enables it temporarily to meet the problem. But it does this with blind disregard for expense. The growth of the city might be illimitable if its purse were illimitable; since the ingenuities of engineering can solve many of our difficulties if we can disregard the expense. The point is that the expense is becoming unbearable. The "overhead" of the city is increasing to a point at which it will outmeasure any of its tangible or intangible benefits. Then something must happen: something which will not be more growth and more expense.

We come now to the breakdown of the street system, and the inability of our overground and underground ways to carry the load of traffic. Our older cities were planned for four-story buildings at most. With the rise of the six-story building in the middle of the last century, traffic difficulties were felt in the shopping district of lower Broadway. An experimental safety bridge was even built. Today, not only in the lower part of Manhattan, but in vast sections between the Pennsylvania and the Grand Central Railroad stations, up Park Avenue and Broadway, and even over in Brooklyn—*today from two to six cities* have been piled up one above the other. This would be bad enough if only foot traffic and public vehicles were considered: the automobile has added the proverbial last straw, for each car, with its two or three occupants, occupies at least twice, and sometimes three or four times the space of pedestrians walking. Since our zoning in the builtup parts of the city has all been done in subservience to rising land values, none of our zoning provisions touch this problem; on the contrary, even in parts of the city where the four-story town has lingered, the twenty-story town is permitted—in fact, is being built. If our avenues were wide enough to carry comfortably the present and potential load of traffic, there would not, in a great many parts of the city, be room for the buildings themselves.

Our city officials and engineers are now hinting that the "solution" lies in building overhead streets. But even if it were conceivable that a complete system of aerial streets could be built for the population, this could be done *only at a cost which would fall back upon the land in the shape of taxes—and in turn this would make it necessary to build higher buildings and more streets!* To call this circle vicious scarcely does it justice. In point of fact no large city, however unbalanced its budget, attempts to keep up with its need for free channels of circulation. Every day the congestion increases—in spite of traffic policeman, curb setbacks, one-way streets, electric traffic signs. Even in Los Angeles, whose growth was coincident with the auto, the cars have multiplied faster than the streets have been widened. The end here is already in sight. There must come a time when every street in New York will be regulated as the streets in the financial district now are: individual vehicles will not be permitted to circulate through the business and industrial sections during the day. This is what happened in prosperous commercial Rome when its congestion reached something like New York's present pitch; and it is inevitable here. It is equally inevitable in Pittsburgh's triangle, where it is now actively discussed, and in Chicago's Loop. And all the while the costs are piling up. The hard, practical men who think they can avoid this conclusion while they continue to congest the population and raise the land values are living in dreamland: they simply have not the courage to face the results of their own handiwork.

The breakdown of the mechanical means of transporation follows hard upon the collapse of the street system; the same causes are at work. As the city increases in height it increases also in area; for the railroad and subway must be introduced to carry the main load of passengers from the central district of skyscraper offices and lofts to the outlying areas. When the vacant land on the outskirts is filled up, the net result is congestion at both ends. This causes a demand for additional means of transportation. Beyond a point which big cities reach at a very early point in their career, more transportation routes mean more congestion. The only way this could be avoided is by duplicating the existing transportation lines; but this method would reduce the earnings of the existing lines by distributing the load, and it is never even considered except when an equal degree of congestion can be assured to the new line. The cost of all these facilities increases steadily as the lines are lengthened into more remote areas so that in one way or another a subsidy must be introduced to support them at a price per ride the ordinary commuter can afford. At the present time New York, with its five cent fare, is losing more than $12,000,000 annually on the money it paid for constructing subways, and it will lose even more on the new lines, which the transit engineers estimate will be three times as costly.

This is one of the concealed costs of living in a great city: it parallels the hidden cost of other services, including sewers, elaborate street paving and complicated utilities but all the while this cost is pressing down on the economic well-being of the average citizen. In addition to the half billion or so that New York is preparing to spend in future on its subways, increased suburban facilities are now needed. D. L. Turner, the engineer of the New York Transit Commission, has suggested an expenditure of some three quarters of a billion dollars, of which he proposes that one-half be paid in taxes, partly by the city and partly by the suburbs: this will, in his opinion, take care only of the increase of traffic in ten years (to April, 1934) when the octopus-city must again face another colossal expenditure, if its bloated growth is to continue. It is possible that the annual saving in man-power, equipment and coal through such a regional redistribution of population as would enable the majority to walk to work, would pay the larger part of the necessary plant and equipment for new communities.

As things go now, on the other hand, there is no way in any of the large centers of avoiding a continuous breakdown in its transit facilities. They are, and they must remain, perpetually inadequate so long as people and industries, instead of being redistributed into planned communities, are sucked blindly into the metropolitan areas.

But perhaps all this congestion is justified by the fact that industry is conducted more efficiently in the big city? Perhaps this more than equals the other losses? Not at all; just the contrary in fact. In most industries it actually costs more to carry on manufacturing on the congested island of Manhattan than it does in smaller industrial centers. The reasons are plain. The transportation of goods through the streets and on railways is the very life-blood of industry; and in all our big centers these arteries are clogged. Lacking streets to keep pace with the multiple-city, the trucks in New York city spend less time in active hauling than in unproductive work—locked in congested streets, or waiting at the crowded loading stations and stores. The few hours a day that the trucks actually move at snail's pace has already made the automobile uneconomical; and so the greater part of trucking is still done by horsepower in order to lower the overhead charges. The periodic congestion of freight terminals and docks—with the spoiling and rotting of perishable foods—present another facet of the same difficulty. At the pier, in the railway yard, at the factory, congestion obstructs the normal processes of industry.

Finally, the crowded conditions of the city have increased the overhead within the factory. The garment industry, for example, stands fourth among New York's manufacturers; and many of its shops have moved into great skyscrapers in the central district. Here the high rent, the high taxes, and the high cost of fireproof structures have so raised the overhead costs that New York manufacturers, on their own confession, already find it difficult to compete with those in smaller cities, where these costs are lower. The higher cost of housing in the metropolitan area is likewise reflected in proportionately higher wages for the same type of work—or else it is borne by the worker in impoverished living conditions.

Certain industries are inevitably associated with great seaport and traffic junctions, like Philadelphia, New York and Chicago; but as the city increases in population the disadvantages for other kinds of manufacturing tend to counterbalance the advantages of the local market. When the local overhead cannot be shifted, and when smaller centers are, in spite of their poorer financial and business facilities, able to make their industrial advantages felt, the great city's industries will have to migrate or declare bankruptcy. We are still in the day of postponement; but the day of reckoning will come; and it behooves us to anticipate it. The question then will be whether industries are to migrate into the free area that lies immediately around the great city, or whether it will not pay, once moving must be faced, to locate at some point in a much larger area, where land values are not so high and where a finer environment may be provided more easily, without the risk of being gobbled up eventually—as Pullman was gobbled up by Chicago, and as Yonkers and Mt. Vernon are now being gobbled up by New York in its steady growth.

Inadequate housing facilities, inadequate water supplies, inadequate sewage, inadequate streets and inadequate transportation—these are but the larger and more obvious ills that derive from the congestion of population. They are enough, however, to show that the great city, as a place to live and work in, breaks down miserably; that it is perpetually breaking down; and that it will continue to do so as long as the pressure of population within a limited area remains. I have used New York merely for the sake of concrete example. New York's problem of housing in 1850 was Chicago's problem in 1890; New York's transit solution of 1900 is now Chicago's solution of 1925—and promises no better; and so on with the other details in the breakdown. Other cities can avoid New York's breakdown only by making an effort to avoid New York's "greatness."

Now all these breakdowns are costly in themselves; unfortunately the effort to put them off becomes even more costly. The result is that money and effort which should go into making the city more liveable—the money that should be spent on the education of children, on the maintenance of health, upon art, education, and culture—all this money and effort is devoted to expenditures which do no more than make the physical side of congestion barely tolerable. It is not merely that the effort to supply sufficient transportation routes, to widen streets sufficiently, is inevitably doomed to failure: what is worse is that even if it were successful it would be foolish and extravagant.

If we saw a family with ragged and neglected children, in a tumbledown shack, half of which was unfit for habitation, spending all its income and savings in providing a tiled bathroom and an automobile, we should conclude that this expenditure was unbalanced: the house should be put in order, the children clothed, the rooms sunned, aired and dusted, and the toilet arrangements adjusted to a decent sanitary minimum. Yet the expenditures of the great city are quite as wild and unbalanced as this. In order to reduce the horrors that result from the breakdown of housing and transportation, the city spends all its funds on futile palliatives. It lives in the midst of a sort of perpetual cataclysm. The great city—if I may sum up the case in a different metaphor—is like a man afflicted with hardening of the arteries, a man so conscious of his condition and so preoccupied with carrying out the incidental medical treatment (hopeless though it be) that he has no time to work, to think, to play, to create, or to perform any of those acts which separate a state of invalidism from a state of health.

All the breakdowns we have been studying are the result of a congestion of population; and the greater the magnitude of that congestion the more chronic the breakdown becomes, and the more completely does it embrace all the activities of the city. The big city is bankrupt. The little city that has adopted a program of mere expansion—and where is the little city that does not boast its first skyscraper—is headed in the same direction.

Once we actually face the situation, we shall, I am confident, be roused to the drastic public efforts that are necessary to deal with it. The day of the palliatives and the patent medicines is passing—in city-growth as in the fight on disease. We must do all that is necessary to combat the forces of congestion at their source. For in that direction lie the fundamental things that men and women care most deeply for—a beautiful environment, a home for children, an opportunity to enjoy the day's leisure and the ability to ride on the Juggernaut of industry, instead of being prostrated under its wheels.

Report of the New York State Commission of Housing and Regional Planning

by Henry Wright*

The ever-increasing concentration of population in cities and towns and the continuous depopulation of the countryside have given rise to problems in both city and country in which the State as a whole has a vital interest. The onward march to the city has resulted in rising urban land costs, a consequent intensification of land use which, in turn, further increases land costs and requires still more intensive use of the land. This unending cycle has already so over-burdened public facilities that every growing city must finance new public improvements in a measure far beyond its ability, with a resulting break down in street traffic and transit facilities, in public school equipment and all other public services. Attempts to relieve street congestion by widening streets and resort to mechanical devices serve only to exhaust the city's tax revenue and increase congestion still further. The staggering cost of needed rapid transit facilities is met by sacrificing schools, parks and playgrounds and even this offers no relief. The experience of New York City in subway construction demonstrates that by the time new subways are completed they are already inadequate. They also serve only to develop new sources of congestion at the center.

The problem of the country is equally vital. Every year thousands of acres of land hitherto cultivated are abandoned to weeds and brush. Within the past forty-five years 5,700,000 acres of farm land in New York State have been withdrawn from cultivation. While the heaping of population into New York City creates the highest land values in the world, within a hundred miles of the lower tip of Manhattan land may be bought for unpaid taxes.

The unplanned, uncoordinated development of the past has given us the problems with which we are wrestling today. While the old forces that have shaped the present State are still operating, new forces have come into being to dominate the future. These new forces may be left free to alter the present mould without direction and without control. On the other hand they may be

*Henry Wright, *Report* of the New York State Commission of Housing and Regional Planning (Albany: State of New York, May 7, 1926).

intelligently controlled. They may be directed toward a more effective utilization of all the resources of the State and thereby profoundly affect the future movement of population.

Two years ago the Commission of Housing and Regional Planning began this preliminary study of the relation of the resources of the State to its economic history. This is no academic study. Its purpose is the practical one of preparing for the future. This report is not a plan. It is a collection and analysis of some small part of the final data that will serve as a basis of future planning. In this study the Commission has attempted to ascertain and measure the forces which have shaped the present State and to evaluate the new forces which are now altering the present mould. Its purpose is to find a basis for a plan for the future development of the State. A plan of the State is not a thing to be willed into being by any one man or Commission or power. It is the result of many forces—physical, economic and social. Although it must rest on the unchanging physical conformation of the State, it is subject to constant revision as a result of changing habits and economic relations of men, and of their ability, through better understanding or invention, to harness nature to their need.

In carrying forward its studies the Commission has been more and more impressed with the need of a permanent agency for planning the physical development of the State. At the present time several State departments are engaged in the preparation of unrelated plans. Coordination may best be accomplished by a planning board in the Executive Department.

The Commission recommends the establishment of such a board with the personnel composed of the heads of the several State departments charged with the expenditure of funds appropriated for permanent public improvements, and representatives of planning boards created under chapters 267 and 539 of the Laws of 1925.

. . . .

NEW FORCES SHAPING THE FUTURE

We have seen that the social and economic organization of the State has passed through two periods. First there was scattered, small-scale industry serving local markets. It was the period of the water-wheel, hand-driven tools, the wagon road and canal and the town. Then came the age of steam, the machine, rail transportation and the city. The small plant gave way to the modern factory, sales forces canvassed the national market, the town declined, the city rose. In New York State the topography which determined the location of rail transportation forced almost all of the growth into one narrow valley that extends from Buffalo east to Albany and thence south to New York.

Electric Power and the Automobile. Within the current century new forces have come into being: Long-distance electric transmission and motor transport are among the most important. These are capable of altering the life of the people of the State in as striking a manner as did steam and the railroad. Electric power, made from the energy of falling water or at great central coal-burning stations and carried long distances at low cost, opens new possibilities of more available energy in the same way that steam did in an era of water-wheels. The automobile, motor bus and truck may have quite as marked an effect on industry as had the railroad.

Long-distance transmission of electric current should make possible the introduction of technical methods that result in the production of cheaper energy. Large scale generation is itself more economical. At the same time it allows the recovery of valuable by-products that are lost in the small plant. The plant may be located at the coal mines or source of water power. The cost of transmitting electrical energy is much lower than that of shipping the equivalent energy in the form of coal. Furthermore the interconnection of generating systems allows the exchange of current between widely separated areas, thus equalizing the load and reducing the effect of a break-down that is a hazard in the case of local generating stations.

Supplementing Steam by Electricity. Electrical energy therefore has the technical and economic possibility of supplanting local steam power. . . . Now the primary horsepower of motors driven by electric current is greater than the power in steam plants and steam power is actually decreasing.

Electric Power and Decentralization. The introduction of electric power and particularly the development of its long-distance transmission have tremendous possibilities of influencing the social and economic pattern. When factories depended on steam power, the machinery had to be located near the boiler. The boiler in turn could only be set up where coal could be delivered cheaply, that is, at tide-water or on a railroad. When local electric generation began, the driving belt was lengthened. The power station needed to be on a railroad siding or tide-water but the factory was free, so far as its power requirements were concerned, to locate within the distributing radius of the station—a matter of miles. Now comes transmission for hundreds of miles. The generating station may be at a source of water power, the mouth of a coal mine or any other point where coal and water may be cheaply brought together. The power requirements of the factory place no practical barrier to its location anywhere. It may have energy at almost the same cost inland or at tide-water, in the valley or the highlands, at the rails or in the country.

The Motor Car and Decentralization. Within the last fifteen years the motor vehicle has become an important means of transport. This year there are about 2,000,000 motor vehicles in New York State—more than one for every six persons. As a result of motor traffic there has been built up a net-work of hard-surfaced roads, miles of which are added every year. The present projected highway system will embrace 14,000 miles of improved road in ten years. Thus we have an entirely new transportation system. Unlike the railroads it can extend as a net over large areas. It is flexible and capable of quick adaptation to new routes. Furthermore, roads may be built with a sharper grade than railways and therefore hills present less of a barrier.

The influence of motor transport has not yet made itself fully felt. The changes which it may introduce in social and economic life are very great. Factories which formerly located on the rails may now make short hauls of both raw materials and finished product by motor. Establishments which were held to congested centers by the proximity of an existing labor supply may now draw workers who come in their cars or buses from greater areas. People themselves may be freed from crowded districts and enabled to get to work from suburban regions.

Enrichment of Farm Life.   Finally both electric power and motor transport remove certain of the objectionable features of farm life. Good roads and the motor break down the isolation of the farm. The motor also extends the area over which farms may serve urban centers with perishable products. Cheap electric power lightens the drudgery of farm life. Certain of the forces which have driven people from the farms to the cities may therefore be removed.

These forces make decentralization possible. They do not compel it. Are there any indications that a redistribution of population is probable? What forces are at work that may lead to a reversal of the trend of population that characterized the last part of the nineteenth century and the early years of the twentieth?

Social Cost of Concentration.   The primary costs of intense city concentration are the loss of human values. New York City shows these costs in more exaggerated form than any other. To a lesser degree they exist in every other city of the State. With the passing of rural or small town life have gone natural facilities for recreation. For the open field is substituted the city street with its constant stream of traffic. For woods and mountains are substituted parks. An artificial recreation grows up: pool rooms, moving picture theatres, dance halls and a host of other good, bad and indifferent forms of commercialized amusement. The home has suffered; the shadows of pyramiding land prices steal across one window after another until in the characteristic tenement in New York City two out of three rooms are sealed in perpetual darkness or twilight. The narrow canyons keep out not only light but air.

The reaction against these conditions is shown in the pressure to escape to suburban life. For the wealthy, the town and country house has long been familiar. The year-round suburban homes of salaried and professional men have been rapidly increasing in number. Since 1920 one of the most marked movements of population has been the attempted escape of the artisan from the congested center to new developments in outlying areas.

Economic Wastes of Congestion.   These costs are imponderables. They have exerted less influence on our development than the economic forces making for concentration. It is possibly indicative of future trends that congestion breeds economic resistance to further growth and has raised physical problems that so far defy solution. The Commission has already shown that land prices increase more rapidly than population and that to maintain the high land prices more and more intensive use must be made of the city land. An industry in a large city can only compete with plants in smaller cities if the city yields some compensating advantages. The lower land prices of the small center give it a great competitive advantage. As the city grows it must inevitably lose some industries which thrived while the city itself was smaller.

Transportation of both persons and freight becomes increasingly expensive as the city grows. The crowding on the New York subways is perhaps one of the imponderable social costs. But the increasing length of the haul is an economic fact whose consequences may be measured in dollars and cents on the tax bill. The congestion of city streets has slowed down the movement of goods. Street widening, one-way streets, non-parking regulations and elaborate traffic control are resorted to—and ultimately in the most congested area private, personal vehicular traffic is forbidden during the day. We are forced to ration the use of our street system. The larger city has higher per capita costs of government. These costs are in large part due to the assumption of new activities by the municipal government: the provision of parks and playgrounds, extended duties of the health authorities. All of these costs must be absorbed in the cost of living.

Factors Impeding City Growth. The large city can maintain its position only through an initially higher productivity that goes to pay for the excess costs of its operation. Any change in technique that breaks down this differential productivity operates against the large city.

It is apparent that there are new forces making for a change in the social and economic pattern. Long-distance electric transmission and the motor remove certain of the limitations that forced economic activity into congested areas. The increasing costs of operation in the large city will impel certain industries to escape to smaller centers now that power and transportation are available there. Not all industries will be effected alike. But change is in the air. What will the pattern in the future be like? What pattern, that is allowed by the state of the technical arts, will carry with it the highest social values? How may the shaping of this most desirable pattern be controlled?

THE NEED OF A PLAN

The economic and social pattern is always in a state of flux. However, there are periods of unusual activity. For decades at a time there may be a marked drift in a particular direction. We now appear to be on the threshold of a period in which a strongly marked new trend will be established. Long-distance electric transmission and motor transport offer potential release from the centralizing pressure. The apparently insoluble problems—physical, economic and social—that are raised by the pyramiding city may force a change.

1. Coordinated or Uncoordinated Development

In such a period the activities of a large number of bodies tend to shape the future pattern. The arrangement and location of transportation facilities is most important. A town becomes stagnant that has held a key position in one transportation system and is relegated to a less important position under a different system. Oswego was an important city during the period of canals. It was the lake terminus of the canal from Syracuse. It still has rail connection with Syracuse, but the rail service gives Oswego a relatively poorer position than did the canal. On the other hand, the Erie Canal made Buffalo the terminal for waterborne freight. In the decade during which the canal was completed (1820-1830) Buffalo increased in population 313 per cent. The development of large areas is now being controlled by the location of transmission lines. Again the location of a large industry may make a town, as when the General Electric Company located in Schenectady. Lackawanna is wholly a city by edict. So also the fixation of rates by public utility commissions has great influence. The uniform freight rate fixed to the harbor of New York has prevented a differential arising that would strengthen the competitive position of New Jersey harbor cities against the New York water front.

The problem therefore arises whether these activities shall be related to a general plan or shall be controlled only by the most proximate considerations. The uncoordinated economic planning that has characterized our past development neglects imponderable social values. A business man can only remotely concern himself with the conditions of life of his workers. Granted equal economic opportunity in two places, he may choose the one in which his workers may lead the fullest life. But he does not balance good homes against productivity. The aim of the State should be clearly to improve the conditions of life rather than to promote opportunities for profit.

Obviously there is need of a plan to which at least activities of the State shall conform. The action of the State will strongly influence some private developments. At this point the effective control by the State ends. The experience of planning organizations has indicated, however, that many individual business men are glad to call upon the knowledge of such authorities in developing their own plans. While such cooperative planning cannot be dictatorial, there is every reason to suppose that it will result in a healthier, better-organized social structure than we now possess as a result of our virtually planless development.

2. Growing Recognition of Need of Planning

Growing recognition of the need of intelligent direction and coordination of future development is evident in recent local planning activities throughout the State. An awakened interest had developed in problems of land utilization, in the control of traffic, of bulk, height and use of buildings, in the provision of adequate recreational and park areas in towns and cities, and in the extensive planning of physical improvements authorized by local, county and State governments. The past two years have marked unusual progress in city planning in Buffalo, New York City, Rochester, Utica, Syracuse, Schenectady and many of the smaller cities of the State. It is significant that in all this planning the dominant motive has been to plan not only the urban, but also the rapidly growing suburban areas where the immediate problem is becoming acute. Planning activities in New York emphasize more and more the relation of the urban area to the suburban countryside and to the entire region. This regional point of view has not always prevailed in the initial stages of the city plan, but has been a logical outgrowth of local planning experience.

At first there has been a desire on the part of city planning authorities to shape the growth of the surrounding areas with relation to the growing needs of the urban center. The need for decentralization and the march to the suburbs has extended the city's influence into all the adjacent towns and villages. The growing influence of the city is responsible for a tendency toward urban domination of suburban life—a tendency which, though understandable, is laden with serious potential dangers. The desire of the city to impose its plan on the surrounding region has led to more than one attempt to extend the city's legal authority and planning control beyond the urban limits. In almost every instance this extension of authority has been opposed by the surrounding towns and by the county, and this opposition has been sufficiently influential to prevent the extension of municipal planning powers by the Legislature.

The opposition to the extension of municipal authority over surrounding areas is more than the familiar repulsion of urban influence. It involves the jealous regard for local autonomy, the objection to loss of any local powers now enjoyed, and the suspicion, sometimes justified, that the city plan extended will mean the loss of all those distinctive values, social as well as economic, which are characteristic of the surrounding area as a whole.

This apparent impasse, created by conflicting interests, demonstrates the ineffectiveness of obsolete forms of local government and the need for a type of government that can function regionally. This need has been emphasized by Thomas H. Reed, Director of the Bureau of Government of the University of Michigan. Speaking before the National Municipal League, with regard to the problems of the Pittsburgh region, he said:

> The most serious question which confronts students of municipal government today is the development of some form of governmental organization through which these problems can be met . . . recognizing that there are certain governmental needs in the region which can be met only by some form of governmental organization extending throughout the region, there are three possible methods by which the extension of such governmental authority can be secured: First, by the creation of special authorities for each particular need (for example, the London Metropolitan Police District); Second, by the consolidation of all powers of local government

throughout the region in a single authority; Third, by the establishment of regional government of limited powers leaving in existence the existing units of local government.

Although the first of these suggested methods has been most frequently used, and despite the recognition of the apparent advantages in efficiency and economy of the second method (that of consolidation of all local powers in a single authority), official regional planning in New York State has progressed through the cooperation of locally autonomous governmental units.

This method has been justified by more than its regard for prevailing local sentiment. It derives from a concept of regional planning dominated by an objective quite different from that of urban or metropolitan planning. This concept is expressed in the following words of Lewis Mumford:

> The forces that have created the great cities make permanent improvement within hopeless. Our efforts to plan them lag pitifully behind the need when indeed they do not foster the very growth that is becoming insupportable. We are providing, in Professor Geddes's sardonic phrase, more and more of worse and worse. Not so with regional planning. Regional planning asks not how wide an area can be brought under the aegis of the metropolis, but how the population and civic facilities can be distributed so as to promote and stimulate a vivid, creative life throughout a whole region—a region being any geographic area that possesses a certain unity of climate, soil, vegetation, industry and culture. The regionalist attempts to plan such an area so that all its sights and resources, from forest to city, from highland to water level may be soundly developed, and so that the population will be distributed so as to utilize, rather than to nullify or destroy, its natural advantages. It sees people, industry and the land as a single unit. Instead of trying, by one desperate dodge or another, to make life a little more tolerable in the congested centers, it attempts to determine what sort of equipment will be needed for the new centers. It does not aim at urbanizing automatically the whole available country side; it aims equally at ruralizing the stony wastes of our cities.

The conservation and the future development of the resources of a region to the end that an economic gain may not involve inevitable social loss, requires the preservation of all existing natural values both of the country and of the city. This does not mean the complete subordination of country to urban influence. It demands for the time being at least, the retention by local governments of all the powers which they now enjoy. But it further requires experience in cooperation and authority to act in concert with local governments.

One year ago, acting on recommendation of the Commission of Housing and Regional Planning, the Legislature amended the Municipal Law to authorize any county or counties to establish and maintain out of local tax revenue a regional planning board to consist of representatives of the cooperating county and local governments. These boards are empowered and directed "to study the needs and conditions of regional and community planning in such county or counties and propose plans to meet such needs and conditions . . ." Their function is advisory only, the appropriation for and the execution of plans being controlled by the local legislative agencies.

Acting under a special statute granting similar powers, the Niagara Frontier Planning Board was established April 9, 1925. The Niagara Frontier, comprising the entire counties of Niagara and Erie, lying along Lake Ontario, the Niagara River and Lake Erie, bordered on the south by Cattaraugus Creek and its gorge and on the east by the counties of Orleans, Genesee and Wyoming, covers approximately 1,550 square miles. It contains one of the most valuable natural resources in the world. The future importance of the region to the rest of the State and to the country as a whole cannot be overestimated.

The Niagara Frontier Planning Board was the direct outgrowth of preliminary conferences held in Buffalo and Tonawanda under the auspices of the Commission of Housing and Regional Planning in 1924. In September of that year a regional planning association was formed with a membership representing all of the cities, towns and villages in the two counties. By action of the association the official Niagara Frontier Planning Board took form without legal sanction in anticipation of legislation authorizing the establishment of such board and appropriations to cover the board's expenses. The board consisted of the mayors of six cities in the region and three representatives from each of the Boards of Supervisors of Niagara and Erie Counties. This board began to function with the cooperation of both local and county governments as early as November, 1924. With the enactment of the special statute a permanent chairman was elected, appropriations were made by the Boards of Supervisors of Niagara and Erie Counties to defray the expense of the Board for the first year of its operation, and a technical staff was appointed and located at Tonawanda. During the first year the Regional Planning Board has acted in a cooperative capacity as an intermediary between the State Council of Parks, the Erie County Park Commission and the State Reservation at Niagara in the development of a system of parkways for the region. The result of the studies of the board, in collaboration with these organizations, has been a proposed system which has been added to the map of the State Council of Parks after formal approval by that body. The board adopted a program for regional planning study in the Niagara Frontier prepared by the Bureau of Housing and Regional Planning and has assembled data, prepared maps and investigated problems relating to and carried forward specific undertakings looking toward the development of a plan for the region as a whole.

Following the lead of the Niagara Frontier, regional organization has been undertaken in other parts of the State during the past year. A movement has been started looking toward the planning of the entire region comprised within the Genesee Valley.

By action of the County Board of Supervisors of Onondaga County with Syracuse as a center, a Regional Planning Board has been established.

A Capitol District Regional Planning Association has been created through the cooperation of mayors, village presidents, and other official representatives of cities, towns and villages together with members of the Boards of Supervisors of Albany, Schenectady and Rensselaer Counties; and a Central Hudson Valley Regional Planning Association was recently organized. Both of these organizations are working toward the creation of official regional planning boards.

From the standpoint of metropolitan planning, the most important regional planning work in the State has been carried forward since 1922 by the Committee on the Plan of New York and Its Environs organized and supported by the Russell Sage Foundation. With the assistance of able technical advisors and planners this voluntary committee has undertaken the planning of a region comprising an area of 5,528 square miles, lying in three States and including about 400 organized communities, of which New York City is the center. This region, within a radius of 50 miles from the Metropolitan Center, in the words of Frederick A. Delano, Chairman of the Committee, "is tied together by common economic and social interests and by many problems not capable of solution except by united action of all authorities within the area." The purpose of the plan has been further described by Mr. Delano as follows:

"The plan being prepared by the Committee has for its general object the formation of the best form of development of areas within the region for industry, business, residence and recreation and the best system of circulation in connection with traffic and transportation. The plan must be comprehensive not only as to the extent of the area to be dealt with, but also as to the estimate of all the inter-related problems of community growth in the area." The Committee has already completed and published many valuable studies and surveys relating to physical and living conditions and has produced a series of monographs in connection with its economic and industrial survey, together with studies of the legal possibilities and limitations of the problem with reference to questions of zoning, city planning and the acquisition of land for public use.

Regional planning in the State of New York is already moving in the direction of a plan for the State as a whole. As has already been pointed out, local agencies control and will continue to control city and regional planning. It remains, however, to fill in the details of a State plan into which regional activities may fit and without which local efforts are likely to be checkmated. State bond issues for roads and other permanent improvements, if they are to be expended with greatest benefit to the State and local communities must be used with reference to a general plan.

3. Controlling Considerations for the Future

The State has a vital interest in planning. But what sort of a plan will be developed? What consideration must control?

The Commission of Housing and Regional Planning attempts in this report only to suggest certain broad outlines in tentative fashion. A plan for the State cannot be mapped in advance in all its details and filed for reference. It must have life; it must grow. Only certain basic principles may be established to which the pattern will conform in its growth.

In planning for the future it might be assumed that on account of the greater flexibility of electric power and motor transportation on the one hand and the problems arising from concentration in large cities on the other, we would drift back into a situation . . . with small centers scattered all over the State. That, however, would be an unwarranted assumption.

It will be remembered that our survey of the State's resources showed that the most valuable regions for intensive utilization, even for agriculture, lie along the valley systems. Furthermore, decentralization of industry even under the new conditions cannot in most cases proceed far from the railroad trunk lines. So far motor transportation has tended to replace the railroad for local shipments and to supplement the short branch feeders of the railroads. What we must visualize is a civilization based on the valley pattern, but making a fuller and more intelligent use of it than at present. The uplands and mountains must also be employed as reserves of forest, for water catchment and recreation. No new conditions have arisen or are likely to arise that will make these areas fit to be primary centers of manufacture, farming or population.

The best utilization of the State must be governed by the physical contour and distribution of resources. Man cannot alter the main outlines of what nature has given him. Only by recognizing the basic natural conditions can he fit himself to exercise intelligently the control which he has over his own activities.

The more fertile soil and the most valuable geological deposits lie almost entirely in the areas below the 1,000-foot level—the L Valley, the Ontario shore, and the narrow strip east of the Adirondacks. In these regions climatic conditions are most favorable to agriculture. . . . farming as well as manufacturing and commerce belongs to the lowlands.

In planning for the future all these factors must be taken into consideration. The extreme scattering of population in epoch one involved an attempted utilization of resources much of which turned out to be low grade. In epoch two much of this area was abandoned. No new forces have developed that make its recovery for other than forestry seem desirable. In fact there are still many hundreds of thousands of acres of substandard land held in use for farming purposes that should be added to our forests. On the other hand, a fuller economic utilization of the better regions of the State is possible today than was attained in epoch two, a utilization that will involve decentralization rather than concentration within the limits of the valley system. In conjunction with this development of the lowlands must come an increasing appreciation of the services which the uplands may render; the potentialities of new scientific lumbering, of a great playground for the millions who live in towns and of the water power stored in the hills. . . .

4. A Broad Forecast

Certain portions of the State are admirably suited to form a complete social organism. The sort of development which should be anticipated may best be illustrated from the region bordering Lake Ontario and the St. Lawrence River. . . .

From Niagara County on the west to St. Lawrence County on the east the low table-land along the water front has excellent soil and a mild climate. In this section of Monroe, Wayne and Cayuga Counties the average growing season is 170 days. A growing season of more than 160 days is found throughout this belt in all counties except St. Lawrence.

Large water power resources are found in the Niagara Falls and in the St. Lawrence and Adirondacks. The power in the last two is capable of operating extensive industry throughout the eastern part of this belt. The belt is served by the railroad, the Barge Canal and Lake Ontario.

At present the lowlands along the water front are devoted to fruit raising, the manufacturing cities are located in the table-land from 400 to 600 feet elevation. On still higher land are other farms. But though the general utilization of the region as thus described conforms to the ideal suggested, the actual developement does not take full advantage of the great resources of the region. The district is not integrated. Cities like Rochester, Buffalo and Syracuse have grown to such a point as to introduce problems of planning, traffic and housing that might be avoided if smaller industrial centers were developed. The vast industrial and agricultural activity of which this entire region is capable must be related to the hinterland. The lower hills, rising 1200 to 1600 feet above sea level are favorable for dairying and grazing. The highlands should serve for forest reserve and water supply. Access to these and to the beautiful Finger Lakes section in the center of the State would provide recreational escape from the cities. With foresight and planning, such a region might take full advantage of all its resources and might provide a setting for a multitude of prosperous and healthful communities.

5. State Planning and Basic Needs

A plan like this is but a broad outline, simple in concept but complicated in application by a multitude of details and difficulties which are bound to modify its form and influence its accomplishment. The scope of the present investigation has not been sufficient to forecast, except in a most general way, the extent and nature of these problems. Yet, once the basic conception is accepted, certain projects fall naturally into place so that we may broadly suggest the more desirable developments.

For example, in the matter of agriculture the dependence of New York on the rest of the United States may be too great. For many years the State has not grown enough food to sustain its population. In many respects, as has been previously shown, it has become more economical for New York to rely on other States for products such as wheat, beef and mutton. But, with the steady increase in population, both within the State and outside it, with increasing transportation costs, and with development of all the best land elsewhere, this tendency may easily be pushed too far. Agricultural authorities have already pointed out that it has again become profitable to raise wheat within the State. With accurate knowledge of soils, climate and modern methods, and with proximity to the cities, New York farmers may little by little find it profitable to raise a larger proportion of the State's food.

But both agricultural authorities and farmers must base their operations, not only on knowledge of methods and soils, but on a logical arrangement of cities, farm zones and transportation routes. If, with a proper decentralization of city population, farming zones could be laid out near the cities, the farmer would have a better chance for a good living and a full life. The State might point out such opportunities to those who are still clinging to unprofitable uplands but do not know where to go unless it be into a factory.

The same principles hold true as to the utilization of forest reserves and the great water-power resources of the State. Their development is interdependent.

Water supply for the cities is intimately connected with the preservation of the forests, and with hydroelectric power, which requires dams, reservoirs and regulated flow. Coordination is necessary among the cities which are beginning to infringe on each other's regions of supply. New York City has not only exploited a large part of the Westchester watershed with the Croton reservoir, but has crossed the Hudson, reached into the Catskills with the Ashokan and Schoharie Reservoirs, and tapped the Mohawk watershed in upper Schoharie. There is now projected a tri-State development of the Delaware River for further needs.

The time is not far distant when we must make an allotment of the limited water supply among the large cities, and adjust it to the needs of hydroelectric power. This is an engineering task which cannot be successfully accomplished without reference to the State plan, having in mind the future distribution of population, with its power and water needs.

The location of public service utilities involves automatically the exercise of powers which must determine future use and value of large areas of the State. A wise control over the exercise of such power and a coordinated plan with respect to distribution of power and other forms of service is essential to the preservation of the State's interest in its own future.

6. A State Plan and Local Planning

Into this general scheme fit the plans and projects which various regions are making for themselves. The local region is the unit which must, in most cases, initiate action and carry out concrete details. A State plan will not attempt to limit this local action with hard-and-fast outlines; it would, rather, attempt to help the several regions solve their problems by bringing out the relationship of their special situations to outside conditions.

In local planning towns, villages and cities have found that they have many common problems which can only be solved by coordinated action, *i. e.,* by regional planning. So also these regional units will find that there are general problems which must be met by the joint action of neighboring regions: *i. e.,* by State planning. This broad plan and policy, whose need has been shown in this report, must grow from the experience and requirements of the integral parts.

The details of a State plan must be based upon accurate and comprehensive knowledge. The first requirement is a complete "land economic survey" such as that which is being undertaken in Michigan. An industrial economic survey is no less necessary.

In order to make the plan a living and growing thing, it must be contributed to and consulted by every important State department and by many private interests as well, whenever an important decision is to be made. The Park Council, the Water Power Commission, the Conservation Commission, the framers of taxation policy, the Public Service Commission, the highway authorities, manufacturers, bankers, railroads, power companies, local governments—all these and more should coordinate their activities because their decisions are related to most of the important planning problems and are actually interdependent. The achievement of such a coordination must be intrusted to some State agency close to the central executive who can keep in touch with all these varied activities and point out their relationship to each other and to the plan whenever a concrete problem arises. Without such an informed agency of liaison, coordination would be impossible. With it the habit of cooperation may be induced among the various authorities concerned, and the means of cooperation provided.

To broaden out the valley belt, to develop logically the undersettled regions, to give aid to farming and lumbering, to prevent further over-centralization in cities while assisting economy for the manufacturers by proper use of hydroelectric power, to coordinate water supply and to furnish a proper basis for local action—these are some of the objectives of a State plan.

The State has no more imperative duty than to foresee, to plan, and to assist in conducting such development. Up to now we have been too greatly at the mercy of blind chance and of our necessities. We have been to a large extent the creatures of circumstances; we have permitted external forces to shape our lives, without making an effort to see how far these forces conformed to useful human purposes. With the powers that are now at our command, with the technical insight and the social vision which the State can now summon to its service, we may reverse this situation: instead of being the passive creatures of circumstance, we may become more and more the creators of our future. By using nature and machinery intelligently, we can make them serve our human purposes. This is the final aim of the State plan.

Townless Highways for the Motorist

by Benton MacKaye and Lewis Mumford*

It is a commonplace to say that the automobile has revolutionized modern transportation. But the truth of the matter is that this revolution has not got beyond the Kerensky stage. The motor car has taken the place of the horse-and-buggy, and the motor bus has wiped out the street car in many sections of the country; but motor car and motor bus are still largely crawling along in the ruts laid down by earlier habits and earlier modes of transportation.

When one says crawl one means crawl. There is scarcely a town in the country where, at least on two days of the week, the traffic does not become a snarl and a nuisance; there is scarcely a street leading to a school where, unless the motorist does crawl, he may not kill a thoughtless child (a loss that offsets the gain from improved methods of treating such a scourge of childhood as measles); there is hardly a major crossing or a bottle-neck on our modern highways where, in the daily confusion, a car may not be wrecked or a body maimed in someone's impatience to move swiftly where movement is almost impossible. Like the fly, the motorist buzzes his wings vigorously; but his feet are stuck to the flypaper of the old-fashioned highway: a spavined horse could often travel as fast as a 120 h.p. car.

Even in the open country, when the cars at last begin to make a little speed, the adaptation of the motor car to civilized ways of life is still incomplete. There is the scorching ugliness of badly planned and laid out concrete roads peppered with impudent billboards; there is the vast, spreading metropolitan slum of multiple gas stations and hot-dog stands; and on the through highways there is the conflict between speed, safety, and pleasure. The October revolution of the automobile, which will effectually transform the physical means of life and make possible a higher type of civilization, has hardly begun.

What has been responsible for the backwardness of the automobile? A glance at the development of the railroad will perhaps give us some notion. When the locomotive was invented it arrested attention as an entirely new kind of contrivance. Except in the design of the original coaches, there was no temptation to compare Stephenson's Rocket with a stagecoach. From the beginning, the steam locomotive traveled on rails: a special kind of road was laid down for it. In order to prevent its wider and more untrammeled use, the British House of Parliament passed a law making it necessary for a locomotive used upon the highways to be preceded by a man waving a red flag. Had it not been for this law, England might have endured the evils and nuisances of the motor age two generations before they actually came into existence.

The internal combustion engine, which gave us the automobile, was unfortunately first attached to an innocent-looking carriage. The first automobiles were in fact called horseless carriages; and even those of us now in middle age can remember at least the stamps of the Buffalo Exposition of 1901, with the chauffeur perched high on the seat of an old-fashioned four-wheeled cab. So slowly and insidiously did the motor car make its way that, at the beginning, no one thought of putting it on a new kind of road. The first effect of the car was to bring a growing demand for filling up the gullies in the dirt road—gullies and ruts that the old-fashioned buggy had taken without a blink. Then came a demand for a binder that would lay the dust, and after that came road-widening, for the motor car could not turn out so easily into the weeds or ditches beside a narrow road. Finally arose the demand for a better surface, and in the last decade the smooth, well-graded concrete road with the banked turn and the center division has come into existence.

Having achieved thousands of miles of wide, concrete-paved highways, having projected many thousands more on almost exactly the same pattern, we lean back complacently in our chairs and fancy we have solved the problems of motor transportation—although our jammed city streets, our run-down suburbs, our spoiled villages, our devastated tracts of countryside, our country homes that are as quiet and peaceful as a boilerworks are all large and ironic commentaries upon our pretensions. Laying roads is one thing, and making movement on them safe and swift and pleasant is another. At present the only point where the automobile is permitted to come within sight of its potential efficiency is in the factory.

Where have we fallen short? Our chief mistake has been that we have not had the acumen of Uncle Harvey, who never saw an automobile. Back in 1892 Uncle Harvey said to one of us, "My boy, I'll make you a prophecy—the railways of the future will be quite different from the present, for instead of riding on trains each household will have its own family locomotive."

The fact is that in designing our new roads we have continued to provide for horseless carriages; whereas in actuality we are confronted by a kind of vehicle completely different from the carriage, something much closer to the steam locomotive. It is no use for us to assert innocently, as does the United States Government Report on the highways of Connecticut: "It is an interesting fact . . . that many of the present Connecticut trunk lines are not only in the same general location but occupy the identical rights-of-way upon which the old turnpikes were built." That is just the nub of the difficulty. We have tried to adapt the instruments of one age to the demands of another. This is what we do, it is true, when we are thoughtless enough to put an electric-light bulb into an oil lamp or a colonial candlestick; but in dealing with the automobile the results are not quite so innocuous. The loss of efficiency, the loss of life, the destruction of beauty, the dulling of pleasure that attend the spread of motor transportation call for a thorough re-orientation. When we try to travel swiftly in the old ruts we are ditched.

Now, if we had been thinking of the family locomotive instead of the horseless carriage we should have profited by both the good points and the mistakes of the railroad age. The chief merit of the railroad was that it created an independent system of transportation which, for the most part, did not even parallel the existing system of highways. The roadbed was specially designed for the new type of vehicle; a special right of way was created; large tracts of land were laid aside for yards and terminals; stations and junctions were specially designed with facilities for storage and switching, and on the bigger systems the local tracks were separated from the express tracks.

The defects of the original railway system equally merited study: they had much to teach the motor age. The passage of railroad tracks and railroad yards at grade through the center of the community is a blight and an obstruction: once done, it requires many thousands of dollars to undo; and in the meanwhile, the man-hours wasted, the property that has been ruined by fronting the tracks, and the loss of lives all mount up to an incalculable but plainly dreadful total. The other great menace of the railroad is the grade crossing. Where the railroad crosses a main artery, it should do so, we see now, by a bridge or a cut. With other weaknesses of the railroad, such as the neglect of feeder lines and the consequent deterioration of the inaccessible back country, one need not deal here: the transformation of the railroad *line* into a closely articulated motor *mesh* is one of the important contributions of the motor age itself.

Once we have grasped the essential notion of the automobile as a private locomotive, the example of the railroad will give us a clue to its proper treatment. It must have a related but independent road system of its own, and this system must be laid down so as to bring into use all the potential advantages of the automobile for both transportation and recreation. This means a kind of road that differs from the original turnpike, from the railroad and, above all, from the greater part of the existing automobile highways. One can perhaps characterize it best by calling it the Townless Highway, to denote its principal feature—the divorce of residence and transport. But this phrase does not cover all the aspects of modern road planning, as opposed to the muddle and chaos of the past: so let us examine one by one the various parts of the new system.

Let us first consider the motor road as a long-distance form of transportation. Following the existing network of roads, we have in the past put through our highways from one large urban center to another. We all know the results of that process. All the time that is saved in the country stretches is lost once the car enters the city streets: the bigger and more important the trunk road, the larger and more cluttered the town, the greater amount of time that is lost. Since aviation fields are naturally on the outskirts of the city—where they will remain unless the autogiro completely supplants the existing types—this clogging of the motor roads also diminishes the success of aerial transportation. One can fly from Philadelphia to Newark as quickly as one can come in by car from Newark to Times Square.

Our cities sometimes make feeble attempts to accelerate through traffic by routing it off the main avenues. But the first principle of the townless highway goes a long step farther: it requires that the highway avoid passing through the town. The demand for this kind of planning has already come from the motorist and is being met by the more progressive highway engineers. Take Federal Route No. 1 along the Atlantic coast, from Eastport, Maine, to Miami, Florida. Plans are in the making to relocate several sections of this route so that instead of going through the big cities along the Atlantic Coast it will pass them by on the inland side. Other plans would connect these revised sections by revised locations between cities. And so, by these two awkward back steps, Route No. 1 would be relocated farther inland and turned from an old-fashioned turnpike into what it should have been from the beginning—a townless highway.

The by-pass, or belt-line, is part of the big regional plan for New York City and its environs, as envisaged by the planners of the Russell Sage Foundation; it is likewise part of the Philadelphia Tri-State Plan, and of the Boston Bay Circuit project. The State of New Jersey has put through an almost complete system of such by-pass highways. More than once this sort of plan has been opposed by near-sighted business men, against their own better interests. In attempting to keep long-distance traffic on their own Main Street, they would not merely congest avenues that are already congested, with tourists and travelers who are not in the mood for shopping, but they would make access to their own district almost impossible to the local shopper—who would thereby be tempted to travel by train or motor to some larger center.

Intelligent highway planning would prevent such a reckless misuse of local thoroughfares. Local traffic needs ample parking space, as the Sears Roebuck stores have been intelligent enough to discover and to provide for in the layout of their new buildings; through traffic, on the other hand, should go completely outside a town, be it big or little. This is a fundamental maxim of sound motor-way planning. Where it is forgotten only confusion and congestion can result.

If the passage of a trunk-line highway through a town is against the best interests of the shopkeeper and merchant, what shall we say of its relation to the suburban center and to the village? Here the case is even more emphatically against it. Already people are demanding to be rid of the endless stream of gasoline locomotives that pass under domestic windows—the private locomotive, pleasure car, or truck, with its hum, its dust, its exhaust, its constant threat to the lives of little children who have for the moment escaped the eye of their mothers and nurses, to say nothing of grown adults, confronted by much greater hazards on the peaceful highway than the bold highwaymen who terrorized the Pony Express. The demand for relief has been increasing in volume; let us take one state—Massachusetts.

In the famous little village of Deerfield the Connecticut River thoroughfare was relocated eastward, both to relieve the residents of a nuisance and to preserve one of America's truly colonial towns, in effect almost an historic museum. In Harvard, Massachusetts, a main road from Worcester northward was put through the village center before its residents had awakened to its cacophonous possibilities. Very soon after, a vigorous local movement started to demand its relocation outside the village. Meanwhile the next village of Still River was asking why the heavy traffic should pass before *its* doors—and the logical answer is another relocation. From Fitchburg, a city of forty thousand, has come the demand to relocate the "Mohawk Trail" from Boston to Troy, New York, by making a by-pass southward, and so relieving the intolerable congestion of Main Street.

This sort of demand from the small town and village is important, and it points to an interesting fact. In the days of the horse and buggy the highroad served as company. As the cart or carriage joggled by, the farmer in the field or the housewife on her porch could hail it; the horse would stop almost of his own accord, and a chat would follow. But once the country road becomes a main highway, filled with fast traffic a good part of the day and even of the night, when the cars themselves are driven mostly by strangers, not neighbors, the whole situation is changed: the road ceases to be a symbol of sociability; it becomes very largely a curse. We know a suburban real estate man who suddenly became aware of this fact. His property adjoined a large through highway; and thinking in terms of the old-fashioned road of the past, he had put the highest values on the corner houses that were on the highway. It turned out that these houses were the last to be sold, and they did not sell until their prices were reduced. Living on a trunk motor road is like living on the railroad. More and more the sensible property owner is shying off the wide and handsome highway. He wants to travel on it, not to settle there.

Unfortunately, the by-pass is not by itself the solution of the problem of motor transportation. As our roads develop now, the usefulness of the by-pass is checkmated by the roadtown—sometimes called the motor town or the motor slum. We refer to the familiar row of frontage developments—the peanut stand, the hot-dog kennel, the dewdrop inns, the superfluous filling stations with their cut whiskey and applejack and their cut-price gasoline, and the smear of badly designed bungalows which make up such a large part of what on Sundays we prayerfully call the great outdoors.

What is the use of a road's by-passing a town, only to find that the road itself has turned into a town—and a cheap, nasty town at that? This is the question that confronts the motorist who chooses the car instead of the railroad because he likes to be in the country; it is the question that the city dweller ruefully asks himself each Sunday as his car follows the slow procession out of the town that never, somehow, no matter how far away he manages to steal, escapes into the open country. This mean frontage or ribbon development is not merely an American product; they have the same eyesore in England. Mr. Raymond Unwin, the chief consultant on the Greater London plan, after a thorough investigation condemns this development on three counts: it is unsafe, it is inefficient, and it is destructive of the amenities. To all of this one can only say Amen. How will an intelligent road program meet this situation?

So far American opinion has not given much attention to the factors of danger and inefficiency in this roadside development: the danger that comes from the too-numerous entrances and exits from roadtown, and the inefficiency of duplicating equipment or of providing it at the wrong points. In America we have been most aware, perhaps, of the distressing lack of amenity, the hasty, sordid, shantytown look which used to be characteristic of pioneer mining towns in the midst of a quick boom.

The first way of meeting this, by competitions designed to improve the looks of hot-dog stands or filling tanks, has very little to commend it; chaos would still be chaos, though each of the badly related units were as fine in itself as the Parthenon. A second way shows a little more realistic sense of the situation; it takes the form of attempting to "get there first" by obtaining open spaces along the wayside in the form of public parks and forests. The State of Massachusetts got there first on the Mohawk Trail up the east side of Hoosac Mountain in the Berkshires by purchasing the wayside land as a State forest: on the other hand, the State allowed roadtown to get there first by neglecting to purchase the summit and the west side of the mountain—the result being a development that differs only in its primitive background from the purlieus behind Scollay Square. At the present time the same race is starting on the new highway over the Taconic Range. In New Hampshire a campaign has been started to secure gifts of public woodlands along the wayside. But the only satisfactory way of guarding against the roadtown slum is that taken by, for example, the Bronx River and Westchester County Parkways—providing no place on the road system for its existence.

This brings us to the second important principle of modern motorway planning. Not merely must the motor road make up an independent system which by-passes the existing towns; it must be provided with enough land on both sides of the road to insulate it from the surrounding area, whether rural or urban. There are various ways of obtaining this land: some have been explored, others have just been projected. In Massachusetts the suggestion has been made to zone the land a certain distance back from the motor roads on exactly the same principle as is now applied to the zoning of urban land. This would perhaps do away with that early speculation in suburban and bungalow sites along main highways which now encourages slum development and leads to an early deterioration of the rural quality of the environment. But perhaps the most important and feasible means is the acquisition by purchase of a rural strip on each side of the main highway as a necessary part of its original development.

The through road must be a parkway. This would increase the original cost of such roads, but the increased value of the neighborhood tends to offset the original cost of the road itself, and where parallel roads exist, it tends to do away with slum development, since the value of the land lifts it out of the cheaper forms of exploitation. If the further expense of this method counteracted the tendency to spend money lavishly on aimless and unimportant highways, not demanded either by traffic or the beauties of the natural scenery, this would be all to the good. The wastes of bad planning and extravagant planning which we now cheerfully pay for to-day would probably more than pay for the cost of necessary and efficient planning on the lines here suggested.

But the planners of effective motorways cannot rest content with by-passes and an improved wayside environment, much though these would contribute by themselves to the speed and pleasure of the run. This is only a part of the revolution to be effected by the motor car. Both of these measures are working backward to what this revolution demanded in the first place: a roadway located quite apart from the towns with a wayside free from the eyesores of town growth: in short, a townless highway. Both of these measures are schemes for building this highway backward. Better that way, of course, than not at all.

Nevertheless, such hindsight is expensive. Has any definite project yet been undertaken which recognizes all the implications of the motor revolution? Yes; there is at least one. It is a town in New Jersey near Paterson, which has been built by the City Housing Corporation, a limited dividend company, and has been working successfully for over two years. Its name is Radburn. Seen near at hand, Radburn is merely a fairly closely builtup suburban town, of well-planned but very modest houses, surrounded by an unusual amount of communal open space in the form of a communal park. One can wander over its pedestrian paths for half an hour, perhaps, before one is suddenly struck by the fact that one has not crossed a road and has not seen an automobile. On, on the other hand, one may drive up and down the concrete highways and lanes of Radburn for an equal time before realizing that one has not encountered a pedestrian—has not even had him for company on the sidewalk, if only for the reason that on the motor avenues no sidewalk has been provided for him. What is the secret of this unique sense of safety and freedom of movement?

By going up in an airplane or by looking at an aerial map of this little town one discovers that one has been in a new kind of city—a town deliberately built for the motor age. In an ordinary city the streets form a continuous system, and wherever the street goes, through traffic can go, too. Not so in Radburn. In Radburn through traffic is confined to the through avenues; from these main avenues, which define the Radburn superblocks, there stems a system of motor lanes each of which comes to a dead end. The greater number of residences can be reached only by motor lanes, and no car is tempted to enter a motor lane unless the driver has definite business there. Such a town was unthinkable before the coming of the automobile; the motor car not merely makes it thinkable, but expedient and necessary.

By dedicating the wide through avenues to through traffic, by likewise dedicating the narrow local motor lanes to local traffic only, the two different purposes are automatically separated. Result: quiet homes and fast motor travel, not by ignoring the advantages of motor transportation but by boldly facing them and providing for them. Where pedestrian traffic must cross motor traffic within the great superblocks that make up the residential sections, the deadly grade crossing is eliminated and a bridge or an underpass separates the two systems: they cross but very rarely meet. Since playgrounds, a school, and other community facilities are provided in each superblock, no child need ever cross a traffic artery on its way to school or to the playground; indeed, the housewife who goes to market on foot is equally safe.

The insulation of highways from residential neighborhoods and the connection of these two elements by side lanes are a necessary complement in urban planning to our modern system of transportation. It is only by such a bold and radical departure in the plannng of new cities or the extension of old ones that the congestion brought by motor transportation can be permanently relieved. If every city were side-laned within its limits, and if it were itself connected with the main trunk routes by side lanes, the congestion and danger that now make motor transportation so inefficient would be lowered. How much they would be lowered it is impossible to estimate. In smaller centers like Radburn both items would probably approach close to zero. The side lane in motor transportation corresponds to the switch in railroad systems: it is the only orderly way of entering a main line.

Harvard, Massachusetts, which has already been cited, is considering a plan for being side-laned. This will show how the principle concerns the external relations of the town as well as its internal planning. The proposed Harvard plan is to relocate the main road now going through the village, to establish a mile away on the new main road a separate group of buildings, a station for gas, food, rest rooms, and other needed roadside utilities, and to connect this wayside station by means of a side lane with the old residential village of Harvard Center. The station here, you will note, corresponds exactly to the railroad station. The principal function of such a station is transport and commerce, not residence; and the motor car has dispensed with the need, slow as we have been to acknowledge it, for the "two minutes' walk" to the station—in two minutes one can go a mile with a timorous driver and a new car!

The side lane would not in this case be a blind alley; for it would connect with other local roads. This would be true of the planning of such lanes in existing towns and villages generally. The point to remember is this: it is only by a deliberate separation of local and through roads, of traffic and residential functions, that the motor road itself can attain its maximum efficiency in the number of vehicles served at the highest safe speed, and that the community can attain its maximum efficiency as a place for living, recreation, sleep, and the care of the young. It is sheer habit that makes us expect to live on through roads: that was convenient and efficient only when the horse was our quickest means of transportation and when, lacking concrete surfaces and motor plows, it was impossible to clear the country roads of snow. The speed of the automobile has increased our effective radius at least tenfold. To be a mile from a main highway by automobile is to be no farther away than five hundred feet on foot. Separating through traffic from local traffic by side lanes not merely increases safety but increases the total speed of a journey. Turning off is a quicker way of reaching the center of a city, all other things being equal, than remaining on a main highway that attempts the hopeless task of going through.

There is still, however, one problem that remains to be taken care of: that is the road between the stations. To concentrate the roadside services in definite units, instead of letting them dribble inefficiently along its entire length is an important step; the next is to follow the example of the railroad and keep the road itself absolutely free.

It is physically impossible on a railroad for the rolling stock to enter the track between switches. Since no other vehicles can enter, there is no occasion for frontage development, and such does not occur between stations except by some chance unrelated to the railroad. On the other hand, the basic cause of frontage development on the ordinary motor road is that vehicles can enter and depart at any point. This makes for the danger, the inefficiency, and the impaired amenities pointed out by Mr. Raymond Unwin. But every motorist is his own authority on this subject: he knows what a hazard crossroads are, how his foot moves toward the brake as he approaches intersecting streets, how often he has almost sideswiped another car in the effort to avoid a careless driver slipping out of an unsuspected gas station.

Plainly, then, the fewer the intersections the safer and faster will it be for long-distance traffic. The only way to dispose once and for all of roadtown is to make it physically impossible to enter or leave the motorway except at properly planned stations. Chairman Edward Bassett, of the National Council on City Planning, has suggested this simple device and given it the name of the freeway. On high-speed arteries, the stations on these freeways would undoubtedly be at considerable distances apart—perhaps as much as ten miles or more—and ordinary traffic would usually cross the express road by the overpass or the underpass.

The Townless Highway would, like Radburn, recognize the motor revolution and attempt to meet at every point the new situation it has raised. None of the principles embodied in the Townless Highway is altogether new or untried: the main element of uniqueness in the proposal is the putting of all of them into a coherent plan. The Townless Highway would be, like the railway, an institution in itself, a system. It would always be a through highway and not a local road. It must follow its own lines of topography. It must be based upon motor-age principles, not stagecoach methods or even railroad methods, much though we can learn by imitation or avoidance from both of these. It must disregard all previous turnpikes and local roads, unless these by chance should be suited to its special purpose. It will avoid towns big and little, not by dodging around them via by-passes, but by following the less developed territory. It would have its stations adjacent to the several towns within this territory, the two in each case being connected by side lanes. Between stations the road would constitute a freeway.

In connection with the planning or design or regulation of each of these features various problems would, of course, arise. Should the stations be designed as part of the highway and controlled by some regional authority? Should they be built and owned by the government—or merely planned? How are we to prevent slum towns from springing up around the stations, as they tended to, seventy-five years ago, around the new railroad stations? These are all important and difficult questions; but we cannot go into them here.

Let us rather try to picture the working out of the main elements in the system as they would touch the motorist himself. He awakens after a good sleep: the rumble and wheeze of long-distance traffic is at least a mile from his residence. He glides out with his car on to the relatively narrow local road, which need no longer be wide enough to take care of the heavy cross-country traffic, and he remembers, with a smile, how his local tax bill has gone down since the assessment for the widening of these local roads has been removed and the tax for their upkeep has gone down with the decreased wear and tear. He heads his car for the nearest station on Route No. 1. When he reaches the station he remembers that he is low on gas. As he pauses for a minute to have his tank filled up he watches a group of tourists eating their breakfast on the veranda of the well-equipped restaurant which has supplanted the half a dozen greasy hot-dog incubators that used to be scattered over the roadside. The food at this particular station is good enough to acquire a local reputation, and often people come out from town for a shore dinner; the restaurant itself, turned away from the road, looks out on to a pleasant vista of fields and salt meadows. He now approaches the road, but he must wait for the lights to change before he can turn in from the local road. Now he is off; in a minute the car is doing close to sixty on the flat stretches where the curves have all been smoothed out. With no danger of anyone suddenly cutting across, with no officious advertiser begging him to halt and change his tires or his underwear, or to patronize a hotel in the town he has just left, with unobstructed right of way and unobstructed vision, our motorist has less anxiety and more safety at sixty miles an hour than he used to have in the old roadtown confusion at twenty-five. Even the intersections do not mar his pleasure: they are far enough apart to warrant traffic lights, and unless the red signal is set—in this respect we are at last getting abreast of the railroad!—he speeds past the crossing blithely.

The motorist reaches the country quickly; he sees the country when he is in it. Whether he is traveling for sheer pleasure or to get somewhere, his major purposes are served by the Townless Highway; the motor car has become an honor to our mechanical civilization and not a reproach to it. When our motorist arrives at his destination he is still smiling and fresh; he has been irritated neither by threatened accidents nor by unexpected delays nor by tedious battles with the congestion of Main Street, attempting to rival all the mistakes of Fifth Avenue and Broadway. This is not utopia any more than the efficiency of a limited train on a fine railroad is utopia: it is merely intelligence, effectively applied. A civilization that can achieve the Twentieth Century or the Broadway Limited will not be content forever to wallow in the confusion and chaos of antiquated motorways and all their ugly accompaniments.

How shall we achieve the Townless Highway? The most feasible means, perhaps, would be through Federal direction. Let the Federal aid law of 1916 be brought abreast of the planning needs of the nineteen-thirties. A simple proviso would do it. Let the Federal moneys flow to the States, as now, for weaving together a national system of motor thoroughfares—provided that the specific principles here outlined be applied to such thoroughfares within each State. This would be a genuine recognition of the motor revolution. For the helpless and bewildered efforts of the past, good though they were in intention, it would substitute a conscious and well-directed intelligence, capable of assimilating all the lessons we have learned in fifteen years. That would be the October revolution of the automobile.

The Regional Survey of New York and Its Environs

by Thomas Adams*

The preparation of a Regional Plan for New York and Its Environs has entailed the making of extensive studies, during the past five years, of existing physical, economic, and social conditions. Reports based on these studies are being published in a series of volumes. This statement appears at the beginning of the first volume. It may justly be said that these studies and reports will form a contribution toward that science of regional and city planning in relation to modern conditions of urban growth which is still in its infancy.

The art of city planning, however, as expressed by the solution of problems of engineering and architectural design, has been practised since ancient times. Every planned city of which we have records teaches the engineer and the architect something about design. We can see that some of the principles of design have always been recognized, but that at different periods of time the application of these principles has taken different forms. In ancient Palestine, Egypt, Macedonia, Greece, Italy, and China formal planning in the limited physical sense was done on a scale and in a way that proves the genius of the older civilizations to have been remarkably successful in dealing with problems of design. The remnants that remain of the picturesque towns of the Middle Ages show how the craftsmanship of those times applied itself to city building.

In the Renaissance period in Europe the art of municipal design took new forms as a result of the advance of learning and of the interest which princely rulers then took in the subject, and it expressed itself in cities, of which many still stand. These were considered as models by Washington, Jefferson, and L'Enfant when, towards the end of the eighteenth century, they planned the capital city of Washington, and by those who, almost simultaneously, promoted the planning of the extension of Edinburgh, Scotland.

The replanning of Paris, and the extension of Italian, Swedish, and German cities during the nineteenth century, were carried forward in obedience to the same influences and principles of design. Indeed, it can hardly be said that the

*Thomas Adams, "Preface to the Regional Survey," *Regional Survey of New York and Its Environs,* Vol. 1 (New York: Committee on Regional Plan of New York and Its Environs, 1928), vii-xvii.

art of city planning in modern times, so far as it concerns itself with architectural or engineering design, contains anything in its approach to or conception of the problem that has not been thought of and used in city building for many centuries. But apart from lessons of design the planner of today cannot obtain much guidance from the methods used in planning cities in past times.

In this century and on this Continent Burnham's Plan of Chicago stands out as a great presentation of a grand architectural conception of city building and extension. Probably no other plan, as a plan, has achieved more than this as an inspiration to a people. But much more than an architectural conception, however brilliant, is needed to guide the right building of modern cities. The health and general well-being of masses of people, and the highly complicated economic and social structure of the urban community of the present time, call for the recognition of many factors that either were neglected or did not enter into the problems of cities of past times. One of the problems is, as it always has been, how can beauty and order be achieved in the building of the city? In a broader sense it is also how can the external aspects of the city be made to minister to aesthetic enjoyment and civic pride without detracting from the strength of those economic and ethical forces on which depend the prosperity, comfort, bodily health, and convenience of the inhabitants of the city. That structural beauty and public health may be conflicting rather than complementary is shown in all city building since the days when the Greeks and Romans laid out their magnificent civic centers and processional ways and neglected the dwellings of the common people. Today there are many cities that have planned and created beauty in their public places at the expense of the environment of the homes of their poorer citizens.

How can we harmonize the needs of the spirit and the needs of the body in the city organism? How also can the American city obtain beauty and order without too much constraint of individual liberty and too much interference with rights of persons and property? How can it obtain these things without impairing, but rather while improving, the quality of the home, the spaciousness of the parks and playgrounds, the efficiency of industry, the relief of traffic congestion and the equitable distribution of advantages and opportunities for all its citizens? As Mr. Herbert Hoover says, what is needed is "a new conception of city building."

The art of city building in a country where the sentiment of individual liberty is as strong as it is in the United States is a very different and much more complex thing than it is in countries where constraint by government is more acceptable than here, or where an autocracy, beneficent or otherwise, prevails over the design and management of cities.

The American city must be planned in accordance with the special degree to which it is and may continue to be a center of highly organized and standardized production, in harmony with the unique character of the economic forces that control its policies, and in keeping with its powerful traditions of individualism and its own patterns of local government. Underlying all planning there must be legal restraint on those abuses of land which permit one owner to use his liberty to the injury of the liberty of his neighbors. But restraints must be limited in this country to the things that are essential to human health, safety, and well-being. Where aesthetic purposes are sought to be obtained by public action, they must be paid for by money obtained from taxation.

In an important sense all city planning aims to fix certain legal qualities on the land—here the quality of a public street; there the quality of a park; in another place the quality of private property that is to be built upon only in accordance with certain regulations about the height and bulk of buildings and the uses to which they may be put (such regulations being ordinarily known as zoning ordinances). When the land of a community has been planned and stamped by law with such qualities its skeleton structure is for the time being determined. The building up of the land, the development of communications which then proceed upon the basis of this structure, will be beyond the control of the planning body. They will reflect the taste of the people as guided by their architects and engineers and will also betray the limits which the community's incapacity or unwillingness to defray the cost of betterments imposes upon the situation. No city planner can build a city. All he can do is to say to its citizens, "Here is my conception of what you should do, but it is you who are the builders. In Emerson's words—'Build therefore your own world!' "

The modern city is the world that the citizens have chosen to build. To improve it, where it needs improvement, it is they who must choose the method and means of achievement. The basis of any method is voluntary co-operation but there must be leadership. Sound leadership depends primarily on the recognition by those who lead that all human interests are harmonious and that the culture and enduring qualities of man are both the means and the end of wealth. It depends also on knowledge of the causes, effects and trends of present evils of urban growth, and of the methods necessary to prevent the recurrence of these evils. Here is where the main difficulty arises, for who among the leaders of public opinion, the scientists, and the artists of today have certain knowledge of the underlying causes and of the way out of the impasse towards which great cities like New York seem to be drifting? In making the survey of conditions in the New York Region the staff of the Regional Plan has endeavored to get such knowledge as is possible under present circumstances in order to indicate the way that should be followed, if a solution of the problems of the modern city is to be found.

The survey of the New York Region that has been made is an advance in comprehensiveness over any that has been done hitherto. It has been comprehensive in its functional scope, as related to the many and complex uses of urban land for building, means of communication and recreation, as well as in its geographical scope. It has been based on the recognition of the overlapping character of social and economic functions of each community, of different groups of communities, and of the whole federation of communities that make up the metropolitan region. Each element in the community structure has had to be studied in relation to other elements in order to get proper insight into the composite and complex problem of urban growth. Much of the work done has not only been new in its character but also in the respect that it has been undertaken for an area of exceptional size and density of population.

The unique character and scope of the survey has involved experimentation in methods of collecting and analyzing facts at all stages. Further investigation must be carried on in this and other metropolitan regions until a more highly developed scientific foundation is obtained for the planning of cities. In civic surveys made in the past there has been much collection of facts but, for the most part, those collected have been inadequately related, digested, and analyzed so as to present a satisfactory basis for further studies. Thus, in regard to some of the most important phases of urban growth, those engaged in any comprehensive survey of a modern city or urban region have to proceed without the aid of accumulated basic facts and reasoned study of their relations over a long period of time. This absence of a developed science is one disadvantage to the city planner—another is the presence of entirely new conditions that lessen the value of past experience as a guide to the solution of present problems. Changes that have taken place in this century in forms and masses of building, in methods of communication, in size of urban aggregations, and in standards of living are among the new influences which make the modern city an almost incalculable force facing a future that is as difficult to control as it is to know.

It is a difficult task to collect facts and study relations between comparatively static physical conditions, and dynamic and evolutionary economic and social conditions affecting millions of associated beings. It is obvious that the accomplishment of such a task could be done only in a preliminary way. But the preliminaries are important. The staff of the Regional Plan can claim that it has made a start in traversing the right road to discovery while recognizing the long and unknown stretches of undiscovered country that lie ahead. It has been "blazing a trail," with knowledge that all it could accomplish could not lead to finality.

A city consists largely of indefinite things and "indefinite things do not permit of definite measurements." For instance, one of the difficulties in connection with all social investigation is not being able to measure the unknown quantities, or invisible elements, that lie deeper than the investigator is able to go. Then there are elements of change always going on in the social and therefore in the civic structure which mean that an investigation at one time may reveal conditions that would not apply a year or two earlier or a year or two later. The most thorough investigation may be a failure because it cannot lead to definite conclusions with regard to the dynamic and unknown factors in a particular social problem. It is not that the method of the scientist may be fallible, or that the results of his experience may be questionable. Frequently it is that the subject takes a form at the time he investigates it which is different from the form it takes at other times. One may compare the situation in such a case with the astronomer's view of the planet Saturn. The astronomer knows that Saturn has rings as distinguishing marks of the great star, but when Galileo invented his new telescope he had doubts of its infallibility because he did not see the rings. The reason was that the star had the rings turned edgewise to the earth, and so the telescope gave the true picture of Saturn as it was at the time, but not Saturn as it would appear at another time. In order that investigations into social conditions may yield satisfactory results, they have to be made over long-continuing periods, and checked by wide experience before conclusions can be reached of such a rational and definite character that no one can gainsay them or find justification for prejudices in favor of present bad conditions, however intolerable. So it is that in some directions facts that are right today may be out of date tomorrow and shrewd guesses may be more reliable as an index of needs than methodical inquiries. In developing its transitional stages the city marches on, destroying many truths of yesterday.

These statements are made for the purpose of indicating the difficulty and need of investigation of urban conditions and not by way of apology for limits of accomplishment or lack of value in what has been done by the staff of the Regional Plan of New York. Sufficient facts have been collected, measured, and related to enable members of the staff to go forward to the preparation of a plan with assurance that, in collaboration, they can arrive at approximate estimates of the realities of the problems that have to be faced in order that solutions may be found of the present difficulties. Their purpose is to make these realities known and to indicate why and how they should be faced. The acceptance of these proposals by the Committee may not lead to their acceptance by the public or by those in authority, and therefore to immediate or effective solutions. If, however, it hinders aggressive action in wrong directions, restrains wasteful expenditure of money in bolstering up unsound economic conditions, and on the other hand encourages the coming citizens to face realities, it will do all that those who initiated the survey and plan dared to hope would be achieved.

The character and complexity of the New York Region will be revealed in the various reports. In this place, however, it is considered desirable to name a few outstanding facts regarding the Region, before proceeding to give a brief description of the scope of the survey.

The area of the Region is as large as the State of Connecticut and four and a half times as large as Rhode Island. It is 250 times the size of Manhattan Island. Of its 5,528 square miles, 2,887 are in New York State, and 2,641 are in the States of New Jersey and Connecticut. In this area there are approximately 10,000,000 people, more than there are in any state in the Union except New York State, or in the Dominion of Canada. Its topography is greatly varied and its land areas are so interspersed with waterways as to present unique advantages for transportation, and striking beauty in the natural scenery of its environs, in combination with exceptional difficulties in permitting outward expansion and developing plans for future growth.

Its most central and thickly populated counties are the five self-governing county boroughs comprising the City of New York, with about 6,000,000 people, and the county of Hudson, and City of Newark in the State of New Jersey. These counties have an area of 365 square miles. Beyond these areas a zone within a radius of 20 miles has an additional 536 square miles, and still farther outward there are 4,627 square miles largely virgin territory but economically related to the City and Port of New York.

It is estimated that by the year 1965, which has been selected as the date towards which the Committee should look forward in its planning proposals, the population of the Region will be about double the present population, or say 20,000,000. In any event it is considered desirable that the possibility of such an increase in population should be kept in mind in making a plan.

The manufacturing plants in the Region now number over 60,000, and its harbor facilities include 868 piers spread over 125 miles of waterfront. The foreign trade of its port in 1923 was valued at $3,316,671,910. The 13 railroads that serve the New York Region have 1,890 miles of right of way and carried 241,836,000 passengers to and from the Metropolitan terminals in 1924. The 600 miles of rapid transit tracks and 5,011 miles of laid out streets in the city alone indicate the enormous task of making a study of its system of circulation. Every day 2,870,000 people travel into and out of the part of Manhattan below 59th Street. Schools have to be provided for over a million children in the city alone, and recreation facilities are needed for twice that number of young people.

The whole urban area—comprising such vast economic interests—is constantly replanning and rebuilding itself piecemeal. During the past 25 years large portions of the central area have been remade by the erection of buildings and construction of subways, roads, bridges, and tunnels. Enormous expenditures will be incurred in continuing this process of reconstruction, and it is obvious that great savings and improved conditions would be effected by proceeding on the basis of a well-conceived plan.

Its financial problems are staggering in their scope and ramifications. The annual budget of the city alone has now reached the half-billion mark and nearly two billions circulate through its Treasury every year. Twenty years ago the expenditures of the National Government were less than those of the City of New York today. Public improvements in contemplation by responsible authorities in the Region involve an expenditure of at least three billions in the next fifteen years.

The survey has been made with the general object of examining the growth, characteristics, and needs of the communities in the whole urban region which is economically and socially related to the port of New York, and to summarize and present the results in a form that would afford guidance in the preparation of a plan so designed as to secure the best possible development of the whole Region.

Of necessity the field of study covered by the regional survey has had to be limited to those matters that had the most direct bearing on the making of a graphic regional plan dealing with tangible proposals for improving physical conditions. It was inevitable, however, that in the pursuit of the studies agreed upon by the Committee, many inquiries had to be made regarding current and passing problems and ancillary features for the purpose of obtaining knowledge for the staff, although the results of these secondary studies are not, in themselves, appropriate or condensable enough for presentation in published reports.

The series of Survey and Plan Reports will consist of twelve volumes, the first ten presenting the essence and results of the principal studies carried out as a basis for planning, and the remaining two presenting in text, maps, and diagrams the conclusions and proposals developed as a result of the Survey.

The first volume of Survey Series deals with major economic factors in the New York metropolitan region and discusses trends and tendencies in the assignment to areas of activities in leading industries. Two volumes, supplementary to Volume I, give a description of the detailed studies of the most important fabricating industries and of activities connected with wholesale markets, retail shopping and finance. Succeeding these are being published volumes dealing *inter alia* with distribution of population and land values; highway traffic; transit and transportation; port and industrial areas; public recreation, including studies of the growth, extent and distribution of public open spaces; neighborhood communities and development of new towns; the uses of buildings and spaces about them, including zoning, housing, etc.; sunlight in urban areas; planning and development of unbuilt land; economics of land subdivision; rights in land under water; the maintenance of the integrity of the street plan; and public services and sanitation.

The Plan Volumes will contain an historical summary of planning in the Region; an analysis of the general influences and trends of urban expansion, and of the mechanics and application of planning; a review of functions, circulation and planning methods; a statement of principles and standards to govern city and local planning; a series of architectural studies and proposals for treatment of important concrete problems; and an atlas and description of the Regional Plan dealing comprehensively with utilization of land and circulation in its various forms.

The Plan was originated by Mr. Charles D. Norton in 1921. Since then a Committee, whose members are listed on another page, under the chairmanship first of Mr. Norton until his death in 1923, and later of Mr. Frederic A. Delano, has directed the work. No existing governmental agency could have undertaken the task of making a survey and plan for a region so lacking in political unity as that which includes the area socially and economically related to the Port of New York. The work had to be undertaken by a private group willing to render voluntary service, and financed from other than political sources. A plan prepared by such a group can only be accepted as it commends itself to citizens throughout the Region as well done and useful. The Committee has no power to execute plans. Moreover, there is no body in existence, or likely to be created, to exercise that power. The expectation of the Committee is that the Plan when made will be adopted in separate parts and incorporated, with modifications, by local authorities in plans to be made for their respective areas. The carrying out of any plan must be a gradual process. Before the public will accept the proposals in the Plan it must understand them. This means that much educational work must be undertaken over a considerable period of time. Continual replanning and modifying will be necessary merely to meet changing conditions during the period of execution. The Committee's staff has successfully promoted much of the recent legislation necessary to make planning effective, and is endeavoring to promote a regional wide organization of local planning and park commissions. The cost of making the surveys and plans and of publishing the series of reports has been met by the Russell Sage Foundation of New York.

At the inaugural meeting of the Plan Mr. Robert W. deForest, President of the Russell Sage Foundation, said: "It is that plan which makes the city a better place to live in and a better place to work in that most interests the Foundation." Apart, however, from the objective which particularly interests the Foundation, it may be claimed that the improvement of living conditions for the present and prospective population is a primary requisite of any city or regional plan. This involves consideration of the conditions in which people work and travel as well as those concerned with their housing accommodations, and their recreation facilities. A predominant need in the New York Region is the extension and improvement of the Port of New York, and the maintenance and development of certain major activities in central areas. It is considered to be desirable to have a reasonable degree of concentration for business purposes in which due regard is paid to the requirements of health and the circulation of traffic, combined with a well-balanced distribution of industries not requiring central locations. The development of a unified plan of transit and transportation is also a question of vital importance in promoting the proper development and prosperity of the metropolitan area.

Plans for relieving traffic congestion should emphasize the need of greater mobility rather than more restricted movement, in the interest of industry, business, the convenience and general welfare of the inhabitants, and land values. Everything that is practicable should be done to promote, and not to hamper, the means of communication.

To achieve those ends it is not conceived to be necessary that overcrowding of land and congestion of streets and terminals should continue unchecked. There is ample space in the Region to permit of desirable forms of well-balanced growth of industry and population and to enable measures to be employed to prevent the recurrence of existing evils of congestion in those areas that are now least crowded or undeveloped. Whatever may be the final answer to the question as to what are desirable heights and densities of buildings, it is considered that as buildings become higher the spaces surrounding them for movement, light, and air should be increased. Standards of open space for all purposes of recreation need to be determined. Better distribution and more adequate provision of public open spaces need to be made, particularly in proximity to residential areas.

Certain major problems of design need to be brought to public attention and illustrated by pictures of possibilities. These include the frontages of the East and West waterfronts of Manhattan, the frontage of Brooklyn and New Jersey overlooking Upper Bay, the land on both banks of the Harlem River, the development of new railroad terminals at 60th Street yards and Mott Haven, the planning of Hackensack Meadows, and the creation of model communities and properly planned neighborhood units.

New York has to be considered from several points of view that are of continental significance. These include its commanding position as the portal through which flows the greatest volume of international commerce, with the network and convergence of transportation facilities that this involves; as the metropolis of economic activities of 120,000,000 people; and as the leading center of industry and distribution. These and other economic considerations, coupled with the growing public demand for improved environment, impose upon its leading citizens and civic rulers a great responsibility for making the structural development of the city commensurate in dignity and grandeur with its power and wealth.

PART III

An Urban Nation,
1945–1965

CHAPTER FIVE

METROPOLIS: SUBURB AND CORE

The most striking and significant feature of the modern American city is the divided social and physical pattern of its metropolitan form. In the course of the 20th century the metropolitan community has undergone important transformations—especially in shifting from an industrial to a postindustrial economy—but its fragmented character has continued to influence physical structure and social organization. This division is manifest in the growing differences between the two component parts of the metropolis—the central or core city and its surrounding region.

The fragmented character of the contemporary metropolis had its origins in the confluence of a number of late 19th-century factors, which brought about the transformation of compact, walking-distance cities into far-flung metropolitan areas. The desire of an emerging industrial middle class to enjoy rural amenities, coupled with the influx of business, industry, and foreign immigrants into the crowded core areas provided the psychological incentive for moving away from the city. The advent first of the railroad and then the electric streetcar, along with the extending of other public utilities to outlying fringes, made suburban subdivision physically possible. The resulting movement of population and housing, followed by commerce and industry, gained momentum in the 1920's when the increased use of the automobile made it possible for even greater numbers of people to live miles from the city. Slowed somewhat during the early years of the depression, this suburbanization movement has continued unabated since the 1940's, particularly after World War II.

But while metropolitan areas have been growing at an amazing pace since the late 19th-century, their component parts have grown at different rates. For the first 20 years of this century central cities grew at a faster pace than their surrounding regions, but since 1920 the suburban and satellite communities have grown faster than the core. In 1900 the population of the central cities of the metropolitan areas was 61.9 percent of the total, while the outer regions made up only 38.1 percent. However, in the five metropolitan regions with a population of 3 million or more, the growth in central cities in the decade 1950-1960

189

was only 1 percent, and in the suburban fringe 71 percent. The Committee for Economic Development estimates that by 1975, only 42 percent of the total metropolitan population will reside in the central city, and 57 percent will live in the suburban fringe—thus reversing the ratio that existed at the beginning of the century.

What is most striking about this population movement today is that it has now assumed a racial dimension. For as whites who could afford to move left the central city, blacks migrating from the rural South have been replacing them in ever greater numbers. The white movement away from the city was a full-fledged flight *before* the black influx into the cities, but Negro migration has spurred the continued decline in the proportion of whites living in the central city. In 1910, 73 percent of the total Negro population in the United States lived in rural areas, but by 1966, 69 percent of the Negroes were urban (as compared to 64 percent of the whites). Between 1950 and 1966, 86 percent of the total increase in Negro population took place in central cities, while 77.8 percent of the increase in white population took place in the suburbs. Furthermore, the concentration of urban blacks has been mostly in the largest cities. Our 12 biggest cities (New York, Chicago, Los Angeles, Philadelphia, Detroit, Baltimore, Houston, Cleveland, Washington D.C., St. Louis, Milwaukee, and San Francisco) contain over two thirds of the Negroes living outside the South. By 1968, seven of these cities were over 30 percent Negro.

Here, then, are the physical and social characteristics of the modern metropolis we are trying to rebuild: a core of dilapidation and poverty surrounded by a ring of relative affluence. There are, of course, various kinds of suburbs. But for the past century the majority of suburbanites have moved from the city for similar reasons: to enjoy greater contact with nature, to preserve the security of private family life, to escape changing conditions in the city, and to retain the integrity and intimacy of small community independence. Whether these ideals are actually realized in the suburbs or not, they form the mental picture or basis upon which many have attempted to shape a "suburban style of life." David Riesman discusses a number of the implications for American society resulting from the effort to develop such an ethos, and finds much lacking in the suburban ideal. From a somewhat more sympathetic perspective, Robert Wood comments on one of the main social and political motives of those who have moved to the suburbs.

The desire for political autonomy, as Wood describes it, and the need to be related to a manageable unit of government in which one can feel involved is, of course, admirable. But if it is gained at the cost of excluding others because of the color of their skin, and at the cost of indifference and blindness to the problems arising in the area of the city recently abandoned, then the price is too high. And this is often just what the flight to the suburb has meant: an ignorant neglect or smug indifference to the growing crisis in the central city. Only recently have many Americans been made aware of the sometimes hopeless, sometimes explosive conditions in the heart of their cities. There were earlier warnings, including the voices of blacks like Marcus Garvey and Malcolm X, or the understanding of a keen observer like Charles Silberman. But the division of our country into two largely distinct societies and the consequences of a dehumanized urban environment have been made real for many only as a result of the rioting on the streets of our cities in the 1960's.

Following numerous urban riots during the summer of 1967 President Lyndon Johnson appointed a National Advisory Commission on Civil Disorders and charged it with finding out what happened, why it had happened, and what should be done to prevent continued violence. The main conclusions of the report issued by the commission (referred to as the Kerner Report after Illinois Governor Otto Kerner who was chairman of the commission) are that, "White racism is essentially responsible for the explosive mixture which has been accumulating in our cities since the end of World War II," and that if action is not taken to alter the direction of current trends the continued division of American society will lead to even more tragic consequences. In the section of the Kerner Report reprinted in this chapter, the commission sets forth a number of alternatives open to us as we face "the future of our cities."

The Suburban Dislocation

by David Riesman*

The suburbs have become so characteristic of life "among democratic nations" that some of our most acute social observers in the post-World War II years have seen in them the shape of the egalitarian future. William H. Whyte, Jr., in his *Fortune* series on "The Transients" has emphasized the poignancy of the relaxed yet inescapable bonds in the new suburbs, notably Park Forest. Others, too, have been struck by a kind of massification of men in Levittown and other housing developments such as was once postulated for the endless residential blocks of the cities created by the industrial revolution. Even in a Canadian suburb, where one might expect slightly more hierarchical traces, a team of social scientists has found "the track of generations" barely visible. In the light of these commentaries, the emphasis on status in *Middletown, Yankee City, Elmtown,* or the New York suburb which marks for Charlie Gray in Marquand's novel the point of no return—this emphasis on graded ranks seems almost archaic. In contrast, the new suburbanite appears to suffer, less from exclusion, than from a surfeit of inclusions.

Yet this is impression, based on a few soundings in a few perhaps strategic and surely highly visible locations. We know very little about the relatively settled suburbs, especially those leapfrogged by the waves of post-World War II growth; and so far as I can see we know almost nothing about the suburbs (old or new) surrounding the smaller cities. The new developments which have altered the physical and moral landscape so strikingly may betoken a trend or a blind alley. They may fascinate us out of our contemporary fears for the loss of liberty and individuality; and intellectuals, seldom unambivalent about the suburbs—whether or not they make them their own domiciles—may generalize from them too readily to middle-class life and leisure as a whole.

Sociological Studies

Such considerations led me to a review of what sociologists have recently written, at their most empirical, about cities, suburbs, and the urban-rural fringe. Much of this work is based on census data or on such repeated explorations as the University of Michigan's Detroit Area Survey or the Metropolitan St. Louis

*David Riesman, "The Suburban Dislocation," *The Annals* of the American Academy of Political and Social Science, 314 (November, 1957), pp. 123-125, 129-146.

Survey. Such studies tend to put a brake on extrapolative generalization. They indicate, for example, the presence of urban elements in rural areas, and vice versa. The city is not necessarily the seat of urbanism, and the suburban way differs from the city way only at the polarities of each and is based on variables not entirely dependent on ecology or visible from a helicopter. Hence these investigations do support the common-sense observation that can find suburban styles in many cities and urban ones in many suburbs; that an urban fringe is growing which is neither country nor city nor quite bedroom suburb in the older mode.

If this is so, then it means that the differences which divide Americans today depend less and less on where one lives, what one does, or who one is in terms of lineage, but more and more it depends on style and social character. Of course, some self-selection will occur towards places to live and towards occupations—especially between the two sectors of our "dual economy" I shall describe later. However the sorting at any given time reflects chance and idiosyncracy and scarcely predicts the life cycle of individuals. Occasional studies of suburban voting and a few intimations concerning suburban worship shed tangential light on such major questions of attitude. On the whole, however, it seems fair to say that empirical investigations—including those recently done on problems of zoning, planning, and recreational needs; on the location of industry and the journey to work; and on problems of suburban and regional administration—scarcely connect with the kinds of writing cited at the outset. Thus, we cannot link nation-wide data on changes in metropolitan areas with Whyte's descriptions of how Park Forest feels toward its pro tem inhabitants. This is the characteristic situation in sociology today—that research in the macrocosmic and in the microcosmic scarcely connect, scarcely inform each other. At any rate, this is my excuse, or my opportunity, for dealing in this paper with quite general themes only illustratively and sporadically pinned down in empirical research: I speak for a point of view—at best for a seasoned subjectivity.

. . . .

Revolt against Industrialism

[Among suburban dwellers and our society in general] . . . we are witnessing a tremendous but tacit revolt against industrialism. It is a very different sort of revolt from either that of the machine smashers of the early nineteenth century or that of the various anti-industrial sects—socialist, anarchist, agrarian, etc.—of an earlier day. Large manufacturing industry is increasingly moving to the luxury side of the "dual economy," and backbreaking toil and harsh physical conditions are vanishing (except in industrialized farming and the service trades) with the coming of electricity, full employment, unions, and personnel men. But the luxury, which is often used to make the work more gregarious and less of an effort, is seldom used to make it less monotonous. Naturally, men treat their work as delinquents treat school though schools are less likely than plants to pioneer the partial truancy of the four-day week, escaping and sabotaging when they can. Managers and foremen try in vain to restore the "old school spirit" to their employees and, failing, seek through automation and quality control to make up for the deliquescence of the "instinct of workmanship" once so painfully built into the labor force. Observers of factory life have repeatedly pointed out that status within the plant is no longer gained by hard work and craftsmanship, but rather by one's consumer skills outside. Men dream, not of rising in the factory, but of starting a small business such as a motel, gas station, or TV repair shop in the shabby and open-shop underside of our dual economy. For youngsters from subsistence farms, for hillbillies, and Southern Negroes, a Detroit or Gary factory is still glamorous or at least a liberation from drastic poverty and insecurity; but for second- and third-generation factory workers, it no longer holds much meaning other than as a (hopefully temporary) source of funds and fringe benefits.

To be sure, there is a new industrialism of electronics, plastics, aviation, and so on, which retains a certain appeal that the older industries have so largely lost. However, the new firms, increasingly located in suburbs or where people want to live: California, and the Southwest and Florida, speed the movement out of heavy industry and merge factory and suburban life in a blend Patrick Geddes would probably disown. But we see in these industries precisely the form that the revolt against industrialism has taken today, namely to partially incorporate the "enemy" so that industrialism is not compartmentalized but rather, in muted form, spreads into all parts of the culture. This is, of course, what happens in so many social struggles: One defeats the enemy by becoming more like him.

Life and Work Values

Let me pursue this further by looking at what is happening to the older form of industrial and commercial metropolis. When, a few years ago, I studied interviews done with several hundred college seniors at twenty representative universities, asking them what they would like or expect to be doing in fifteen years, I was struck by the fact that the great majority planned to live in the suburbs. They expected to be married, and in describing their prospective spouses they hoped for what we might call station-wagon types: educated, companionable, civic-minded, and profoundly domestic. There were few who recognized some incompatability between focus on suburban life and focus on big-city ambitions (for instance, a senior who wanted to go into advertising, yet not live in or near New York). They were—with some exceptions especially among the Southerners—willing to sacrifice the heights of achievement, though not the plateaus of the luxury economy, in favor of their goals of suburban domesticity and peace. Those who hailed originally from the suburbs suffered from no disenchantment and wanted to return to them—often to the same one—while both city-bred and small-town boys also preferred the suburbs. I assume that some of the latter in an earlier day would have wanted to leave Main Street behind and make their mark in the big city, whatever lingering agrarian fears and suspicions of it they still harbored. The city today, for many, spells crime, dirt, and race tensions, more than it does culture and opportunity. While some people still escape from the small town to the city, even more people are escaping from the city to the suburbs.

The successful book and movie, *The Man in the Grey Flannel Suit,* dramatizes these values quite explicitly. The hero chooses unromantic suburban cosiness, with (in the movie version) a not altogether inspiring wife and progeny, in preference to a high-pressure but potentially exciting business opportunity. The head of the business is portrayed as having destroyed his family life and as virtually alienated from all human contact. Very likely, some of his junior executives would describe the company as a "mink-lined rattrap," thus explaining and justifying their withdrawal of affect from the work itself, while recognizing that they are still competitive. A recent fragmentary survey presents evidence that managers are less satisfied with their work even than unskilled workers, and it is conceivable that the middle-class occupations in general will soon be regarded as sources of funds and of periodic contacts and activity, much as the working-class occupations are now largely regarded. If work loses its centrality, then the place where it is done also comes to matter less, and the access to variety in work that the central city provides may also come to matter less. Indeed, so much is this the case already that advertising for engineers in *Scientific American* and in trade journals looks more and more like the vacation advertising in *Holiday.* Minneapolis-Honeywell offers seasons and skiing as a counter-lure to the aircraft and electronic suburbs of the Far West. In this regimen, white-collar and blue-collar move towards one another, as each group now emphasizes the consumption aspects of life.

Suburban Way of Life

This life, as just indicated, is increasingly focused on the suburbs which, since World War II, have grown so in quantity as to change their quality. For, although upper-class and upper-middle-class people have lived in the suburbs of our great cities since the 1880's or earlier, the cities before World War II still retained their hegemony: They engrossed commercial, industrial, and cultural power. The city represented the division and specialization not only of labor but of attitude and opinion: By discovering like-minded people in the city, one developed a new style, a new little magazine, a new architecture. The city, that is, provided a "critical mass" which made possible new combinations—criminal and fantastic ones as well as stimulating and productive ones. Today, however, with the continual loss to the suburbs of the elite and the enterprising, the cities remain big enough for juveniles to form delinquent subcultures, but barely differentiated enough to support cultural and educational activities at a level appropriate to our abundant economy. The elite, moreover, tend to associate with like-income neighbors rather than with like-minded civic leaders, thus dispersing their potential for leadership beyond township boundaries. Ironically, these people sometimes choose to live in communities which might be almost too manageable if millions of others did not simultaneously make the same choice.

Indeed, the suburbs are no longer simply bedroom communities but increasingly absorb the energies of the men as well as the women and children. The men, that is, are not simply being good providers while still attached to the values of the industrial system: They are seekers after the good life in the suburbs on their own account. Early marriage and the rise in the birth rate are so many rivulets of individuals, only barely self-conscious protest against the values inherited from industrialism and the low-birth-rate middle-class metropolis—so many decisions to prefer companionship in the present to some distant goal, and so many mortgages of the future in the benevolent shadow of the luxury economy and its escalator of slow inflation, promotion, and protection. Whereas men once identified themselves with commerce and industry—with its power, its abstractions, its achievements—and forced women to remain identified with domesticity—save for those women who broke through the barrier and became man-imitating career girls—now, as many observers have pointed out, a growing homogenization of roles is occurring. Women take jobs to support the suburban menage periodically while men take part in its work (do-it-yourself), its civic activities (Parent-Teachers Association, and so on), and its spirit. Rather than delegating religion to their womenfolk, men go to church in increasing numbers, occasionally as in an earlier day to be respectable or to climb socially, and occasionally out of a genuine religious call, but more typically because the church, like the high school and the country club, has become a center for the family as a social and civic unit.

Decentralization of Leisure

All this brings with it an increasing decentralization of leisure. Just as the suburban churches tend, within the boundaries of the "three faiths," to an amiable syncretism, ignoring doctrinal or liturgical differences, so too the other leisure activities of the suburbs tend to reduce the specialized differentiations possible in a metropolis. What I mean here can be illustrated with reference to music. A metropolis has enough music lovers to organize highly differentiated groups: Mozart lovers may split off from Bach lovers and would never encounter lovers of Wagner, while in the suburbs the music lovers—if they are to support communal activities at all—must in some measure homogenize their tastes and hence create a local market for "classical music." Indeed, they will be exposed to a good deal of community pressure to support the musical activities of their friends in return for having their own enterprises supported. The same holds, *parri passu,* for the other arts—just as it does for the differentiation of specialty stores, churches, and museums found in a large city. By the same token, the suburban activist can feel that his own contribution matters, as he would likely feel in the big city only when he is very rich, very active, or very influential. People brought up in the suburbs may not realize what they are missing, and they may relate their emotional ties entirely to their locality, not going downtown to shop or to visit friends or to go to the theatre.

Suburbs differ, of course, in what they make available, and so, as we noted at the outset, do central cities; thus, Morris Janowitz showed that many people who, to the visitor's eye, live in Chicago actually live in a small neighborhood that might as well be a suburb. Moreover, central cities are increasingly influenced by suburban styles of life: People trained to a suburban attachment to their cars drive downtown even when good and commodious public transportation is available, and they wear the casual dress of the suburbs when they do.

The suburban dweller believes, in fact, that he has the best of both worlds. In the interviews with college seniors I referred to earlier, in which such stress was placed on suburban domesticity, many students also emphasized their wish not to lose the cultural amenities they had enjoyed in college. Some of these amenities will certainly be distributed in the suburb though frequently in diluted doses: Piped in through television and radio and high-fidelity sets; the suburb may even support a theatre group and, in a few cases, amateur chamber music; the local high school will provide entertainment of a sort, as well as facilities for adult education.

However, as the radii lengthen on which people move away from the city—as they must with the crowding of the suburbs leading to the jump to the exurbs—people either learn as in California to drive great distances for dinner or confine themselves to their immediate environs: The central city as a meeting place disappears—a process which has gone further in Los Angeles and Chicago than in Boston or New York. The neighbors make up little circles based—as William H. Whyte, Jr., showed for Park Forest—largely on propinquity.

Loss of Human Differentiation

The decentralization of leisure in the suburbs goes further than this, however, as the home itself, rather than the neighborhood, becomes the chief gathering place for the family—either in the "family room" with its games, its TV, its informality, or outdoors around the barbecue. And while there are values in this of family closeness and "togetherness," there is also a loss of differentiation as the parents play pals to their children and the latter, while gaining a superficial precocity, lose the possibility of wider contacts. At worst, there is a tendency for family talk and activity to seek the lowest common denominator in terms of age and interest.

Some of these matters are illustrated by an interview with a housewife who had recently bought a house in one of the wealthier suburbs north of Chicago. Her husband had been transferred to Chicago from a southern city and had been encouraged by his company to buy a large house for entertaining customers. Customers, however, seldom came since the husband was on the road much of the time. The wife and three children hardly ever went downtown—they had no Chicago contacts anyway—and after making sporadic efforts to make the rounds of theater and musical activities in the suburbs and to make friends there, they found themselves more and more often staying home, eating outdoors in good weather and looking at TV in bed. Observing that "there is not much formal entertaining back and forth," the wife feared she was almost losing her conversational skills; yet she felt that her family had been pulled closer together by the shared activities, in which the husband joined on weekends, around the home. After listening to her list and discuss the friends made at church and golf, it became evident that her immediate environment just missed providing her with people close enough to her in taste and interest for intimate ties to develop.

One interview, of course, proves little, and many factors are obviously involved in choice of friends; suburban location in an older, nonhomogeneous suburb is only one of them. I recall obtaining such interviews in Kansas City, too, among people who had lived there all their lives and had potential access to wide strata in the metropolitan area. Nevertheless, there seems to me to be a tendency, though not a pronounced one, in the suburbs to lose the human differentiations which have made great cities in the past the centers of rapid intellectual and cultural advance. The suburb is like a fraternity house at a small college—or the "close propinquity" to which Tocqueville referred—in which like-mindedness reverberates upon itself as the potentially various selves within each of us do not get evoked or recognized. For people who move to the suburb to live when adult, of course, matters are different than among those who never knew another milieu. And, to be sure, creative human contact need not be face to face but can often be vicarious, through print or other mediated channels. Certainly, highly differentiated human beings have grown up in locales which gave them minimal support. Moreover, though the nonneighborly seldom seek the suburbs, a few doubtless manage to survive there. Ease of movement, in any case, permits periodic access to others, although as these others themselves scatter to the suburbs, this process becomes more difficult.

Role of the Automobile in Suburbia

Indeed, at least until each of us has his own helicopter or rocket, this pattern of life requires us to spend a great deal of time in automobiles, overcoming decentralization—but driving is itself a terribly "decentralized" activity, allowing at best for car-pool sociability, and at worst mitigated by the quiz-bits, frequent commercials, and flatulent music of AM radio. As compared with the older suburbanites who commuted by train and read the paper, did homework, or even read a book, the present and increasing tendency to travel to work by car seems aggressively vacuous and solipsistic. Whereas in preindustrial cultures and in the lower classes in industrial society, people sometimes just hang on a corner or sit vacantly, it is striking that in a society which offers many alternatives, people will consent to drive vacantly but not refreshingly—woe betide the careless or unspry pedestrian or bicyclist who gets in the way of industrial workers pouring out of the factory parking lots or white-collar workers coming home on a throughway. The human waste here is most important, but the waste of resources and land, the roadside *dreck,* the highways which eat space as railroad yards even in St. Louis or Chicago never did, are not negligible even in a hugh rich country.

Where the husband goes off with the car to work—and often, in the vicious circle created by the car, there is no other way for him to travel—the wife is frequently either privatized at home or to escape isolation must take a job which will help support her own car. Whereas the rental courts of developments like Park Forest provide companionship for the stranded wives—companionship which, given the age and sex homogeneity, is sometimes oppressive—other suburbs are so built and so psychologically "unsociometric" as to limit neighboring and leave many women to the company of Mary Margaret McBride and Arthur Godfrey. Indeed, in a few instances of interviewing in the morning in new suburbs south of Chicago, I have been struck by the eagerness of the housewives to talk to somebody (and not only to a man!) who is not a salesman—once they can be weaned away from the TV which amuses them as a kind of vicarious baby sitter. It is not only the visiting intellectual who finds the lives of these women empty, their associations fragmentary. My colleagues, Donald Horton and R. Richard Wohl, speak of the "parasocial intimacy" they attain with the celebrities of the TV variety shows. The women themselves, if at all sensitive or well educated, complain of having their contacts limited to their young children and to a few other housewives in the same boat. And, as a result of efforts to understand the extraordinary philoprogenitiveness of the suburban middle classes (a theme recurred to below), I have come to entertain the suspicion that, once started on having children, these women continue in some part out of a fear of the emptiness of life without children and of the problems they would face of relating themselves to their menfolk without the static, the noise, the pleasures, the "problems" that the presence of children provides.

The children themselves, in fact, before they get access to a car, are captives of their suburb, save for those families where the housewives surrender continuity in their own lives to chauffeur their children to lessons, doctors, and other services which could be reached via public transport in the city. In the suburban public schools, the young are captives, too, dependent on whatever art and science and general liveliness their particular school happens to have—again contrast the metropolis, with its choice of high schools, as most notably in New York.

Uneven Distribution of Leisure

Let me stress again that the themes I am discussing are peculiar neither to the United States nor to the twentieth century. Just as cities are older than industry so are suburbs, their splendors, and miseries. It is the democratization and exten-

sion of the phenomena I am describing, and the resultant constriction of alternatives, which give them a new and cumulative quality. The modern suburb is the
product of the car, the five-day week, and the "bankers' hours" of the masses.
As hours drop further, we can anticipate that still fewer families with children
will willingly live in the city. Exceptions would be cities like Minneapolis where
the inhabitants can focus their leisure around their cottages on nearby lakes. But
the same developments which have reduced hours for those white-collar and
factory workers who do not go in for "moonlighting" or extra jobs have in turn
put additional pressure on the still limited leisure of certain professional groups.
These latter, in one way or another, cater to those whose enhanced income and
leisure time allows them greatly to increase their consumption of services.
People, that is, can now afford both the time and money for better medical care,
more professional advice (therapeutic and otherwise), additional schooling, and
so on. And the professions and service trades that supply these wants do not
benefit from automation. Thus, the very developments that have increased the
leisure of the masses have greatly reduced that of certain of the classes: Doctors,
civil servants, teachers, school and college administrators, and some groups of
managers and intellectuals work almost as long hours as steelworkers did in the
nineteenth century. While some of these cadres, notably the doctors, have
enough of a monopoly position to earn high incomes in partial revenge for being
overworked, others, notably the civil servants and teachers, are poorly paid both
in money and time. It is these groups who are becoming the principal victims of
the anti-industrial or leisure revolution.

Yet these victims, too, live in the suburbs where they are exposed to the
styles of life of neighbors with at least equal incomes and a far easier schedule—
neighbors, moreover, who need never bring work home at night. This developing
pattern of uneven distribution of leisure has not been channeled into political
slogans. We do not hear cries for the doctors of the world to unite and throw off
their patients (a good many of whom have no better or more socially mobile
ways to spend their time than by absorbing doctors' time!). Few today would
begrudge the masses their claims both on the landscape and on services; but few
have asked what this portends for the leisure of the servicers. Even now, school
superintendents sometimes poignantly say they should never have gotten
married and had children, for they must continuously serve other families and
other children. Nor can such a group partially make it up to their families
through the status and ease that money can buy as, for example, do busy
surgeons or top executives. Ministers and rabbis, too, are victims of the suburban
style in "belongingness"; and they are likewise unprotected by celibacy from
having their own families wish they were in some other line of work.

The Dilemma of Professionals

How do people feel who live in the suburbs without the comforts and indul-
gences the ads tell them they ought to have—and not only the ads, but the

"propaganda of the deed" of their neighbors and their neighbors' children? Visitors to the metropolis have often been struck by the contrast of Gold Coast and slum, of majesty and misery. Suburban contrasts in housing and decor are less stark; majesty rides less high and misery less low. Yet, just because the suburb doesn't present poverty and deprivation as a given, the less self-evident lack of privileges must sometimes rankle and smolder. This is true even though some middle-class suburbanites, weary of the time on their hands, no doubt envy the doctor his busy rounds and his unquestioned usefulness.

Thus it would seem that a polarization is occurring between those who are dispensable to their jobs, and who therefore have a lot of time off, and those who, precisely as a result of this development, have no time off. A hundred years ago, doctors took it easy. In those days few could afford their services or were educated enough to recognize and discover symptoms; today illness is felt to be arbitrary, not one of the givens of life. A hundred years ago, civil servants took it easy: Their jobs were sometimes sinecures for impecunious writers. Today city and suburban officials, planners, highway engineers, and National Park personnel struggle in vain to cope with the problems created by mobile masses of Americans. The struggle is similar to that of a permissive mother with a brood of willful, well-fed, and not wholly socialized children. In the novels of Trollope and other nineteenth-century novelists we glimpse this vanished world in which professional people led a leisurely existence. Today this is available only to those who can turn a deaf ear to importunate clients and customers, to colleaguial pressures, and to their own ambitions.

Of course, I have minimized in this account the fact that doctors and other professionals are often among the happy few who enjoy their work. They like the constellation of activities they perform; they find their colleagues and sometimes their clients stimulating; in the best case, they regard their work as play, with the freedom and creativity of the best play. We cannot speak of "overwork" where the task and the pace are freely chosen—even if there are included some inevitable marginal increments of boredom and compulsion. Yet we must also recognize both that many intellectuals and professional people have entered their careers under some compulsion—even though their horizons are wider than those of most farmers and factory workers—and that the developments here discussed have sometimes trapped them beyond the point of no return. Their image of the career may have been formed on an older, less harrassed model. Furthermore, they may have chosen their careers, in part at least, out of such factors as a distaste for business and industry and ethical, ideological, or snobbish scruples against big business rather than out of a positive pleasure in, for example, scientific work. They may find themselves, then, in a quasi-big business of their own, but with none of the protections big business can give. They may retain the illusion of setting their own pace whereas in actuality the traffic sets it for them. In rejecting industry and commerce, only to be plunged right back into it as is the case with many professors and physicians, they resemble the suburbanite who flees the city and has it catch up with him.

Suburbia's Positive and Negative Aspects

Our Center for the Study of Leisure has been conducting studies of limited scope in several Chicago suburbs in an effort, *inter alia,* to see what happens to people who leave the city for the suburbs in terms of new commitments and new demands. We have also done a very inconclusive study of how people in the city spend their week ends. We have the impression that the suburbanite, tied to his house as the doctor is to his practice, may actually be less likely to take off for a week end in the country than the urban dweller whose janitor can look after his apartment and even the cat. Indeed, it is the city people, freed by industrialism from long hours of grinding work, who (along, of course, with an ample supply of untied suburbanites) make up a large proportion of the outboard population of our lakes and rivers and of the thirty-five million fishermen—more than twice the number of those urban sportsmen, the bowlers. Although air-conditioning makes even the most humid and dirty city potentially habitable, people can't wait to leave town on week ends and during the summer, even though in many parts of the country it means spewing the city into the countryside and fighting with like-minded crowds for space on roads, lakes, and at motels.

As I have indicated, I believe that snobbery and imitation of the rich play a declining part in this exodus to the suburbs and that the quiet revolt against the city and industrialism plays an increasing part. I would argue that there is often less "front" in the new suburbs than in equivalent sections of a metropolis, and less pressure for a lace-curtain life concealing back-stage scrimping and meanness than there once was. People do not usually learn the idea of a garden suburb either from British models or Mumford or Clarence Stein: The idea, in its uncomplicated forms, is an omnipresent dream, carrying overtones of the Bible, peasant life and folk imagery. The urban wish for contact with nature has been crystallized for many Americans around the habits of the British gentry and their middle-class imitators. But, more modest than the aspidistra-lovers of the London suburbs, we prefer not to give fancy names to our own "villas," but to let this dumb show be done for us by the realtors. In the Chicago area, for instance, a great many suburbs have either "Park" or "Forest" in their names, and two of them have both! Furthermore, social mobility means that many, perhaps most urban dwellers will have suburban relatives or friends. The mass production of suburbs, especially in the postwar years, has made them accessible to almost everyone. Only in the rural and impoverished parts of the South and Great Plains farming regions are we likely to find many people who do not know anybody who lives in a suburb and have never had occasion to visit one. Beyond that, the vicarious socialization of Americans into the experiences of consumption they are about to have is the continuous task of the mass media. Many of these, and at a variety of income levels, are devoted to expounding the suburban way of life directly in ads and features; other media are indirect vehicles for suburban styles in the homes pictured in stories, the sport shirts worn, and the idols of consumption portrayed. The whole American ethos, which once revolved about the dialectic of pure country versus wicked but exciting city, seems to me now aerated by the suburban outlook. This produces an homogenization of both city and country, but without full integration.

While on the whole the lower-middle- and middle-income suburbs sponsor the relaxed life, there is one area where they impose an imperative which many city dwellers have not met, namely that of having some sort of garden—less as a cultural amenity than as a minimum contribution to civic decency: A kind of compulsory outdoor housekeeping. Indeed, in the study of gardening in two Chicago suburbs conducted by our Center for the Study of Leisure we gained the impression that garden clubs were not extremely active in either one (though we have found very active and prestigeful clubs on the North Shore); garden clubs are much more characteristic of older communities, where they represent a familiar activity of some of the established families, rather than of the new suburbs, where gardening must compete with many other hobbies and activities, both outdoor and indoor. We found in Fairlawn, a new developer's suburb, for example, that to many housewives the garden was simply one more chore. It represented neither a contrast with the asphalt jungle of the city, nor a pleasure in growing things, nor a rage for order. It was rather a tax imposed by neighborhood consciousness—the neighbors often being interpreted as more concerned and censorious than they, for the most part, were. Thus we find that many people who have moved newly to the suburbs to escape the city come without awareness of the constraints they will find—or mistakenly interpret—in the suburb. Like the appointment in Samara, they meet pressures they had thought to leave behind, though altered in form and impact.

One of these pressures, already adverted to, is the metropolis itself; its traffic, its ethnic minorities, and its tax rates tend to catch up with them. The waves of succession within the city proper do not halt at its boundaries, and many old and established suburbs are finding themselves cut in two by freeways and by the new kinds of people they bring. In this situation, some of the old kinds of people are among those tempted to become exurbanites, putting the ever-approaching city another few miles away and hoping to solve the dilemma of distance versus intimacy by a superhighway.

However, in this quandary the emphasis on superhighways—and on supercars which require them—takes on much of the lunatic quality of an arms race. As highways get bigger and better, they invite more cars, destroy what undeveloped and unschematized country (or central city) remains, and require still more highways in an unending spiral.

Suburban Styles of Life and Thought

People have been drilled by industrialism in the values of efficiency—narrowly defined in terms of speed, performance, and a kind of streamlined look (what Jacques Barzun has referred to as "America's Romance with Practicality"). Thus even when they flee from the cities and the style of life industrialism has brought about, they cannot change the style of thought which sees the solution to ribbon developments in stretching them still further until our East and West coasts threaten to become continuous roadside slums.

What is true of the planning, or lack of it, of our road-centered culture as a whole is also true of domestic architecture. Efficiency here is less stark—and consequently often less attractive—since it must compete with traditional definitions of a suburban free-standing home. But, as many architects have pointed out, the interiors are highly modern in the sense of mechanization. Indeed, one reason why husbands have been willing to become domesticated is that they have been promoted from dishwashers to operators of dishwashers. Similarly, they use power mowers to give crew cuts to handkerchief-sized lawns and pierce their wives' and neighbors' ears with the screams of high-fidelity music. The open plan of the very newest ranch-style homes puts the TV set on a swivel in the center. Here it can be seen from all parts of the house so that urban news, fashions, gossip, and jokes can circulate in the home throughout the daily cycle of the members of the family. But all these improvements are bought at the expense of space for the individual whose bedroom in the suburban development is often smaller than in city tenements. This is especially true, as Albert Roland of *Household* magazine has pointed out to me, of the newest suburban homes. These have both a family room and a living room. The latter, like the old parlor, is used only for state occasions; the family room is big enough for games, the TV, an inside barbecue, and general clutter.

Nor does the lawn or backyard provide a bounteous free space in most of the new developments. In comparison with the size and cost of the house, plots are small (much as they have traditionally been in midwestern cities where people wanted to avoid the row house but not to be too far from their next-door neighbors). Moreover, the fact that there is both a front and a backyard—the latter being, in many developments, the "family room" and the former the "parlor"—means that what space there is becomes divided. And just as the homes have no interstitial spaces, no nooks and crannies, so the lots have no texture taken individually or together. I keep asking myself what the lots will look like when the explosion of our population doubles the numbers in the suburban hegira without, in all probability, increasing proportionately the services that our new expectations crave. Will houses and lots get smaller when people can no longer spread further afield? People have been moving to the suburbs in many cases in pursuit of an inchoate dream of spaciousness. They have looked for a release from urban tensions, from crowded and ugly schools, from indoors. And ordinarily this release has more than compensated for losses in urban qualities which are difficult to sense or describe—qualities of possibility, often, rather than of actual use. What will occur when the urban qualities have been dissipated, while the suburban ones elude all but the rich?

Such questions assume, as I have here been doing, that Americans have ceased being socially inventive outside the corporate or military spheres. They assume that we will not discover the governmental or voluntary channels either to give many people alternative satisfactions to large families or to create forms of life and livelihood appropriate to another age of population expansion—this time with no frontiers left. Certainly, there is now a kind of private inventiveness in the suburbs among people who, having lost "the track of generations" and traditional standards of judgment and taste, are somehow managing, with ambivalent aid from the media, to create new forms and styles. The leaders of Park Forest and several other new communities, surrounded by others as green as they, often managed to develop some communal decencies and controls; in that sense, the town-meeting spirit is far from moribund. It is easy to see the negative and ironical features of the suburbs—harder to see emergent crystallizations.

But one trouble is that the suburbs, like the families within them, can scarcely control their own immediate environs, let alone the larger metropolitan and national orbits that impinge on them and decide their eventual atmosphere. And here is where the suburbanites' immense liking for Ike is portentous. It expresses the wish of so many of the college seniors mentioned above that civics and the Community Chest replace politics; it expresses the hope, built into the very structure of credit and the additive-extrapolative style of thought, that nothing serious will occur, that everything will go on as before. And it expresses this hope, of course, at the very moment when private decisions—irresponsibly influenced—to buy or not to buy, to propagate or not to propagate store up our destinies (quite apart from the similar activities of the rest of our small planet). In interviews done in Chicago suburbs by Louis Harris before the 1956 elections, he asked potential voters how they felt about a part-time, golf-playing president. Many were indignant, saying they would play golf too if they had such problems—though when asked to name serious problems facing the country, they could often get no further than high taxes. Plainly, Ike's complacencies mirrored and supported their own (Eisenhower, of course, like most anyone in Washington, is far less complacent than these constituencies), and their defenses against untoward apprehension were too great to allow thought for the morrow.

The Aimless Quality of Suburban Life

In the days of Lincoln Steffens and later, people emphasized the "shame of the cities," and in the 1920's major novelists emphasized the constraints of small-town and occasionally of small-suburban life. Today, the comparable worry, in the books dealing with the suburbs, is conformity—*Point of No Return,* with its concern for place and competition, strikes a somewhat older note; writers point to the uniformity of the ranch style, the ever-present television antennae, the lamp, if not the crack, in the picture window—which usually provides a view of the nearly treeless street, the cars, and someone else's picture window. Actually, uniformity and conformity are quite different matters as Georg Simmel has observed in his essay on "Fashion." The former may dictate to men only in inessentials, whereas the latter involves some psychological mechanism. And the conformity of the new suburbs is, in some important ways, far less stringent than that of the old; if it is not quite the case that "anything goes," lots of things do go which once would, if known, have brought ostracism. If one does not seek to force the new suburbanite back across the ethnic tracks he has just crossed, he is quite tolerant, even bland. If he is political at all—rather than parochially civic-minded, tending to a "garden" which includes the local schools and waterworks—he is apt to be an Eisenhower Republican, seldom informed, rarely angry, and only spasmodically partisan.

No, what is missing in suburbia, even where the quality of life has not overtly deteriorated, is not the result of claustrophobic conformity to others' sanctions. Rather, there would seem to be an aimlessness, a pervasive low-keyed unpleasure. This cannot be described in terms of traditional sorrows but is one on which many observers of the American scene and the American visage have commented, notably Erich Fromm in *The Sane Society* and the Goodmans in *Communitas*. For millions of people, work no longer provides a central focus for life; and the breadwinner is no longer the chief protagonist in the family saga —just as Saturday night no longer provides a central focus for festivity. In fact, the decentralization of leisure in the suburbs is not only spatial but temporal, as evenings from Thursday through Sunday are oriented to play rather than work and are not individually accented or collectively celebrated.

At the same time, leisure has not picked up the slack—as, in earlier writings, I was too sanguine that it might. Whatever balances of work and play might have been possible for preindustrial man, postindustrial man is keyed, as I remarked earlier, to greater expectations. He has learned more "needs" and cannot in any case reconstitute the institutions industrialism destroyed. It is almost inconceivable, for example, to imagine a reconstitution of the folk arts which everywhere—in Nigeria as in New Orleans, in Damascus as in Tennessee—prove fragile in the face of mass-produced music and imagery. In *Communitas*, the Goodmans devoted much ingenuity to suggesting how, in their New Commune, work could be made more varied and interesting: By job rotation on a grand scale, by alternating supervision and apprenticeship, by scrutiny of all work in terms of means as well as ends. But automation as presently interpreted moves us yet further away from such a re-examination of work routines, even though, were our values different, it could provide an opportunity for eliminating monotonous work and bringing far more variety and spark into it.

The Future of Leisure

I recently had the opportunity to talk about the future of leisure with some thoughtful union leaders and adult educators. They were looking forward, in dismay as much as in hope, to a far shorter working week and a less demanding working day. They were asking specialists on leisure how these vacua of time and energy could be filled with more creativity and less boredom. They were saddling leisure with the burden which indeed it did carry for a small minority of the leisure class in some aristocratic eras—the burden of supporting life's total commitment and significance. Suggestions were made for better adult education courses, even for sabbaticals for everybody or short periods of residence in an Aspen-like setting. And one leader spoke of efforts to link workers possessing underused craft skills with groups such as nursery schools possessing substandard facilities—groups which could greatly benefit from the energies and capabilities of people who would in their free time build jungle gyms, chairs, or other needed equipment. But it was clear from the tone of the meeting that these notions, valuable as they were, could not even claim the status of palliatives. It was not that they could not (given workers as they now are) complete with commercial recreation or polishing the car, but also that they did not provide the "moral equivalent of work." We can see in the bored teen-agers who don't like school, and are already sated with sex unmitigated by love, what leisure is like for most people when life lacks the accent and structure given it by work—not simply stand-by "work" but some effortful and periodically challenging activity.

In the studies of unemployed men made during the great depression, the observation of the demoralizing nature of being without work was often made, but it was sometimes assumed that this was mostly a matter of status and of poverty which forced the unemployed man to hang uselessly about the house. And in the studies of men who have retired, the same theme recurs. They are demoralized because the job gave status and income, and also because they grew up in a work-minded era and were not prepared for the age of leisure. I myself had thought that when a whole generation had been reared which was not driven to work by the agreed-upon motives of hunger and gain—often unconsciously driven because work-mindedness was instilled, so to speak, with mother's bottle feeding on schedule—such people could retire more comfortably than the elderly now do because they would have been preparing for it all life long. Presently, however, I am inclined to believe that work is still necessary because our inventiveness has not found ways of relating masses of men to creative activity or to each other outside of work. Though the artist, of whatever sort and for whom there is no real division between work and play, indicates what may someday be possible, even the artist, whatever his ideology of *l'art pour l'art,* needs usually to feel he is being of some use—if only in acting out a counterpoint to Philistine utilitarianism.

With these considerations in mind, I asked the union leaders whether they might not do more for leisure by increasing the pressure on management for meaningful work—that is, for reorganization of the factory along the lines sketched by the Goodmans in the New Commune—than by direct focus on leisure itself. I argued that if work were more demanding (without being, other than occasionally, totally exhausting) leisure would present slightly less unmanageable prospects. It could at least begin to be seen as discontinuous with work and could be enlivened by the vigor and play of mind and muscle at work. If men, instead of standing at a row of dials or on an assembly line, could have the freedom of the plant that maintenance men have, and their opportunity to set their own schedules; if they could work under pressure at times, without being charged with rate-busting, they might then leave their work without feeling resentful of industrialism, only to pepper away at deer with elephant rifles, or to seek a second job sometimes allowing independence from a boss without diminishing monotony. I stressed this because of my belief that the boundaries which once separated our problems from each other (as other boundaries separated city from country, men from women, middle class from lower class, sociology from politics, and economics from anthropology) have been disappearing, along with many forms of parochialism and isolationism.

City planners are, of course, among the few people who are forced to know this already, try as some of them do to act like highway engineers or administrative efficiency experts. Some of them know that the motives which once gave structure to both work and leisure, and the interchanges and journeys between them, have also been disappearing, even though millions of people, shorn of other rationales for activity, still go after money. At present they do this not in the form of capital but in the form of consumer goods. Our new middle-class large families are, in part, an effort to fill this gap. Similarly, our suburbs are an effort to build a life not based on work but instead on the family and on voluntary associations. It is surely an advance to prefer children to capital gains, and suburban *Gemütlichkeit* to urban pavements (though, as British planners discovered in building the New Towns and as writers for the *Architectural Review* have insisted, there were values concealed in the most seemingly depressed urban conglomerations which were lost in the move to the more hygienic and aseptic planned communities—much as farmers for a long time failed to realize that worms and other "varmint" were essential to a well-nourished soil). But the advances cannot be consolidated unless they are made on a broader front; otherwise, people may quickly oscillate again towards such apparent security as industrialism gave them. Faced with the mounting depreciations of the crowded suburbs and aware of their own powerlessness, they may turn to strong authority which promises to clean up the already foreseeable mess. Even now, drivers in a traffic jam, frustrated by each other's presence, are not the most amiable of men. This, despite the fact that, once on the move again, it is largely the sense of moving rather than anything they actively do or enjoy which gives them pleasure and release.

Tensions on the Suburban Scene

One of the findings of our gardening study comes to mind here, and it may serve as a coda to these adumbrations. I have remarked above on the tendency for families in the new suburb of Fairlawn to assume that their neighbors, who were in fact quite tolerant, were putting pressure on them to have not merely a passable garden but a good one. Actually, the neighbor's visual sense was not that highly developed, nor their emulative sense either. They were tolerant of each other's gardens as of each other's life in general. I asked myself then what was the source of the extensive misinterpretation which led to such comments as the following by a Fairlawn housewife. She described to the interviewer an ambitious plan for a rose garden and large beds of flowers all around the house as follows:

> I really hate gardening; we both do. My husband never plays golf any more and we do nothing all weekend but work in the garden. I mean work.

I recalled analogous comments made by students who were working allegedly to prepare for an exam which their intelligence told them they could not easily fail; I recalled other such comments by business and professional men who created anxieties in their work in order to give it drama and bite. I realized that, since we are not really attached to anything we are doing, we look for spurs when life no longer automatically provides them. Perhaps the housewife just quoted cannot make herself (or her spouse) work at all without picturing dire consequences for failure. Or perhaps she has in this case simply projected her own moralism or malice into her neighbors—possibly also as a part of an internal family argument with an indifferent or indolent husband. Games, the arts, conversation are all activities which have institutionalized short bursts of effort as the price both of pleasure and performance. The suburbs, however, in seeking to take the place of the city, provide insufficient comparable agendas, and housewives such as those we saw who gardened with neither pleasure nor skill still clung to the demand that neighbors and nature seemed to make.

I have lost any sanguinity that they will learn better simply by sticking it out; they may only get more bored, more destructive. Their pleasure in flowers, or in the arrangements of nature, cannot be very intense if they put up, as they seem ready enough to do, with the visual blight of so much of our suburbscape, the roads that take them there, the cars they drive in. I am not speaking of "taste," in the sense of high taste, but rather of the quality with which visual experience is assimilated. And I am certainly not speaking of the uniformity of the Levittowns as such. The row houses in Baltimore or Philadelphia are often handsome in ways which our suburbs, varied in a most studied fashion, fail to achieve. In the course of the industrial revolution and the rise of the middle classes, both elite taste and traditional taste declined. Today, despite frequent improvement in advertising and magazine layout, in interior decoration, and in corporate and public building, the sense for visual imagery of Americans remains stunted, and the children of the suburbs grow up accepting the neat, the new, the shiny, but with minimal awareness of vista, proportion, or independent critical judgment of the look of life around them.

Conclusion

Writing ten years ago about the Goodmans' book, [Percival and Paul Goodman, *Communitas: Means of Livelihood and Ways of Life,* 1947] I was up against the perennial planners problem: How to get from here to there, when "here" is the omnipresent educator, the agent of socialization. Yet, as makers of goods and ideas know, Americans are almost too ready to abandon one thing for another, provided they are persuaded by the media or friends that the other is somehow "better" or, preferably, "the best," along a dimension which is already given. To be sure, the range of such persuasion is not terribly wide, and it is wider of course in inessentials or externals, though the last ten years have seen radical changes in food habits, men's clothes, child rearing, and other (one might suppose) tenacious things. More problematic is the persuasion itself. When mobilized for the planners' good ends it is frequently self-defeating because it almost inevitably uses the given means such as appeals to snobbery or to a fake efficiency. Yet the fear of this problem, with its practical and ethical dilemmas, seems to me at present to have intimidated thinking about what the good ends are. Thus, even if people could be persuaded, there is nothing to persuade them of. Plans, as history occasionally shows, have their own persuasive power, particularly in unexpected historical junctures. Many Americans will soon discover the loss of urban and suburban texture and might then be ready to do something, were a model available. The social processes I have touched upon in this paper are moving people into the service trades and professions and out of industry and farming. We need to find meaningful work for the displaced ones rather than locating still more of them in selling, public relations, and looking after each other. The country can "use" poets, painters, planners, and prophets in virtually unlimited amounts. With poets in recent years the country has not done too badly; with painters—despite all I have said about visual blight and the country of the blind—not too badly, either. But planners and prophets?

The Image of Suburbia

by Robert C. Wood*

Suburbia as Looking Glass

Strictly speaking, suburbs are places and suburbanites are people. Even more strictly speaking, suburbs are places in the country immediately outside a city and suburbanites are the inhabitants of that country. Suburbs depend upon the special technological advances of the age: the automobile and rapid transit line, asphalt pavement, delivery trucks, septic tanks, water mains, and motor-driven pumps. Suburbanites have habits which distinguish them more or less sharply from other Americans: they are commuters, they tend to own their own homes, which have at least some access to open space, and they have more children than the average American family. These definitions and characteristics indicate in concrete ways what suburbs and suburbanites are.

They do not, however, explain *why* suburbs exist, or, aside from simple progress, what accounts for the extraordinary explosion of our large cities into the countryside. To understand the underlying motives and aspirations which gave momentum to the massive shift of population another definition is necessary. We have to explain an abstraction, a concept of the mind, with elusive and subtle connotations. We have to explain "suburbia."

The most fashionable definition of suburbia today is that it is a looking glass in which the character, behavior, and culture of middle class America is displayed. When we look at suburbs we see our homes; when we look at suburbanites we see ourselves. Suburbia, according to this interpretation, reflects with fidelity modern man, his way of living, his institutions and beliefs, his family and his social associations. Because forty-seven million of us live in suburbs—more than in the cities or in isolated towns or on the farms—the suburbanite is, by statistical definition, the average American. Because over twelve million of us have moved to the suburbs in the last ten years—marking the greatest migration in the shortest time of the nation's history—the suburban trend should typify our contemporary way of life.

Many of the specialists who have looked carefully into the mirror find a man who is not appealing. The old images of national life seem to them to have

*Robert C. Wood, *Suburbia: Its People and Their Politics* (Boston: Houghton, Mifflin Company, 1958), pp. 3-19. Reprinted by permission of the publisher.

disappeared; the stern Puritan, the sturdy yeoman, the hard-working capitalist are gone. In their place is a prototype whom it is difficult to idealize: a man without direction or ambition except for his desire for a certain portion of material security, a man so conscious of his fellows that he has no convictions of his own. Lacking the stern code of conduct of the "inner directed" man of the nineteenth century, separated from the Protestant ethic that maintained individuality fifty years ago, the suburbanite seeks direction from a passing parade of "experts" who, in the rapid succession of changing fashions, dictate the design of his house, the education of his children, the choice of his friends, and the use of his income. He willingly turns the direction of community affairs over to others. But since his neighbors are just as uncertain as he is, few real individualists appear to guide civic destinies. In the suburbs, in the opinion of its prominent investigators, the modern American exchanges individuality, privacy, the certain satisfactions of pride of craftsmanship and work well done, for something obscurely defined as the social ethic, being a good fellow, and group cooperation.

In this context, the suburb is the home of the modern man, the big organization on his doorstep. Suburban culture and the pattern of suburban life are designed to intensify the pressures on the individual. They encourage conformity, and subtly rearrange the use of space and time, the relations of the family, the activities of social and political organizations for the higher purpose of "the group." Each characteristic and institution of suburban life bears witness to the fact that David Riesman's lonely crowd is everywhere.

Thus, John Seeley and his associates point out that the suburbanite lives not in a house that expresses his individuality or that blends landscape and architecture to emphasize man's oneness with nature. Instead, he builds a house which expresses values of real estate experts but never his own, or he settles in a big development constructed on too little land. In either case, except for trivial detail, he builds his house as much like his neighbor's as possible. He whistles up the bulldozers, in John Keats' words, "to knock down all the trees, bat the lumps off the terrain, and level the ensuing desolation." He becomes lost in "squads and platoons" of little boxes on concrete slabs each surrounded by "a patch of bilious sod and two rusty dwarf cedars struggling for life beside each identical doorstep." If income permits, the houses are larger, though their lots are proportionately the same, and crammed with mechanical conveniences that testify to a pre-occupation with consumption. They are arranged to "stage" elaborate displays of entertainment, built to encourage family and neighborhood sociability, erected as symbols of material well-being. The disappearance of clean styles of architecture, the rise of the modified Cape Cod—ranch-type Colonials, their uniform reproduction row on row, the violence done to the natural terrain—all these are taken to document "togetherness," the new social ethic in practice.

The use of time in the suburbs is described as a further indication of the new

America. Most observers find an implacable array of schedules which seem to testify to the suburbanite's inability to live as an individual and as he chooses. The commuter schedule for the husband, the nursery and social schedule for the wife, the school day for the growing child, these govern suburban life relentlessly. There are no longer any options, but instead unbreakable patterns for the day, the week, the year, and the generation. Time spent going to and from work, time spent in hauling children, time spent in class, the weekday for work, the weekend for "career maneuvering" or "improving" social status, all are by the clock. To the reporters of Crestwood Heights, one of the suburbs most meticulously observed, time is apparently the master of each and every inhabitant. Endlessly active, constantly harassed, the suburbanite hurries everywhere, caught up in a chain of events never of his own making but from which he cannot withdraw. He is plunged into a "hotbed of participation," an endless circle of meetings, appointments, arrivals, departures, and consultations.

Suburban institutions provide further ammunition for the looking-glass theory. They are shown as monuments of a society in which each member is attuned to the others but never to himself. The school emerges as the all-important focus of existence, and from the school, to children and parents alike, comes the constant message of "life adjustment." As "opinion leaders," teachers strive to inculcate cooperation, belongingness, togetherness. Courses aim at "socializing" the child through a process by which he learns specific skills at the same time that he is taught to use them only in an overtly friendly manner. Competition is subdued; so is individuality; the cry is for a common outlook, and discipline is achieved by indirect measures of ostracism. The generalization has even been made that by the time he gets to college, a suburban student chooses his career in business administration or science, where there are human relations to be cultivated or where there are facts, but where there are never values.

The aim of learning to get along with others, of advancing oneself only as a member of the group, infects, it is said, family life and leisure hours. The commuter-father is no longer the figure of authority; stern measures of discipline are not countenanced, and even if they were, the father is not home enough to use them in the proper time and place. Although family life is "important," and love and constant association are expected, the means for holding the family together are obscure. It is left to the mother and the schools, and the experts on whom both rely, to rear the child and run the suburb. Educated women, wanting motherhood but expecting something more, anxious to put their talents to use beyond the family circle, are in charge. Skipping from one meeting to another, indulging or wanting to indulge in extramarital affairs, ceaselessly expunging their feelings of guilt by over-protecting their children, they rule suburbia. So the desires and demands of children—space for their play, their training, their future careers, their happiness—become the predominant force in suburbia.

The decline of individuality is also found, according to most reports, in adult associations and activities. Suburban friendships are determined, by and large, by the physical layout of the neighborhoods in which they take place, or dictated by career maneuvering necessary in big-organization office politics. In the politics of public life, suburbanites are passive consumers of the national issues of the day or "inside-dopesters" on what the issues really are. On the local scene their political activity is frenzied but ineffective, for suburbanites are always ultimately manipulated by the shrewd, calculating developer, the old residents, or the school superintendent.

From this pattern of character, space, time, and the interaction of these institutions and beliefs, most observers go on to say, has come a new type of culture. Self-consciously friendly, in constant association, afraid or unable to differentiate themselves from their neighbors, the suburban residents form a classless society. Suburbia is a melting pot of executives, managers, white-collar workers, successful or unsuccessful, who may be distinguished only by subtle variations in the cars they drive, the number of bedrooms in their houses, or the tables they set. Their consumption is inconspicuous because they cannot deviate too far from the standards of their neighbors—but for the same reason it has a common quality. It is never ceasing, and for almost all suburbanites, time payments for purchases in an already overextended budget have replaced the savings account.

By this interpretation the life of suburbanites is "outgoing" in the sense that, lacking internal resources, they search for status and reassurance from the group around them, and that life is pathetic in the same sense. A fundamental transformation of American society is in full swing, and since the suburbs are seen to represent the transformation with such fidelity, they should be taken as the symbol and sign of the future.

Holdouts in Suburbia

Intriguing as the looking-glass interpretation is, it cannot be taken as a precise definition of suburbia. It is more a commentary on middle class Americans wherever they live: on the farms now equipped with central heating and television, within the city limits, in Peyton Place, Middletown updated, or the growing Southern town absorbing the second industrial revolution in the United States. As a generalization, the group-man theory is far too sweeping to take into account the suburbs which are not residential. It cannot explain the industrial suburb, where more people work than live, the slum suburb, deserted by the middle class and fallen on evil days, the racetrack suburb, the honky-tonk suburb of night clubs, amusement parks and used-car lots. It deals only with the dormitory suburb, and principally with the better type of dormitory suburb.

Even in the residential suburb, there are limitations to the theory. Against the broad wave of mass culture, mass values, and mass society, there is at least one stubborn holdout. While residential suburban living and individual suburbanites may represent modern character and behavior, their suburban governments do not. They join the other suburban political units around our large cities in clinging persistently to the independence they received when they were isolated villages and hamlets in a rustic countryside. If the suburb is a brand new development taking the place of forest or potato farm, the inhabitants insist on creating governments modeled after their older autonomous neighbors. These rural neighbors, far from acquiescing to the cult of size, turn their backs on progress and resist the influences of modernity. Though they accept the homes of the organization man, they insist on retaining the legal form and the public institutions which are relics of a bygone age.

This superimposition of provincial government on cosmopolitan people provides a strange pattern of incongruity. Within this single economic and social complex we have come to call a metropolitan area, hundreds and hundreds of local governments jostle one another about. Counties overlie school districts, which overlie municipalities, which overlie sanitary and water districts, which sometimes overlie townships and villages. Except for the special-purpose "districts," each suburban government maintains its own police force, its fire station, its health department, its library, its welfare service. Each retains its authority to enact ordinances, hold elections, zone land, raise taxes, grant building licenses, borrow money, and fix speed limits.

The spectacle of these ancient jurisdictions careening merrily on their way is often amusing and more frequently disturbing. By ordinary standards of effective, responsible public services, the mosaic of suburban principalities creates governmental havoc. Across a typical suburban terrain, twenty or thirty or fifty volunteer fire departments buy equipment and, with varying degrees of efficiency, put out fires. A welter of semi-professional police forces, usually poorly equipped and inadequately staffed, jealously compete or lackadaisically cooperate, uncertain of the limits of their jurisdiction. Independent school systems build costly plants, some crammed to capacity, others with excess space. In one municipality the water table dips perilously low; in another, foresighted or fortunate enough to have access to a reservoir, sprinklers turn all summer long. And, always, for suburban governments taken together, there is the extra and apparently unnecessary cost of doing individually what might be done collectively: the additional expense of making separate purchases without benefit of . quantity discounts, of administrative and political overhead, of holding local elections and hiring city managers, of reporting, accounting, and auditing these separate activities.

The anachronisms of suburban governments have long been apparent and long decried. For almost half a century, the conditions of inefficiency, confusion, duplication, overla)pping and waste have been under fire. For at least twenty-five years, reform movement after reform movement has moved against the antiquated political structures, proposing their consolidation, advancing one scheme after another to bring together their conflicting activities. Again and again the call has rung out for a king-sized government to fit the king-sized metropolitan community. Some critics emphasize the inequities of tax burdens and public services among the suburbs, some point to their incapacity to solve common problems of water supply and mass transportation, some underscore the absence of a responsible region-wide political process and system of representation. All condemn the compounding of confusion which the array of municipalities, boroughs, and districts brings about as they play hob with the orderly provision of municipal services and public finance.

Yet with extraordinarily few exceptions the ranks of suburban governments hold fast. They cling to their independence, stand successfully against the demands for efficiency and economy, and resist the lure of the big organization. More numerous than at any time in our history, their boundaries bursting with new inhabitants, their administrative and tax structure apparently strained to capacity or beyond, suburban political institutions remain adamant. They reject the prospect of consolidation with the larger society; they continue to hold out when every other influence in modern life calls for their absorption.

Suburbia as Renaissance

The paradox which suburban government presents to suburban society sharply limits the theory of suburbia as the looking glass and suburbanites as the advance guard of the new America. A social order apparently built upon a commitment to the virtues of large organizations, indoctrinated to the advantages of size and scale, still tolerates tiny, ineffective governments which seem almost willfully bent on producing chaos, and which are still multiplying. As political entities, suburbs represent an order unwilling to join in the change going on about them; they flout the modern ideology attributed to suburban man.

They flout this ideology, moreover, by raising an ancient and honorable standard straight out of American political folklore. The justification of suburban legal independence rests on the classic belief in grassroots democracy, our long-standing conviction that small political units represent the purest expression of popular rule, that the government closest to home is best. The defense of suburban autonomy is that no voter is a faceless member in a political rally, but an individual citizen who knows his elected officials, can judge their performance personally and hold them accountable.

In the suburb, according to the folklore, the school board is likely to be composed of neighbors or friends, or at least friends of friends or neighbors of neighbors. Its members do not come from another part of a large city; they are available and accessible. So are the mayor, the county clerk, the commissioners, the councilmen, and selectmen. So are the chief of police, the water superintendent, the plumbing inspector, and the health officers. In this way, elected officials, bureaucrats, party leaders—the entire apparatus of democratic politics—are exposed to view, recognized and approached as they never are in a great metropolis. In politics, the suburb dwellers hold fast to a conviction that the small organization, run by a group of relatively few individuals, provides the best management of public affairs that is possible.

The strength of this conviction has been powerful enough, at least to date, to blunt the edge of all the reform efforts to bring suburban governments into the twentieth century. In spite of statistics indicating that the metropolitan area in which suburbia exists is actually a single community, in spite of the obvious organizational chaos brought on by this political multiplicity, even the most ardent efficiency expert hesitates to deny the values small governments represent. Instead of recommending outright abolition of suburban jurisdictions, he presents one ingenious scheme after another—federations, special authorities, new systems of representation, new complexities of local government—designed to provide some measure of administrative rationality while still maintaining suburban autonomy. At rock bottom he accepts the value of small size and he works to preserve the suburb as a legal entity even if its powers must be reduced in the face of the realities of the modern world.

So, as yet there is little sign that this array of small municipalities merely represents a cultural lag. On the contrary, the statistics point in exactly the opposite direction, for every census report shows more—and smaller—and more self-consciously independent suburban governments than existed ten years earlier. And those which the looking-glass theory selects as the best examples of the home of modern man are also the ones which exhibit the most independent political institutions.

There are also signs that this renaissance of small-scale autonomy is not confined to suburban governments alone. Even the most confirmed advocate of the New American Character still finds signs of small town behavior throughout the suburbs he studies. So William H. Whyte, Jr., in investigating the organization man at home, discovers two sides to every coin he examines, notes something old as well as something new, remains ambivalent in his judgment of the suburb in a way which contrasts sharply with his indictment of the organizational world in general.

Whyte's residents are, of course, transients, newcomers to the town in which they live, and they are soon to move on to other, better suburbs. Nonetheless, they try to put down roots and they succeed to some degree; even though the roots are shallow. To Whyte there is something admirable in the vigor with which they respond to the advertisements that call their suburb a friendly small town, as contrasted to the lonely big city, and in the way they work to make the advertisement a reality. The suburbanite penchant for joining his neighbors to agitate against the town hall indifference and the developer may be participation for participation's sake, but it also may express citizenship of the highest sort. Small roots are better than none, civic spirit is to be preferred to apathy, and the chance to "chew on real problems" in public affairs is desirable, for it creates allegiances that have purpose.

Whyte does not scorn community affairs then. He approves of the suburbanite's self-conscious efforts to guide his town's future, even though he is only passing through and cannot stay to enjoy it. It is still an indication of older values, however sugar-coated in new jargon, and so is the classlessness of his suburbia. The melting-pot analogy is, after all, another cherished American ideal. It seems a laudable fact that the suburb often promotes better understanding among inhabitants with different ethnic origins, religions, and backgrounds, even though they are all within the middle class, that it helps prevent the emergence of classes and furthers the ideal of equality. It is to be preferred to the jarring hostility of groups wrangling among themselves in the large cities and it is a sign of small town life as it has always been known.

The pattern of inconspicuous consumption, the web of friendship, and the outgoing life that Whyte describes also have something of the flavor of a renaissance. Although "keeping down with the Joneses" may indicate group tyranny, it is still better than keeping up with them. At least it displays disapproval of overt snobbishness and obvious symptoms of city superciliousness; it harks back once again to the frontier spirit of equality. While suburbanites should probably manage their budgets more prudently than they do, at least their desire for improvement and progress is a sturdy American trait. Even suburban friendships have their admirable qualities so far as the observers are concerned. They may be largely determined by the location of play areas, the placement of driveways and lawns, and the size of the living room, and they may impose a surveillance that makes privacy clandestine and the way of the introvert hard. But here are old-time qualities of warmth, helpfulness, and service to others. While Whyte finds pressures for benevolent conformity, he also discovers brotherhood. He sees that the church may have sacrificed theology for acceptance and the school may stress adjustment at the expense of the liberal arts, but he sees also that it is good to have churches and schools. These provide a sense of community, institutions that are socially useful, and it is not surprising that in the end Whyte speaks of his suburbanites as pioneers.

Even more impressive than the fragments of small town culture still persisting in the suburb is the ideal that every analyst of suburbia seems to cherish of what suburbia ought to be. There is a special temper in the rage which the looking-glass philosopher expresses when he uncovers the organization man at home, for to him there is a special irony and incongruity in making the suburb synonymous with modern life.

John Keats sketches the idealized suburb most clearly. Following Mary and John Drone through their weary succession of inadequate, overpriced homes in suburbs inhabited by directionless people who do not know they are unhappy, he is angry not at suburbia but at what has been done to it. He objects not a whit to the popular demand for space, for relatively small neighborhoods, for private homes, for roots, however temporary. He protests only against the degradation of these aspirations by greedy, selfish contractors and by the foolish, undisciplined residents themselves. He describes developments, and he wants communities.

Keats' prescription is not to tear suburbia apart, but to build it better. He wants homes arranged so that the illusions of privacy and aesthetics can be cultivated in small space. He wants suburbanites to join together to build libraries and swimming pools, where truly useful and common purposes are served. He would encourage the flight from the city so long as it is properly done, with taste and recognition of family budgetary limits and with awareness of the public problems to be faced. He would surround with regulations and controls the builder who remains the sturdy nineteenth century individualist and is responsible for the damage suburbs do. What suburbia ought to be, for Keats, is a carefully designed constellation of small towns, each with its own community center, each self-contained, each controlling its local affairs at the local level with polite regard for the larger region to which it belongs.

The small town, the small community, this is what seems good about the suburb to most observers, what needs to be preserved, and what the large organization should not be permitted to despoil. Spontaneous collaboration, voluntary neighborliness, purposeful participation, these are the goals of real suburbanites. And all of the observers seem to cherish the hope that in the suburbs we can re-create the small communities we have lost in our industrial sprawl since the Civil War. The irony they find is that our suburbanites do not discriminate between the type of association a small town can give and that which Madison Avenue promotes. The ambivalence of Whyte is genuine; to him suburban virtues lie in the degree to which the suburb approximates the small town, and vices lie in deviation from this ideal. The image of the small community shines through the condemnation of modern life. If it is faithful to this ideal, the suburb may save us all from the artificial group without reestablishing the unpalatable culture of the rugged individualist.

Even the harshest critic of our modern suburb is not insensitive to this appeal. Although the great organization seems essential to contemporary society, and the pressures of mass society appear overwhelming, no analysis counsels surrender. For the most pessimistic there is, it seems, still a chance for an individual to fight the organization, even if he has to cheat. And the best way to fight is on home ground where the suburbanite can try to fuse the political ideology of the small government with the social mores of the small community.

Thus, while the looking-glass theory protests the onrush of modern culture, it takes comfort in the hope that suburbia can somehow hold out against it. It is encouraged by the possibility that the suburbs may break up the sprawling metropolitan area into discrete units distributing here an industrial area, here a low-income neighborhood, here a retail center, here an exclusive residential area, but everywhere permitting a closer communion within the small localities. It applauds newspaper editorials which warn against making governments and communities "so big that no one counts" and speaks out for "the concept of people working together in identifiable units in a community with a cohesive past and future . . . of which the individual can feel a part and for the life of which he can feel a sense of participation and responsibility."

These hopes are imperfectly realized today, of course; modern circumstances always threaten them and frequently combine to subvert them. But the vision is powerful; it helps move the ordinary citizen to suburbia, the sociologist to protect it, and the political scientist to preserve it. The ancient symbol of the "republic in miniature" persists, and the suburb is its contemporary expression. For all our changes in culture and behavior, for all the heavy price we pay in inadequate local public services, nonexistent metropolitan services, and high taxes, the good life and the good government still come for us in small packages. Although minimum adjustments to the demands of urban life must be made, it seems the job of the suburb, either by social resistance or political compromise, to ensure the preservation of these values.

Suburbia, defined as an ideology, a faith in communities of limited size and a belief in the conditions of intimacy, is quite real. The dominance of the old values explains more about the people and the politics of the suburbs than any other interpretation. Fundamentally, it explains the nature of the American metropolis. It indicates why our large urban complexes are built as they are, why their inhabitants live the way they do, and why public programs are carried out the way they are. If these values were not dominant it would be quite possible to conceive of a single gigantic metropolitan region under one government and socially conscious of itself as one community. The new social ethic, the rise of the large organization, would lead us to expect this development as a natural one. The automobile, the subway, the telephone, the power line certainly make it technically possible; they even push us in this direction.

But the American metropolis is not constructed in such a way; it sets its face directly against modernity. Those who wish to rebuild the American city, who protest the shapeless urban sprawl, who find some value in the organizational skills of modern society must recognize the potency of the ideology. Until these beliefs have been accommodated reform will not come in the metropolitan areas nor will men buckle down to the task of directing, in a manner consonant with freedom, the great political and social organizations on which the nation's strength depends. A theory of community and a theory of local government are at odds with the prerequisites of contemporary life and, so far, theory has been the crucial force that preserves the suburb. There is no economic reason for its existence and there is no technological basis for its support. There is only the stubborn conviction of the majority of suburbanites that it ought to exist, even though it plays havoc with both the life and government of our urban age.

The Beer Can in the Cotton Patch

by Charles E. Silberman*

Migration to the large city has always been painful, both to the migrants and to the people among whom they settled. A good many sociologists, city planners, and others concerned with urban problems have concluded, therefore, that the difficulties Negroes are having with the city, and the city with its Negro residents, represent simply one more chapter in the long saga of urban migration—a chapter which will end as happily as the preceding ones. The foremost proponent of this point of view is Professor Philip M. Hauser, Chairman of the Sociology Department of the University of Chicago, and Director of its Population Research and Training Center. According to Professor Hauser, "The problems which confront the Negro today, although perhaps differing in degree, are essentially the same kinds of problems which confronted our migrant groups in the past," and they will be solved in essentially the same way. Professor Hauser concedes that Negro migrants do not need "Americanization," as did their European predecessors, but he argues that they *do* need "acculturation" (some professors prefer the term "urbanization" or "accommodation"). This need for acculturation, in his view, forms the heart of the Negro problem of the large city. For Negroes have "been drawn from a primitive folk culture into a metropolitan way of life" in little more than a single generation—"as severe a problem of acculturation," Hauser argues, "as any group in history has ever faced." To solve "the Negro problem," he concludes, "the older residents must teach the newcomers what is expected of them in the city," thereby equipping them "to enter into the opportunities of the dominant culture." Unless the new Negro residents receive the proper instruction from their cultural superiors—so the theory runs—they are bound to make undesirable neighbors; for their "primitive folk culture" permits or even encourages behavior that clashes with the needs and standards of city life. "A Negro in the Mississippi Delta," Hauser suggests by way of illustration, "tosses his empty whiskey bottle or beer can in a cotton patch, and what difference does it make? But on the asphalt pavements of a city it can make a difference, esthetically and with respect to safety. If physical violence is accepted in the south as a means of resolving conflict," Hauser continues, "nobody cares much; but in the urban community, such acts become

---

*Charles E. Silberman, *Crisis in Black and White,* Vintage Edition (New York: Random House, 1964), pp. 36-57. Reprinted by permission of Random House, Inc.

felonies, with much more serious consequences." In one variant or another this theory that Negroes need "acculturation" underlies most of the public and private programs now being developed in Northern cities to ameliorate the Negro-urban problem. The Ford Foundation, for example, has committed a portion of its huge resources and influence to an attempt "to do in one generation for the urban newcomer what until now has taken three." The Foundation makes no distinction between the problems faced by Negroes and those faced by other contemporary migrants. The metropolis, Dr. Paul N. Ylvisaker, Director of the Foundation's Public Affairs Program, has told city planners and civic leaders, should be viewed "as a continuous system of attracting the newcomer (once the Scotch, the Irish, the Jews, the Italians, now the Negroes, the Puerto Ricans, the mountain whites, the Mexicans, and the American Indians) and of assimilating this newcomer to all that is up-to-date and sought after in the urban culture."

The "acculturation theory" can provide a useful perspective. Measured against the backdrop of history, the gangs and crime and squalor of today seem almost benign. Americans who have been shocked to read that women employees of the Supreme Court have been officially advised to secure a police escort before leaving the Court building at night should at the very least know that muggings and robberies in the capital antedate the recent Negro influx. In 1858, for example, when the Negro residents of the nation's capital still wore the fetters of slavery, a Senate committee investigated the city's rising crime rate. "Riot and bloodshed are of daily occurrence," the committee reported, "innocent and unoffending persons are shot, stabbed, and otherwise shamefully maltreated, and not infrequently the offender is not even arrested." And during the week-long Draft Riots in New York in 1863, when the Irish immigrants of Hell's Kitchen revolted against authority, federal troops had to be recalled from the front to restore order. Ninety-seven years later, the grandson of Irish immigrants was elected President of the United States. If the most backward, downtrodden, and discriminated-against European immigrant groups have now all moved up into the great American middle class—so the reasoning seems to go—then why not the Negroes, too?

Reasoning by analogy can be dangerously misleading, however; history does not usually repeat itself. Too many historians and sociologists—and far too many civic leaders—are using the "acculturation theory" as a license to look away from the uncomfortable fact of race and so to avoid the hard and painful decisions. Government officials can hardly be blamed for taking the easy way when academic authorities offer the bland reassurance that time and history will solve everything. To be sure, Hauser admits that the Negro's problem of adjustment may be more difficult than that of the European immigrants. But "forces are in motion," he assured the United States Civil Rights Commission, "that will enable the Negro to win his place as a full-fledged member of the American society." The motion Hauser is talking about is a lot slower than Negroes may be willing to accept, however. The process of acculturation, he told a Washington,

D.C., audience in 1961, "requires time—time measured in human generations rather than years. I am displeased to report this," he dutifully added, "but it is the only honest thing to do."

Harvard's Professor Oscar Handlin offers much rosier lenses. "The experience of the past," he wrote at the end of *The Newcomers,* a study of Negro and Puerto Rican migration to New York City, "offers a solid foundation for the belief that the newest immigrants to a great metropolis will play as useful a role as any of their predecessors. They themselves need only show the will and energy, and their neighbors the tolerance, to make it possible."

It will take a lot more than that. To suggest that good will alone will solve the urban Negro problem is fatuousness of the worst sort. Good will can never be relied upon to solve any hard problem, and the question of the Negro's place in America is the hardest problem this country has ever faced. It is equally fatuous to pretend that color is irrelevant, as so many adherents of the "acculturation theory" seem to do. The plain fact is that the Negro faces a problem different in kind, and far more complex, than that faced by any of his European predecessors.

There are many differences. For one thing, the United States has far less need for unskilled labor today than it had when European immigrants were flooding our shores. It took no great transfer of skill for an Irish or Italian peasant to become a laborer on a construction gang. It takes an enormous transfer of skill, however, to enable a sharecropper from Mississippi to find a job as a computer programmer. And the gap is widening between Negro education and training, on the one hand, and the requirements of the labor market, on the other. Automation, new management techniques, and changes in consumer spending patterns are all reducing the demand for unskilled and semiskilled labor and increasing employment in professional, managerial, clerical, and sales jobs, many of which require considerable education and training. These white-collar occupations account for no less than 97 per cent of the total increase in employment that occurred between 1947 and 1963. The professionalization of the labor force accelerated during the mid-fifties, and will pick up momentum in the middle and late sixties. But Negroes are badly prepared for this change. Seven Negro men in ten now work in unskilled or semiskilled blue-collar jobs, compared to three out of ten white men; and more than half the Negro men over the age of twenty-five (*vs.* 21 per cent of white men) have had less than a grammar school education. Small wonder that in Northern industrial centers one out of every three Negro workers has suffered unemployment in the last several years, or that in some Negro neighborhoods, the unemployment rate may run as high as 40 per cent. To anyone walking through the Negro neighborhoods of any large city—and to the children who grow up in them—few sights are more familiar than the groups of idle Negro men congregating at street corners, or the lonely Negroes sitting on their front stoops all day long, sipping wine from bottles discreetly hidden in brown paper bags.

Negroes' lack of education and training and their concentration in unskilled occupations—conditions produced by past discrimination—do not entirely account for Negro poverty, however. Neither does the inadequate growth of the economy, which has caused high unemployment among unskilled whites as well as among Negroes. On the contrary, the Negro unemployment rate is higher than the white rate in *every* major occupational group. Among craftsmen and fore-men, for example, Negro unemployment ran to 9.7 per cent in 1962, compared to 4.8 per cent for whites; among clerical workers, 7.1 per cent *vs.* 3.8 per cent; among unskilled laborers, 15.8 per cent *vs.* 11 per cent. While a great many Negroes cannot find jobs because they lack the necessary skills, all too many Negroes who do have the education and training are unable to put their skills to work.

It is a lot harder for Negroes today to bear their poverty and lack of status than it was for the European immigrants. If you have to be poor, John Kenneth Galbraith has quipped, at least have the good sense to be born during a time when *everybody* is poor. The European immigrants showed this good judgment; they arrived at a time when the great majority of the population was poor. The Negro migration, by contrast, is occurring in an affluent society. Hence the Negroes are an economic as well as a racial minority—the first minority poor the world has ever known. Two out of three Negro households earn less than $4,000 a year, and one Negro male in nine is out of work. This poverty and insecurity are particularly galling to the Negro, who sees the white society that surrounds him grow increasingly affluent while he remains mired in squalor. Contrary to popular impression, the Negroes' economic position has actually deteriorated over the last ten years, relative to that of whites. Negroes did make enormous advances during World War Two and the boom years that followed, for the shortage of labor drew them into factory and white-collar jobs that had always been barred to them. As a result, Negro income increased 80 per cent faster than white income, and the median income of Negro families jumped from only 37 per cent of white income in 1939 to 57 per cent in 1952. But this escalation halted with the general slowdown of the economy after the Korean war. As a result, the median income of Negro families dropped from its high of 57 per cent of white income in 1952 to 53 per cent in 1962.

The slum in which the Negro lives, moreover, has been bequeathed to him by the Italians and Poles, the Slovaks and Jews of yesteryear who have left for greener pastures. In contrasting his lot with theirs, the Negro is positive that "the man"—the white man—has stacked the cards against him.

Among the great mass of working-class Negroes, therefore, and among many of the middle class as well, apathy exists side by side with a growing, festering resentment of their lot. These Negroes are more and more convinced that they should have a better life; they are less and less convinced that they themselves can do anything about it.

Most important of all, however, the Hauser-Handlin-Ylvisaker approach, which sees the Negro problem as similar in kind to the problem faced by European immigrants in the past, or white migrants today, diverts attention from what is surely the central fact. The Negro is unlike any other immigrant group in one crucial regard: he is colored. And that makes all the difference. The Irish immigrants, to be sure, faced job discrimination as severe as the Negro faces today. A century ago, in fact, Negroes apparently were preferred over Irishmen. A want ad in the New York *Daily Sun* of May 11, 1853, for example, seeking a woman for general housework, specified, "English, Scotch, Welsh, German or any country or color except Irish." But once the Irishman was "Americanized," his problem could be fairly easily resolved. He could lose his brogue and, if he so desired, change his name; and when his income permitted, he could move away from the slum and lose himself in the crowd. So, today, can the Appalachian whites and even most Puerto Ricans. But no Negro has ever made that much money in the United States; no matter how wealthy—or how educated, how "acculturated"—he may become, he cannot lose himself in the crowd. He remains a Negro. Sociologists and political scientists, for example, commonly refer to "Irish-Americans" or "Italian-Americans" or "Polish-Americans"—but to "American Negroes." The accent is always on "Negro."

The European ethnic groups, in short, could move into the main stream of American life without forcing beforehand any drastic rearrangements of attitudes or institutions. For the Negro to do so, however, will require the most radical changes in the whole structure of American society. The mere presence of a Negro in a white residential neighborhood unleashes fears and hatreds of the most elemental sort, and leads almost without exception to an exodus of the white residents. Residential segregation of Negroes has actually increased over the past several decades, despite the improvement in their economic position. This is in sharp contrast with the experience of European immigrant groups—or with the current experience of Puerto Rican immigrants. Traditionally, migrants have settled initially in ethnic ghettos in the slums of the central city and worked at the worst-paid and most menial occupations; but as they and their descendants move up the occupational ladder, they also move away from the ghetto to less and less segregated neighborhoods. Not so with the Negroes; the contrast between Negro experience and that of other immigrant groups is all the more striking in view of the fact that ethnic organizations generally have tried to *maintain* their ethnic colonies intact, whereas most major Negro organizations have been fighting for residential dispersal. And there seems to be little doubt that residential segregation in turn helps bar the Negro's assimilation into the economy and society at large.

The problem is double-barreled. On the one hand, "acculturation" is not enough; for all his culture or wealth, the educated Negro remains an alien in his own land. But on the other hand, the process of acculturation doesn't seem to "take." Thus, Negroes have not been moving up the socio-economic ladder as rapidly as might have been expected; second- and third-generation Negro city dwellers achieve less in school than the second- and third-generation offspring of immigrants; the crime rate in settled Negro areas is high and rising; and so on. Consider the following report:

It cannot be denied that the main results of the development of the Philadelphia Negro since the war have on the whole disappointed his well-wishers. They do not pretend that he has not made great advance in certain lines, or even that in general he is not better off today than formerly . . . Yet there is a widespread feeling that more might reasonably have been expected in the line of social and moral development than apparently has been accomplished. Not only do they feel that there is a lack of positive result, but the relative advance compared with the period just before the war is slow, if not an actual retrogression; an abnormal and growing amount of crime and poverty can justly be charged to the Negro; he is not a large taxpayer, holds no conspicuous place in the business world or the world of letters, and even as a workingman seems to be losing ground.

The war in question was the Civil War, not World War Two; the writer was the great Negro sociologist, W. E. B. Du Bois, in his classic study of *The Philadelphia Negro,* published in 1899.

Du Bois' observations remain uncomfortably pertinent. An increasing proportion of Negroes, moreover, are city-born and raised, but too many occupy the same relative position in society as did their parents and grandparents. In 1960, for example, 44 per cent of the Negro residents of Chicago were born in Illinois, and perhaps two-thirds of the older Negroes (those over forty-five) had lived in metropolitan areas for twenty years or more. Yet fully one-quarter of the Negro families in Chicago are receiving public welfare assistance; Negroes account for 25 per cent of the city's population, but over 80 per cent of the relief recipients. Negroes also account for a disproportionate amount of crime.

Much the same is true of Harlem, once the largest Negro community in the United States and still in a sense the intellectual and cultural center of American Negroes. Harlem receives a steady flow of migrants from the South (some seventy-five hundred came between 1955 and 1960), but it is predominantly a community of established city dwellers, with over two hundred fifty churches and some fifty-four social agencies in its service. Only 4 per cent are recent migrants from the South—yet Harlem's juvenile delinquency rate is nearly two and one half times the city average, its venereal disease rate is nearly seven times as high. Considerably more than one-third of all Harlem births are illegitimate, a ratio nearly five times that of the city as a whole. Harlem's infant mortality rate—generally considered the best single measure of the state of a community's health—is nearly twice as high as that for New York City as a whole.

By any measure of social disorganization, in short, Harlem is a slum sunk in apathy and steeped in crime, narcotics addiction, poverty, and disease. "Don't let this Harlem git you," a motherly Harlem matron advises the young hero of Ellison's *Invisible Man,* just recently arrived from the South. "I'm in New York, but New York ain't in me, understand what I mean? Don't get corrupted." But many do. And the worst corruption of all is not the crime but the apathy; not even the Black Muslims can attract any sizable membership in Harlem. The hopelessness seems to increase with the passage of time. "Yes, we've progressed," James Baldwin has quipped. "When I was a boy in Harlem, Negroes got drunk and cursed each other out. Now they become junkies and don't say anything."

They do not read anything, either—in part because they never learn to read fluently. In the New York City public schools, New York-born Negro youngsters read as poorly as in-migrant youngsters; by the sixth grade, both groups, on average, score at about the fourth-grade level, nearly two years below the national norm. The fact that the city-born youngsters read no better than recent arrivals from the South is all the more striking in view of the fact that the former have somewhat higher IQs—in the sixth grade, an average of 90, compared to 85.8 for the in-migrants. Thus, the native-born children perform at a lower level relative to capacity than the newcomers. Residence in the Northern city seems to dull rather than to stimulate achievement.

If Negroes remain outside the main stream of city life, therefore—if they appear amoral, if their behavior clashes with city standards—the blame can be placed less and less on what Professor Hauser calls the "primitive folk culture" of the Negro South. A growing body of research—most notably, the studies of the Negro family in Washington, D.C., by Hylan Lewis and associates—suggests that urban Negroes in fact do share in middle-class values and aspirations. They, too, value financial success; they, too, want their children to be educated; they, too, are ashamed of illegitimacy, to cite a few examples. To be sure, lower-class Negroes do not always act accordingly; they do drop out of schools and they do have more illegitimate children than members of the middle class. But the reason, in many cases, is that their poverty—intellectual and cultural as well as financial—gets in the way. Some Negroes know what they want (according to middle-class standards) but do not know how to achieve these wants. Others know both, but their daily struggle for existence drains them of the energy they need to achieve their aspirations. These people, in Hylan Lewis' phrase, are "frustrated victims of middle-class values." Precisely because they have been acculturated into middle-class values, their inability to climb out of the lower-class slum persuades them that the cards are stacked against them, or reinforces their sense of worthlessness. In either case, the evidence of their lives suggests that there is no use in trying.

But the slum-dwelling Negro's behavior stems from something deeper-rooted, and harder to overcome, than poverty: his hatred of "the man," the white man, who seems determined to keep him in his place. Take Professor Hauser's tale of the Negro from Mississippi, who once threw his empty whiskey bottle or beer can in the cotton patch and who, as Hauser puts it, now must be taught not to hurl it out his Chicago tenement window. There may well be some Negroes in Chicago who throw beer cans out of windows because they do not know any better; the great majority who do so, however, know perfectly well that their act is antisocial; that is precisely why they do it! They throw the beer can not through ignorance but through hate—because throwing it out the window is an act of defiance, a readily available means of social protest. There are other means of protest, of course; misbehaving in school, or dropping out of school altogether; not showing up for work on time, or not showing up at all (and lying about the reason); breaking school windows or ripping telephone receivers out of outdoor phone booths; or the oldest form of protest of all, apathy—a flat refusal to co-operate with the oppressor or to accept his moral code. "You can force a man to live in a prison," says Saul Alinsky of the Industrial Areas Foundation, "but you can't make him contribute to its upkeep."

Against what are the beer-can throwers or the drop-outs protesting? In a word, everything: the world about them, which dooms them to defeat and humiliation (or which they believe dooms them, which amounts to the same thing); and the weakness in themselves, which accepts humiliation, and so makes defeat inevitable. Something happens to the Negro in Harlem (or the South Side of Chicago, or North Philadelphia, or their equivalents in a dozen cities) —something which stifles the ambition and kills the spirit, and suffuses the whole personality with despair and emptiness. Like the immigrants of old, the Negro migrants, many of them, come in search of the promised land. But their aspirations are quickly trampled on. In one of the short stories in his *Eight Men,* the late Richard Wright described what moving to Chicago did to him:

> While working as a porter in Memphis I had often stood aghast as a friend of mine had offered himself to be kicked by the white men; but now, while working in Chicago, I was learning that perhaps even a kick was better than uncertainty . . . I had elected, in my fevered search for honorable adjustment to the American scene, not to submit and in doing so I had embraced the daily horror of anxiety, of tension, of eternal disquiet.
>
> To solve this tangle of balked emotion, I loaded the empty part of the ship of my personality with fantasies of ambition to keep it from toppling over into the sea of senselessness. Like any other American, I dreamed of going into business and making money; I dreamed of working for a firm that would allow me to advance until I reached an important position . . . Yet I knew—with that part of my mind that the whites had given me—that none of my dreams were possible. Then I would hate myself for allowing my mind to dwell upon the unattainable. Thus the circle would complete itself.
>
> Slowly I began to forge in the depths of my mind a mechanism that repressed all the dreams and desires that the Chicago streets, the newspapers, the movies were evoking in me. I was going through a second childhood; a new sense of the limit of the possible was being born in me. What could I dream of that had the barest possibility of coming true? I could think of nothing. And, slowly, it was upon exactly that nothingness that my mind began to dwell, that constant sense of wanting without having, or being hated without reason. A dim notion of what life meant to

a Negro in America was coming to consciousness in me, not in terms of external events, lynchings, Jim Crowism and the endless brutalities, but in terms of crossed-up feeling, of emotional tension.

Despair and apathy, of course, are basic ingredients of any lower-class community, and a good many problems attributed to Negroes because of their race in fact are due to their class. But there is a special quality to the despair of the Negro slum that distinguishes it from any other. For the youngster growing up in Harlem or any other Negro slum, the gates of life clang shut at a terrifyingly early age. For one thing, the children become aware almost from infancy of the. opprobrium Americans attach to color. They feel it in their parents' voices as they are warned to behave when they stray beyond the ghetto's wall. They become aware of it as they begin to watch television, or go to the movies, or read the mass-circulation magazines; beauty, success, and status all wear a white skin. They learn to feel ashamed of their color as they learn to talk, and thereby to absorb the invidiousness our very language attaches to color. White represents purity and goodness, black represents evil. The white lie is the permissible misstatement, the black lie the inexcusable falsehood; the black sheep is the one who goes astray (and when he goes astray, he receives a black mark on his record); defeat is black (the stock market crashed on "Black Thursday"), victory white. Even James Weldon Johnson's "Negro National Anthem" speaks of Negroes "treading our path through the blood of the slaughtered/ . . . Till now we stand at last/*Where the white gleam of our bright star is cast.*" [Emphasis added]

Language aside, Negro children learn soon enough—from their father's menial job, or lack of it, from his mixture of fear and deference and hate of "the man"—that the world is white and they are black. And the odds are small indeed that a Negro child can grow up without being abused or patronized, without being convinced by a hundred big and small humiliations, that he has no worth and no chance. "One did not have to be very bright," Baldwin has written of his childhood in Harlem, "to realize how little one could do to change one's situation; one did not have to be abnormally sensitive to be worn down to a cutting edge by the incessant and gratuitous humiliation and danger one encountered every working day, all day long." He continues:

> The humiliation did not apply merely to working days, or workers; I was thirteen and was crossing Fifth Avenue on my way to the Forty-second Street library, and the cop in the middle of the street muttered as I passed him, "Why don't you niggers stay uptown where you belong?" When I was ten, and didn't look, certainly, any older, two policemen amused themselves by frisking me, making comic (and terrifying) speculations concerning my ancestry and probable sexual prowess, and for good measure, leaving me flat on my back in one of Harlem's empty lots.

And if the child should grow up somehow without confronting prejudice and discrimination directly, he meets it soon enough as an adult. He meets it whether he stays in the slum or moves to the top, for white men in authority do not always distinguish between Negroes who are "acculturated" and those who are not. The police are an ever-present threat; there is hardly a Negro community in the United States which does not regard the local police with suspicion, if not with hate. Consider the following report from the New York City *Amsterdam News* of December 8, 1962:

> Two young white cops were suspended from the New York City Police force last Wednesday after they were indicted and arrested on charges of brutal assault on a 30-year-old prominent Negro engineer in a West Side police station when he went in to complain about being unlawfully searched and assaulted by them earlier in the street . . .
>
> Victim of the police brutality was Marshal Whitehead, 30, of 116 W. 87 St., a prominent designing engineer with a Hempstead, L.I., firm.
>
> The brutality incident occurred last August 8 when Whitehead after returning home from a neighborhood softball game decided to run around the block and loosen up.
>
> As he was trotting in the area of 87th St. and Amsterdam Ave., the tactical police force car with four officers stopped, and several got out and slugged him and searched him, and then told him to get off the street.
>
> Whitehead, whose photo is to be on the cover of the forthcoming Emancipation issue of a popular magazine, wrote the police car number down and went home.
>
> Whitehead later went to the stationhouse to complain and was sent to a Detective Keogh, who after interviewing him, denied any knowledge of the police car number and tore up the slip containing the license number.
>
> As Whitehead was about to leave, he saw the four cops who had slugged him earlier, entering the stationhouse and identified [them].
>
> The cops reportedly said: "If you want something to complain about, then we'll give you something to complain about" and allegedly took him to the basement of the stationhouse, where Whitehead was brutally assaulted about the head and body, and later arrested for disorderly conduct and resisting arrest. [The charges were later dismissed.]

The occasional acts of police brutality, however, hurt less than the constant flow of petty indignities—indignities that seem to demonstrate, a dozen times a year, that no matter what a Negro does, no matter what he achieves, no matter what he is, the white world will never accept him. He can be Ralph Bunche, and still be refused a room in an Atlanta hotel while his secretary's reservation is immediately accepted. He can be a distinguished sociologist, yet in a restaurant two blocks from the White House be ushered to a table alongside the kitchen door while the front tables are all unoccupied. Experiencing hostility wherever they go, many Negroes begin to *expect* hostility wherever they go. They lose their ability to distinguish a real from a fancied injury; as James Baldwin has put it, "every American Negro risks having the gates of paranoia close on him," and he takes affront from anything and everything. Appearing in court to answer charges of assaulting a white musician, for example, the band-leader Charlie Mingus angrily turned on his own lawyer, who had described Mingus as "a great jazz musician." "Don't call me a *jazz* musician," he told the startled lawyer. "To me the word *jazz* means nigger, discrimination, second-class citizenship, the whole back-of-the-bus bit . . . I'm just a musician, man."

The worst indignity of all is being patronized by whites who "know how to handle Negroes." The housekeeper inspecting my wife's hospital room was obviously pleased with the way the Negro porter had cleaned the room. "You're a good boy, Jimmy," she told him by way of compliment; and Jimmy said, "Thank you, Ma'am." Jimmy was forty-eight years old. Perhaps he had become so used to being treated like a boy that he took the insult as a compliment. Or perhaps he had merely learned, for his own well-being, to hide his anger behind a mask of servility. In any case, he knew that no supervisor would say, "You're a good boy, Jack," if the white orderly did a good job of mopping up after a patient. "There is a form of oppression which is more painful and more scathing than physical injury or economic privation," Rabbi Abraham Heschel told the first National Conference on Religion and Race. "It is public humiliation." Ancient Jewish law understood and underscored this fact. According to the Talmud, one should prefer to throw oneself alive into a burning furnace than to embarrass another person publicly. Indeed, the same Hebrew word denotes both murder and insult.

Negroes are given humiliation, insult, and embarrassment as a daily diet, and without regard to individual merit. They are convinced, as a result, that most whites never see them as individuals, that all Negroes look alike to whites; the theme of "facelessness" and "invisibility" runs through Negro literature. "No more fiendish punishment could be devised, were such a thing physically possible," the philosopher William James once wrote, "than that one should be turned loose in society and remain unnoticed by all the members thereof." The Negro is noticed, of course, for in rejecting him, white society must thereby notice him. But the Negro, too often, is noticed only to be rejected. "The dehumanized image of the Negro which white Americans carry in their minds, the anti-Negro epithets continuously on their lips," Richard Wright has written, "exclude the contemporary Negro as truly as though he were kept in a steel prison."

This sense of rejection by American society, a sense which dominates the lower-class Negro's life, tends to destroy his feeling of responsibility to law and authority; law and authority are always white and middle class and always seem designed to keep the lower-class Negro in his place. It also creates a good deal of class conflict and antagonism within the Negro community. Lower-class Negroes tend to resent Negroes who have achieved economic success, especially if the success is in the white world, for they are convinced that whites have so stacked the cards against Negroes that none can rise through ability or merit. Hence, if another Negro has "made it" in the white world it must be because of favoritism, because he pandered to white prejudice or white vanities, and thereby betrayed his own race. (Since ability counts for naught in the white world, why else has he advanced while I'm held back?) This kind of intra-group hostility is fairly typical of disadvantaged groups—witness the "shanty Irish" resentment of the "lace-curtain Irish" a generation or two ago. And lower-class Negroes' resentment of "dickety" Negroes frequently exists side-by-side with a vicarious delight that "one of our boys has made it."

Most important of all, however, the Negro reacts to exclusion with anger and hate. Nor is it just the sullen, apathetic tenement dweller who hates "the man." On the contrary, it is hard to imagine how any Negro American, no matter how well born or placed, can escape a deep sense of anger and a burning hatred of things white. Some are better able to repress it than others, but few escape its demonic force. "To be a Negro in this country and to be relatively conscious," James Baldwin has written, "is to be in a rage almost all the time." With those Negroes who deny their hatred, the essayist-novelist J. Saunders Redding has written, "I have no quarrel . . . it is simply that I do not believe them." Some Negroes, he concedes, may be able to order their lives so as to avoid the experience of prejudice and discrimination—but to do so, in his view, requires an effort so great as to bring them to a psychopathic brink. "One's heart is sickened," he writes, "at the realization of the primal energy that goes into the sheer business of living as a Negro in the United States—in any one of the United States." It is impossible, in Redding's view, for a Negro to avoid a dual personality; inevitably, one part of him reacts to people and events as an individual, the other part reacts as a Negro.

The inevitability and the horror of this fact—the unending consciousness of color—were driven home to Redding by a traumatic experience he describes in his moving essay, "On Being Negro In America." The incident occurred during the thirties, when Redding was teaching at a Negro college in Louisville. His office window overlooked a white slum beginning at the edge of the campus. Standing at the office window one quiet winter Saturday, he saw a young woman lurching and staggering in his back yard, until she fell face down in the snow. He couldn't tell whether she was sick or drunk. "Pity rose in me," he relates, "but at the same time something else also—a gloating satisfaction that she was white. Sharply and concurrently felt, the two emotions were of equal strength, in perfect balance, and the corporeal I, fixed in a trance at the window, oscillated between them." The gloating won out. Redding decided not to go to her aid, but salved his conscience by calling the police to report "a drunken woman lying in the back yard of a house on Eighth Street." An hour later, the police came—and the next morning, Redding read on a back page of a newspaper that the woman had died of exposure following an epileptic seizure. "One can wash his hands," Redding concludes, "but the smudges and scars on the psyche are different."

Redding was troubled by the conflict between his instincts as a Negro and his instincts as a human being, and scarred by his decision to follow the former. A good many Negroes would have felt no such qualms of conscience afterward, nor would they have felt beforehand the tug of war Redding describes, between his desire to help the woman and his glee that a white person was in trouble. On Sunday, June 3, 1962, when news was flashed around the United States that a chartered airplane bound from Paris to Atlanta had crashed, killing 130 of the 132 aboard, Malcolm X, then the number two man in the Black Muslim movement, now leader of his own black nationalist group, was delivering a sermon to fifteen hundred Muslims in Los Angeles. He immediately shared the good news with his audience:

> I would like to announce a very beautiful thing that has happened . . . Somebody came and told me that [God] had answered our prayers in France. He dropped an airplane out of the sky with over 120 white people in it because the Muslims believe in an eye for an eye and a tooth for a tooth. But thanks to God, or Jehovah or Allah, we will continue to pray and we hope that every day another plane falls out of the sky . . . We call on our God—He gets rid of 120 of them at one whop.

Whites have generally been shocked by the animal-like hatred Muslim leaders have expressed on this and other occasions. They should be upset; but they shouldn't be surprised. There's no reason to assume that black men are more immune to the cancer of hate than white men, and we have seen more than enough examples of white hatred and brutality in recent years: in mobs rioting in Oxford, Mississippi, to block James Meredith's admission to the University, and in the obscene insults flung at him by his fellow students—the flower of Mississippi gentry—throughout his stay there; in the famous pictures of three Birmingham policemen forcing a single Negro woman to the ground, and pinning her there with their knees; in crowds in Chicago hurling rocks to try to stop a Negro from moving into a previously all-white neighborhood. And Malcolm X's pleasure at the plane crash was no more vengeful than the glee expressed by Eugene "Bull" Connor, then-Commissioner of Public Safety of Birmingham, Alabama, when he learned that Rev. Fred T. Shuttlesworth, Alabama Negro leader, had been injured by a spray of water from police hoses. Connor was sorry that he hadn't been present to see the event—he'd been waiting all week to see Shuttlesworth hurt, he said—and he expressed regret that Shuttlesworth was carried away in an ambulance instead of a hearse. The Black Muslims' hatred, in short, is the mirror image of white hatred.

To be sure, the Muslims have been able to enroll no more than 100,000, and perhaps as few as 50,000, Negroes as active members. But they have captured the sympathy of an enormous segment of Northern urban Negroes, who are unwilling to embrace the Muslim's strict discipline and religious tenets but who are delighted to hear the anger they feel being expressed so clearly. "I don't know how many followers he's got," a Harlem cabdriver told *Life* photographer Gordon Parks, who had just left Malcolm X, "but he has sure got a hell of a lot of well wishers." The cabbie was one of the latter. "Those Muslims or Moslems, 'ever what you call 'em, make more sense to me than the NAACP and Urban League and all the rest of them put together," he told Parks. "They're down on the good earth with the brother. They're for their own people and that Malcolm ain't afraid to tell Mr. Charlie, the FBI or the cops or nobody where to get off. You don't see him pussyfootin' 'round the whites like he's scared of them." Asked whether the Muslims hated all white men, the cabbie replied succinctly that "if they don't, they should, 'cause [the whites] sure don't waste no love on us. I used to live in Mobile and I lived in Memphis and I've lived in New York for fifteen years," the driver finished, "and I've come to one conclusion. No matter where the white man is, he's the same—the only thing he respects is force. And the only things gonna change him is some lead in the belly."

Nor are the relatively uneducated the only ones to respond to the Muslim's siren song of hate. On the contrary, the Muslims have struck a responsive chord in the most sophisticated Negro circles—among men and women in the forefront of the drive for integration, as well as in those who have held themselves aloof from any contact with "the problem." "Malcolm says things you or I would not say," a former president of the New York NAACP chapter confesses in admiration. "When he says those things, when he talks about the white man, even those of us who are repelled by his philosophy secretly cheer a little outside ourselves, because Malcolm X really does tell 'em, and we know he frightens the white man. We clap."

The Future of the Cities

by The National Advisory Commission on Civil Disorders*

INTRODUCTION

We believe action of the kind outlined in preceding pages can contribute substantially to control of disorders in the near future. But there should be no mistake about the long run. The underlying forces continue to gain momentum.

The most basic of these is the accelerating segregation of low-income, disadvantaged Negroes within the ghettos of the largest American cities.

By 1985, the 12.1 million Negroes segregated within central cities today will have grown to approximately 20.3 million—an increase of 68 percent.

Prospects for domestic peace and for the quality of American life are linked directly to the future of these cities.

Two critical questions must be confronted: Where do present trends now lead? What choices are open to us?

THE KEY TRENDS

Negro Population Growth

The size of the Negro population in central cities is closely related to total national Negro population growth. In the past 16 years, about 98 percent of this growth has occurred within metropolitan areas, and 86 percent in the central cities of those areas.

A conservative projection of national Negro population growth indicates continued rapid increases. For the period 1966 to 1985, it will rise to a total of 30.7 million, gaining an average of 484,000 a year, or 7.6 percent more than the increase in each year from 1960 to 1966.

Central Cities. Further Negro population growth in central cities depends upon two key factors: in-migration from outside metropolitan areas, and patterns of Negro settlement within metropolitan areas.

From 1960 to 1966, the Negro population of all central cities rose 2.4 million, 88.9 percent of total national Negro population growth. We estimate that

* *Report of the National Advisory Commission on Civil Disorders* (Washington: United States Government Printing Office, March 1, 1968), pp. 215-226.

natural growth accounted for 1.4 million, or 58 percent of this increase, and in-migration accounted for one million, or 42 percent.

As of 1966, the Negro population in all central cities totaled 12.1 million. By 1985, we have estimated that it will rise 68 percent to 20.3 million. We believe that natural growth will account for 5.2 million of this increase and in-migration for 3.0 million.

Without significant Negro out-migration, then, the combined Negro populations of central cities will continue to grow by an average of 274,000 a year through 1985, even if no further in-migration occurs.

Growth projected on the basis of natural increase and in-migration would raise the proportion of Negroes to whites in central cities by 1985 from the present 20.7 percent to between an estimated 31 and 34.7 percent.

Largest Central Cities. These, however, are national figures. Much faster increases will occur in the largest central cities where Negro growth has been concentrated in the past two decades. Washington, D.C., Gary, and Newark are already over half Negro. A continuation of recent trends would cause the following 10 major cities to become over 50 percent Negro by the indicated dates:

New Orleans	1971	St. Louis	1978
Richmond	1971	Detroit	1979
Baltimore	1972	Philadelphia	1981
Jacksonville	1972	Oakland	1983
Cleveland	1975	Chicago	1984

These cities, plus Washington, D.C. (now over 66 percent Negro) and Newark, contained 12.6 million people in 1960, or 22 percent of the total population of all 224 American central cities. All 13 cities undoubtedly will have Negro majorities by 1985, and the suburbs ringing them will remain largely all white, unless there are major changes in Negro fertility rates, in-migration, settlement patterns, or public policy.

Experience indicates that Negro school enrollment in these and other cities will exceed 50 percent long before the total population reaches that mark. In fact, Negro students already comprise more than a majority in the public elementary schools of 12 of the 13 cities mentioned above. This occurs because the Negro population in central cities is much younger and because a much higher proportion of white children attend private schools. For example, St. Louis' population was about 36 percent Negro in 1965; its public elementary school enrollment was 63 percent Negro. If present trends continue, many cities in addition to those listed above will have Negro school majorities by 1985, probably including:

Dallas	Indianapolis	Harrisburg
Pittsburgh	Kansas City, Mo.	Hartford
Buffalo	Cincinnati	New Haven
Louisville		

Thus, continued concentration of future Negro population growth in large central cities will produce significant changes in those cities over the next 20 years. Unless there are sharp changes in the factors influencing Negro settlement patterns within metropolitan areas, there is little doubt that the trend toward Negro majorities will continue. Even a complete cessation of net Negro in-migration to central cities would merely postpone this result for a few years.

Growth of the Young Negro Population

We estimate that the Nation's white population will grow 16.6 million, or 9.6 percent, from 1966 to 1975, and the Negro population 3.8 million, or 17.7 percent, in the same period. The Negro age group from 15 to 24 years of age, however, will grow much faster than either the Negro population as a whole, or the white population in the same age group.

From 1966 to 1975, the total number of Negroes in this age group nationally will rise 1.6 million, or 40.1 percent. The white population aged 15 to 24 will rise 6.6 million, or 23.5 percent.

This rapid increase in the young Negro population has important implications for the country. This group has the highest unemployment rate in the Nation, commits a relatively high proportion of all crimes and plays the most significant role in civil disorders. By the same token, it is a great reservoir of underused human resources which are vital to the Nation.

The Location of New Jobs

Most new employment opportunities do not occur in central cities, near all-Negro neighborhoods. They are being created in suburbs and outlying areas—and this trend is likely to continue indefinitely. New office buildings have risen in the downtowns of large cities, often near all-Negro areas. But the out-flow of manufacturing and retailing facilities normally offsets this addition significantly—and in many cases has caused a new loss of jobs in central cities while the new white collar jobs are often not available to ghetto residents.

Providing employment for the swelling Negro ghetto population will require society to link these potential workers more closely with job locations. This can be done in three ways: By developing incentives to industry to create new employment centers near Negro residential areas; by opening suburban residential areas to Negroes and encouraging them to move closer to industrial centers; or by creating better transportation between ghetto neighborhoods and new job locations.

All three involve large public outlays.

The first method—creating new industries in or near the ghetto—is not likely to occur without Government subsidies on a scale which convinces private firms that it will pay them to face the problems involved.

The second method—opening up suburban areas to Negro occupancy—obviously requires effective fair housing laws. It will also require an extensive program of federally aided, low-cost housing in many suburban areas.

The third approach—improved transportation linking ghettos and suburbs—has received little attention from city planners and municipal officials. A few demonstration projects show promise, but carrying them out on a large scale will be very costly.

Although a high proportion of new jobs will be located in suburbs, there are still millions of jobs in central cities. Turnover in those jobs alone can open up a great many potential positions for Negro central-city residents—if employers cease racial discrimination in their hiring and promotion practices.

Nevertheless, as the total number of Negro central-city jobseekers continues to rise, the need to link them with emerging new employment in the suburbs will become increasingly urgent.

The Increasing Cost of Municipal Services

Local governments have had to bear a particularly heavy financial burden in the two decades since the end of World War II. All U.S. cities are highly dependent upon property taxes that are relatively unresponsive to changes in income. Consequently, growing municipalities have been hard pressed for adequate revenues to meet rising demands for services generated by population increase. On the other hand, stable or declining cities have not only been faced with steady cost increases, but also with a slow-growing, or even declining, tax base.

As a result of the population shifts of the postwar period, concentrating the middle class in residential suburbs while leaving the poor in the central cities, the increasing burden of municipal taxes frequently falls upon that part of the urban population least able to pay them.

Increasing concentrations of urban growth have called forth greater expenditures for every kind of public service: Education, health, police protection, fire protection, parks, sanitation, etc. These expenditures have strikingly outpaced tax revenues.

The story is summed up below:

Local Government Revenues, Expenditures, and Debt
(billions of dollars)

	1950	1966	Increase
Revenues	11.7	41.5	+29.8
Expenditures.	17.0	60.7	+43.7
Debt outstanding	18.8	77.5	+58.7

Despite the growth of Federal assistance to urban areas under various grant-in-aid programs, the fiscal plight of many cities is likely to grow even more serious in the future. Local expenditures inevitably will continue to rise steeply as a result of several factors, including the difficulty of increasing productivity in the predominantly service activities of local governments, together with the rapid technologically induced increases in productivity in other economic sectors.

Traditionally, individual productivity has risen faster in the manufacturing, mining, construction, and agricultural sectors than in those involving personal services. However, since all sectors compete with each other for talent and personnel, wages and salaries in the service-dominated sectors generally must keep up, with those in the capital-dominated sectors. Since productivity in manufacturing has risen about 2.5 percent per year compounded over many decades, and even faster in agriculture, the basis for setting costs in the service-dominated sectors has gone up too.

In the postwar period, costs of the same units of output have increased very rapidly in certain key activities of local government. For example, education is the single biggest form of expenditure by local governments (including school districts), accounting for over 40 percent of their outlays. From 1947 to 1967, costs per pupil-day in U.S. public schools rose at a rate of 6.7 percent per year compounded—only slightly less than doubling every 10 years. This major cost item is likely to keep on rising rapidly in the future, along with other government services like police, fire, and welfare activities.

Some increases in productivity may occur in these fields, and some economies may be achieved through use of assistants such as police and teachers' aides. Nevertheless, the need to keep pace with private sector wage scales will force local government costs to rise sharply.

This and other future cost increases are important to future relations between central cities and suburbs. Rising costs will inevitably force central cities to demand more and more assistance from the Federal Government. But the Federal Government can obtain such funds through the income tax only from other parts of the economy. Suburban governments are, meanwhile, experiencing the same cost increases along with the rising resentment of their constituents.

CHOICES FOR THE FUTURE

The complexity of American society offers many choices for the future of relations between central cities and suburbs and patterns of white and Negro settlement in metropolitan areas. For practical purposes, however, we see two fundamental questions:

Should future Negro population growth be concentrated in central cities, as in the past 20 years, thereby forcing Negro and white populations to become even more residentially segregated?

Should society provide greatly increased special assistance to Negroes and other relatively disadvantaged population groups?

For purposes of analysis, the Commission has defined three basic choices for the future embodying specific answers to these questions:

The Present Policies Choice

Under this course, the Nation would maintain approximately the share of resources now being allocated to programs of assistance for the poor, unemployed and disadvantaged. These programs are likely to grow, given continuing economic growth and rising Federal revenues, but they will not grow fast enough to stop, let alone reverse, the already deteriorating quality of life in central-city ghettos.

This choice carries the highest ultimate price, as we will point out.

The Enrichment Choice

Under this course, the Nation would seek to offset the effects of continued Negro segregation and deprivation in large city ghettos. The enrichment choice would aim at creating dramatic improvements in the quality of life in disadvantaged central-city neighborhoods—both white and Negro. It would require marked increases in Federal spending for education, housing, employment, job training, and social services.

The enrichment choice would seek to lift poor Negroes and whites above poverty status and thereby give them the capacity to enter the mainstream of American life. But it would not, at least for many years, appreciably affect either the increasing concentration of Negroes in the ghetto or racial segregation in residential areas outside the ghetto.

The Integration Choice

This choice would be aimed at reversing the movement of the country toward two societies, separate and unequal.

The integration choice—like the enrichment choice—would call for large-scale improvement in the quality of ghetto life. But it would also involve both creating strong incentives for Negro movement out of central-city ghettos and enlarging freedom of choice concerning housing, employment, and schools.

The result would fall considerably short of full integration. The experience of other ethnic groups indicates that some Negro households would be scattered in largely white residential areas. Others—probably a larger number—would voluntarily cluster together in largely Negro neighborhoods. The integration choice would thus produce both integration and segregation. But the segregation would be voluntary.

Articulating these three choices plainly oversimplifies the possibilities open to the country. We believe, however, that they encompass the basic issues—issues which the American public must face if it is serious in its concern not only about civil disorder, but the future of our democratic society.

THE PRESENT POLICIES CHOICE

Powerful forces of social and political inertia are moving the country steadily along the course of existing policies toward a divided country.

This course may well involve changes in many social and economic programs—but not enough to produce fundamental alterations in the key factors of Negro concentration, racial segregation, and the lack of sufficient enrichment to arrest the decay of deprived neighborhoods.

Some movement toward enrichment can be found in efforts to encourage industries to locate plants in central cities, in increased Federal expenditures for education, in the important concepts embodied in the "War on Poverty," and in the Model Cities Program. But Congressional appropriations for even present Federal programs have been so small that they fall short of effective enrichment.

As for challenging concentration and segregation, a national commitment to this purpose has yet to develop.

Of the three future courses we have defined, the present policies choice—the choice we are now making—is the course with the most ominous consequences for our society.

The Probability of Future Civil Disorders

We believe that the present policies choice would lead to a larger number of violent incidents of the kind that have stimulated recent major disorders.

First, it does nothing to raise the hopes, absorb the energies, or constructively challenge the talents of the rapidly growing number of young Negro men in central cities. The proportion of unemployed or under-employed among them will remain very high. These young men have contributed disproportionately to crime and violence in cities in the past, and there is danger, obviously, that they will continue to do so.

Second, under these conditions, a rising proportion of Negroes in disadvantaged city areas might come to look upon the deprivation and segregation they suffer as proper justification for violent protest or for extending support to now isolated extremists who advocate civil disruption by guerrilla tactics.

More incidents would not necessarily mean more or worse riots. For the near future, there is substantial likelihood that even an increased number of incidents could be controlled before becoming major disorders, if society undertakes to improve police and National Guard forces so that they can respond to potential disorders with more prompt and disciplined use of force.

In fact, the likelihood of incidents mushrooming into major disorders would be only slightly higher in the near future under the present policies choice than under the other two possible choices. For no new policies or programs could possibly alter basic ghetto conditions immediately. And the announcement of new programs under the other choices would immediately generate new expectations. Expectations inevitably increase faster than performance. In the short run, they might even increase the level of frustration.

In the long run, however, the present policies choice risks a seriously greater probability of major disorders, worse, possibly, than those already experienced.

If the Negro population as a whole developed even stronger feelings of being wrongly "penned in" and discriminated against, many of its members might come to support not only riots, but the rebellion now being preached by only a handful. Large-scale violence, followed by white retaliation could follow. This spiral could quite conceivably lead to a kind of urban *apartheid* with semimartial law in many major cities, enforced residence of Negroes in segregated areas, and a drastic reduction in personal freedom for all Americans, particularly Negroes.

The same distinction is applicable to the cost of the present policies choice. In the short run, its costs—at least its direct cash outlays—would be far less than for the other choices.

Social and economic programs likely to have significant lasting effect would require very substantial annual appropriations for many years. Their cost would far exceed the direct losses sustained in recent civil disorders. Property damage in all the disorders we investigated, including Detroit and Newark, totaled less than $100 million.

But it would be a tragic mistake to view the present policies choice as cheap. Damage figures measure only a small part of the costs of civil disorder. They cannot measure the costs in terms of the lives lost, injuries suffered, minds and attitudes closed and frozen in prejudice, or the hidden costs of the profound disruption of entire cities.

Ultimately, moreover, the economic and social costs of the present policies choice will far surpass the cost of the alternatives. The rising concentration of impoverished Negroes and other minorities within the urban ghettos will constantly expand public expenditures for welfare, law enforcement, unemployment, and other existing programs without arresting the decay of older city neighborhoods and the breeding of frustration and discontent. But the most significant item on the balance of accounts will remain largely invisible and incalculable—the toll in human values taken by continued poverty, segregation, and inequality of opportunity.

Polarization

Another and equally serious consequence is the fact that this course would lead to the permanent establishment of two societies: one predominantly white and located in the suburbs, in smaller cities, and in outlying areas, and one largely Negro located in central cities.

We are well on the way to just such a divided nation.

This division is veiled by the fact that Negroes do not now dominate many central cities. But they soon will, as we have shown, and the new Negro mayors will be facing even more difficult conditions than now exist.

As Negroes succeed whites in our largest cities, the proportion of low-income residents in those cities will probably increase. This is likely even if both white and Negro incomes continue to rise at recent rates, since Negroes have much lower incomes than whites. Moreover, many of the ills of large central cities spring from their age, their location, and their obsolete physical structures. The deterioration and economic decay stemming from these factors have been proceeding for decades and will continue to plague older cities regardless of who resides in them.

These facts underlie the fourfold dilemma of the American city:

Fewer tax dollars come in, as large numbers of middle-income taxpayers move out of central cities and property values and business decline;

More tax dollars are required to provide essential public services and facilities, and to meet the needs of expanding lower income groups;

Each tax dollar buys less, because of increasing costs;

Citizen dissatisfaction with municipal services grows as needs, expectations and standards of living increase throughout the community.

These are the conditions that would greet the Negro-dominated municipal governments that will gradually come to power in many of our major cities. The Negro electorates in those cities probably would demand basic changes in present policies. Like the present white electorates there, they would have to look for assistance to two basic sources: the private sector and the Federal Government.

With respect to the private sector, major private capital investment in those cities might have ceased almost altogether if white-dominated firms and industries decided the risks and costs were too great. The withdrawal of private capital is already far advanced in most all-Negro areas of our large cities.

Even if private investment continued, it alone would not suffice. Big cities containing high proportions of low-income Negroes and block after block of deteriorating older property need very substantial assistance from the Federal Government to meet the demands of their electorates for improved services and living conditions.

It is probable, however, that Congress will be more heavily influenced by representatives of the surburban and outlying city electorate. These areas will comprise 40 percent of our total population by 1985, compared with 31 percent in 1960; and central cities will decline from 32 percent to 27 percent.

Since even the suburbs will be feeling the squeeze of higher local government costs, Congress might resist providing the extensive assistance which central cities will desperately need.

Thus the present policies choice, if pursued for any length of time, might force simultaneous political and economic polarization in many of our largest metropolitan areas. Such polarization would involve large central cities—mainly Negro, with many poor, and nearly bankrupt—on the one hand and most suburbs—mainly white, generally affluent, but heavily taxed—on the other hand.

Some areas might avoid political confrontation by shifting to some form of metropolitan government designed to offer regional solutions for pressing urban problems such as property taxation, air and water pollution, refuse disposal, and commuter transport. Yet this would hardly eliminate the basic segregation and relative poverty of the urban Negro population. It might even increase the Negro's sense of frustration and alienation if it operated to prevent Negro political control of central cities.

The acquisition of power by Negro-dominated governments in central cities is surely a legitimate and desirable exercise of political power by a minority group. It is in an American political tradition exemplified by the achievements of the Irish in New York and Boston.

But such Negro political development would also involve virtually complete racial segregation and virtually complete spatial separation. By 1985, the separate Negro society in our central cities would contain almost 21 million citizens. That is almost 68 percent larger than the present Negro population of central cities. It is also larger than the current population of every Negro nation in Africa except Nigeria.

If developing a racially integrated society is extraordinarily difficult today when 12.1 million Negroes live in central cities, then it is quite clearly going to be virtually impossible in 1985 when almost 21 million Negroes—still much poorer and less educated than most whites—will be living there.

Can Present Policies Avoid Extreme Polarization?

There are at least two possible developments under the present policies choice which might avert such polarization. The first is a faster increase of incomes among Negroes than has occurred in the recent past. This might prevent central cities from becoming even deeper "poverty traps" than they now are. It suggests the importance of effective job programs and higher levels of welfare payments for dependent families.

The second possible development is migration of a growing Negro middle class out of the central city. This would not prevent competition for Federal funds between central cities and outlying areas, but it might diminish the racial undertones of that competition.

There is, however, no evidence that a continuation of present policies would be accompanied by any such movement. There is already a significant Negro middle class. It grew rapidly from 1960 to 1966. Yet in these years, 88.9 percent of the total national growth of Negro population was concentrated in central cities—the highest in history. Indeed, from 1960 to 1966, there was actually a net total in-migration of Negroes from the urban fringes of metropolitan areas into central cities. The Commission believes it unlikely that this trend will suddenly reverse itself without significant changes in private attitudes and public policies.

THE ENRICHMENT CHOICE

The present policies choice plainly would involve continuation of efforts like Model Cities, manpower programs, and the War on Poverty. These are in fact enrichment programs, designed to improve the quality of life in the ghetto.

Because of their limited scope and funds, however, they constitute only very modest steps toward enrichment—and would continue to do so even if these programs were somewhat enlarged or supplemented.

The premise of the enrichment choice is performance. To adopt this choice would require a substantially greater share of national resources—sufficient to make a dramatic, visible impact on life in the urban Negro ghetto.

The Effect of Enrichment on Civil Disorders

Effective enrichment policies probably would have three immediate effects on civil disorders.

First, announcement of specific large-scale programs and the demonstration of a strong intent to carry them out might persuade ghetto residents that genuine remedies for their problems were forthcoming, thereby allaying tensions.

Second, such announcements would strongly stimulate the aspirations and hopes of members of these communities—possibly well beyond the capabilities of society to deliver and to do so promptly. This might increase frustration and discontent, to some extent canceling the first effect.

Third, if there could be immediate action on meaningful job training and the creation of productive jobs for large numbers of unemployed young people, they would become much less likely to engage in civil disorders.

Such action is difficult now, when there are about 585,000 young Negro men aged 14 to 24 in the civilian labor force in central cities—of whom 81,000 or 13.8 percent, are unemployed and probably two or three times as many are underemployed. It will not become easier in the future. By 1975, this age group will have grown to approximately 700,000.

Given the size of the present problem, plus the large growth of this age group, creation of sufficient meaningful jobs will require extensive programs, begun rapidly. Even if the Nation is willing to embark on such programs, there is no certainty that they can be made effective soon enough.

Consequently, there is no certainty that the enrichment choice would do much more in the near future to diminish violent incidents in central cities than would the present policies choice. However, if enrichment programs can succeed in meeting the needs of residents of disadvantaged areas for jobs, education, housing, and city services, then over the years this choice is almost certain to reduce both the level and frequency of urban disorder.

The Negro Middle Class

One objective of the enrichment choice would be to help as many disadvantaged Americans as possible—of all races—to enter the mainstream of American prosperity, to progress toward what is often called middle-class status. If the enrichment choice were adopted, it could certainly attain this objective to a far greater degree than would the present policies choice. This could significantly change the quality of life in many central-city areas.

It can be argued that a rapidly enlarging Negro middle class would also promote Negro out-migration, and that the enrichment choice would thus open up an escape hatch from the ghetto. This argument, however, has two weaknesses.

The first is experience. Central cities already have sizable and growing numbers of middle-class Negro families. Yet only a few have migrated from the central city. The past pattern of white ethnic groups gradually moving out of central-city areas to middle-class suburbs has not applied to Negroes. Effective open-housing laws will help make this possible, but it is probable that other more extensive changes in policies and attitudes will be required—and these would extend beyond the enrichment choice.

The second weakness in the argument is time. Even if enlargement of the Negro middle class succeeded in encouraging movement out of the central city, it could not do so fast enough to offset the rapid growth of the ghetto. To offset even *half* the growth estimated for the ghetto by 1975 an out-migration from central cities of 217,000 persons a year would be required. This is eight times the annual increase in suburban Negro population—including natural increase— that occurred from 1960 to 1966. Even the most effective enrichment program is not likely to accomplish this.

A corollary problem derives from the continuing migration of poor Negroes from the Southern to Northern and Western cities. Adoption of the enrichment choice would require large-scale efforts to improve conditions in the South sufficiently to remove the pressure to migrate. Under present conditions, slightly over a third of the estimated increase in Negro central-city population by 1985 will result from in-migration—3.0 million out of total increase of 8.2 million.

Negro Self-Development

The enrichment choice is in line with some of the currents of Negro protest thought that fall under the label of "Black Power." We do not refer to versions of Black-Power ideology which promote violence, generate racial hatred, or advocate total separation of the races. Rather, we mean the view which asserts that the American Negro population can assume its proper role in society and overcome its feelings of powerlessness and lack of self-respect only by exerting power over decisions which directly affect its own members. A fully integrated society is not thought possible until the Negro minority within the ghetto has developed political strength—a strong bargaining position in dealing with the rest of society.

In short, this argument would regard predominantly Negro central cities and predominantly white outlying areas not as harmful, but as an advantageous future.

Proponents of these views also focus on the need for the Negro to organize economically as well as politically, thus tapping new energies and resources for self-development. One of the hardest tasks in improving disadvantaged areas is to discover how deeply deprived residents can develop their own capabilities by participating more fully in decisions and activities which affect them. Such learning-by-doing efforts are a vital part of the process of bringing deprived people into the social mainstream.

Separate but Equal Societies?

The enrichment choice by no means seeks to perpetuate racial segregation. In the end, however, its premise is that disadvantaged Negroes can achieve equality of opportunity with whites while continuing in conditions of nearly complete separation.

This premise has been vigorously advocated by Black-Power proponents. While most Negroes originally desired racial integration, many are losing hope of ever achieving it because of seemingly implacable white resistance. Yet they cannot bring themselves to accept the conclusion that most of the millions of Negroes who are forced to live racially segregated lives must therefore be condemned to inferior lives—to inferior educations, or inferior housing, or inferior status.

Rather, they reason, there must be some way to make the quality of life in the ghetto areas just as good—or better—than elsewhere. It is not surprising that some Black-Power advocates are denouncing integration and claiming that, given the hypocrisy and racism that pervade white society, life in a black society is, in fact, morally superior. This argument is understandable, but there is a great deal of evidence that it is unrealistic.

The economy of the United States and particularly the sources of employment are preponderantly white. In this circumstance, a policy of separate but equal employment could only relegate Negroes permanently to inferior incomes and economic status.

The best evidence regarding education is contained in recent reports of the Office of Education and Civil Rights Commission which suggest that both racial and economic integration are essential to educational equality for Negroes. Yet critics point out that certainly until integration is achieved, various types of enrichment programs must be tested, and that dramatically different results may be possible from intensive educational enrichment—such as far smaller classes, or greatly expanded preschool programs, or changes in the home environment of Negro children resulting from steady jobs for fathers.

Still others advocate shifting control over ghetto schools from professional administrators to local residents. This, they say, would improve curricula, give students a greater sense of their own value, and thus raise their morale and educational achievement. These approaches have not yet been tested sufficiently. One conclusion, however, does seem reasonable: Any real improvement in the quality of education in low-income, all-Negro areas will cost a great deal more money than is now being spent there—and perhaps more than is being spent per pupil anywhere. Racial and social class integration of schools may produce equal improvement in achievement at less total cost.

Whether or not enrichment in ghetto areas will really work is not yet known, but the enrichment choice is based on the yet-unproven premise that it will. Certainly, enrichment programs could significantly improve existing ghetto schools if they impelled major innovations. But "separate but equal" ghetto education cannot meet the long-run fundamental educational needs of the central-city Negro population.

The three basic educational choices are: Providing Negro children with quality education in integrated schools; providing them with quality education by enriching ghetto schools; or continuing to provide many Negro children with inferior education in racially segregated school systems, severely limiting their lifetime opportunities.

Consciously or not, it is the third choice that the Nation is now making, and this choice the Commission rejects totally.

In the field of housing, it is obvious that "separate but equal" does not mean really equal. The enrichment choice could greatly improve the quantity, variety, and environment of decent housing available to the ghetto population. It could not provide Negroes with the same freedom and range of choice as whites with equal incomes. Smaller cities and suburban areas together with the central city provide a far greater variety of housing and environmental settings than the central city alone. Programs to provide housing outside central cities, however, extend beyond the bounds of the enrichment choice.

In the end, whatever its benefits, the enrichment choice might well invite a prospect similar to that of the present policies choice: separate white and black societies.

If enrichment programs were effective, they could greatly narrow the gap in income, education, housing, jobs, and other qualities of life between the ghetto and the mainstream. Hence, the chances of harsh polarization—or of disorder—in the next 20 years would be greatly reduced.

Whether they would be reduced far enough depends on the scope of the programs. Even if the gap were narrowed from the present, it still could remain as a strong source of tension. History teaches that men are not necessarily placated even by great absolute progress. The controlling factor is relative progress—whether they still perceive a significant gap between themselves and others whom they regard as no more deserving. Widespread perception of such a gap—and consequent resentment—might well be precisely the situation 20 years from now under the enrichment choice, for it is essentially another way of choosing a permanently divided country.

THE INTEGRATION CHOICE

The third and last course open to the Nation combines enrichment with programs designed to encourage integration of substantial numbers of Negroes into the society outside the ghetto.

Enrichment must be an important adjunct to any integration course. No matter how ambitious or energetic such a program may be, relatively few Negroes now living in central-city ghettos would be quickly integrated. In the meantime, significant improvement in their present environment is essential.

The enrichment aspect of this third choice should, however, be recognized as interim action, during which time expanded and new programs can work to improve education and earning power. The length of the interim period surely would vary. For some it may be long. But in any event, what should be clearly recognized is that enrichment is only a means toward the goal; it is not the goal.

The goal must be achieving freedom for every citizen to live and work according to his capacities and desires, not his color.

We believe there are four important reasons why American society must give this course the most serious consideration. First, future jobs are being created primarily in the suburbs, while the chronically unemployed population is increasingly concentrated in the ghetto. This separation will make it more and more difficult for Negroes to achieve anything like full employment in decent jobs. But if, over time, these residents began to find housing outside central cities, they would be exposed to more knowledge of job opportunities, would have much shorter trips to reach jobs, and would have a far better chance of securing employment on a self-sustaining basis.

Second, in the judgment of this Commission, racial and social-class integration is the most effective way of improving the education of ghetto children.

Third, developing an adequate housing supply for low-income and middle-income families and true freedom of choice in housing for Negroes of all income levels will require substantial out-movement. We do not believe that such an out-movement will occur spontaneously merely as a result of increasing prosperity among Negroes in central cities. A national fair housing law is essential to begin such movement. In many suburban areas, a program combining positive incentives with the building of new housing will be necessary to carry it out.

Fourth, and by far the most important, integration is the only course which explicitly seeks to achieve a single nation rather than accepting the present movement toward a dual society. This choice would enable us at least to begin reversing the profoundly divisive trend already so evident in our metropolitan areas—before it becomes irreversible.

CONCLUSIONS

The future of our cities is neither something which will just happen nor something which will be imposed upon us by an inevitable destiny. That future will be shaped to an important degree by choices we make now.

We have attempted to set forth the major choices because we believe it is vital for Americans to understand the consequences of our present drift:

Three critical conclusions emerge from this analysis:

1. The nation is rapidly moving toward two increasingly separate Americas.

Within two decades, this division could be so deep that it would be almost impossible to unite:

a white society principally located in suburbs, in smaller central cities, and in the peripheral parts of large central cities; and
a Negro society largely concentrated within large central cities.

The Negro society will be permanently relegated to its current status, possibly even if we expend great amounts of money and effort in trying to "gild" the ghetto.

2. In the long run, continuation and expansion of such a permanent division threatens us with two perils.

The first is the danger of sustained violence in our cities. The timing, scale, nature, and repercussions of such violence cannot be foreseen. But if it occurred, it would further destroy our ability to achieve the basic American promises of liberty, justice, and equality.

The second is the danger of a conclusive repudiation of the traditional American ideals of individual dignity, freedom, and equality of opportunity. We will not be able to espouse these ideals meaningfully to the rest of the world, to ourselves, to our children. They may still recite the Pledge of Allegiance and say "one nation . . . indivisible." But they will be learning cynicism, not patriotism.

3. We cannot escape responsibility for choosing the future of our metropolitan areas and the human relations which develop within them. It is a responsibility so critical that even an unconscious choice to continue present policies has the gravest implications.

That we have delayed in choosing or, by delaying, may be making the wrong choice, does not sentence us either to separatism or despair. But we must choose. We will choose. Indeed, we are now choosing.

CHAPTER SIX

MEGALOPOLIS: CRISIS AND CHALLENGE

In the preceding chapters the conditions of modern urban life have been scrutinized in order to decipher the impact of city growth upon urban dwellers. The relationship of the human personality to these new conditions, the ordering of space and spatial factors within the city, and the attempt to promote societal stability among the urbanites seem to represent the major concern of those who study and examine the city. Perhaps the most demanding task for the student of urbanism is to disentangle the intricate web of contradiction and paradox which is the contemporary urban crisis. Close proximity and personal involvement in the baneful results of urbanism—congestion, pollution, disorder, and racial conflict—have deadened our capacity to sort out objectively either the causes or primary problems engendered by urbanization.

The discovery of newer dimensions to the urbanization process further confuses the attempt to define the problems. No longer is the "city" an adequate term to describe the dense congregations of humans in areas in which nonagricultural pursuits are followed. We have advanced from the conceptualization of the city as metropolis and region to the recognition of a different, more imposing and gargantuan urban complexity, the city as "megalopolis." This concept, popularized by the French geographer Jean Gottman, refers to the cluster of metropolitan areas linked together along the northeastern seaboard of the United States. Gottman, a professor at the University of Paris who had made a comprehensive survey of the state of Virginia, was selected by the Twentieth Century Fund to present an interdisciplinary approach to the study of modern urban life.

A more precise term for this urban conglomerate is "connurbation," coined at the turn of the century by Scottish biologist and regional planner, Patrick Geddes. Connurbation more readily symbolizes the fantastic concentration of population within a series of urban areas running from southern New Hampshire to northern Virginia. The notion of overlapping metropolitan areas raises broad and complex questions relating to population density and movement, suburban sprawl, land use, municipal politics, metropolitan resource use and regional plan-

251

ning. This new insight further complicates the attempt to isolate the primary factors contributing to the intensities of urban life.[1]

Clearly, the notion of what a city is, or should be, needs amplification before urban problems can be successfully challenged. The critics of American city planning contend that for too long the urban milieu has been considered primarily as a marketplace or production center, and that the human needs of urban dwellers demand priority over developmental progress. In addition, sociologist Nathan Glazer maintains that city-planners operating under the misguided idea of the "garden city" contributed to the urban malaise because they planned for the suburb and not the city. By imposing a system of order based upon decentralization, planners have stimulated the flight to suburbia and the creation of inner city ghettos. Jane Jacobs argues that the resulting suburban sprawl breeds conformity, but more significantly, destroys the richness of variety and texture which is to be found only in the city. Thus, according to these authors, unenlightened city planning has accelerated the tenor of the urban crisis.

Everyone agrees that there are urban problems, but a consensus seems to be lacking as to whether these problems represent a "crisis." Indeed, some noted urbanologists,[2] in an attempt to preserve an objective approach, point out that in actual fact the condition of urban life has improved considerably in the last 50 years. Even a cursory examination of available statistics vividly demonstrates that increases of family income, higher standards of living, health, housing and educational improvements, and, curiously, the reduction of crime have taken great strides in the last half century. This "improvement" process has been due to the tremendous technological progress which has occurred. Ironically, however, the evident material progress seems to have resulted in a worsening urban condition. This dismal vision may signify a healthy insight: a crisis seems at hand because of the recognition that man has the technological power to improve or revamp society but seems unwilling to use this instrument of change, except in a halting and often destructive manner.

Technology, or the control over inanimate sources of energy to produce goods and services, is completely dependent for direction upon the caprice or wisdom of the society for which it operates. The institutional and cultural mores of American society are based upon a value structure of individualism and private enterprise, which determines (or vitiates) all attempts at utilizing our technological dexterity to resolve collective urban problems. All the programs of government aimed at redressing the worst conditions of urban life—whether they be urban renewal, public housing, or welfare subsidies—seem to flounder ineffectively. This congenital lack of effectiveness is highlighted by the apparent failure of the major federal program initiated to eliminate slums—urban renewal. In his

---

[1]Not all students of the metropolis find Gottmann's characterization accurate for describing developments taking place in the United States. See, for example, Hans Blumenfeld, "The Modern Metropolis," *Scientific American,* 213 (September, 1965) pp. 64-74.

[2]Among those who have noted this phenomena of progress are Nathan Glazer, Richard Wade, Blake McKelvey, and Constance McLaughlin Green.

trenchant commentary on urban renewal, Herbert Gans clarifies the inherent misdirection of a national policy based upon local control and private incentive. His study of Boston's West End neighborhood, *The Urban Villagers,* illustrated how a stable and thriving low-income community could be torn apart by such ill-conceived federal/municipal actions. The pessimistic prognosis of the National Advisory Commission on Civil Disorders seems to be borne out by the incapacity of governmental and private forces to cope with urban growth. "We believe that the present policies choice would lead to a larger number of violent incidents of the kind that have stimulated major disorders."

There is no simple solution; in fact, the clarification of the "dilemmas" of urban America needs to be stressed. The summation of these dilemmas, such as housing and integration, by Robert Weaver, the first cabinet officer designated to cope with urban affairs, reveals the stark and frightening impasse at which we have arrived. What emerges is a plea for a reconsideration of those institutions and cultural forces which predispose our response to the threatening factors spawned by urbanization. It is our hope that the readings in this book will contribute to the difficult but imperative process of a national self-awareness.

Megalopolis

by Jean Gottmann*

The Northeastern seaboard of the United States is today the site of a remarkable development—an almost continuous stretch of urban and suburban areas from southern New Hampshire to northern Virginia and from the Atlantic shore to the Appalachian foothills. The processes of urbanization, rooted deep in the American past, have worked steadily here, endowing the region with unique ways of life and of land use. No other section of the United States has such a large concentration of population, with such a high average density, spread over such a large area. And no other section has a comparable role within the nation or a comparable importance in the world. Here has been developed a kind of supremacy, in politics, in economics, and possibly even in cultural activities, seldom before attained by an area of this size.

A Very Special Region: Megalopolis

This region has indeed a "personality" of its own, which for some three centuries past has been changing and evolving, constantly creating new problems for its inhabitants and exerting a deep influence on the general organization of society. The modern trends in its development and its present degree of crowding provides both examples and warnings for other less urbanized areas in America and abroad and call for a profound revision of many old concepts, such as the usually accepted distinctions between city and country. As a result new meanings must be given to some old terms, and some new terms must be created.

Great, then, is the importance and significance of this section of the United States and of the processes now at work within it. And yet it is difficult to single this area out from surrounding areas, for its limits cut across established historical divisions, such as New England and the Middle Atlantic states, and across political entities, since it includes some states entirely and others only partially. A special name is needed, therefore, to identify this special geographical area.

*Jean Gottmann, *Megalopolis: The Urbanized Northeastern Seaboard of the United States* (Cambridge: The MIT Press, 1961 and 1966), pp. 3-16. Reprinted with permission of the Twentieth Century Fund.

This particular type of region is new, but it is the result of age-old processes, such as the growth of cities, the division of labor within a civilized society, the development of world resources. The name applied to it should, therefore, be new as a place name but old as a symbol of the long tradition of human aspirations and endeavor underlying the situations and problems now found here. Hence the choice of the term *Megalopolis,* used in this study.

Some two thousand years before the first European settlers landed on the shores of the James River, Massachusetts Bay, and Manhattan Island, a group of ancient people, planning a new city-state in the Peloponnesus in Greece, called it *Megalopolis,* for they dreamed of a great future for it and hoped it would become the largest of the Greek cities. Their hopes did not materialize. Megalopolis still appears on modern maps of the Peloponnesus but it is just a small town nestling in a small river basin. Through the centuries the word *Megalopolis* has been used in many senses by various people, and it has even found its way into Webster's dictionary, which defines it as "a very large city." Its use, however, has not become so common that it could not be applied in a new sense, as a geographical place name for the unique cluster of metropolitan areas of the Northeastern seaboard of the United States. There, if anywhere in our times, the dream of those ancient Greeks has come true.

An Urbanized Area with a Nebulous Structure

As one follows the main highways or railroads between Boston and Washington, D.C., one hardly loses sight of built-up areas, tightly woven residential communities, or powerful concentrations of manufacturing plants. Flying this same route one discovers, on the other hand, that behind the ribbons of densely occupied land along the principal arteries of traffic, and in between the clusters of suburbs around the old urban centers, there still remain large areas covered with woods and brush alternating with some carefully cultivated patches of farmland. These green spaces, however, when inspected at closer range, appear stuffed with a loose but immense scattering of buildings, most of them residential but some of industrial character. That is, many of these sections that look rural actually function largely as suburbs in the orbit of some city's downtown. Even the farms, which occupy the larger tilled patches, are seldom worked by people whose only occupation and income are properly agricultural. And yet these farm areas produce large quantities of farm goods!

Thus the old distinctions between rural and urban do not apply here any more. Even a quick look at the vast area of Megalopolis reveals a revolution in land use. Most of the people living in the so-called rural areas, and still classified as "rural population" by recent censuses, have very little, if anything, to do with agriculture. In terms of their interests and work they are what used to be classified as "city folks," but their way of life and the landscapes around their residences do not fit the old meaning of urban.

In this area, then, we must abandon the idea of the city as a tightly settled and organized unit in which people, activities, and riches are crowded into a very small area clearly separated from its nonurban surroundings. Every city in this region spreads out far and wide around its original nucleus; it grows amidst an irregularly colloidal mixture of rural and suburban landscapes; it melts on broad fronts with other mixtures,of somewhat similar though different texture, belonging to the suburban neighborhoods of other cities. Such coalescence can be observed, for example, along the main lines of traffic that link New York City and Philadelphia. Here there are many communities that might be classified as belonging to more than one orbit. It is hard to say whether they are suburbs, or "satellites," of Philadelphia or New York, Newark, New Brunswick, or Trenton. The latter three cities themselves have been reduced to the role of suburbs of New York City in many respects, although Trenton belongs also to the orbit of Philadelphia. . . .

The "standard metropolitan areas," first used by the U. S. Bureau of the Census in 1950, have clarified this confused situation somewhat but not entirely. For example, the New York-Northeastern New Jersey standard metropolitan area cuts across political boundaries to reveal the relationships of this vast region to the core city of New York. And yet the mechanical application of the term "standard metropolitan area" has resulted in the establishment of separate areas for Trenton, which is closely tied to both Philadelphia and New York, and for Bridgeport, which is for many practical purposes part of the New York area. Similar problems can be found in other parts of Megalopolis.

Thus an almost continuous system of deeply interwoven urban and suburban areas, with a total population of about 37 million people in 1960, has been erected along the Northeastern Atlantic seaboard. It straddles state boundaries, stretches across wide estuaries and bays, and encompasses many regional differences. In fact, the landscapes of Megalopolis offer such variety that the average observer may well doubt the unity of the region. And it may seem to him that the main urban nuclei of the seaboard are little related to one another. Six of its great cities would be great individual metropolises in their own right if they were located elsewhere. This region indeed reminds one of Aristotle's saying that cities such as Babylon had "the compass of a nation rather than a city."

Megalopolis—Main Street and Crossroads of the Nation

There are many other large metropolitan areas and even clusters of them in various parts of the United States, but none of them is yet comparable to Megalopolis in size of population, density of population, or density of activities, be these expressed in terms of transportation, communications, banking operations, or political conferences. Megalopolis provides the whole of America with so many essential services, of the sort a community used to obtain in its "downtown" section, that it may well deserve the nickname of "Main Street of the nation." And for three centuries it has performed this role, though the transcontinental march of settlement has developed along east-west axes perpendicular to this section of the Atlantic seaboard.

In recent times Megalopolis has had concentrated within it more of the Main Street type of functions than ever, and it does not yet seem prepared to relinquish any of them. Witness, for example, the impact of the Federal government in Washington, D.C., as it tightens up over many aspects of national life; the continued crowding of financial and managerial operations into Manhattan; New York's dominance of the national market for mass communication media, which resists all attempts at erosion; and the pre-eminent influence of the universities and cultural centers of Megalopolis on American thinking and policy-making. Megalopolis is also the country's chief façade toward the rest of the world. From it, as from the Main Street of a city, local people leave for distant travel, and to it arriving strangers come. For immigrants it has always served as the chief debarkation wharf. And just as passing visitors often see little of a city except a few blocks of its Main Street, so most foreign visitors see only a part of Megalopolis on their sojourns in the United States.

Just as Main Street lives for and prospers because of the functions of the whole city, rather than because of any purely local advantages of its own, so is Megalopolis related to the whole United States and its rich resources. In general, Megalopolis itself was blessed only moderately by nature. It has no vast expanse of rich soils (there are some good soils but more poor ones), no special climatic advantages (its cyclonic climate is far from ideal), and no great mineral deposits (though there are some). In these respects it cannot compare with the generous natural potential of the Middle West or Texas or California. But it does excel in locational advantages—deep harbors of a drowned shoreline, on which its principal cities were early established, and a connecting-link relationship between the rich heart of the continent and the rest of the world. By hard work man has made the most of these locational resources, the most outstanding ones in an otherwise average natural endowment. As a result, early in its history Megalopolis became a dynamic hub of international relations, and it has maintained and constantly expanded that role to the present day. It is now the most active crossroads on earth, for people, ideas, and goods, extending its influence far beyond the national borders, and only as such a crossroads could it have achieved its present economic pre-eminence.

Megalopolis as a Laboratory of Urban Growth

Modern technology and social evolution provide increasing opportunity in urban pursuits on the one hand, and on the other steadily improving means of producing more agricultural goods with less manpower. The forces at work in our time, coupled with the growth in population, are, therefore, bound to channel a rising flow of people toward urban-type occupations and ways of life. As this tide reaches more and more cities they will burst out of old bounds to expand and scatter all over the landscape, taking new forms like those already observable throughout Megalopolis. This region serves thus as a laboratory in which we may study the new evolution reshaping both the meaning of our traditional vocabulary and the whole material structure of our way of life.

Tomorrow's society will be different from that in which we grew up, largely because it will be more urbanized. Nonagricultural ways of life will be followed by more and more people and will occupy much more space than they ever did, and such changes cannot develop without also deeply modifying agricultural life and production. So great are the consequences of the general evolution heralded by the present rise and complexity of Megalopolis that an analysis of this region's problems often gives one the feeling of looking at the dawn of a new stage in human civilization. The author has visited and studied various other regions of the world but has not experienced such a feeling anywhere else. Indeed, the area may be considered the cradle of a new order in the organization of inhabited space. This new order, however, is still far from orderly; here in its cradle it is all in flux and trouble, which does not facilitate the analyst's work. Nevertheless, a study of Megalopolis may shed some light on processes that are of great importance and interest.

A Study in Entangled Relationships

As the work of data-gathering and analysis progressed it became evident that the key to most of the questions involved in this study of Megalopolis lies in the interrelationships between the forces and processes at work within the area rather than in the trends of growth or the development of techniques. Thus the trend of population increase, easy to measure and perhaps to forecast approximately, provides less insight into the nature of the area than do the interrelations existing between the processes that caused the local population to grow, those that attracted certain kinds of people to Megalopolis, and those that supplied the swelling crowds with the means to live and work together there. Many of these processes are statistically measurable and some of them can be mapped, but the degree to which each of them stems from the others or determines them is a much more subtle matter, and is more basic to an understanding of what is going on and what can be done about it.

Most regional studies stay on the safer and more superficial grounds of statistical description and functional classifications. Had this report followed that pattern it would have been devoted mainly to summing up the abundant data available from the Censuses and other sources of general information about the various characteristics of Megalopolis. A description of natural conditions, such as topography, climate, hydrography, and vegetation, would have introduced a historical sketch to be followed by chapters on population, industries, trade, transportation and communications, the real estate market, other occupations, and descriptions of the main cities and of the general features of "rural areas." Such a report would have concluded with a description of present problems and forecasts of the future presented by means of graphs, based on the assumption that the trends of the past twenty to fifty years will continue for the next twenty years.

A mere compilation of such data would probably be of service to some people but it could hardly help those who need further insight into and understanding of the basic problems of the area. By attempting to find out more about the deeper processes and their entanglements, one may hope to achieve a more fundamental kind of knowledge, which can be applied to another area or projected into the future more safely, though not always more easily. This is why the present report is organized along a somewhat less classical outline, its goal being a more reasoned discussion and an objective analysis. For such complicated phenomena as the social and economic processes at work in Megalopolis there are, of course, numerous and interlocking determining factors. The author has endeavored to search for *all* these factors, keeping in mind their multiplicity and entanglements and avoiding any arbitrary choices among them.

Outline of This Report

Part One presents a sketch of the *dynamics of urbanization* and attempts to show, in terms of the region's history, why things have come to be as they are and where they are. Although this section is largely descriptive it cannot avoid raising some new questions.

Part Two takes up what may be called the *"modern revolution in land use."* The new mixture of urban and rural must be dissected and each part related to the others in the newly developing system. Separation between place of work and place of residence creates within the area the system of daily "tidal" movements involved in commuting. Over these are superimposed other currents, some seasonal and some irregularly recurrent. These reflect relations between different parts of Megalopolis that stem from more complicated needs than the simple journey from home to work. These other needs grow more complicated and more general as average family income rises and both goods and activities that were once considered dispensable come to be regarded as necessary by large numbers of Megalopolitans. As Montesquieu observed two centuries ago, on the eve of the Industrial Revolution, "It is the nature of commerce to make the superfluous useful and the useful necessary." Perhaps it is not commerce but just human nature that produces this sequence. At any rate it has certainly been proven true of the consumption of goods, and now it seems to apply to the consumption of activities and space. The modern urban revolution, so apparent already in the affluent society of Megalopolis, devours time and space as well as food and industrial goods, and the fulfilling of these needs requires many types of movements.

These various tidal movements involve a reshaping of land use. Much agricultural land has been taken over by residential and industrial development. On the remaining farms a new specialized type of agriculture is developing, which requires less space than did the old system of farming. Woods have spread over much of the land abandoned by the farms, and this expansion of forests calls for new methods and concepts of forestry management, to provide for recreational and other suburban needs and for a better conservation of the landscape and of wildlife. Simultaneously the old city cores or "downtowns" are evolving toward decline or renewal, while uptowns, suburbs, and outer suburbia are becoming interlocked in a new and still constantly changing web of relationships. Regional integration is taking on forms unknown a generation or two ago, and the old system of local, state, and national authorities and jurisdictions, which has changed little, is poorly suited to present needs.

New *patterns of intense living* that have become normal in Megalopolis affect not only land use. They also exert a strong influence on the economic and social foundations of society, and Part Three endeavors to describe the problems thus created. The density of activities and of movement of all kinds is certainly the most extraordinary feature of Megalopolis, more characteristic even than the density of population and of skyscrapers. It has become a means of maintaining economic growth and stabilizing society; but how far can it go without destroying itself? For example, the growth of Megalopolis owes much to the automobile, but highway traffic jams are beginning to strangle city activities and to take the pleasure and efficiency out of driving a car. At the same time cars contribute to the ruination of other means of transportation, made more necessary than ever by the massive tidal currents of people and goods. The self-defeating effect of dense concentrations may be observed also in other fields than transportation. Many industries, for example, are now aiming at decentralization. The intense living of Megalopolis makes a great deal of waste inescapable, waste of space and time as well as of materials. For a long time such waste may have seemed justifiable, for, paradoxically, the crowding that caused it brought higher economic yields. Now this crowding seems at times to defeat its own aims. Why and how does such intense living grow and threaten itself? Answers to these queries build up a general picture of a dynamic and prosperous society, obviously responsible for maintaining the growth of large-scale urbanization but responsible also for the problems the process creates and for finding the badly needed solutions.

It is easier to accept responsibility for solutions than to provide them. The many millions of people who find themselves *neighbors in Megalopolis,* even though they live in different states and hundreds of miles from one another, are barely becoming aware of the imperatives of such a "neighborhood." Part Four attempts to point them out. Responsible public opinion is becoming conscious of the problems involved, and the struggle to find solutions has started. It is especially difficult because no one problem can be tackled without affecting the others. Transportation, land use, water supply, cultural activities, use and development of resources, government and politics—all are interrelated.

Today it is essential that solutions be found to save this area from decay and to reassure the nation and the world about the kind of life modern urbanization trends presage for the future. Megalopolis has been built and often reshaped by its people. These people are now wealthier, better educated, and better endowed with technological means than ever. They ought to be able to find ways of avoiding decline of the area.

For the Better or for the Worse?

The preceding paragraph may seem to imply an unwarranted optimism about society's ability to control itself. True, history records a long list of brilliant civilizations that have sunk under the pressure of internal decay and external jealousy. We remember their names: Babylon, Corinth, Sparta, Athens, Rome, and many others. In the shadowy vistas of ancient times they vanished into the distance like shipwrecked ships loaded with ambition and precious cargo. Can such a fate be looming in the offing for Megalopolis? Modern urban sprawl is viewed by many as a threat to progress and general welfare. What is happening in Megalopolis today has been described as a pathological phenomenon, a sickness, a cancer. Such views are held by distinguished and respectable citizens of the area. One may well be alarmed by their invectives, all the more so as one does not have to go far away from Megalopolis to hear expressions of distrust and jealousy inspired by the amazing concentration of wealth and power in the great seaboard cities. Are people both in and out of this extraordinary region united in condemning it?

Urban growth in general has been discussed and condemned on moral grounds for a long time. Such debate is expectable and desirable, but on the whole history has shown the condemnation to be unjust, as can be seen by a brief review of some of the consequences of crowding.

Contrasts between rich and poor, for example, are especially striking in the crowded communities of cities. These may exist in rural areas too, but there they are diluted by scattering and veiled in greenery. The growth of urban pursuits (industries, trade, services) sharpens the contrasts by condensing them into a smaller area. Rich and poor live within short distances of one another and mix together in the streets in a way that often arouses righteous indignation. It seems brutally amoral to witness destitution neighboring on elegant sophistication, poverty mixing with prosperity. And yet, alas, a growing city's environment can hardly escape offering such sights. For many centuries there was an enormous difference between the advancement possible in trade and industry on the one hand and in farming on the other (though modern farm mechanization and subsidies to agriculture have substantially increased the profit possibilities of farming), and so to rise economically within the span of one lifetime has traditionally been easier in cities than in rural areas. The affluence of those who have so risen draws to the city large groups of humbler people, who come there to profit by the local abundance of money and the volume of spending and to serve the wealthier. In contrast to the more conservative "open" country, the "closed-in" city offers a more dynamic environment, socially and economically.

In cities, too, other vicious aspects of economic growth and social life have always been more evident than in the country. As urban development was accelerated by the Industrial Revolution, some of these vicious aspects became increasingly obvious. Slums and mobs grew worse than ever, making the urban landscape ethically and aesthetically shocking to those who cared about the people. From his sojourns in an industrializing western Europe, and especially from Paris during the French Revolution, Thomas Jefferson brought back impressions that reinforced his normal Virginian opposition to great cities and the development of manufactures or large-scale commerce. As slums and mobs became more general in European cities in the first half of the nineteenth century there arose more awareness about the classes of society and social injustice. There was more discussion of these matters, and the early Socialist doctrines were largely inspired by them. Then came the teachings of such philosophers as Fourier and Proudhon in France and Engels and Karl Marx in Germany, opposing great urban concentration as much as great concentration of capital. Engels' writings on the slums and working conditions in the then fast-developing British cities, such as Manchester, are well known. Because urban conditions of living and working were largely at the root of nineteenth-century Socialist doctrines, Karl Marx stressed that his theories applied much more to the industrialized countries of western Europe, which had accumulated large amounts of capital, than to the rural, little-urbanized countries to the east. Twentieth-century events have proved him wrong on this score, however, for communism has conquered the mainly rural countries, and the forms of socialism that developed in the more urban and capitalistic countries of the West have turned away from Marxism.

Crowding of population within a small area creates shortages of various resources, and most of the crowded people are bound to suffer in some ways because of the shortages. To alleviate them, to make crowding more bearable and the population happier, ways and means of constantly better distribution must be found. Otherwise no lasting growth can develop, and the whole enterprise will soon be doomed. From the struggle against such shortages have come some of mankind's most important advances. In the arid areas of the Middle East, for example, early civilization arose when people first congregated around the main springs and permanent rivers. As the settlement grew, the supply of both water and irrigable land became scarce. To insure survival of the people a proper distribution system had to be achieved, and rules and regulations had to be set up and accepted. Thus organized society, ruled by law, was born. Because authorities were needed to enforce law, political power arose, and people organized themselves to avoid more oppression than was necessary. Everywhere, the more crowded people have become in cities the more they have craved both security and freedom. Modern political life and its concepts of liberty, self-government, and democracy are the products of urban growth, the inheritance of cities in process of growth and development—places such as Jerusalem,

Athens, Rome, Bruges, Florence, Paris, London, to mention only those that have been most studied by historians. And the same places, or similar urban centers, have contributed most of our scientific and technological developments, either because people there were struggling to solve pressing problems or because urban societies make possible a leisurely enough elite, some of whose members can devote themselves to disinterested research and a search for a better understanding of the universe.

Thus urban crowding and the slums and mobs characteristic of it may be considered growing pains in the endless process of civilization.

In the same way, the picture of Megalopolis is not as dark as the outspoken pessimists and frequent protests would seem to paint it. Crowded within its limits is an extremely distinguished population. It is, *on the average,* the richest, best educated, best housed, and best serviced group of similar size (i.e., in the 25-to-40-million-people range) in the world. The area is still a focus of attraction for successful or adventurous people from all over America and beyond. It is true that many of its sections have seen pretty rural landscapes replaced by ugly industrial agglomerations or drab and monstrous residential developments; it is true that in many parts of Megalopolis the air is not clean any more, the noise is disturbing day and night, the water is not as pure as one would wish, and transportation at times becomes a nightmare. Many of these problems reflect the revolutionary change that has taken place as cities have burst out of their narrow bounds to scatter over the "open" countryside. In some ways this suburban sprawl may have alleviated a crowding that had threatened to become unbearable, for residential densities of population per square mile have decreased. But new problems have arisen because of the new densities of activities and of traffic in the central cities and because the formerly rural areas or small towns have been unprepared to cope with the new demands made upon their resources. New programs are needed to conserve the natural beauty of the landscape and to assure the health, prosperity, and freedom of the people. In spite of these problems, however, available statistics demonstrate that in Megalopolis the population is on the average healthier, the consumption of goods higher, and the opportunity for advancement greater than in any other region of comparable extent.

Thus the type of urban growth experienced here generates many contrasts, paradoxes, and apparently contradictory trends. It calls for debate and naturally excites passionate opinions for and against it. Are its results for the better or for the worse? It is not for our generation to moralize on the matter, but to strive to make the outcome be for the better, whatever obstacles may be in the way. Megalopolis stands indeed at the threshold of a new way of life, and upon solution of its problems will rest civilization's ability to survive. In the search for such solutions there will be found no easy keys to success, no "gimmicks" or "open-sesames." Solutions must be thought out, ironed out, and constantly revised in the light of all the knowledge that can be acquired by all concerned. It is the author's hope that this report, a systematic and sometimes critical analysis of the past and present of Megalopolis, will contribute to the gathering of such knowledge and to its distribution. At the same time, it will tell the story of an extraordinary region as its people have made it.

Why City Planning Is Obsolete

by Nathan Glazer*

Modern city planning has completely failed to plan for big cities in the twentieth century. It has failed because it has not yet broken loose from the "garden city" dream with which the planning movement began—an essentially small-town vision concerned with small-town values. What passes for city planning today is fundamentally a rejection of the big city and of all it means—its variety, its peculiarities, its richness of choice and experience—and a yearning for a bucolic society.

Solutions to the problems of the twentieth century big city are still to be found. But they will not be found unless we discard the outdated diagnoses and irrelevant solutions on which the planning movement grew, and which have been given sufficient trial to demonstrate their shortcomings. By now, there is a growing awareness of these inadequacies, on the part of some planners, but it may be helpful to explore how city planning wandered from the mark, and to suggest the kind of problems that must be faced if planning is to deal properly with big cities.

The garden city idea—which remains the strongest force in city planning even though it has taken on new guises and has been adapted to high population densities—was launched in 1899 in England by Ebenezer Howard, a court stenographer whose avocation was planning, as an effort to overcome the horrors of life in the nineteenth-century city. Howard's aim was to destroy the uniformity of the great city, to break it up into a series of small communities, places in which people could again live close to nature, in which they would be closer to their work, in which overcrowding would be reduced and anonymity replaced by small-town feeling. The image was the English country town—with the manor house and its park replaced by a community center, and with some factories hidden behind a screen of trees, to supply work.

The "garden city," from its inception, was thus suburban planning, not city planning, and the garden cities were physically placed outside the city proper. Nevertheless the garden city was conceived as an alternative to the city, and as a solution to city problems; this was, and is still, the foundation of its immense power as a planning idea.

*Nathan Glazer, "Why City Planning is Obsolete," *Architectural Forum,* 109 (July, 1958), pp. 96-98. Reprinted from the Architectural Forum, Copyright July 1958 by Time, Inc.

Made in America

The man in American town planning who stands closest to Howard in the character of his work, and his influence, is Architect and Planner Clarence Stein, now 76 years of age. Like Howard, Stein has been more than a propagandist for the values of the planned community. During the 1920's and 1930's he actually built new communities expressing his ideas and values. These communities demonstrated advantages over the customary suburb. There were superblocks, which were more varied than the gridiron street pattern, and which made it possible to merge back yards into parks and playgrounds in the middle of blocks. In Radburn, N.J. . . . , Stein's most impressive superblocks were built, separating motor traffic and pedestrian traffic.

It was obviously impossible to copy such planned garden communities *within* the dense city. This would have been much too expensive for the private philanthropic builders who were supporting the schemes of Stein and his colleagues. The power of eminent domain was also unavailable to Stein's backers. So these communities were built on the city outskirts. "This we should do," Stein wrote, "until such time as we have adequately demonstrated, by contrast, how unworkable and wasteful are the obsolete patterns of the old cities, and how completely they demand replacement."

The Skyscraper Town

Before the planned community could invade the city, however, some way had to be found by which population densities might be raised far beyond those envisaged by the garden city planners. The needed idea was dramatized by the French architect, Le Corbusier, who was fascinated by the vision of residential skyscrapers in a park. . . .

The Le Corbusier idea is in some respects diametrically opposed to the garden city idea; it is a scheme for building vertically instead of horizontally, for centralizing instead of dispersing. And yet, crucial concepts are common to both these main lines of planning: the notion of locating buildings in a park; and the corollary to this idea, the attack on the continuous row of linked buildings, lining the city street, which had been the major visual characteristic of cities throughout history. Even more fundamental was the idea, common to both approaches, that the city could be improved by replacing its chaos and confusion with a single plan, different from the urban plans of the past in that it was not conceived as a general outline of streets and major public institutions, but as a placement of every residence, every facility, every plot of green.

The fundamental kinship between the garden city and the towers in a park is demonstrated by the fact that today the most advanced planning ideas call for a mixture of the two, as in the English "New Towns" built since the war . . . , or in such American examples as Fresh Meadows, Long Island; Mill Creek, Philadelphia; Lafayette Park in Detroit.

These ideas have influenced a vast amount of new building: low-rent housing projects, cooperative apartment projects, government-insured "garden apartment" developments, and housing tracts developed by private builders.

How Far Have We Come?

It is true that the ideas have been applied mechanically and tastelessly; that the superblocks now very often enclose only garages; that the pedestrian paths neither bridge nor pass under the roads for vehicles; that the green has been reduced to tiny patches; that the overcrowding is so great that even these patches must be protected by fences or be trampled into dust by the too numerous children. Certainly Clarence Stein and the small band of energetic planners and reformers that worked with him would have hoped for much more.

But even if all these attempts to rebuild the city were as good as Radburn or Sunnyside, how far would we have actually come in dealing with the problems of the huge, metropolitan twentieth-century city? Certain problems of the nineteenth-century city have indeed been overcome; we have more green, more air, less dirt, fewer people living in cellars. But the startling result is that the planned developments have also in large measure destroyed the central values of the city—its value as meeting place, as mixing place, as a creator and consumer of culture at all levels. And the destruction would have been no less great if all the new interior-city developments had somehow been as good as Radburn or Sunnyside, or as refined as Le Corbusier's skyscraper schemes.

Of course the city does not exist only to create and consume culture, to supply a center for meeting and mixing. Is it not true, then, that other values have been enhanced, that the city as a place to live now satisfies more people who live in it?

Even this proposition seems questionable.

Consider, to begin with, the condition of the poor. The great experiment of the destruction of the slums has taught us something unexpected: that it is no simple matter to plan an environment for the poor that is any better than that which the slums provided. We have cleaner and better public housing apartments, but no less crime, drunkenness, or social disorder. And if there is less disease, this is because of advances in medicine which have reduced death rates dramatically, regardless of the social conditions under which the people live. There were values in the slum areas, it now appears. People lived in them even if they could afford better because they liked the neighborhoods. And when slums were destroyed, many people did not leave them willingly; they had to be forced out. The former slum-dwellers may now be secured from having prostitutes and drug pushers for neighbors—but they also no longer have poets, politicians, and businessmen for neighbors. They can now shop in supermarkets, but they can no longer enjoy the stimulus of the coffee house or bar, the grocery or bakery oriented to an ethnic group. And they no longer have the rows of stores in which they established storefront churches, radical political headquarters, or whatever else they willed. In short, it was not so easy to plan a better neighborhood than the one that had grown up chaotically, unplanned, under the impact of private profit-seeking and pleasure-seeking.

So much for the poor. What have the middle classes gained? Their apartment houses and two-family row houses have been replaced by small, fragilely built, freestanding houses on distant plots—and again consider how little would be different if they were all Radburns. The inhabitants' trip to the city has been lengthened; their neighborhood narrowed and impoverished; even the amount of covered living space they have is often less than they possessed in the six-room tenement flats or in once-fashionable apartments which had filtered down to the middle class. Indeed, the most desirable living space a middle-class family can generally find today in the city is one of the old houses or apartments built long before planners had any influence, and when private profit seekers were unrestrained by government control, unaided by government subsidy, and uninfluenced by the ideas of city planners. Uncontrolled capitalism may have had less to do with the problems of our cities than we assume it did.

And finally, what has happened to the city core, the center that people visit, that eager migrants want to live in, that produces what is unique in the city, both good and bad? It has been losing the vitality that gave it its attraction; and the greater the suburbanization of the city, the weaker the city's core has grown.

In short, city living is still, for most people, as difficult as it ever was, and for many it is more difficult. If the poor have gains to set against their losses, the rich and middle-classes are worse off. Artists, intellectuals, and professors have poorer quarters, or enjoy those they have less, as city centers weaken and can no longer match their former array of pleasures and services.

This is where the great effort that began with Howard, at the end of the last century, seems to have left us. What went wrong?

No Plan for the City

The main thing that went wrong was this: the planners did not plan for the city at all. They confined themselves to carefully worked out suburbs. They made the diagnosis: something is dreadfully wrong with the big city. The cure: let us build better towns.

But nothing much was wrong with the *town* to begin with. Since land values were low in towns, people could enjoy big lawns and gardens. Since towns were small, they had easy access to the country. But the main point in building Radburn—when towns as attractive as Morristown and Madison were not far off—was not to revolutionize the town. Radburn was built to influence the city core. The trouble was that in working to influence the city, the planners did not plan for cities.

How does one plan for cities, with all their variety, richness, and life, and yet retain such simple pleasures as space, light, and natural things? Or put another way: how do we plan for space and light, and simultaneously retain the city's quality of being a city?

Even to begin, we must examine the crucial factors affecting our big cities and disentangle from them the assumptions bequeathed to us by the garden city planners. Among the most crucial factors are these four: size, texture, traffic, and taste.

Sprawl versus Density

Size is the most overwhelming fact about the modern city, and we have failed to come to grips with it because we have continued to misconceive the problem as being mainly a question of density, of numbers of people per acre.

But size itself was, and remains, the problem—not density as such. Even if London had been successfully broken up into garden cities of 50,000 population each, what would have been gained? It would have required 200 garden cities. It would have sprawled over even a larger area than it now does, and the city— London itself—would have disappeared in the process. A city needs a center, and its center must be characterized by the highest possible density: theaters, stores, offices, organization headquarters, hotels, restaurants, residences, town houses, apartment houses, even slums (the Bohemians must live somewhere). All these must be crowded together to have a city. This richness, this crowding together of many different things, cannot be accomplished by reducing density. Had the planners really been successful in reducing population densities to 50 people per acre, or some such ideal, we would not have to save our great cities; we would have to create them!

The problem was that cities, as a result of the enormous population growth and the industrial revolution of the nineteenth century, became so large that it was no longer possible to combine great density with access to country, as the great cities of the past had done. The problem was that the cities spread far over the landscape, destroying the values of wild land, farmland, countryside. And this problem, far from being solved, is only intensified by reducing population density, for lowered densities cause the city to spread out even further.

Perhaps one answer lies in attempting models of much larger cities than have ever been planned, plans maintaining the variety, density, and richness of a city, yet limited by green belts: cities of a half-million people, rather than 50 thousand, with an urban variety of residental quarters, cultural amenities, and economic opportunities. In effect, this would be to multiply the population of the garden city by ten, and aim at the character of a city rather than that of a suburb or a town.

Whims of a Multitude

The characteristic texture of the true city, its liveliness and variety, is the second great factor to be considered. This aspect of the city has not been fostered by planners. Instead, the planners saw this simply as disorder, a negative factor. The garden city planners thought it was capitalism—the unrestrained activities of private individuals, seeking private profits and private convenience—that was at the root of the nineteenth-century city's difficulties, and they reasoned that a central intelligence, unconcerned with the profit motive, would inevitably produce a better city for all. "The shape and appearance of things," wrote Stein, an imposer of order, "and the relation of the parts that make the chaotic accidents called cities, are the summation of the haphazard, independent whims of a multitude of individuals. They ultimately determine the pattern for living by filling in the cubbyholes marketed by the subdivider; and for the individual there seems to be no alternative."

The diagnosis was faulty. For the free enterprise that the early planners viewed with suspicion was not the explanation of what went wrong with the nineteenth-century city. In Athens, Florence, Venice, or Bath, private profit was also a consideration. There too "developers" sold either plots or houses. There too the "independent whims of a multitude of individuals" worked, but in a framework set upon the basis of a combination of utility and the desire for beauty in order. And indeed, were it not for the "independent whims of a multitude of individuals," there would be no way to develop the density and richness of texture that defines the city.

To get this richness of texture it is necessary to allow far more free play to individuality, to allow many more functions to crowd together, and jumble together, and rub against each other, than even the best plans have permitted. No plan has ever come within hailing distance of recreating what are in some respects the best and richest parts of our cities—Greenwich Village in New York, North Beach in San Francisco. Such areas seem to require a mixture of lower-class residential area, preferably Italian, as a base—with its stores, coffee shops, churches, and the like—offering cheap living for poor young people, combined with expensive apartments or town houses, combined with art stores, used furniture and antique stores, night clubs, restaurants, all kinds of shops. This kind of thing, one of the glories of the city, no planner can plan.

Traffic and Taste

Motor traffic is now well recognized as a crucial city problem, but so long as we cling to garden city concepts of planning, the full seriousness of motor traffic in the city will not be realized. The dense texture of the city is destroyed by motorcars if the streets are widened and parking lots opened up for cars. It is questionable whether we can retain city centers at all if they are adapted to private automobiles. The most hopeful idea to have emerged in planning in recent years is the proposal that downtown streets be turned into malls and pedestrian ways, and the car banned from the city center. But this is not a complete solution. Perhaps to the shopping centers and to city centers which require that the car be left outside, we shall add new urban residential areas, of urban texture and density.

Finally, a fourth factor in the unsatisfying state of our cities must be faced: the catastrophic decline in taste that has accompanied the industrial revolution. This is the most difficult thing to talk about. Aside from its controversial nature, what can possibly be done about it? What can be done about the fact that buildings, neighborhoods, squares, and streets lack beauty, variety and exhilaration? One very small thing that can be done, and is done increasingly, is for people to become aware of the minor virtues in design that turn up almost continually in old buildings, old neighborhoods, old streets (and they need not be very old to compare favorably with much contemporary design). We must be more careful about destroying these to build new areas that will very often be inferior. Certainly the encouragement of better city design is of first importance but, in the meantime, even a defensive or holding operation has some virtues.

Whatever solutions we find to deal with these urgent problems of our cities, one thing is sure: nothing will be cured by bringing the suburb, even in its best forms, into the city. And yet this was the main objective in the program of a whole generation of city planners. We have come to the end of that road, and we must now discover or invent forms of planning appropriate to the great city.

The Generators of Diversity

by Jane Jacobs*

Classified telephone directories tell us the greatest single fact about cities: the immense numbers of parts that make up a city, and the immense diversity of those parts. Diversity is natural to big cities.

"I have often amused myself," wrote James Boswell in 1791, "with thinking how different a place London is to different people. They, whose narrow minds are contracted to the consideration of some one particular pursuit, view it only through their medium . . . But the intellectual man is struck with it, as comprehending the whole of human life in all its variety, the contemplation of which is inexhaustible."

Boswell not only gave a good definition of cities, he put his finger on one of the chief troubles in dealing with them. It is so easy to fall into the trap of contemplating a city's uses one at a time, by categories. Indeed, just this—analysis of cities, use by use—has become a customary planning tactic. The findings on various categories of use are then put together into "broad, overall pictures."

The overall pictures such methods yield are about as useful as the picture assembled by the blind men who felt the elephant and pooled their findings. The elephant lumbered on, oblivious to the notion that he was a leaf, a snake, a wall, tree trunks and a rope all somehow stuck together. Cities, being our own artifacts, enjoy less defense against solemn nonsense.

To understand cities, we have to deal outright with combinations or mixtures of uses, not separate uses, as the essential phenomena. We have already seen the importance of this in the case of neighborhood parks. Parks can easily—too easily—be thought of as phenomena in their own right and described as adequate or inadequate in terms, say, of acreage ratios to thousands of population. Such an approach tells us something about the methods of planners, but it tells us nothing useful about the behavior or value of neighborhood parks.

A mixture of uses, if it is to be sufficiently complex to sustain city safety, public contact and cross-use, needs an enormous diversity of ingredients. So the first question—and I think by far the most important question—about planning cities is this: How can cities generate enough mixture among uses—enough

*Jane Jacobs, *The Death and Life of Great American Cities,* Vintage Edition (New York: Random House, 1961), pp. 143-151. Reprinted by permission of Random House, Inc.

diversity—throughout enough of their territories, to sustain their own civilization?

It is all very well to castigate the Great Blight of Dullness and to understand why it is destructive to city life, but in itself this does not get us far. Consider the problem posed by the street with the pretty sidewalk park in Baltimore, which I mentioned back in Chapter Three. My friend from the street, Mrs. Kostritsky, is quite right when she reasons that it needs some commerce for its users' convenience. And as might be expected, inconvenience and lack of public street life are only two of the by-products of residential monotony here. Danger is another—fear of the streets after dark. Some people fear to be alone in their houses by day since the occurrence of two nasty daytime assaults. Moreover, the place lacks commercial choices as well as any cultural interest. We can see very well how fatal is its monotony.

But having said this, then what? The missing diversity, convenience, interest and vitality do not spring forth because the area needs their benefits. Anybody who started a retail enterprise here, for example, would be stupid. He could not make a living. To wish a vital urban life might somehow spring up here is to play with daydreams. The place is an economic desert.

Although it is hard to believe, while looking at dull gray areas, or at housing projects or at civic centers, the fact is that big cities *are* natural generators of diversity and prolific incubators of new enterprises and ideas of all kinds. Moreover, big cities are the natural economic homes of immense numbers and ranges of small enterprises.

The principal studies of variety and size among city enterprises happen to be studies of manufacturing, notably those by Raymond Vernon, author of *Anatomy of a Metropolis,* and by P. Sargant Florence, who has examined the effect of cities on manufacturing both here and in England.

Characteristically, the larger a city, the greater the variety of its manufacturing, and also the greater both the number and the proportion of its small manufacturers. The reasons for this, in brief, are that big enterprises have greater self-sufficiency than small ones, are able to maintain within themselves most of the skills and equipment they need, can warehouse for themselves, and can sell to a broad market which they can seek out wherever it may be. They need not be in cities, and although sometimes it is advantageous for them to be there, often it is more advantageous not to. But for small manufacturers, everything is reversed. Typically they must draw on many and varied supplies and skills outside themselves, they must serve a narrow market at the point where a market exists, and they must be sensitive to quick changes in this market. Without cities, they would simply not exist. Dependent on a huge diversity of other city enterprises, they can add further to that diversity. This last is a most important point to remember. City diversity itself permits and stimulates more diversity.

For many activities other than manufacturing, the situation is analogous. For example, when Connecticut General Life Insurance Company built a new headquarters in the countryside beyond Hartford, it could do so only by dint of providing—in addition to the usual working spaces and rest rooms, medical suite and the like—a large general store, a beauty parlor, a bowling alley, a cafeteria, a theater and a great variety of games space. These facilities are inherently inefficient, idle most of the time. They require subsidy, not because they are kinds of enterprises which are necessarily money losers, but because here their use is so limited. They were presumed necessary, however, to compete for a working force, and to hold it. A large company can absorb the luxury of such inherent inefficiencies and balance them against other advantages it seeks. But small offices can do nothing of the kind. If they want to compete for a work force on even terms or better, they must be in a lively city setting where their employees find the range of subsidiary conveniences and choices that they want and need. Indeed, one reason, among many others, why the much-heralded postwar exodus of big offices from cities turned out to be mostly talk is that the differentials in cost of suburban land and space are typically canceled by the greater amount of space per worker required for facilities that in cities no single employer need provide, nor any one corps of workers or customers support. Another reason why such enterprises have stayed in cities, along with small firms, is that many of their employees, especially executives, need to be in close, face-to-face touch and communication with people outside the firm—including people from small firms.

The benefits that cities offer to smallness are just as marked in retail trade, cultural facilities and entertainment. This is because city populations are large enough to support wide ranges of variety and choice in these things. And again we find that bigness has all the advantages in smaller settlements. Towns and suburbs, for instance, are natural homes for huge supermarkets and for little else in the way of groceries, for standard movie houses or drive-ins and for little else in the way of theater. There are simply not enough people to support further variety, although there may be people (too few of them) who would draw upon it were it there. Cities, however, are the natural homes of supermarkets and standard movie houses *plus* delicatessens, Viennese bakeries, foreign groceries, art movies, and so on, all of which can be found co-existing, the standard with the strange, the large with the small. Wherever lively and popular parts of cities are found, the small much outnumber the large. Like the small manufacturers, these small enterprises would not exist somewhere else, in the absence of cities. Without cities, they would not exist.

The diversity, of whatever kind, that is generated by cities rests on the fact that in cities so many people are so close together, and among them contain so many different tastes, skills, needs, supplies, and bees in their bonnets.

Even quite standard, but small, operations like proprietor-and-one-clerk hardware stores, drug stores, candy stores and bars can and do flourish in extraordinary numbers and incidence in lively districts of cities because there are enough people to support their presence at short, convenient intervals, and in turn this convenience and neighborhood personal quality are big parts of such enterprises' stock in trade. Once they are unable to be supported at close, convenient intervals, they lose this advantage. In a given geographical territory, half as many people will not support half as many such enterprises spaced at twice the distance. When distance inconvenience sets in, the small, the various and the personal wither away.

As we have transformed from a rural and small-town country into an urban country, business enterprises have thus become more numerous, not only in absolute terms, but also in proportionate terms. In 1900 there were 21 independent nonfarm businesses for each 1,000 persons in the total U.S. population. In 1959, in spite of the immense growth of giant enterprises during the interval, there were 26½ independent nonfarm businesses for each 1,000 persons in the population. With urbanization, the big get bigger, but the small also get more numerous.

Smallness and diversity, to be sure, are not synonyms. The diversity of city enterprises includes all degrees of size, but great variety does mean a high proportion of small elements. A lively city scene is lively largely by virtue of its enormous collection of small elements.

Nor is the diversity that is important for city districts by any means confined to profit-making enterprises and to retail commerce, and for this reason it may seem that I put an undue emphasis on retail trade. I think not, however. Commercial diversity is, in itself, immensely important for cities, socially as well as economically. Most of the uses of diversity on which I dwelt in Part I of this book depend directly or indirectly upon the presence of plentiful, convenient, diverse city commerce. But more than this, wherever we find a city district with an exuberant variety and plenty in its commerce, we are apt to find that it contains a good many other kinds of diversity also, including variety of cultural opportunities, variety of scenes, and a great variety in its population and other users. This is more than coincidence. The same physical and economic conditions that generate diverse commerce are intimately related to the production, or the presence, of other kinds of city variety.

But although cities may fairly be called natural economic generators of diversity and natural economic incubators of new enterprises, this does not mean that cities *automatically* generate diversity just by existing. They generate it because of the various efficient economic pools of use that they form. Wherever they fail to form such pools of use, they are little better, if any, at generating diversity than small settlements. And the fact that they need diversity socially, unlike small settlements, makes no difference. For our purposes here, the most striking fact to note is the extraordinary unevenness with which cities generate diversity.

On the one hand, for example, people who live and work in Boston's North End, or New York's Upper East Side or San Francisco's North Beach-Telegraph Hill, are able to use and enjoy very considerable amounts of diversity and vitality. Their visitors help immensely. But the visitors did not create the foundations of diversity in areas like these, nor in the many pockets of diversity and economic efficiency scattered here and there, sometimes most unexpectedly, in big cities. The visitors sniff out where something vigorous exists already, and come to share it, thereby further supporting it.

At the other extreme, huge city settlements of people exist without their presence generating anything much except stagnation and, ultimately, a fatal discontent with the place. It is not that they are a different kind of people, somehow duller or unappreciative of vigor and diversity. Often they include hordes of searchers, trying to sniff out these attributes somewhere, anywhere. Rather, something is wrong with their districts; something is lacking to catalyze a district population's ability to interact economically and help form effective pools of use.

Apparently there is no limit to the numbers of people in a city whose potentiality as city populations can thus be wasted. Consider, for instance, the Bronx, a borough of New York containing some one and a half million people. The Bronx is woefully short of urban vitality, diversity and magnetism. It has its loyal residents, to be sure, mostly attached to little bloomings of street life here and there in "the old neighborhood," but not nearly enough of them.

In so simple a matter of city amenity and diversity as interesting restaurants, the 1,500,000 people in the Bronx cannot produce. Kate Simon, the author of a guidebook, *New York Places and Pleasures,* describes hundreds of restaurants and other commercial establishments, particularly in unexpected and out-of-the-way parts of the city. She is not snobbish, and dearly likes to present her readers with inexpensive discoveries. But although Miss Simon tries hard, she has to give up the great settlement of the Bronx as thin pickings at any price. After paying homage to the two solid metropolitan attractions in the borough, the zoo and the Botanical Gardens, she is hard put to recommend a single place to eat outside the zoo grounds. The one possibility she is able to offer, she accompanies with this apology: "The neighborhood trails off sadly into a no man's land, and the restaurant can stand a little refurbishing, but there's the comfort of knowing that . . . the best of Bronx medical skill is likely to be sitting all around you."

Well, that is the Bronx, and it is too bad it is so; too bad for the people who live there now, too bad for the people who are going to inherit it in the future out of their lack of economic choice, and too bad for the city as a whole.

And if the Bronx is a sorry waste of city potentialities, as it is, consider the even more deplorable fact that it is possible for whole cities to exist, whole metropolitan areas, with pitifully little city diversity and choice. Virtually all of urban Detroit is as weak on vitality and diversity as the Bronx. It is ring superimposed upon ring of failed gray belts. Even Detroit's downtown itself cannot produce a respectable amount of diversity. It is dispirited and dull, and almost deserted by seven o'clock of an evening.

So long as we are content to believe that city diversity represents accident and chaos, of course its erratic generation appears to represent a mystery.

However, the conditions that generate city diversity are quite easy to discover by observing places in which diversity flourishes and studying the economic reasons why it can flourish in these places. Although the results are intricate, and the ingredients producing them may vary enormously, this complexity is based on tangible economic relationships which, in principle, are much simpler than the intricate urban mixtures they make possible.

To generate exuberant diversity in a city's streets and districts, four conditions are indispensable:

1. The district, and indeed as many of its internal parts as possible, must serve more than one primary function; preferably more than two. These must insure the presence of people who go outdoors on different schedules and are in the place for different purposes, but who are able to use many facilities in common.

2. Most blocks must be short; that is, streets and opportunities to turn corners must be frequent.

3. The district must mingle buildings that vary in age and condition, including a good proportion of old ones so that they vary in the economic yield they must produce. This mingling must be fairly close-grained.

4. There must be a sufficiently dense concentration of people, for whatever purposes they may be there. This includes dense concentration in the case of people who are there because of residence.

The necessity for these four conditions is the most important point this book has to make. In combination, these conditions create effective economic pools of use. Given these four conditions, not all city districts will produce a diversity equivalent to one another. The potentials of different districts differ for many reasons; but, given the development of these four conditions (or the best approximation to their full development that can be managed in real life), a city district should be able to realize its best potential, wherever that may lie. Obstacles to doing so will have been removed. The range may not stretch to African sculpture or schools of drama or Rumanian tea houses, but such as the possibilities are, whether for grocery stores, pottery schools, movies, candy stores, florists, art shows, immigrants' clubs, hardware stores, eating places, or whatever, they will get their best chance. And along with them, city life will get its best chances.

The Failure of Urban Renewal

by Herbert J. Gans*

Suppose that the government decided that jalopies were a menace to public safety and a blight on the beauty of our highways, and therefore took them away from their drivers. Suppose, then, that to replenish the supply of automobiles, it gave these drivers a hundred dollars each to buy a good used car and also made special grants to General Motors, Ford, and Chrysler to lower the cost—although not necessarily the price—of Cadillacs, Lincolns, and Imperials by a few hundred dollars. Absurd as this may sound, change the jalopies to slum housing, and I have described, with only slight poetic license, the first fifteen years of a federal program called urban renewal.

Since 1949, this program has provided local renewal agencies with federal funds and the power of eminent domain to condemn slum neighborhoods, tear down the buildings, and resell the cleared land to private developers at a reduced price. In addition to relocating the slum dwellers in "decent, safe, and sanitary" housing, the program was intended to stimulate large-scale private rebuilding, add new tax revenues to the dwindling coffers of the cities, revitalize their downtown areas, and halt the exodus of middle-class whites to the suburbs.

For some time now, a few city planners and housing experts have been pointing out that urban renewal was not achieving its general aims, and social scientists have produced a number of critical studies of individual renewal projects. These critiques, however, have mostly appeared in academic books and journals; otherwise there has been remarkably little public discussion of the federal program. Slum-dwellers whose homes were to be torn down have indeed protested bitterly, but their outcries have been limited to particular projects; and because such outcries have rarely been supported by the local press, they have been easily brushed aside by the political power of the supporters of the projects in question. In the last few years, the civil rights movement has backed protesting slum-dwellers, though again only at the local level, while rightists have opposed the use of eminent domain to take private property from one owner in order to give it to another (especially when the new one is likely to be from out-of-town and financed by New York capital).

*Herbert J. Gans, "The Failure of Urban Renewal: A Critique and Some Proposals," *Commentary*, 39 (April, 1965), pp. 29-37. Reprinted from *Commentary*, by permission; copyright © 1965 by the American Jewish Committee.

Slum clearance has also come under fire from several prominent architectural and social critics, led by Jane Jacobs, who have been struggling to preserve neighborhoods like Greenwich Village, with their brownstones, lofts, and small apartment houses, against the encroachment of the large, high-rise projects built for the luxury market and the poor alike. But these efforts have been directed mainly at private clearance outside the federal program, and their intent has been to save the city for people (intellectuals, and artists, for example) who, like tourists, want jumbled diversity, antique "charm," and narrow streets for visual adventure and aesthetic pleasure. (Norman Mailer carried such thinking to its farthest point in his recent attack in the *New York Times Magazine* on the physical and social sterility of high-rise housing; Mailer's attack was also accompanied by an entirely reasonable suggestion—in fact the only viable one that could be made in this context—that the advantages of brownstone living be incorporated into skyscraper projects.)

But if criticism of the urban renewal program has in the past been spotty and sporadic, there are signs that the program as a whole is now beginning to be seriously and tellingly evaluated. At least two comprehensive studies, by Charles Abrams and Scott Greer, are nearing publication, and one highly negative analysis—by an ultra-conservative economist and often irresponsible polemicist—has already appeared: Martin Anderson's *The Federal Bulldozer*. Ironically enough, Anderson's data are based largely on statistics collected by the Urban Renewal Administration. What, according to these and other data, has the program accomplished? It has cleared slums to make room for many luxury-housing and a few middle-income projects, and it has also provided inexpensive land for the expansion of colleges, hospitals, libraries, shopping areas, and other such institutions located in slum areas. As of March 1961, 126,000 dwelling units had been demolished and about 28,000 new ones built. The median monthly rental of all those erected during 1960 came to $158, and in 1962, to $192—a staggering figure for any area outside of Manhattan.

Needless to say, none of the slum-dwellers who were dispossessed in the process could afford to move into these new apartments. Local renewal agencies were supposed to relocate the dispossessed tenants in "standard" housing within their means before demolition began, but such vacant housing is scarce in most cities, and altogether unavailable in some. And since the agencies were under strong pressure to clear the land and get renewal projects going, the relocation of the tenants was impatiently, if not ruthlessly, handled. Thus, a 1961 study of renewal projects in 41 cities showed that 60 per cent of the dispossessed tenants were merely relocated in other slums; and in big cities, the proportion was even higher (over 70 per cent in Philadelphia, according to a 1958 study). Renewal sometimes even created new slums by pushing relocatees into areas and buildings which then became overcrowded and deteriorated rapidly. This has principally been the case with Negroes who, both for economic and racial reasons, have been forced to double up in other ghettos. Indeed, because almost two-thirds of the cleared slum units have been occupied by Negroes, the urban renewal program has often been characterized as Negro clearance, and in too many cities, this has been its intent.

Moreover, those dispossessed tenants who found better housing usually had to pay more rent than they could afford. In his careful study of relocation in Boston's heavily Italian West End, Chester Hartman shows that 41 per cent of the West Enders lived in good housing in this so-called slum (thus suggesting that much of it should not have been torn down) and that 73 per cent were relocated in good housing—thanks in part to the fact that the West Enders were white. This improvement was achieved at a heavy price, however, for median rents rose from $41 to $71 per month after the move.

According to renewal officials, 80 per cent of all persons relocated now live in good housing, and rent increases were justified because many had been paying unduly low rent before. Hartman's study was the first to compare these official statistics with housing realities, and his figure of 73 per cent challenges the official claim that 97 per cent of the Boston West Enders were properly rehoused. This discrepancy may arise from the fact that renewal officials collected their data after the poorest of the uprooted tenants had fled in panic to other slums, and that officials also tended toward a rather lenient evaluation of the relocation housing of those actually studied in order to make a good record for their agency. (On the other hand, when they were certifying areas for clearance, these officials often exaggerated the degree of "blight" in order to prove their case.)

As for the substandard rents paid by slum-dwellers, this is true in only a small proportion of cases, and then mostly among whites. Real-estate economists argue that families should pay at least 20 per cent of their income for housing, but what is manageable for middle-income people is a burden to those with low incomes who pay a higher share of their earnings for food and other necessities. Yet even so, Negroes generally have to devote about 30 per cent of their income to housing, and a Chicago study cited by Hartman reports that among non-white families earning less than $3,000 a year, median rent rose from 35 per cent of income before relocation to 46 per cent afterward.

To compound the failure of urban renewal to help the poor, many clearance areas (Boston's West End is an example) were chosen, as Anderson points out, not because they had the worst slums, but because they offered the best sites for luxury housing—housing which would have been built whether the urban renewal program existed or not. Since public funds were used to clear the slums and to make the land available to private builders at reduced costs, the low-income population was in effect subsidizing its own removal for the benefit of the wealthy. What was done for the slum-dwellers in return is starkly suggested by the following statistic: *only one-half of one per cent* of all federal expenditures for urban renewal between 1949 and 1964 was spent on relocation of families and individuals; and 2 per cent if payments are included.

Finally, because the policy has been to clear a district of all slums at once in order to assemble large sites to attract private developers, entire neighborhoods have frequently been destroyed, uprooting people who had lived there for decades, closing down their institutions, ruining small businesses by the hundreds, and scattering families and friends all over the city. By removing the structure of social and emotional support provided by the neighborhood, and by forcing people to rebuild their lives separately and amid strangers elsewhere, slum clearance has often come at a serious psychological as well as financial cost to its supposed beneficiaries. Marc Fried, a clinical psychologist who studied the West Enders after relocation, reported that 46 per cent of the women and 38 per cent of the men "give evidence of a fairly severe grief reaction or worse" in response to questions about leaving their tight-knit community. Far from "adjusting" eventually to this trauma, 26 per cent of the women remained sad or depressed even two years after they had been pushed out of the West End.

People like the Italians or the Puerto Ricans who live in an intensely group-centered way among three-generation "extended families" and ethnic peers have naturally suffered greatly from the clearance of entire neighborhoods. It may well be, however, that slum clearance has inflicted yet graver emotional burdens on Negroes, despite the fact that they generally live in less cohesive and often disorganized neighborhoods. In fact, I suspect that Negroes who lack a stable family life and have trouble finding neighbors, shopkeepers, and institutions they can trust may have been hurt even more by forcible removal to new areas. This suspicion is supported by another of Fried's findings—that the socially marginal West Enders were more injured by relocation than those who had been integral members of the old neighborhood. Admittedly, some Negroes move very often on their own, but then they at least do so voluntarily, and not in consequence of a public policy which is supposed to help them in the first place. Admittedly also, relocation has made it possible for social workers to help slum-dwellers whom they could not reach until renewal brought them out in the open, so to speak. But when only a few cities have so far used social workers to make relocation a more humane process.

These high financial, social, and emotional costs paid by the slum-dwellers have generally been written off as an unavoidable by-product of "progress," the price of helping cities to collect more taxes, bring back the middle class, make better use of downtown land, stimulate private investment, and restore civic pride. But as Anderson shows, urban renewal has hardly justified these claims either. For one thing, urban renewal is a slow process: the average project has taken twelve years to complete. Moreover, while the few areas suitable for luxury housing were quickly rebuilt, less desirable cleared land might lie vacant for many years because developers were—and are—unwilling to risk putting up high- and middle-income housing in areas still surrounded by slums. Frequently, they can be attracted only by promises of tax write-offs, which absorb the increased revenues that renewal is supposed to create for the city. Anderson reports that, instead of the anticipated four dollars for every public dollar, private investments have only just matched the public subsidies, and even the money for luxury housing has come forth largely because of federal subsidies. Thus, all too few of the new projects have produced tax gains and returned suburbanites, or generated the magic rebuilding boom.

Anderson goes on to argue that during the fifteen years of the federal urban renewal program, the private housing market has achieved what urban renewal has failed to do. Between 1950 and 1960, twelve million new dwelling units were built, and fully six million substandard ones disappeared—all without government action. The proportion of substandard housing in the total housing supply was reduced from 37 to 19 per cent, and even among the dwelling units occupied by non-whites, the proportion of substandard units has dropped from 72 to 44 per cent. This comparison leads Anderson to the conclusion that the private market is much more effective than government action in removing slums and supplying new housing, and that the urban renewal program ought to be repealed.

It would appear that Anderson's findings and those of the other studies I have cited make an excellent case for doing so. However, a less biased analysis of the figures and a less tendentious mode of evaluating them than Anderson's leads to a different conclusion. To begin with, Anderson's use of nationwide statistics misses the few good renewal projects, those which have helped both the slum-dwellers and the cities, or those which brought in enough new taxes to finance other city services for the poor. Such projects can be found in small cities and especially in those where high vacancy rates assured sufficient relocation housing of standard quality. More important, all the studies I have mentioned deal with projects carried out during the 1950's, and fail to take account of the improvements in urban renewal practice under the Kennedy and Johnson administrations. Although Anderson's study supposedly covers the period up to 1963, much of his data go no further than 1960. Since then, the federal bulldozer has moved into fewer neighborhoods, and the concept of rehabilitating rather than clearing blighted neighborhoods is more and more being underwritten by subsidized loans. A new housing subsidy program—known as 221(d) (3)—for families above the income ceiling for public housing has also been launched, and in 1964, Congress passed legislation for assistance to relocatees who cannot afford their new rents.

None of this is to say that Anderson would have had to revise his findings drastically if he had taken the pains to update them. These recent innovations have so far been small in scope—only 13,000 units were financed under 211(d) (3) in the first two years—and they still do not provide subsidies sufficient to bring better housing within the price range of the slum residents. In addition, rehabilitation unaccompanied by new construction is nearly useless because it does not eliminate overcrowding. And finally, some cities are still scheduling projects to clear away the non-white poor who stand in the path of the progress of private enterprise. Unfortunately, many cities pay little attention to federal pleas to improve the program, using the local initiative granted them by urban renewal legislation to perpetuate the practices of the 1950's. Yet even with the legislation of the 1960's, the basic error in the original design of urban renewal remains: it is still a method for eliminating the slums in order to "renew" the city, rather than a program for properly rehousing slum-dwellers.

Before going into this crucial distinction, we first need to be clear that private housing is not going to solve our slum problems. In the first place, Anderson conveniently ignores the fact that if urban renewal has benefited anyone, it is private enterprise. Bending to the pressure of the real-estate lobby, the legislation that launched urban renewal in effect required that private developers do the rebuilding, and most projects could therefore get off the drawing board only if they appeared to be financially attractive to a developer. Thus, his choice of a site and his rebuilding plans inevitably took priority over the needs of the slum-dwellers.

It is true that Anderson is not defending private enterprise *per se* but the free market, although he forgets that it only exists today as a concept in reactionary minds and dated economic texts. The costs of land, capital, and construction have long since made it impossible for private developers to build for anyone but the rich, and some form of subsidy is needed to house everyone else. The building boom of the 1950's which Anderson credits to the free market was subsidized by income-tax deductions to homeowners and by F.H.A. 2nd V.A. mortgage insurance, not to mention the federal highway programs that have made the suburbs possible.

To be sure, these supports enabled private builders to put up a great deal of housing for middle-class whites. This in turn permitted well-employed workers, including some non-whites, to improve their own situation by moving into the vacated neighborhoods. Anderson is quite right in arguing that if people earn good wages, they can obtain better housing more easily and cheaply in the not-quite-private market than through urban renewal. But this market is of little help to those employed at low or even factory wages, or the unemployed, or most Negroes who, whatever their earnings, cannot live in the suburbs. In consequence, 44 per cent of all housing occupied by non-whites in 1960 was still substandard, and even with present subsidies, private enterprise can do nothing for these people. As for laissez faire, it played a major role in creating the slums in the first place.

The solution, then, is not to repeal urban renewal, but to transform it from a program of slum clearance and rehabilitation into a program of urban rehousing. This means, first, building low- and moderate-cost housing on vacant land in cities, suburbs, and new towns beyond the suburbs, and also helping slum-dwellers to move into existing housing outside the slums; and then, *after* a portion of the urban low-income population has left the slums, clearing and rehabilitating them through urban renewal. This approach is commonplace in many European countries, which have long since realized that private enterprise can no more house the population and eliminate slums than it can run the post office.

Of course, governments in Europe have a much easier task than ours in developing decent low-income projects. Because they take it for granted that housing is a national rather than a local responsibility, the government agencies are not hampered by the kind of real-estate and construction lobbies which can defeat or subvert American programs by charges of socialism. Moreover, their municipalities own a great deal of the vacant land, and have greater control over the use of private land than do American cities. But perhaps their main advantage is the lack of popular opposition to moving the poor out of the slums and into the midst of the more affluent residents. Not only is housing desperately short for all income groups, but the European class structure, even in Western socialist countries, is still rigid enough so that low- and middle-income groups can live near each other if not next to each other, and still "know their place."

In America, on the other hand, one's house and address are major signs of social status, and no one who has any say in the matter wants people of lower income or status in his neighborhood. Middle-class homeowners use zoning as a way of keeping out cheaper or less prestigious housing, while working-class communities employ less subtle forms of exclusion. Consequently, low-income groups, whatever their creed or color, have been forced to live in slums or near-slums, and to wait until they could acquire the means to move as a group, taking over better neighborhoods when the older occupants were ready to move on themselves.

For many years now, the only source of new housing for such people, and their only hope of escaping the worst slums, has been public housing. But this is no longer a practical alternative. Initiated during the Depression, public housing has always been a politically embattled program; its opponents, among whom the real-estate lobby looms large, first saddled it with restrictions and then effectively crippled it. Congress now permits only 35,000 units a year to be built in the entire country.

The irony is that public housing has declined because, intended only for the poor, it faithfully carried out its mandate. Originally, sites were obtained by slum clearance; after the war, however, in order to increase the supply of low-cost housing, cities sought to build public housing on vacant land. But limited as it was to low-income tenants and thus labeled and stigmatized as an institution of the dependent poor, public housing was kept out of vacant land in the better neighborhoods. This, plus the high cost of land and construction, left housing officials with no other choice but to build high-rise projects on whatever vacant land they could obtain, often next to factories or along railroad yards. Because tenants of public housing are ruled by a set of strict regulations—sometimes necessary, sometimes politically inspired, but always degrading—anyone who could afford housing in the private market shunned the public projects. During the early years of the program, when fewer citizens had that choice, public housing became respectable shelter for the working class and even for the unemployed middle class. After the war, federal officials decided, and rightly so, that public housing ought to be reserved for those who had no other alternative, and therefore set income limits that admitted only the really poor. Today, public housing is home for the underclass—families who earn less than $3000-$4000 annually, many with unstable jobs or none at all, and most of them non-white.

Meanwhile the enthusiasm for public housing has been steadily dwindling and with it, badly needed political support. Newspaper reports reinforce the popular image of public-housing projects as huge nests of crime and delinquency—despite clear evidence to the contrary—and as the domicile of unregenerate and undeserving families whose children urinate only in the elevators. The position of public housing, particularly among liberal intellectuals, has also been weakened by the slurs of the social and architectural aesthetes who condemn the projects' poor exterior designs as "sterile," "monotonous," and "dehumanizing," often in ignorance of the fact that the tightly restricted funds have been allocated mainly to make the apartments themselves as spacious and livable as possible, and that the waiting lists among slum-dwellers who want these apartments remain long. Be that as it may, suburban communities and urban neighborhoods with vacant land are as hostile to public housing as ever, and their opposition is partly responsible for the program's having been cut down to its present minuscule size.

The net result is that low-income people today cannot get out of the slums, either because they cannot afford the subsidized private market, or because the project they could afford cannot be built on vacant land. There is only one way to break through this impasse, and that is to permit them equal access to new subsidized, privately built housing by adding another subsidy to make up the difference between the actual rent and what they can reasonably be expected to pay. Such a plan, giving them a chance to choose housing like all other citizens, would help to remove the stigma of poverty and inferiority placed on them by public housing. Many forms of rent subsidy have been proposed, but the best one, now being tried in New York, is to put low- and middle-income people in the same middle-income project with the former getting the same apartments at smaller rentals.

Admittedly, this approach assumes that the poor can live with the middle class and that their presence and behavior will not threaten their neighbors' security or status. No one knows whether this is really possible, but experiments in education, job training, and social-welfare programs do show that many low-income people, when once offered *genuine* opportunities to improve their lives and given help in making use of them, are able to shake off the hold of the culture of poverty. Despite the popular stereotype, the proportion of those whom Hylan Lewis calls the clinical poor, too ravaged emotionally by poverty and deprivation to adapt to new opportunities, seems to be small. As for the rest, they only reject programs offering spurious opportunities, like job-training schemes for non-existent jobs. Further, anyone who has lived in a slum neighborhood can testify that whatever the condition of the building, most women keep their apartments clean by expenditures of time and effort inconceivable to the middle-class housewife. Moving to a better apartment would require little basic cultural change from these women, and rehousing is thus a type of new opportunity that stands a better chance of succeeding than, say, a program to inculcate new child-rearing techniques.

We have no way of telling how many slum-dwellers would be willing to participate in such a plan. However poor the condition of the flat, the slum is home, and for many it provides the support of neighboring relatives and friends, and a cultural milieu in which everyone has the same problems and is therefore willing to overlook occasional disreputable behavior. A middle-income project cannot help but have a middle-class ethos, and some lower-class people may be fearful of risking what little stability they have achieved where they are now in exchange for something new, strange, demanding, and potentially hostile. It would be hard to imagine an unwed Negro mother moving her household to a middle-income project full of married couples and far removed from the mother, sisters, and aunts who play such an important role in the female-centered life of lower-class Negroes. However, there are today a large number of stable two-parent families who live in the slums only because income and race exclude them from the better housing that is available. Families like these would surely be only too willing to leave the Harlems and Black Belts. They would have to be helped with loans to make the move, and perhaps even with grants to buy new furniture so as not to feel ashamed in their new surroundings. They might be further encouraged by being offered income-tax relief for giving up the slums, just as we now offer such relief to people who give up being renters to become homeowners.

Undoubtedly there would be friction between the classes, and the more affluent residents would likely want to segregate themselves and their children from neighbors who did not toe the middle-class line, especially with respect to child-rearing. The new housing would therefore have to be planned to allow some voluntary social segregation for both groups, if only to make sure that enough middle-income families would move in (especially in cities where there was no shortage of housing for them). The proportion of middle- and low-income tenants would have to be regulated not only to minimize the status fears of the former, but also to give the latter enough peers to keep them from feeling socially isolated and without emotional support when problems arise. Fortunately, non-profit and limited dividend institutions, which do not have to worry about showing an immediate profit, are now being encouraged to build moderate-income housing; they can do a more careful job of planning the physical and social details of this approach than speculative private builders.

If the slums are really to be emptied and their residents properly housed elsewhere, the rehousing program will have to be extended beyond the city limits, for the simple reason that that is where most of the vacant land is located. This means admitting the low-income population to the suburbs; it also means creating new towns—self-contained communities with their own industry which would not, like the suburbs, be dependent on the city for employment opportunities, and could therefore be situated in presently rural areas. Federal support for the construction of new towns was requested as part of the 1964 Housing

Act, and although Congress refused to pass it, the legislation will come up again in 1965.

To be sure, white middle-class suburbanites and rural residents are not likely to welcome non-white low-income people into their communities even if the latter are no longer clearly labeled as poor. The opposition to be expected in city neighborhoods chosen for mixed-income projects would be multiplied a hundredfold in outlying areas. Being politically autonomous, and having constituencies who are not about to support measures that will threaten their security or status in the slightest, the suburbs possess the political power to keep the rehousing program out of their own vacant lots, even if they cannot stop the federal legislation that would initiate it. On the other hand, experience with the federal highway program and with urban renewal itself has demonstrated that few communities can afford to turn down large amounts of federal money. For instance, New York City is likely to build a Lower Manhattan Expressway in the teeth of considerable local opposition, if only because the federal government will pay 90 per cent of the cost and thus bring a huge sum into the city coffers. If the rehousing program were sufficiently large to put a sizable mixed-income project in every community, and if the federal government were to pick up at least 90 per cent of the tab, while also strengthening the appeal of the program by helping to solve present transportation, school, and tax problems in the suburbs, enough political support might be generated to overcome the objections of segregationist and class-conscious whites.

Yet even if the outlying areas could be persuaded to cooperate, it is not at all certain that slum-dwellers would leave the city. Urban renewal experience has shown that for many slum-dwellers, there are more urgent needs than good housing. One is employment, and most of the opportunities for unskilled or semi-skilled work are in the city. Another is money, and some New York City slum residents recently refused to let the government inspect—much less repair their buildings because they would lose the rent reductions they had received previously. If leaving the city meant higher rents, more limited access to job possibilities, and also separation from people and institutions which give them stability, some slum residents might very well choose overcrowding and dilapidation as the lesser of two evils.

These problems would have to be considered in planning a rehousing program beyond the city limits. The current exodus of industry from the city would of course make jobs available to the new suburbanites. The trouble is that the industries now going into the suburbs, or those that would probably be attracted to the new towns, are often precisely the ones which use the most modern machinery and the fewest unskilled workers. Thus, our rehousing plan comes up against the same obstacle—the shortage of jobs—that has frustrated other programs to help the low-income population and that will surely defeat the War on Poverty in its present form. Like so many other programs, rehousing is finally seen to depend on a step that American society is as yet unwilling to take: the deliberate creation of new jobs by government action. The building of new towns especially would have to be coordinated with measures aimed at attracting private industry to employ the prospective residents, at creating other job opportunities, and at offering intensive training for the unskilled after they have been hired. If they are not sure of a job before they leave the city, they simply will not leave.

The same social and cultural inhibitions that make slum residents hesitant to move into a mixed-income project in the city would, of course, be even stronger when it came to moving out of the city. These inhibitions might be relaxed by moving small groups of slum residents en masse, or by getting those who move first to encourage their neighbors to follow. In any case, new social institutions and community facilities would have to be developed to help the erstwhile slum-dweller feel comfortable in his new community, yet without labeling him as poor.

Despite its many virtues, a rehousing program based on the use of vacant land on either side of the city limits would not immediately clear the slums. Given suburban opposition and the occupational and social restraints on the slum-dwellers themselves, it can be predicted that if such a program were set into motion it would be small in size, and that it would pull out only the upwardly mobile—particularly the young people with stable families and income—who are at best a sizable minority among the poor. What can be done now to help the rest leave the slums?

The best solution is a public effort to encourage their moving into existing neighborhoods within the city and in older suburbs just beyond the city limits. Indeed, a direct rent subsidy like that now given to relocatees could enable people to obtain decent housing in these areas. This approach has several advantages. It would allow low-income people to be close to jobs and to move in groups, and it would probably attract the unwed mother who wanted to give her children a better chance in life. It would also be cheaper than building new housing, although the subsidies would have to be large enough to discourage low-income families from overcrowding—and thus deteriorating—the units in order to save on rent.

There are, however, some obvious disadvantages as well. For one thing, because non-white low-income people would be moving into presently white or partially integrated areas, the government would in effect be encouraging racial invasion. This approach would thus have the effect of pushing the white and middle-income people further toward the outer edge of the city or into the suburbs. Although some whites might decide to stay, many would surely want to move, and not all would be able to afford to do so. It would be necessary to help them with rent subsidies as well; indeed, they might become prospective middle-income tenants for rehousing projects on vacant land.

Undoubtedly, all this would bring us closer to the all-black city that has already been predicted. For this reason alone, a scheme that pushes the whites further out can only be justified when combined with a rehousing program on vacant land that would begin to integrate the suburbs. But even that could not prevent a further racial imbalance between cities and suburbs.

Yet would the predominantly non-white city really be so bad? It might be for the middle class which needs the jobs, shops, and cultures that the city provides. Of course, the greater the suburban exodus, the more likely it would become that middle-class culture would also move to the suburbs. This is already happening in most American cities—obvious testimony to the fact that culture (at least of the middlebrow kind represented by tent theaters and art movie-houses) does not need the city in order to flourish; and the artists who create high culture seem not to mind living among the poor even now.

Non-white low-income people might feel more positive about a city in which they were the majority, for if they had the votes, municipal services would be more attuned to their priorities than is now the case. To be sure, if poor people (of any color) were to dominate the city, its tax revenues would decrease even further, and cities would be less able than ever to supply the high quality public services that the low-income population needs so much more urgently than the middle class. Consequently, new sources of municipal income not dependent on the property tax would have to be found; federal and state grants to cities (like those already paying half the public-school costs in several states) would probably be the principal form. Even under present conditions, in fact, new sources of municipal income must soon be located if the cities are not to collapse financially.

If non-whites were to leave the slums en masse, new ghettos would eventually form in the areas to which they would move. Although this is undesirable by conventional liberal standards, the fact is that many low-income Negroes are not yet very enthusiastic about living among white neighbors. They do not favor segregation, of course; what they want is a free choice and then the ability to select predominantly non-white areas that are in better shape than the ones they live in now. If the suburbs were opened to non-whites—to the upwardly mobile ones who want integration now—free choice would become available. If the new ghettos were decent neighborhoods with good schools, and if their occupants had jobs and other opportunities to bring stability into their lives, they would be training their children to want integration a generation hence.

In short, then, a workable rehousing scheme must provide new housing on both sides of the city limits for the upwardly mobile minority, and encouragement to move into older areas for the remainder. If, in these ways, enough slum-dwellers could be enabled and induced to leave the slums, it would then be possible to clear or rehabilitate the remaining slums. Once slum areas were less crowded, and empty apartments were going begging, their profitability and market value would be reduced, and urban renewal could take place far more cheaply, and far more quickly. Relocation would be less of a problem, and with land values down, rebuilding and rehabilitation could be carried out to fit the resources of the low-income people who needed or wanted to remain in the city. A semi-suburban style of living that would be attractive to the upper-middle class could also be provided.

At this point, it would be possible to begin to remake the inner city into what it must eventually become—the hub of a vast metropolitan complex of urban neighborhoods, suburbs, and new towns, in which those institutions and functions that have to be at the center—the specialized business districts, the civil and cultural facilities, and the great hospital complexes and university campuses—would be located.

Even in such a city, there would be slums—for people who wanted to live in them, for the clinical poor who would be unable to make it elsewhere, and for rural newcomers who would become urbanized in them before moving on. But it might also be possible to relocate many of these in a new kind of public housing in which quasi-communities would be established to help those whose problems were soluble and to provide at least decent shelter for those who cannot be helped except by letting them live without harassment until we learn how to cure mental illness, addiction, and other forms of self-destructive behavior.

This massive program has much to recommend it, but we must clearly understand that moving the low-income population out of the slums would not eliminate poverty or the other problems that stem from it. A standard dwelling unit can make life more comfortable, and a decent neighborhood can discourage some anti-social behavior, but by themselves, neither can effect radical transformations. What poor people need most are decent incomes, proper jobs, better schools, and freedom from racial and class discrimination. Indeed, if the choice were between a program solely dedicated to rehousing, and a program that kept the low-income population in the city slums for another generation but provided for these needs, the latter would be preferable, for it would produce people who were able to leave the slums under their own steam. Obviously, the ideal approach is one that coordinates the elimination of slums with the reduction of poverty.

As I have been indicating, an adequate rehousing program would be extremely costly and very difficult to carry out. Both its complexity and expense can be justified, however, on several grounds. Morally, it can be argued that no one in the Great Society should have to live in a slum, at least not involuntarily.

From a political point of view, it is urgently necessary to begin integrating the suburbs and to improve housing conditions in the city before the latter becomes an ominous ghetto of poor and increasingly angry Negroes and Puerto Ricans, and the suburbs become enclaves of affluent whites who commute fearfully to a downtown bastion of stores and offices. If the visible group tensions of recent years are allowed to expand and sharpen, another decade may very well see the beginning of open and often violent class and race warfare.

But the most persuasive argument for a rehousing program is economic. Between 50 and 60 per cent of building costs go into wages and create work for the unskilled who are now increasingly unemployable elsewhere. A dwelling unit that costs $15,000 would thus provide as much as $9000 in wages—one-and-a-half years of respectably paid employment for a single worker. Adding four-and-a-half million new low-cost housing units to rehouse half of those in substandard units in 1960 would provide almost seven million man-years of work, and the subsequent renewal of these and other substandard units yet more. Many addi-

.tional jobs would also be created by the construction and operation of new shopping centers, schools, and other community facilities, as well as the high-ways and public transit systems that would be needed to serve the new suburbs and towns. If precedent must be cited for using a housing program to create jobs, it should be recalled that public housing was started in the Depression for precisely this reason.

The residential building industry (and the real-estate lobby) would have to be persuaded to give up their stubborn resistance to government housing programs, but the danger of future underemployment, and the opportunity of participating profitably in the rehousing scheme, should either convert present builders or attract new ones into the industry. As for the building trades unions, they have always supported government housing programs, but they have been unwilling to admit non-whites to membership. If, however, the rehousing effort were sizable enough to require many more workers than are now in the unions, the sheer demand for labor—and the enforcement of federal non-discriminatory hiring policies for public works—would probably break down the color barriers without much difficulty.

While the federal government is tooling up to change the urban renewal program into a rehousing scheme, it should also make immediate changes in current renewal practices to remove their economic and social cost from the shoulders of the slum-dwellers. Future projects should be directed at the clear-ance of *really harmful* slums, instead of taking units that are *run down but not demonstrably harmful* out of the supply of low-cost housing, especially for downtown revitalization and other less pressing community improvement schemes. Occupants of harmful slums, moreover, ought to be rehoused in decent units they can afford. For this purpose, more public housing and 221(d) (3) projects must be built, and relocation and rent assistance payments should be increased to eliminate the expense of moving for the slum-dweller. Indeed, the simplest way out of the relocation impasse is to give every relocatee a sizable grant, like the five-hundred dollars to one thousand dollars paid by private builders in New York City to get tenants out of existing structures quickly and painlessly. Such a grant is not only a real incentive to relocatees but a means of reducing opposition to urban renewal. By itself, however, it cannot reduce the shortage of relocation housing. Where such housing now exists in plentiful supply, renewal ought to move ahead more quickly, but where there is a short-age that cannot be appreciably reduced, it would be wise to eliminate or post-pone clearance and rehabilitation projects that require a large amount of reloca-tion.

Nothing is easier than to suggest radical new programs to the overworked and relatively powerless officials of federal and local renewal agencies who must carry out the present law, badly written or not, and who are constantly pres-sured by influential private interests to make decisions in their favor. Many of these officials are as unhappy with what urban renewal has wrought as their armchair critics and would change the program if they could—that is, if they received encouragement from the White House, effective support in getting new legislation through Congress, and, equally important, political help at city halls to incorporate these innovations into local programs. But it should be noted that little of what I have suggested is very radical, for none of the proposals involves conflict with the entrenched American practice of subsidizing private enterprise to carry out public works at a reasonable profit. The proposals are radical only in demanding an end to our no less entrenched practice of punishing the poor. Yet they also make sure that middle-class communities are rewarded financially for whatever discomfort they may have to endure.

Nor are these suggestions very new. Indeed, only last month President Johnson sent a housing message to Congress which proposes the payment of rent subsidies as the principal method for improving housing conditions. It also requests federal financing of municipal services for tax-starved communities, and aid toward the building of new towns. These represent bold and desirable steps toward the evolution of a federal rehousing program. Unfortunately, however, the message offers little help to those who need it most. Slum-dwellers may be pleased that there will be no increase in urban renewal activity, and that relocation housing subsidies and other grants are being stepped up. But no expansion of public housing is being requested, and to make matters worse, the new rent subsidies will be available only to households above the income limits for public housing. Thus, the President's message offers no escape for the mass of the non-white low-income population from the ghetto slums; in fact it threatens to widen the gap between such people and the lower-middle-income population which will be eligible for rent subsidies.

On the other hand, as in the case of the War on Poverty, a new principle of government responsibility in housing is being established, and evidently the President's strategy is to obtain legislative approval for the principle by combining it with a minimal and a minimally controversial program for the first year. Once the principle has been accepted, however, the program must change quickly. It may have taken fifteen years for urban renewal even to begin providing some relief to the mass of slum-dwellers, but it cannot take that long again to become a rehousing scheme that will give them significant help. The evolution of federal policies can no longer proceed in the leisurely fashion to which politicians, bureaucrats, and middle-class voters have become accustomed, for unemployment, racial discrimination, and the condition of our cities are becoming ever more critical problems, and those who suffer from them are now considerably less patient than they have been in the past.

Dilemmas of Urban America

by Robert C. Weaver*

It is generally recognized that race is a principal factor in many aspects of urban development. James Q. Wilson, for example, identifies the color issue as one of the three major problems of our cities, and Charles E. Silberman has observed that "the urban problem is in large measure a Negro problem."

Government at all levels is addressing itself more and more to racial policy in housing; and civil rights groups, as well as citizens' committees, are busily engaged in pressing for equal opportunity in housing. Nonwhites and those concerned with eradicating poverty are championing more and better housing for the disadvantaged at the same time that many of them are highly critical of racial ghetto patterns of living.

Some, whose main concern is other than housing or poverty, become involved because of the pervasive impact of racial residential patterns. Proponents of school integration, for example, realize that their objective is frustrated by residential segregation; thus they become champions of integrated housing. At the same time some of the trade groups in the housing industry are equally active in attempting to prevent or vitiate public action for open occupancy in housing.

There are few among those seriously concerned with equal opportunity who would not insist that all ethnic groups in American society should have free access to housing throughout the communities in which they live. Ability to pay should be the only criterion for entrance, and individual acceptance of established behavior patterns should be the only requirement for continued occupancy.

If there were an adequate amount of decent shelter at prices which those in the market can pay, obviously a much larger proportion of the population could find "standard" accommodations—that is, sound physical structures having adequate plumbing and sanitary facilities and sufficient space for the household affected. But we have long recognized that private enterprise, unassisted, has not, cannot, and will not provide standard housing for a large proportion of the less affluent. Thus governmental programs have been established to provide the needed assistance.

*Robert C. Weaver, *Dilemmas of Urban America* (Cambridge: Harvard University Press, 1965), pp. 78-112. Reprinted by permission of the publishers from Robert C. Weaver, *Dilemmas of Urban America*, Cambridge, Mass.: Harvard University Press, Copyright, 1965, by the President and Fellows of Harvard College.

Questions arise as to what public policy should be and how effective it will be in achieving the desired results. Even more fundamental is the issue of what specifically we want to achieve. Most who speak and act from the liberal point of view would probably assert that they want more and better housing available to nonwhites, a dissolvement of ghettos, and integrated residential patterns. But few have taken the time to inquire whether or not these necesssarily are consistent goals. If some of these objectives are now competitive with others, or if inflexible commitment to one may delay another, which is to be selected? On what basis is it to be chosen, and by whom? Or, finally, is this a matter of one approach versus another, or the most desirable mixture of approaches?

As long as there was little effective action in this sphere of American life, such questions were academic. Today when there is action and when changes are occurring, the answers become extremely important. If, for example, rapid development of stable integrated neighborhoods will do only little to increase the supply of decent houses for nonwhites in the foreseeable future, is such action more important and socially desirable than rapid expansion of housing opportunities for nonwhites at the cost of meaningful (as contrasted to transitional) integration? On the other hand, in light of the influence of upper-class suburbia upon our values, can suburban patterns of racial occupancy be neglected?

A part of the problem is a difference of opinion as to how governmental housing programs operate and their impact upon racial residential patterns. Urban renewal offers a good example, for, as Lyle E. Schaller, a perceptive observer of the program, observed: "Thousands of Negroes think of . . . [it] as a synonym for 'Negro removal' while many whites are thoroughly convinced that their block would have remained all white if it had not been for urban renewal. Integrationists contend that urban renewal officials have been negligent by not pushing fair housing policies while segregationists read the open occupancy clauses written into redevelopment contracts and are convinced that urban renewal is but another device developed by the federal bureaucracy to break down the separation of the races."

Public housing is criticized because it does not yet have a firm policy of making certain that locations are chosen to encourage integration. And Whitney Young, Executive Director of the National Urban League, has stated that urban renewal, slum clearance, and highway construction will result in Negroes' being more segregated in the unattractive areas of the city.

Actually, during the decade 1950 to 1960, the degree of racial residential segregation did not increase; it declined slightly. In addition, its incidence grew in the cities of the South and lessened slightly in the North, reflecting the greater political power of nonwhites in the North and the utilization of residential segregation in the South as a means of vitiating judicial action that prohibits segregation in public facilities, especially public schools. During the ten years from 1950 to 1960, over-all progress toward open occupancy was slight, and my observations would lead me to believe that although it has been accelerated since

1960, the amount of interracial housing has remained quantitatively small. Yet there are unmistakable evidences of changing patterns and changing attitudes toward nonwhite neighbors. The situation is not static and, as in many aspects of race relations, statistical averages and index numbers do not reflect the total situation.

Not only has there been a liberalization of attitude toward open occupancy but significant institutional developments have occurred. The first of these is the recent spontaneous rise of about a thousand fair housing committees, largely in the suburbs. These are groups of middle-class whites who have organized to recruit and welcome nonwhites as neighbors. President Kennedy's Executive Order on Equal Opportunity in Housing (1962), despite its limited coverage, has slowly opened new neighborhoods to nonwhites, supplementing the eighteen state laws, three territory laws, and thirty-four municipal ordinances for fair housing practices. Most recently, several thousand Americans have organized to provide financial resources in support of nonsegregated housing on a national scale. It is important to observe that, for reasons that will be discussed later, most of the progress toward open occupancy in housing has involved the more affluent.

Of all the industry groups in housing, the National Association of Real Estate Boards has been the most outspoken foe of fair housing legislation. It justifies its position on the ground of concern for property rights and freedom of choice in the disposition of real estate. State and local real estate boards have supplemented the widespread activities of the national body in this field. For example, the California organization of real estate boards drew up the language and supplied the principal support for Proposition 14 in that state, a proposition which not only prevents enforcement of the state fair housing law but also requires a statewide referendum before any additional legislation in this field can be enacted.

Early in March 1965 the lobbyist for the Texas Real Estate Association identified himself and his organization as the proponents of a similar constitutional amendment in Texas. Texas has no fair housing legislation; so in this case the proposed amendment was designed to prevent passage of such a law. This legislation was killed in committee. Nine additional states had similar legislation before them in the spring of 1965, and in every instance it had strong support from the state real estate boards. However, by June none of these bills had been passed.

Local real estate boards have supported similar action in Akron, Dayton, and elsewhere. Yet there have been a few exceptions among real estate boards. Several years ago the Real Estate Board of Greater Boston was a champion of fair housing legislation in Massachusetts, and, more recently, the Real Estate Board of Greater Baltimore urged extension of the Executive Order for Equal Opportunity in Housing to include conventional lending on home mortgages by federally chartered and insured institutions.

Concurrently the masses of nonwhites, keenly conscious of their housing deprivations, press to remove them. Thus there is, within the Negro community, growing pressure for relief, and the riots in Negro ghettos during the summer of 1964 were unmistakable expressions that tempers had grown short.

All of the efforts which improve the status of low-income Americans will also affect racial housing problems. As the antipoverty program succeeds, an increasing number of nonwhites not only will have more money to spend for housing but will develop even greater dissatisfaction with their present shelter and neighborhoods.

In such a setting, it is not enough to report that attitudes and patterns are changing. For men and women who are living under intolerable conditions, such changes seem remote. They want action, and for them action is significant only if it upgrades their own housing.

Relaxation of racial ghetto patterns of living will have immediate impact primarily upon those nonwhites who are more affluent. Such a development might have offered hope for all nonwhites had it happened a generation ago. Today the tempo in civil rights is such that these relaxations in the color line, as important as they may be over the long run, do little to reduce the social pressure in the ghettos.

There is a new realization in many parts of American society that existing racial housing patterns throughout the urban complex are crucial. Bernard Weissbourd, president of Chicago's Metropolitan Structures and a large-scale builder and redeveloper, writing for the Center for the Study of Democratic Institutions, aptly stated:

> "Present segregation practices are a serious obstacle . . . ; at the same time they provide an additional reason why a program designed to create heterogeneous communities both within the city and beyond the suburbs has become imperative . . . The question of segregation is always present when the character and location of public housing and urban renewal projects are being determined. An unwillingness to face up to it has paralyzed city planning. It is necessary to deal with the question not only for the sake of civil rights for Negroes but in order to free city planning from some unspoken assumptions that underlie almost everything that happens about housing in our cities."

CURRENT PARADOXES

Urban renewal is the one public activity occasioning large-scale dislocation that has high standards for relocation. And it is now enforcing them. Yet is the *one* public program which is constantly criticized for its relocation activities, largely in terms of their impact upon minorities.

Proponents of racial integration in housing oppose slum clearance and, frequently, advocate rehabilitation of existing structures; but rehabilitation tends to perpetuate existing residential racial patterns. Some of those who attack ghetto patterns demand that housing built in redevelopment areas be exclusively for low-income occupancy; still, in cities with large nonwhite populations, such housing usually becomes predominantly, or exclusively, nonwhite.

In an effort to break down racial concentrations, some groups look to dispersion of displacees into integrated neighborhoods. Unfortunately, the consequence of their efforts, if successful, is, sometimes, to expand the patterns of residential segregation over a larger segment of the city.

In one community or in one area, urban renewal is opposed because it is said to mean nonwhite displacement; in another its defeat is lamented because lack of urban renewal is said to be sure to cause nonwhite displacement.

Some who champion open occupancy would utilize "benign" quotas to achieve racial integration; others eschew the use of quotas, citing the ideological conflict between quotas and the concept of open occupancy.

In many cities, fair housing committees bemoan the paucity of takers among nonwhites. Yet these committees concentrate for the most part upon the placement of upper-income nonwhites. Regardless of the reasons for this (and there may be a rational basis for it, given the committees' objectives), by neglecting lower-income minority families the committees automatically limit their potential.

The most stable interracial neighborhoods are inhabited by upper-income nonwhites. Such areas, while promoting racial integration, do little directly to upgrade the housing of the mass of nonwhites.

We should not be surprised by these paradoxes of race in the field of housing or in other aspects of our society. *There are problems of race because there is prejudice. And prejudice is always irrational and illogical. Those who are the butt of extreme prejudice can hardly be expected to react in terms of detached logic. Nor do consistent lines of approach emerge from these circumstances.*

THE PROBLEMS OF SITES

The paradoxes just listed now must be examined in more detail.

The *location* of housing is perhaps the most crucial single factor in its racial occupancy. If new residential construction or rehabilitation is carried out in a site which is an integral part of nonwhite concentration, the occupancy usually becomes either exclusively or almost exclusively nonwhite. The one general exception occurs where an entire neighborhood is cleared and a new (and higher) income group is housed there.

These circumstances have led to the current pressure from civil rights and associated groups to secure locations for public housing beyond the boundaries of existing nonwhite neighborhoods. Several problems emerge.

The first problem is a reflection of both class and racial attitudes. Regardless of color, the residents of middle-income neighborhoods generally oppose the location of public housing projects in their midst. In addition, white neighborhoods of all income composition usually oppose such projects on the basis of racial concerns. Emulating largely the attitudes of upper-income groups and reflecting the racial exclusiveness of suburbia, most residents of white areas oppose public housing primarily because they fear nonwhite inundation. And all of this is complicated by the fact that because of the very racial attitudes that have led to residential segregation, public housing projects having a policy of open occupancy frequently become predominantly, or exclusively, nonwhite. In small communities with limited nonwhite populations, or in developments removed from concentrations of nonwhites, this need not occur. Where it does happen, however, it, in turn, accentuates the fears delineated above.

Selection of sites for public housing is primarily a local responsibility, but the Public Housing Administration now lists promotion of racially democratic housing patterns as one criterion. This is sometimes effective; it does not, however, guarantee locations which will facilitate mixed racial patterns. Though the federal government can refuse to approve a site, it cannot take the initiative and select one.

Situations increasingly arise where a locality will approve for public housing only sites now occupied by nonwhites or in areas undergoing racial transition. The choice for local groups concerned with housing for low-income and nonwhite families is often between (1) public housing that will be primarily nonwhite and (2) only a small amount of new low-income public housing. The principal impact of federal policy in this situation comes out of its requirement that those displaced by urban renewal and public housing be relocated in decent, safe, and sanitary accommodations. Often this requirement cannot be met without additional public housing. Usually it is facilitated if such low-rent housing is constructed on vacant land, most of which is outside existing nonwhite neighborhoods.

The selection of vacant sites is, of course, desirable from many points of view. It avoids dislocation; it provides a net expansion in the supply of low-rent accommodations; it relieves the pressures of a growing nonwhite population upon the existing supply of housing as was noted above. But, since public housing is initiated by local governments, there are slight prospects of its being constructed in the suburbs. Within the central city, the supply of vacant land is often restricted, and most that exists is so located as to assure strong opposition to public housing. Yet sound housing policy would dictate use of vacant sites or those that are appropriate for residential redevelopment but now in other uses.

The greatest progress toward integration in public housing is occurring in existing projects which were formerly tenanted exclusively by one racial group. As a consequence of the Executive Order on Equal Opportunity in Housing, a few changes were made. Under Section VI of the Civil Rights Act of 1964, all local housing authorities must agree to open occupancy in all public housing accommodations. Already the pace of integration has been stepped up. Interestingly, had there been an open-occupancy policy at the time the affected projects were constructed, many of the developments now subject to integration would never have been built.

The resolving of issues about sites for public housing brings to the surface differences in outlook between the more affluent nonwhites and the less affluent ones. The affluent tend to be more insistent on integration, whereas the less affluent may feel that their primary need is more decent housing and their situation so critical that they cannot afford the luxury of pressing for integration. When public housing outside, but not far removed from, nonwhite concentration becomes increasingly occupied by nonwhites, as it frequently does, little is gained for integration, but the supply of shelter and the land area available to low-income nonwhites is augmented. As a practical matter, in some localities there are relatively few sites available to public housing today which will assure stable interracial occupancy. Thus the dilemma.

I have noted above that when the advent of nonwhite residents accelerates abandonment of an area by whites, the cause of residential integration is set back. To meet this issue voluntary groups are sometimes formed to discourage panic selling and abandonment of established neighborhoods by white residents; and such action presents no dilemmas. But there are a few people who would restrain rather than merely discourage the movement of whites. This, of course, is inconsistent with our announced concern for maximum freedom of choice in selecting a place to live. And, unfortunately, it would frequently serve to delay the expansion of housing available to nonwhites. For under current patterns of racially homogeneous neighborhoods, the principal method used by nonwhites to augment the supply of shelter available to them is to succeed or displace whites. The only effective way to discourage panic selling and rapid racial succession in neighborhoods is to secure *de facto* open occupancy in a wide sector of the housing market. When that is achieved, all will be able to move freely but the exercise of this choice will not assure residence in a permanently ethnically homogeneous neighborhood: thus the racial motivation for moving will be greatly reduced.

There is real irony in that urban renewal, a program identified on the basis of its earlier performance as "Negro clearance," has recently made some significant contributions toward desirable sites for public housing. Many of these have been so redeveloped as to encourage biracial occupancy. To date, the volume of public housing on urban renewal sites has not been quantitatively or relatively large. It is, however, growing. Prior to the fiscal year ending June 30, 1961, contracts for public housing in urban renewal areas had been signed for 66 projects involving 12,098 dwelling units. During the succeeding three years between 1961 and 1964, 117 additional ones involving 14,988 dwelling units were placed under contract. More important, the patterns of occupancy which evolve are significant. Biracial occupancy of public housing occurred in the urban renewal programs of a score of cities, including Louisville and Newport, in Kentucky; Easton, Farrell, and Philadelphia, in Pennsylvania; New York City; Minneapolis; and Morristown, New Jersey.

Urban renewal has made its greatest contribution to the site problem in the realm of moderate-income housing. Here the relative demand among nonwhites for housing is not so overwhelming as to offer the same threat of innundation by the minorities. In addition, there is a sizable white demand at this income level. Thus, the moderate-income housing program referred to in Chapter 3, which provides housing bargains through below-the-market interest rates on long-term mortgages, is economically attractive to whites as well as nonwhites. Since the program began in 1961 an increasing volume of this housing has been planned, built, and occupied in urban renewal areas. A significant segment of it is racially mixed and appears to be fairly stable in this respect.

The reason why the most stable biracial neighborhoods are those of upper-income occupancy is that the possibility of nonwhite inundation is less real, reflecting the relative paucity of higher-income nonwhites in most cities. Unquestionably stable interracial neighborhoods have emerged in Washington, St. Louis, New York City, Boston, Chicago, Detroit, New Haven, Jersey City, Newark, Paterson, Philadelphia, Harrisburg, York, Minneapolis, San Francisco, Richmond (California), and in a growing number of redevelopments elsewhere.

Even in the South, urban renewal has facilitated new racial patterns. In the Landmark luxury apartments constructed in the Butler Street urban renewal site in Atlanta, Georgia, two Negro families were in occupancy in February 1965. In the redevelopment of East Nashville, three Negro households were living in a new downtown apartment building. In these and other cities of the South the novelty is not interracial patterns of living, but such patterns in newly constructed high-income and moderate-income neighborhoods.

As of June 30, 1964, some 54,875 dwelling units in urban renewal areas were occupied. About 90 percent had been privately financed; the rest were public housing. Whites lived in 32,796 units, nonwhites in 19,617, and color was not reported in the remaining 2,462. Thirty-five projects had all-white occupancy, thirty-six were occupied exclusively by nonwhites, and ninety-three had some degree of racial mixture. Fourteen of these "mixed" developments with 7,077 dwelling units were from 95 to 99 percent white; seven were 95 to 99 percent nonwhite; and seventy-two, housing 35,528 households, were integrated in the sense that over 5 percent of the occupants were of a second ethnic origin. These "integrated" developments housed some 22,000 white and 11,000 nonwhite families. The developments for which race was not reported were located in Puerto Rico; they housed some 2,500 additional families and were racially integrated. These data are the basis of my earlier observation that "urban renewal is providing, for the first time, a sizable supply of new racially integrated housing in a growing number of our cities . . . [It] is slowly affording nonwhites (most of whom are middle-income) a chance to move out of racial ghettos into what, for the most part, seem to be stable ethnically integrated neighborhoods. Non-white families involved—far too few to date—are thereby able at long last to begin to emulate the residential mobility of earlier migrants to urban centers.

Although this may offer some encouragement to integrationists, it has ex-
tracted a real cost, the impact of which has been concentrated upon low-income
non-whites. The first element, of course, is the forced displacement of households and small businesses. In addition, urban renewal has torn down ten times
more low-income and moderate-income housing units than it has helped to
produce. Until recently, most redevelopment housing has been so highly priced
as either to exclude or greatly restrict nonwhite occupancy.

An interesting dilemma faces efforts to effect open occupancy in new construction facilitated by the Veterans Administration and the Federal Housing
Administration. It has been suggested that such construction should be identified by a sign which would announce its availability to all ethnic groups. Aside
from the technical difficulty inherent in the fact that a given development may
use several types of financing (including conventional, which is not now covered
by the Executive Order), there are policy questions. With less than 20 percent of
new starts now affected by federal open-occupancy requirements, such signs
might discourage white purchasers or renters (who would go to competing developments). Were the coverage of the Executive Order more extensive, this problem would be less troublesome. But, if the coverage were more extensive, signs
of identification might not be necessary, since nonwhite purchasers or renters
could assume that any new project would be available to them and behave
accordingly.

In any discussion of site selection, a word should be added about the relative
desirability of existing ghettos for redevelopment. Because of the historic concentration of newcomers near the core of the city and the long-time occupancy
of desirably located sites by nonwhites, particularly in cities of the Old South,
theirs are often prime locations. Proposals to clear such sites (and low-income
racially mixed sites) and rehouse higher-income whites on them were the basis
for coining the phrases "Negro removal" and "Negro clearance." Yet at the very
moment that nonwhites and others opposed such action, some of them also
opposed the redevelopment (either with or without urban renewal) of these
areas with public housing.

INCOME AND INTEGRATION

The basic urban dilemma of income and race has already been mentioned. It
is a choice between (1) housing a large number of nonwhites in low-rent accommodations, (2) housing a somewhat smaller number in moderate-income housing, and (3) housing a much smaller number in high-income structures. This
dilemma is most sharply presented when decisions are being made relative to the
income distribution to be achieved in the redevelopment of an urban renewal
area, although it exists also when construction occurs elsewhere. There is, of
course, an option of some of each type of housing, but it is seldom considered
by those who engage in this colloquy. Because the degree and the potential

stability of racial mixture varies, in any one site, inversely with the level of income served by redevelopment, the choice, again, frequently appears to be between racial integration and the augmentation of new housing available to nonwhites. This issue presents itself in several forms.

In a Midwestern city where a vast urban renewal project is largely completed, and where half of the newly constructed 3,700 dwelling units are occupied by nonwhites, there was a question about income groups to be served by the future construction on the remaining undeveloped land. Originally it was proposed that over half the additional new units should be for moderate-income households. The redevelopers of somewhat higher-rent housing now in occupancy wanted a lower proportion of moderate-income housing and a larger proportion of higher-income accommodations. The Negro community was split, with most preferring the maximum degree of moderate-income housing. Civil rights groups and liberals were more sharply split.

There was no question that in proportion as a larger amount of moderate-income housing was provided, the degree of nonwhite occupancy would increase. Some feared that it might become so pronounced as to endanger the stability of the existing interracial pattern. At the same time, many who live in the vicinity of the renewal area still believe that since it was originally a Negro slum, the proportion of nonwhites rehoused should be significantly larger than it has been to date.

After much discussion and the consideration of a number of proposals, the city council finally approved the sale of thirty acres in the urban renewal areas. The redeveloper will construct over 1,100 dwelling units in high-rise apartments and town houses. Up until the final action of the city council, the economic mix of the redevelopment remained fluid. At the end there was a relaxation from the previous requirement of 55 percent moderate-income accommodations; the contract with the developer specified no more than 40 percent and no less than 20 percent of such housing.

This apparent imbalance was partially offset by the plans for moderate-income construction elsewhere in the area of nonwhite concentration. By June 1965 some 1,200 units of 221(d) (3) housing was completed, under construction, or planned for this section of the city.

In a somewhat smaller city in the East a different manifestation of the same problem has arisen. As in the Midwestern community, the renewal area was previously a Negro slum. Original plans envisioned redevelopment for high-income occupancy. This occasioned a storm of protest on the part of civil rights groups. Further analysis indicated that there would not be a market for high-income housing and plans were revised.

At this point there was a split between the protesting groups. One wanted moderate-income redevelopment on the grounds that it would provide housing within the reach of many nonwhites while lending itself to integration. Another group championed public housing because it would not occasion economic dislocation in the area.

It was decided to achieve economically diversified housing, with concentration upon moderate-income accommodations. But the controversy continued to rage. The organization and the individuals who supported the decision took the position that it would not only provide a significant volume of housing for nonwhites but also create a stable interracial neighborhood. They said that if nothing but public housing was built, the result would be an economic and ethnic ghetto. Also, they feared that it would be difficult to market integrated housing on the site of a former Negro slum if a large volume of low-income housing were provided there.

The champions of public housing redevelopment claimed that it was only equitable that the same people who previously lived in the area should move back into it. When they were told that, on the basis of past experience, only a few of the displaced would seek shelter there, they replied that the adverse impact of urban renewal had been concentrated upon poor Negroes and that this same group, suffering from a lack of decent housing, should benefit directly from the redevelopment. They added that relocation would only aggravate the shelter deprivation of this class, immediately reducing the supply of low-income housing in the city.

There were some interesting fringe benefits incident to the controversy. Relocation will take place in stages. Redevelopment on the site will include an economically diversified range of housing, some within the means of displaced families. Relocation planning now calls for short-term property improvements within the project area to serve better the needs of those who reside there during most of the relocation period. During this interim a community center will be provided for their use, and it will offer extensive social services, including a number of programs typical of the antipoverty campaign.

One could describe many other cases in which there appears to be a choice between augmenting to the maximum degree the supply of housing for nonwhites and obtaining less housing for them while fostering integration. In some instances, as in the extensive West Side rehabilitation and redevelopment in New York, an effort is made to achieve something of both goals. Redevelopment there will provide a relatively small volume of newly constructed high-rent units, a sizable volume of new and rehabilitated middle-income and moderate-income housing, and a slightly smaller amount of low-income housing. Even this solution fails to avoid dilemmas. What, for example, should be the mix? What criteria should be selected as the basis for the decision? And these questions, if they could be answered definitely, would not be determining. Any range of choices is limited by the response of the marketplace; and a mix that might work in the West Side of Manhattan would probably not be economically possible in Harlem or the Bronx, let alone the South Side of Chicago. Experience in New York City, San Francisco, and other cities has demonstrated that political pressure, too, exerts a significant influence upon the ultimate decisions.

Related decisions must be faced outside urban renewal areas. For some time public housing has been under attack. Much of the criticism is somewhat similar to the disenchantment with urban renewal: the program failed to realize the high hopes and promises of its earlier proponents. This has generated great disillusionment, and disillusionment usually leads to condemnation. The truth is that, with all its limitations, public housing has significantly upgraded the shelter of almost 600,000 American families, half of which are nonwhite. It has also perpetuated economic ghettos and developed a poor image in some localities.

In an effort to offset both of these weaknesses, many propose mixing public and moderate-income housing. This has a surface appeal, seeming to provide the best of both worlds, that is, an increase in low-income housing and at the same time the provision of racially integrated neighborhoods. Indeed, there is a slowly growing number of successful combinations of this type and they may provide an arrangement which will be a viable answer in many areas of the central cities. This is always a real possibility in sites which are well located, such as the West Side of Manhattan or the Western Addition area in San Francisco.

Yet there are dilemmas here too. They cannot be wished away, and they may as well be understood. In those localities where there is the fear and possibility of nonwhite inundation, the public housing sector in such a development could easily become all nonwhite, creating a pattern that might spread to the moderate-income accommodations as well. In many areas and in many sites, serious difficulties arise in marketing an interracial moderate-income development. If such a development is confused or identified with public housing, these difficulties can be aggravated.

Thus, in an effort to achieve two laudable objectives, low-income and moderate-income housing on the one hand and integration on the other, there is the danger that neither will be accomplished. Outside urban renewal areas as well as in them, zoning relaxations and public acquisition of land for housing occur only after local public hearings. One of the questions asked at these hearings is the type of construction or redevelopment that is envisioned. In many cities, neither zoning adjustments nor utilization of eminent domain will be approved if the re-use is to include public housing. Thus its proposed mixture with moderate-income housing may defeat attempts to construct either.

As suggested above, if moderate-income housing is decided upon, it may be successful at the cost of failure to alleviate to the maximum degree the quantitative needs of nonwhites. Such construction, however, is not without a significant indirect contribution to this objective. It greatly facilitates the filter-down process. For unlike high-cost additions to the housing supply, moderate-income additions are priced fairly close to what the poor are paying for substandard housing. Thus, as the volume of such new housing increases and vacancies occur, it is possible that lower-income families may move in before the house has depreciated over a long period of time. Such depreciation, of course, is what has defeated filtering-down in the past. By the time high-priced housing has depreciated enough to be within the financial reach of the poor, it is pretty bad housing, either in terms of its physical condition or its overcrowded pattern of occupancy.

The principal existing and proposed moderate-income housing programs of the federal government are restricted to nonprofit and limited-profit sponsors for rental units, and to individual or cooperative ownership for others. Insofar as such housing is constructed in former slum areas, it will have a revolutionary impact upon the neighborhoods. A radical change in ownership results. More important, slum landlords are replaced by nonprofit or limited-profit organizations.

In certain cities, "Negro housing" is a most profitable investment: some individuals and firms operate as many as 500 units each. This large-scale ownership contrasts with the ineffectual bargaining power of poor Negro tenants and perpetuates possibilities of economic exploitation. Federally assisted moderate-income housing is a real threat to the slumlords, and they recognize it. In one state they are said to have exchanged information from city to city and to have been discussing strategy to kill any and all forms of urban renewal. In this instance slum clearance, via urban renewal, can be a real benefit to nonwhites and contribute significantly to the upgrading of housing in the affected cities. Of course, public housing has long operated to serve the same purpose.

There is a much more basic philosophical argument in favor of moderate-income housing. It starts from the premise that cities need to manufacture a middle class. Moderate-income housing is consistent with the true aims of the city, according to this concept. Actually, those, like Charles Silberman, who accept this point of view would look beyond housing. "It's doubtful," he writes, "whether any simple, dramatic approach can solve the Negro housing problem. So long as the great majority of Negroes have slum incomes, they are going to live in slums. In the long run, therefore, the only way to solve the problem of Negro housing is to solve the problem of Negro people—to raise the economic and social level of the Negro community."

Of course, something has to be done over the short run. An approach which would be consistent with this analysis has already been proposed. It is to utilize, through rent supplements, existing housing as a source of shelter for low-income families. This proposal, however, leans upon several assumptions. The first is that there is a supply of available housing that can be upgraded. One of two conditions would have to exist: either there would be a loose housing market or a low-income and moderate-income housing program which would encourage an easement in the housing market for less affluent families.

Recognizing the difficulties of obtaining sites for public housing, there are those who advocate a bold program for moderate-income housing. Both in the central city and, to a lesser degree in the suburbs, the problem of obtaining sites for moderate-income housing is more manageable. Thus the proponents of this approach state that if such housing is augmented, it will be possible to relieve the pressure for accommodations in the ghettos, reduce the degree of economic exploitation therein, and upgrade the supply of existing low-income housing while increasing the supply of moderate-income structures available to minorities and others.

Once this prospect is suggested, there are pressures to abolish the federal public housing program and leave low-cost construction to private nonprofit organizations. I am opposed to these pressures. In the first place, the financial formula of public housing provides a unique machinery for low-cost construction loans. This is achieved through the use of federally guaranteed tax-exempt bonds issued by local governments. With the money raised by these low-interest loans, they pay for the land and the construction of public housing developments. Secondly, the number, expertise, and capacity of nonprofit organizations in this country are still small. To look to them for exclusive or primary sponsorship, construction, and operation would automatically limit the volume of low-income housing. Finally, we are recognizing that there is a need for greater social services and humanly oriented management in low-income housing developments. Public bodies can often best provide these, and they are apt to be more readily available to public housing than to developments by nonprofit organizations.

The proposal for a bold program of moderate-income housing and an end to the public housing program is, in fact, an expression of an "either-or"—a categorically logical—solution to a problem for which there is no single solution. While we expand the medium-income housing approaches, we also need to improve and redirect the public housing program. Until the war on poverty is won, we shall continue to have many families and individuals whose housing needs can best be met by public housing.

REHABILITATION AND RACE

The increasing importance of rehabilitation in urban renewal was discussed in the preceding chapter. The initial reaction to this has been generally favorable on the part of those who decry "Negro removal." There is a question as to how long it will be popular with those whose principal concern is integration.

By its very nature rehabilitation that is cost-conscious, in the sense that it avoids pricing former residents out of the area, tends to perpetuate existing patterns of living. This means that although it would minimize the displacement of nonwhites from localities where they now live, it would contribute little to their entering new areas. But it would vastly upgrade and improve their present environment. Here the dilemma seems to be avoiding "Negro clearance" at the price of making little progress toward integration. Actually, much more is involved. Real and spurious issues of political power and questions of Negro businesses must be considered as well.

There is a prevalent attitude among Negro politicians that efforts to destroy the ghetto are designed, in part at least, to dilute the political power of nonwhites. It seems to me that this is of limited validity. In city-wide or state-wide elections such concentrations are meaningless, and in precinct or other smaller area-based contests, nonwhites would have greater political power if so distributed as to be deciding factors in several such contests rather than being the totality in one contest. However, the fact that such opinion exists creates a vested interest in preserving existing neighborhoods. On the other hand there is great validity in opposing minority group displacement on the grounds that it uproots and often destroys nonwhite businesses. These are usually small, somewhat marginal establishments, catering to a market peculiar to their location. Relocation is always difficult for them and often impossible.

Wide-scale rehabilitation under urban renewal requires a significant degree of neighborhood citizen participation, and the population involved is, for the most part, the same before and after the activity. Thus any economic class conflict as to objectives is minimized. The present residents want to preserve the current economic composition of the affected area. If they are lower-income renters, they usually oppose radical upgrading lest it appreciably inflate rents. Most of the occupants of the deteriorating gray areas outside the central business district, once there is the prospect of area-wide upgrading, are primarily concerned with their continued occupancy with the minimum increase in housing costs.

Proponents of integration may react differently. Rehabilitation of the gray areas with a concern for avoiding displacement of former residents will, ultimately, have effects somewhat similar to building public housing in nonwhite neighborhoods: it will tend to perpetuate economic and ethnic ghettos. But it will not cause the same degree of economic and ethnic displacement that widespread rebuilding will cause, nor will it create a physical setting that will last for sixty years, as public housing construction will create. It may be, therefore, that the proponents of integration will find rehabilitation under urban renewal more palatable than demolition, relocation, and redevelopment. Indeed some socially motivated organizations are championing rehabilitation and residential integration as complementary goals.

There is, of course, less chance of whites' moving into an area that was once a nonwhite slum if its former residents remain after rehabilitation than when it is demolished and both the physical and human symbols of its past are removed. Where there are pockets of low-income nonwhite concentration, rehabilitation that prices former residents out of the market can, and has, become a tool for minority displacement.

Thus rehabilitation can occasion controversy over racial patterns. For example, in the Hyde Park area of Chicago, redevelopment which involved much "spot rehabilitation" was criticized because it had failed to rehouse a large proportion of low-income nonwhite residents. A crusading Negro champion of civil rights challenged this criticism, affirming that the redevelopment in Hyde Park was making a basic contribution to residential integration in Chicago. Actually, he was right: but there had been displacement of low-income nonwhites at the same time that higher-income Negroes entered the area. Here, it seems, the effect of rehabilitation was similar to that of new construction, reflecting the impact of the cost of the housing provided.

In Washington, D.C., an urban renewal plan featuring rehabilitation was supported by low-income residents. This came to public notice when the

National Capital Planning Commission rejected the long-discussed Adams-Morgan urban renewal proposal calling for spot clearance and spot rehabilitation in a large area of Northwest Washington. Most of the low-income Negro residents in the proposed project area, many liberals, the local Negro press (which frequently characterized urban renewal as "Negro clearance"), as well as the leading daily paper, deplored the Planning Commission's action. The small businesses in the area, a private so-called rehabilitation firm, and some resident upper-income nonwhites applauded it.

These different reactions followed from the fact that the renewal plan would have provided low-income and moderate-income housing for many of the present less affluent Negro residents in the area. The forces of the private market and code enforcement, which the Planning Commission expected to carry out the upgrading of the area, would dislocate permanently many of the low-income residents without giving them any relocation assistance. These forces would also permit many small businesses to remain—businesses that would be displaced or forced to remodel by any effective site plan concerned with compatible land-use patterns.

If an area is in nonwhite occupancy, it cannot become integrated without some displacement, even if the treatment is code enforcement or rehabilitation. The situation is complicated by the fact that urban renewal has been used as an instrument for displacing all—or most—nonwhites from desirable areas of a city. Although this seldom happens today, the fact that it has happened created an image of the program. Thus any displacement of nonwhites automatically conjures up the concept of pushing minorities out of desirable locations—and usually without any compensation for the inconvenience.

One may conjecture that of all the possible compromises in racial housing issues, the compromise that will be least difficult to live with, for now, will be rehabilitation. This will be true, however, only if the real impact of this approach is realized—an understanding which I doubt exists today. The point is that, provided this approach is supplemented by positive action to achieve the objectives of democratic housing patterns elsewhere in a community, rehabilitation which avoids general economic displacement is not too damaging to these goals.

MEETING THE HOUSING NEEDS OF NONWHITES

It requires no detailed analysis to demonstrate that in our urban centers where the nonwhite population is growing, now primarily because of natural increase rather than migration, adequate housing for minorities can be obtained only by expanding the space they occupy. Additional pressures are generated by new highway construction and urban renewal, as well as additional locally sponsored programs which displace nonwhites. But, so far, stable biracial residential patterns seem to require gradual change in neighborhood ethnic composition, and that, *if restricted to only a few parts of a city,* results in too slow a pace of change to provide the volume of housing needed by nonwhites.

One device suggested to ease the situation is the entrance of nonwhites into the suburbs. So far this has been a trickle, limited primarily to the more affluent. A more fundamental approach, outlined above, would be to provide a large volume of lower-cost housing on an open-occupancy basis in the suburbs. Both economic and psychological benefits would follow. The economic benefits have been shown earlier in this chapter. Equally important would be the resulting modification of the homogeneous patterns of suburbia and the tendency to reduce the prestige of such residential arrangements throughout the urban complex. There would be other benefits as well. In Chapter 2, I referred to the costs of continued exclusion of lower-income families from the suburbs. Also, as more and more employment opportunities appear outside the central cities, such exclusion accentuates the already serious problems of transportation.

But, in addition to white suburbia's opposition to nonwhite neighbors, there are complications to the outward-movement approach, too. An immediate one is the apparent disinclination of many nonwhites to move away from the central city. This may be a short-run phenomenon, reflecting the cultural security the ghetto affords to many who feel rejected elsewhere; it is an adjustment to enforced residential segregation. In any event, there is nothing innate about the behavior and if new opportunities were to arise, it is probable that they would be embraced by the majority who may be hesitant to pioneer today.

Some upper-income nonwhites do have a strong attachment to their present central-city locations. They have economic, political, and social motivations for remaining in a nonwhite community. But a much larger number of lower-income persons who are economically and socially mobile probably have lesser ties with the ghetto and provide a much greater potential for movement to the suburbs. Certainly, as a recent article reminds us, there is a real possibility that the opening of lower-income housing to nonwhites in the suburbs would significantly ease the quantitative pressure on housing in the central cities while not necessarily raising issues of color and class simultaneously in suburbia. This suggests that the middle-class orientation of most fair housing committees has greatly limited their efficacy.

It suggests, also, a redirection of the committees' programs. This would be consistent with recent advocacy of a more effective spatial distribution of higher-income nonwhites—one which would involve their continued occupancy in the central city. For some time most nonwhites will be central-city residents. It is claimed, therefore, that the better-trained and more successful nonwhites can be most helpful in accelerating the movement of other nonwhites into the mainstream of American life by remaining in those parts of the metropolitan areas where nonwhites are concentrated.

Again the issue does not call for an "either-or" approach but one that involves both phenomena. Actually, regardless of ideology, both are occurring and increasingly will occur. In Boston, for example, the older, long-term middle-class residents of a Negro area undergoing rehabilitation and redevelopment indicated a preference to remain there. The younger, better-trained, and occupationally integrated households were the pioneers in entering suburban and central-city biracial neighborhoods.

As we move toward realization of widespread open occupancy—the only residential pattern consistent with the philosophy and promise of a democracy— we shall encounter many contradictory developments. There will be frequent instances when efforts to achieve a stated objective may result in the realization of another. Or we may achieve one goal without contributing significantly to another equally important one. Perhaps the most frustrating development will be occasions when mixed racial residential patterns that have involved great dedication and effort will prove to be but transitional stages in the process of augmenting the inventory of shelter available to nonwhites.

But without abandoning or repudiating our commitment to equal opportunity in housing, we cannot ignore the supply of existing facilities. This is no less valid in housing than in education. For both, there is wisdom in Kenneth Clark's recent dictum that the goals of integration and quality of existing facilities must be sought together. In both of these basic areas of American life, each supports the other.